THE
IMPEACHMENT
REPORT

THE
IMPEACHMENT
REPORT

The
HOUSE INTELLIGENCE COMMITTEE'S
REPORT ON ITS INVESTIGATION INTO
DONALD TRUMP AND **UKRAINE**

INTRODUCTION BY
JON MEACHAM

B\D\W\Y
BROADWAY BOOKS
NEW YORK

INTRODUCTION

JON MEACHAM

The weather was hot, the stakes high, the debates fraught. In the long Philadelphia summer of 1787, in the stuffy confines of the Pennsylvania State House (later known as Independence Hall), the members of the Constitutional Convention were framing a new government for the nascent United States of America. In conversations about executive power, James Madison of Virginia spoke of the presidency as a unique office that would ideally transcend sectional jealousies. In a speech on Saturday, July 21, Madison argued, "The Executive Magistrate would be considered as a national officer, acting for and equally sympathizing with every part of the U. States."

From an executive to whom much was given, though, much would be expected, for Madison and his colleagues in Philadelphia shared a tempered, often pessimistic view of human nature. "If men were angels," Madison was to write in *The Federalist*, "no government would be necessary."

And since men were decidedly unangelic, government would require divisions of sovereignty and detailed sanctions to keep things in balance. Hence an entire constitutional structure was created, one that has served the nation well for nearly two and a half centuries.

Impeachment and removal from office were the ultimate check on presidential power. "Shall any man be above justice?" George Mason asked at the convention. "Above all, shall that man be above it who can commit the most extensive injustice?"

For the Founders, the answer was no. As the report that follows shows, it is an issue that confronts us even now. The presidency of Donald Trump has challenged or upended innumerable American conventions; in this season, the country is facing a reckoning. Given the story told by the House Intelligence Committee in this document, do Americans believe that such conduct by a president is acceptable? That is the question that lies before the Congress—and before the nation.

A bit more history. In 1776, in *Common Sense,* Thomas Paine used the term "President" to describe a chief magistrate. Scholars believe that Paine was the first to use this term for a head of an American government. Even then, more than a decade before the Constitutional Convention, reservations were expressed about investing too much power in a single man. "But where, say some, is the king of America?" Paine wrote. "I'll tell you, friend, he reigns above, and doth not make havoc of mankind like the royal brute of Great Britain. . . . [I]n America the law is king." Paine went on to write, "For as in absolute governments the king is law, so in free countries the law ought to be king; and there ought to be no other."

The potential power of the presidency, for good or for ill, was always clear. "His person, countenance, character, and actions, are made the daily contemplation and conversation of the whole people," John Adams wrote in 1790. To Alexander Hamilton, writing in *The Federalist,* "Energy in the executive is a leading character in the definition of good government. It is essential to . . . the security of liberty against the enterprises and assaults of ambition, of faction, and of anarchy."

By 1810, after eight years in the office himself, Thomas Jefferson would write, "In a government like ours it is the duty of the Chief-magistrate, in order to enable himself to do all the good which his station requires, to endeavor, by all honorable means, to unite in himself the confidence of the whole people. This alone, in any case where the energy of the nation is required, can produce a union of the powers of the whole, and point them in a single direction, as if all constituted but one body & one mind: and this alone can render a weaker nation unconquerable by a stronger one."

But how to create this "union of the powers of the whole" while maintaining a balance among the branches of government? It was this balance that Madison believed essential to safeguarding liberty from overreaching legislators or from grasping presidents, and it remains a perennial and consuming issue.

To Madison, foreign interference in elections was a threat from the beginning. It would be, he warned, "an object of great moment with the great rival powers of Europe . . . to have at the head of our government a man attached to their respective policies & interests." And what about once the president was in office? The power to impeach was crucial.

"Mr. Madison thought it indispensable," he wrote in a third-person entry in his Constitutional Convention notes, "that some provision should be made for defending the community against the incapacity, negligence, or perfidy of the chief magistrate." Madison's fears? A president "might betray his trust to foreign powers. . . . [L]oss of capacity or corruption was . . . within the compass of probable events, and either of them might be fatal to the Republic." The convention settled on impeachment by the House with conviction in the Senate—an instance of Madisonian checks and balances.

In our time we are living in a moment marked by demagoguery, reflexive partisanship, and a Hobbesian world of constant and total political warfare. We know all the factors: the return of the kind of partisan media that shaped us in the eighteenth and nineteenth centuries, relentless gerrymandering of election districts that has produced few swing congressional seats, and the allure of reality-TV programming that has blurred lines between entertainment and governance.

So what to do? We can begin by reading the following report. In so doing we will find ourselves at once oriented and informed. "When the mariner has been tossed for many days in thick weather, and on an unknown sea," Daniel Webster said in 1830, "he naturally avails himself of the first pause in the storm, the earliest glance of the sun, to take his latitude, and ascertain how far the elements have driven him from his true course." The fate of this presidency, of the ensuing future elections, and of our true course, lies in two sets of hands. The first is the House and the Senate. The second is the electorate that will determine the outcome of the 2020 campaign. People of good will can disagree about impeachment, but one hopes that we can at least agree on what happened even if some choose to excuse it or dismiss it.

Divisions of opinion are inherent elements in a democracy. There was never a once-upon-a-time in American life, and there will never be a happily-ever-after. The world doesn't work that way. Andrew Johnson survived impeachment; Richard Nixon's support held until the very last moment of Watergate; Joe McCarthy's anticommunist reign lasted not a season or a single cycle but four long years—and even after he'd fallen into disgrace, 34 percent of the country still supported him.

Yet the free flow of information and a respect for facts over opinion, for reason over tribe, are critical to the life of the Republic. As Theodore Roosevelt remarked, "To announce that there must be no criticism of the president, or that we are to stand by the president, right or wrong, is not only unpatriotic and servile, but is morally treasonable to the American public." Even with their manifold failings, lawmakers and journalists who seek to report and to illuminate rather than to opine and to divide are essential. "Publicity is the very soul of justice," the English philosopher Jeremy Bentham wrote. "It is the keenest spur to exertion, and the surest of all guards against improbity. . . . Without publicity, all other checks are fruitless: in comparison with publicity, all other checks are of small account."

Which, more than a century and a half later, President John F. Kennedy understood. "I think [the press] is invaluable, even though . . . it is never pleasant to be reading things that are not agreeable news," Kennedy told a group of network interviewers in December 1962. "But I would say that it is an invaluable arm of the Presidency, as a check really on what is going on in the administration, and more things come to my attention that cause me concern or give me information. . . . [T]here is a terrific disadvantage to not having the abrasive quality of the press applied to you daily. . . . Even though we never like it, and even though we wish they didn't write it, and even though we disapprove, there isn't any doubt that we could not do the job at all in a free society without a very, very active press."

To say nothing of a very, very active legislature, which is currently at work exercising its constitutional obligation to check and balance the executive. Politicians tend to mirror rather than mold the public, however, which means the nation at large is also on trial.

The past and the present tell us that demagogues can thrive only when a substantial portion of the *demos*—the people—wants them to. In his nineteenth-century classic *The American Commonwealth,* the English scholar and statesman Lord Bryce warned of the dangers of a renegade president. His view, however, was not that the individual himself, from the White House, could overthrow the Constitution. Rather, Bryce believed, disaster would come at the hands of a demagogic president with an enthusiastic public base. "A bold President who knew himself to be supported by a majority in the country, might be tempted to override the law, and deprive the minority of the protection which the law affords it," Bryce wrote. "He might be a tyrant, not against the masses, but with the masses."

The cheering news is that hope is not lost. "The people have often made mistakes," Harry Truman once said, "but given time and the facts, they will make the corrections."

Here, in this volume, are the facts—and as John Adams remarked, facts are stubborn things. Reflecting on the Constitutional Convention, Madison recalled, "There never was an assembly of men, charged with a great & arduous trust, who were more pure in their motives, or more exclusively or anxiously devoted to the object committed to them, than were the members of the Federal Convention of 1787." What history will say about how this Congress and this generation discharge their own "great & arduous trust" in the wake of this report is an open—and urgent—question.

THE TRUMP-UKRAINE
IMPEACHMENT INQUIRY REPORT

Report of the House Permanent Select Committee on Intelligence,
Pursuant to H. Res. 660 in Consultation with the
House Committee on Oversight and Reform and the
House Committee on Foreign Affairs

December 2019

House Permanent Select Committee on Intelligence

Rep. Adam B. Schiff (CA), Chairman

Rep. Jim Himes (CT)
Rep. Terri Sewell (AL)
Rep. André Carson (IN)
Rep. Jackie Speier (CA)
Rep. Mike Quigley (IL)
Rep. Eric Swalwell (CA)
Rep. Joaquin Castro (TX)
Rep. Denny Heck (WA)
Rep. Peter Welch (VT)
Rep. Sean Patrick Maloney (NY)
Rep. Val Demings (FL)
Rep. Raja Krishnamoorthi (IL)

Rep. Devin Nunes (CA), Ranking Member
Rep. Mike Conaway (TX)
Rep. Michael Turner (OH)
Rep. Brad Wenstrup (OH)
Rep. Chris Stewart (UT)
Rep. Elise Stefanik (NY)
Rep. Will Hurd (TX)
Rep. John Ratcliffe (TX)
Rep. Jim Jordan (OH)

Majority Staff
Timothy S. Bergreen, Staff Director
Daniel S. Goldman, Director of Investigations
Maher Bitar, General Counsel
Rheanne Wirkkala, Deputy Director of Investigations
Patrick M. Boland, Communications Director

Impeachment Inquiry Investigative Staff

William M. Evans
Patrick Fallon
Sean A. Misko
Nicolas A. Mitchell

Daniel S. Noble
Diana Y. Pilipenko
Ariana N. Rowberry

Carly A. Blake, Deputy Staff Director
William Wu, Budget and Policy Director
Wells C. Bennett, Deputy General Counsel

Oversight Staff

Linda D. Cohen
Thomas Eager
Abigail C. Grace
Kelsey M. Lax
Amanda A. Rogers Thorpe

Lucian D. Sikorskyj
Conrad Stosz
Kathy L. Suber
Aaron A. Thurman
Raffaela L. Wakeman

Non-Partisan Security and Information Technology Staff

Kristin Jepson

Kimberlee Kerr

Claudio Grajeda

House Committee on Oversight and Reform

Rep. Carolyn B. Maloney (NY), Chairwoman
Rep. Elijah E. Cummings (MD), Chairman

Rep. Eleanor Holmes Norton (DC)
Rep. Wm. Lacy Clay (MO)
Rep. Stephen Lynch (MA)
Rep. Jim Cooper (TN)
Rep. Gerald E. Connolly (VA)
Rep. Raja Krishnamoorthi (IL)
Rep. Jamie Raskin (MD)
Rep. Harley Rouda (CA)
Rep. Debbie Wasserman Schultz (FL)
Rep. John Sarbanes (MD)
Rep. Peter Welch (VT)
Rep. Jackie Speier (CA)
Rep. Robin Kelly (IL)
Rep. Mark DeSaulnier (CA)
Rep. Brenda Lawrence (IL)
Rep. Stacey Plaskett (VI)
Rep. Ro Khanna (CA)
Rep. Jimmy Gomez (CA)
Rep. Alexandria Ocasio-Cortez (NY)
Rep. Ayanna Pressley (MA)
Rep. Rashida Tlaib (MI)

Rep. Jim Jordan (OH), Ranking Member
Rep. Paul Gosar (AZ)
Rep. Thomas Massie (KY)
Rep. Virginia Foxx (NC)
Rep. Mark Meadows (NC)
Rep. Jody Hice (GA)
Rep. Glenn Grothman (WI)
Rep. James Comer (KY)
Rep. Michael Cloud (TX)
Rep. Bob Gibbs (OH)
Rep. Clay Higgins (LA)
Rep. Ralph Norman (SC)
Rep. Chip Roy (TX)
Rep. Carol Miller (WV)
Rep. Mark Green (TN)
Rep. Kelly Armstrong (ND)
Rep. Greg Steube (FL)
Rep. Fred Keller (PA)

Majority Staff
Dave Rapallo, Staff Director
Susanne Sachsman Grooms, Deputy Staff Director & Chief Counsel
Peter Kenny, Chief Investigative Counsel
Krista A. Boyd, General Counsel
Janet H. Kim, Chief Counsel for Investigations
Russell Anello, Chief Oversight Counsel
Aryele Bradford, Communications Director

Investigative Staff

S. Tori Anderson
Aaron D. Blacksberg
Chioma Chukwu
Cassie Fields
Greta Gao
Michael Gordon
Jessica L. Heller

Gina Kim
Jason Powell
Dan Rebnord
Ricardo Brandon Rios
Erinn L. Sauer, Detailee
Amish A. Shah
Laura Waters

Operations and Press Team

Zachary Barger, Intern
Jamitress Bowden
Kristen Charley, Intern
Kenyatta Collins
James Darlson, Intern
Emma Dulaney
Evan Elizabeth Freeman, Intern
Christophe Godshall, Intern
Brandon Jacobs
Elisa LaNier

Kellie Larkin
Olivia Letts, Intern
Anna Rose Marx, Intern
Courtney Miller
Noah Steimel, Intern
Travis Stoller, Intern
Amy Stratton
Laura Trevisani, Intern
Joshua Zucker

House Committee on Foreign Affairs

Rep. Eliot L. Engel (NY), Chairman

Rep. Brad Sherman (CA)
Rep. Gregory Meeks (NY)
Rep. Albio Sires (NJ)
Rep. Gerald Connolly (VA)
Rep. Theodore Deutch (FL)
Rep. Karen Bass (CA)
Rep. William Keating (MA)
Rep. David Cicilline (RI)
Rep. Ami Bera (CA)
Rep. Joaquin Castro (TX)
Rep. Dina Titus (NV)
Rep. Adriano Espaillat (NY)
Rep. Ted Lieu (CA)
Rep. Susan Wild (PA)
Rep. Dean Phillips (MN)
Rep. Ilhan Omar (MN)
Rep. Colin Allred (TX)
Rep. Andy Levin (MI)
Rep. Abigail Spanberger (VA)
Rep. Chrissy Houlahan (PA)
Rep. Tom Malinowski (NJ)
Rep. David Trone (MD)
Rep. Jim Costa (CA)
Rep. Juan Vargas (CA)
Rep. Vicente Gonzalez (CA)

Rep. Michael McCaul (TX) *Ranking Member*
Rep. Christopher Smith (NJ)
Rep. Steve Chabot (OH)
Rep. Joe Wilson (SC)
Rep. Scott Perry (PA)
Rep. Ted Yoho (FL)
Rep. Adam Kinzinger (IL)
Rep. Lee Zeldin (NY)
Rep. James Sensenbrenner (WI)
Rep. Ann Wagner (MO)
Rep. Brian Mast (FL)
Rep. Francis Rooney (FL)
Rep. Brian Fitzpatrick (PA)
Rep. John Curtis (UT)
Rep. Ken Buck (CO)
Rep. Ron Wright (TX)
Rep. Guy Reschenthaler (PA)
Rep. Tim Burchett (TN)
Rep. Greg Pence (IN)
Rep. Steve Watkins (KS)
Rep. Michael Guest (MS)

Majority Staff
Jason Steinbaum, Staff Director
Doug Campbell, Deputy Staff Director
Laura Carey, Senior Professional Staff Member, State Department Oversight
Tim Mulvey, Communications Director
Jacqueline Ramos, Senior Professional Staff Member, Europe and Russia

Operations and Press Staff

Evan Bursey
Jacqueline Colvett

Rachel Levitan

TABLE OF CONTENTS

PREFACE

This report reflects the evidence gathered thus far by the House Permanent Select Committee on Intelligence, in coordination with the Committee on Oversight and Reform and the Committee on Foreign Affairs, as part of the House of Representatives' impeachment inquiry into Donald J. Trump, the 45th President of the United States.

The report is the culmination of an investigation that began in September 2019 and intensified over the past three months as new revelations and evidence of the President's misconduct towards Ukraine emerged. The Committees pursued the truth vigorously, but fairly, ensuring the full participation of both parties throughout the probe.

Sustained by the tireless work of more than three dozen dedicated staff across the three Committees, we issued dozens of subpoenas for documents and testimony and took more than 100 hours of deposition testimony from 17 witnesses. To provide the American people the opportunity to learn and evaluate the facts themselves, the Intelligence Committee held seven public hearings with 12 witnesses—including three requested by the Republican Minority—that totaled more than 30 hours.

At the outset, I want to recognize my late friend and colleague Elijah E. Cummings, whose grace and commitment to justice served as our North Star throughout this investigation. I would also like to thank my colleagues Eliot L. Engel and Carolyn B. Maloney, chairs respectively of the Foreign Affairs and Oversight and Reform Committees, as well as the Members of those Committees, many of whom provided invaluable contributions. Members of the Intelligence Committee, as well, worked selflessly and collaboratively throughout this investigation. Finally, I am grateful to Speaker Nancy Pelosi for the trust she placed in our Committees to conduct this work and for her wise counsel throughout.

I also want to thank the dedicated professional staff of the Intelligence Committee, who worked ceaselessly and with remarkable poise and ability. My deepest gratitude goes to Daniel Goldman, Rheanne Wirkkala, Maher Bitar, Timothy Bergreen, Patrick Boland, Daniel Noble, Nicolas Mitchell, Sean Misko, Patrick Fallon, Diana Pilipenko, William Evans, Ariana Rowberry, Wells Bennett, and William Wu. Additional Intelligence Committee staff members also assured that the important oversight work of the Committee continued, even as we were required to take on the additional responsibility of conducting a key part of the House impeachment inquiry. Finally, I would like to thank the devoted and outstanding staff of the Committee on Oversight and Reform, including but not limited to Dave Rapallo, Susanne Sachsman Grooms, Peter Kenny, Krista Boyd, and Janet Kim, as well as Laura Carey from the Committee on Foreign Affairs.

* * *

In his farewell address, President George Washington warned of a moment when "cunning, ambitious, and unprincipled men will be enabled to subvert the power of the people and to usurp for themselves the reins of government, destroying afterwards the very engines which have lifted them to unjust dominion."

The Framers of the Constitution well understood that an individual could one day occupy the Office of the President who would place his personal or political interests above those of the nation. Having just won hard-fought independence from a King with unbridled authority, they were attuned to the dangers of an executive who lacked fealty to the law and the Constitution.

In response, the Framers adopted a tool used by the British Parliament for several hundred years to constrain the Crown—the power of impeachment. Unlike in Britain, where impeachment was typically reserved for inferior officers but not the King himself, impeachment in our untested democracy was specifically intended to serve as the ultimate form of accountability for a duly-elected President. Rather than a mechanism to overturn an election, impeachment was explicitly contemplated as a remedy of last resort for a president who fails to faithfully execute his oath of office "to preserve, protect and defend the Constitution of the United States."

Accordingly, the Constitution confers the power to impeach the president on Congress, stating that the president shall be removed from office upon conviction for "Treason, Bribery, or other high Crimes and Misdemeanors." While the Constitutional standard for removal from office is justly a high one, it is nonetheless an essential check and balance on the authority of the occupant of the Office of the President, particularly when that occupant represents a continuing threat to our fundamental democratic norms, values, and laws.

Alexander Hamilton explained that impeachment was not designed to cover only criminal violations, but also crimes against the American people. "The subjects of its jurisdiction," Hamilton wrote, "are those offenses which proceed from the misconduct of public men, or, in other words, from the abuse or violation of some public trust. They are of a nature which may with peculiar propriety be denominated political, as they relate chiefly to injuries done immediately to the society itself."

Similarly, future Associate Justice of the United States Supreme Court James Wilson, a delegate from Pennsylvania at the Constitutional Convention, distinguished impeachable offenses from those that reside "within the sphere of ordinary jurisprudence." As he noted, "impeachments are confined to political characters, to political crimes and misdemeanors, and to political punishments."

* * *

As this report details, the impeachment inquiry has found that President Trump, personally and acting through agents within and outside of the U.S. government, solicited the interference of a foreign government, Ukraine, to benefit his reelection. In furtherance of this scheme, President Trump conditioned official acts on a public announcement by the new Ukrainian President, Volodymyr Zelensky, of politically-motivated investigations, including one into President Trump's domestic political opponent. In pressuring President Zelensky to carry out his demand, President Trump withheld a White House meeting desperately sought by the Ukrainian President, and critical U.S. military assistance to fight Russian aggression in eastern Ukraine.

8

The President engaged in this course of conduct for the benefit of his own presidential reelection, to harm the election prospects of a political rival, and to influence our nation's upcoming presidential election to his advantage. In doing so, the President placed his own personal and political interests above the national interests of the United States, sought to undermine the integrity of the U.S. presidential election process, and endangered U.S. national security.

At the center of this investigation is the memorandum prepared following President Trump's July 25, 2019, phone call with Ukraine's President, which the White House declassified and released under significant public pressure. The call record alone is stark evidence of misconduct; a demonstration of the President's prioritization of his personal political benefit over the national interest. In response to President Zelensky's appreciation for vital U.S. military assistance, which President Trump froze without explanation, President Trump asked for "a favor though": two specific investigations designed to assist his reelection efforts.

Our investigation determined that this telephone call was neither the start nor the end of President Trump's efforts to bend U.S. foreign policy for his personal gain. Rather, it was a dramatic crescendo within a months-long campaign driven by President Trump in which senior U.S. officials, including the Vice President, the Secretary of State, the Acting Chief of Staff, the Secretary of Energy, and others were either knowledgeable of or active participants in an effort to extract from a foreign nation the personal political benefits sought by the President.

The investigation revealed the nature and extent of the President's misconduct, notwithstanding an unprecedented campaign of obstruction by the President and his Administration to prevent the Committees from obtaining documentary evidence and testimony. A dozen witnesses followed President Trump's orders, defying voluntary requests and lawful subpoenas, and refusing to testify. The White House, Department of State, Department of Defense, Office of Management and Budget, and Department of Energy refused to produce a single document in response to our subpoenas.

Ultimately, this sweeping effort to stonewall the House of Representatives' "sole Power of Impeachment" under the Constitution failed because witnesses courageously came forward and testified in response to lawful process. The report that follows was only possible because of their sense of duty and devotion to their country and its Constitution.

Nevertheless, there remain unanswered questions, and our investigation must continue, even as we transmit our report to the Judiciary Committee. Given the proximate threat of further presidential attempts to solicit foreign interference in our next election, we cannot wait to make a referral until our efforts to obtain additional testimony and documents wind their way through the courts. The evidence of the President's misconduct is overwhelming, and so too is the evidence of his obstruction of Congress. Indeed, it would be hard to imagine a stronger or more complete case of obstruction than that demonstrated by the President since the inquiry began.

The damage the President has done to our relationship with a key strategic partner will be remedied over time, and Ukraine continues to enjoy strong bipartisan support in Congress. But the damage to our system of checks and balances, and to the balance of power within our three branches of government, will be long-lasting and potentially irrevocable if the President's ability to stonewall Congress goes unchecked. Any future President will feel empowered to resist an investigation into their own wrongdoing, malfeasance, or corruption, and the result will be a nation at far greater risk of all three.

* * *

The decision to move forward with an impeachment inquiry is not one we took lightly. Under the best of circumstances, impeachment is a wrenching process for the nation. I resisted calls to undertake an impeachment investigation for many months on that basis, notwithstanding the existence of presidential misconduct that I believed to be deeply unethical and damaging to our democracy. The alarming events and actions detailed in this report, however, left us with no choice but to proceed.

In making the decision to move forward, we were struck by the fact that the President's misconduct was not an isolated occurrence, nor was it the product of a naïve president. Instead, the efforts to involve Ukraine in our 2020 presidential election were undertaken by a President who himself was elected in 2016 with the benefit of an unprecedented and sweeping campaign of election interference undertaken by Russia in his favor, and which the President welcomed and utilized.

Having witnessed the degree to which interference by a foreign power in 2016 harmed our democracy, President Trump cannot credibly claim ignorance to its pernicious effects. Even more pointedly, the President's July call with Ukrainian President Zelensky, in which he solicited an investigation to damage his most feared 2020 opponent, came the day after Special Counsel Robert Mueller testified to Congress about Russia's efforts to damage his 2016 opponent and his urgent warning of the dangers of further foreign interference in the next election. With this backdrop, the solicitation of new foreign intervention was the act of a president unbound, not one chastened by experience. It was the act of a president who viewed himself as unaccountable and determined to use his vast official powers to secure his reelection.

This repeated and pervasive threat to our democratic electoral process added urgency to our work. On October 3, 2019, even as our Committee was engaged in this inquiry, President Trump publicly declared anew that other countries should open investigations into his chief political rival, saying, "China should start an investigation into the Bidens," and that "President Zelensky, if it were me, I would recommend that they start an investigation into the Bidens." When a reporter asked the President what he hoped Ukraine's President would do following the July 25 call, President Trump, seeking to dispel any doubt as to his continuing intention, responded: "Well, I would think that, if they were honest about it, they'd start a major investigation into the Bidens. It's a very simple answer."

By doubling down on his misconduct and declaring that his July 25 call with President Zelensky was "perfect," President Trump has shown a continued willingness to use the power of his office to seek foreign intervention in our next election. His Acting Chief of Staff, Mick Mulvaney, in the course of admitting that the President had linked security assistance to Ukraine to the announcement of one of his desired investigations, told the American people to "get over it." In these statements and actions, the President became the author of his own impeachment inquiry. The question presented by the set of facts enumerated in this report may be as simple as that posed by the President and his chief of staff's brazenness: is the remedy of impeachment warranted for a president who would use the power of his office to coerce foreign interference in a U.S. election, or is that now a mere perk of the office that Americans must simply "get over"?

* * *

Those watching the impeachment hearings might have been struck by how little discrepancy there was between the witnesses called by the Majority and Minority. Indeed, most of the facts presented in the pages that follow are uncontested. The broad outlines as well as many of the details of the President's scheme have been presented by the witnesses with remarkable consistency. There will always be some variation in the testimony of multiple people witnessing the same events, but few of the differences here go to the heart of the matter. And so, it may have been all the more surprising to the public to see very disparate reactions to the testimony by the Members of Congress from each party.

If there was one ill the Founding Founders feared as much as that of an unfit president, it may have been that of excessive factionalism. Although the Framers viewed parties as necessary, they also endeavored to structure the new government in such a way as to minimize the "violence of faction." As George Washington warned in his farewell address, "the common and continual mischiefs of the spirit of party are sufficient to make it the interest and duty of a wise people to discourage and restrain it."

Today, we may be witnessing a collision between the power of a remedy meant to curb presidential misconduct and the power of faction determined to defend against the use of that remedy on a president of the same party. But perhaps even more corrosive to our democratic system of governance, the President and his allies are making a comprehensive attack on the very idea of fact and truth. How can a democracy survive without acceptance of a common set of experiences?

America remains the beacon of democracy and opportunity for freedom-loving people around the world. From their homes and their jail cells, from their public squares and their refugee camps, from their waking hours until their last breath, individuals fighting human rights abuses, journalists uncovering and exposing corruption, persecuted minorities struggling to survive and preserve their faith, and countless others around the globe just hoping for a better life look to America. What we do will determine what they see, and whether America remains a nation committed to the rule of law.

As Benjamin Franklin departed the Constitutional Convention, he was asked, "what have we got? A Republic or a Monarchy?" He responded simply: "A Republic, if you can keep it."

Adam B. Schiff
Chairman, House Permanent Select Committee on Intelligence

EXECUTIVE SUMMARY

The impeachment inquiry into Donald J. Trump, the 45th President of the United States, uncovered a months-long effort by President Trump to use the powers of his office to solicit foreign interference on his behalf in the 2020 election. As described in this executive summary and the report that follows, President Trump's scheme subverted U.S. foreign policy toward Ukraine and undermined our national security in favor of two politically motivated investigations that would help his presidential reelection campaign. The President demanded that the newly-elected Ukrainian president, Volodymyr Zelensky, publicly announce investigations into a political rival that he apparently feared the most, former Vice President Joe Biden, and into a discredited theory that it was Ukraine, not Russia, that interfered in the 2016 presidential election. To compel the Ukrainian President to do his political bidding, President Trump conditioned two official acts on the public announcement of the investigations: a coveted White House visit and critical U.S. military assistance Ukraine needed to fight its Russian adversary.

During a July 25, 2019, call between President Trump and President Zelensky, President Zelensky expressed gratitude for U.S. military assistance. President Trump immediately responded by asking President Zelensky to "do us a favor though" and openly pressed for Ukraine to investigate former Vice President Biden and the 2016 conspiracy theory. In turn, President Zelensky assured President Trump that he would pursue the investigation and reiterated his interest in the White House meeting. Although President Trump's scheme intentionally bypassed many career personnel, it was undertaken with the knowledge and approval of senior Administration officials, including the President's Acting Chief of Staff Mick Mulvaney, Secretary of State Mike Pompeo, and Secretary of Energy Rick Perry. In fact, at a press conference weeks after public revelations about the scheme, Mr. Mulvaney publicly acknowledged that the President directly tied the hold on military aid to his desire to get Ukraine to conduct a political investigation, telling Americans to "get over it."

President Trump and his senior officials may see nothing wrong with using the power of the Office of the President to pressure a foreign country to help the President's reelection campaign. Indeed, President Trump continues to encourage Ukraine and other foreign countries to engage in the same kind of election interference today. However, the Founding Fathers prescribed a remedy for a chief executive who places his personal interests above those of the country: impeachment. Accordingly, as part of the House of Representatives' impeachment inquiry, the Permanent Select Committee on Intelligence, in coordination with the Committees on Oversight and Reform and Foreign Affairs, were compelled to undertake a serious, sober, and expeditious investigation into whether the President's misconduct warrants that remedy.

In response, President Trump engaged in an unprecedented campaign of obstruction of this impeachment inquiry. Nevertheless, due in large measure to patriotic and courageous public servants who provided the Committees with direct evidence of the President's actions, the Committees uncovered significant misconduct on the part of the President of the United States. As required under House Resolution 660, the Intelligence Committee, in consultation with the Committees on Oversight and Reform and Foreign Affairs, has prepared this report to detail the evidence uncovered to date, which will now be transmitted to the Judiciary Committee for its consideration.

SECTION I—THE PRESIDENT'S MISCONDUCT

The President Conditioned a White House Meeting and Military Aid to Ukraine on a Public Announcement of Investigations Beneficial to his Reelection Campaign

The President's Request for a Political Favor

On the morning of July 25, 2019, President Donald Trump settled in to the White House Executive Residence to join a telephone call with President Volodymyr Zelensky of Ukraine. It had been more than three months since President Zelensky, a political neophyte, had been swept into office in a landslide victory on a platform of rooting out corruption and ending the war between his country and Russia. The day of his election, April 21, President Zelensky spoke briefly with President Trump, who had called to congratulate him and invite him to a visit at the White House. As of July 25, no White House meeting had materialized.

As is typical for telephone calls with other heads of state, staff members from the National Security Council (NSC) convened in the White House Situation Room to listen to the call and take notes, which would later be compiled into a memorandum that would constitute the U.S. government's official record of the call. NSC staff had prepared a standard package of talking points for the President based on official U.S. policy. The talking points included recommendations to encourage President Zelensky to continue to promote anti-corruption reforms in Ukraine, a pillar of American foreign policy in the country as far back as its independence in the 1990s when Ukraine first rid itself of Kremlin control.

This call would deviate significantly from that script. Shortly before he was patched through to President Zelensky, President Trump spoke with Gordon Sondland, who had donated $1 million to President Trump's 2016 presidential inauguration and whom the President had appointed as the United States Ambassador to the European Union. Ambassador Sondland had helped lay the groundwork for a very different kind of call between the two Presidents.

Ambassador Sondland had relayed a message to President Zelensky six days earlier that "assurances to run a fully transparent investigation" and "turn over every stone" were necessary in his call with President Trump. Ambassador Sondland understood these phrases to refer to two investigations politically beneficial to the President's reelection campaign: one into former Vice President Joe Biden and a Ukrainian gas company called Burisma, on which his son sat on the board, and the other into a discredited conspiracy theory alleging that Ukraine, not Russia, interfered in the 2016 U.S. election. The allegations about Vice President Biden were without evidence, and the U.S. Intelligence Community had unanimously determined that Russia, not Ukraine, interfered in the 2016 election to help the candidacy of Donald Trump. Despite the falsehoods, Ambassador Sondland would make it clear to Ukrainian officials that the public announcement of these investigations was a prerequisite for the coveted White House meeting with President Trump, an effort that would help the President's reelection campaign.

The White House meeting was not the only official act that President Trump conditioned on the announcement of these investigations. Several weeks before his phone call with President Zelensky, President Trump ordered a hold on nearly $400 million of congressionally-

13

appropriated security assistance to Ukraine that provided Kyiv essential support as it sought to repel Russian forces that were occupying Crimea and inflicting casualties in the eastern region of the country. The President's decision to freeze the aid, made without explanation, sent shock waves through the Department of Defense (DOD), the Department of State, and the NSC, which uniformly supported providing this assistance to our strategic partner. Although the suspension of aid had not been made public by the day of the call between the two Presidents, officials at the Ukrainian embassy in Washington had already asked American officials about the status of the vital military assistance.

At the outset of the conversation on July 25, President Zelensky thanked President Trump for the "great support in the area of defense" provided by the United States to date. He then indicated that Ukraine would soon be prepared to purchase additional Javelin anti-tank missiles from the United States as part of this defense cooperation. President Trump immediately responded with his own request: "I would like you to do us a favor though," which was "to find out what happened" with alleged Ukrainian interference in the 2016 election.

President Trump then asked President Zelensky "to look into" former Vice President Biden's role in encouraging Ukraine to remove a prosecutor widely viewed by the United States and numerous European partners to be corrupt. In so doing, President Trump gave currency to a baseless allegation that Vice President Biden wanted to remove the corrupt prosecutor because he was investigating Burisma, a company on whose board the Vice President's son sat at the time.

Over the course of the roughly thirty-minute call, President Trump repeated these false allegations and pressed the Ukrainian President to consult with his personal attorney, Rudy Giuliani, who had been publicly advocating for months for Ukraine to initiate these specific investigations. President Zelensky promised that he would "work on the investigation of the case." Later in the call, he thanked President Trump for his invitation to join him at the White House, following up immediately with a comment that, "[o]n the other hand," he would "ensure" that Ukraine pursued "the investigation" that President Trump had requested.

During the call, President Trump also disparaged Marie Yovanovitch, the former U.S. ambassador to Ukraine, who championed anti-corruption reforms in the country, and whom President Trump had unceremoniously removed months earlier following a smear campaign waged against her by Mr. Giuliani and others. President Trump claimed that she was "bad news" and was "going to go through some things." He praised the current prosecutor at the time, who was widely viewed as corrupt and who helped initiate the smear campaign against her, calling him "very good" and "very fair."

Hearing the call as it transpired, several White House staff members became alarmed. Far from giving the "full-throated endorsement of the Ukraine reform agenda" that had been hoped for, the President instead demanded a political investigation into an American—the presidential candidate he evidently feared most, Joe Biden.

Lieutenant Colonel Alexander Vindman, an NSC staff member responsible for Ukraine policy who listened to the call, immediately reported his concerns to NSC lawyers. His supervisor, NSC Senior Director for Europe and Russia Timothy Morrison, also reported the call to the lawyers, worrying that the call would be "damaging" if leaked publicly. In response, the lawyers placed the memorandum summarizing the call onto a highly classified server, significantly limiting access to the materials.

The call record would not remain hidden forever. On September 25, 2019, facing immense public pressure to reveal the contents of the call and following the announcement the previous day of a formal impeachment inquiry in the House of Representatives into President Trump's actions toward Ukraine, the White House publicly released the memorandum of the July 25 call.

The record of the call would help explain for those involved in Ukraine policy in the U.S. government, the Congress, and the public why President Trump, his personal attorney, Mr. Giuliani, his hand-picked appointees in charge of Ukraine issues, and various senior Administration officials would go to great lengths to withhold a coveted White House meeting and critical military aid from Ukraine at a time when it served as a bulwark against Russian aggression in Europe.

The answer was as simple as it was inimical to our national security and election integrity: the President was withholding officials acts while soliciting something of value to his reelection campaign—an investigation into his political rival.

The story of that scheme follows.

* * *

The President Removed Anti-Corruption Champion Ambassador Yovanovitch

On April 24, 2019, President Donald Trump abruptly called back to Washington the United States Ambassador to Ukraine, Marie "Masha" Yovanovitch, after a ruthless smear campaign was waged against her. She was known throughout Ukraine and among her peers for aggressively advocating for anti-corruption reforms consistent with U.S. foreign policy and only recently had been asked to extend her stay in Ukraine. Her effectiveness in anti-corruption efforts earned her enemies in Kyiv and in Washington. As Deputy Assistant Secretary of State George Kent testified in praising Ambassador Yovanovitch: "You can't promote principled anticorruption action without pissing off corrupt people."

Beginning on March 20, *The Hill* newspaper published several op-eds attacking Ambassador Yovanovitch and former Vice President Joe Biden, relying on information from a Ukrainian prosecutor, Yuriy Lutsenko, who was widely viewed to be corrupt. Mr. Lutsenko had served as the chief prosecutor in Ukraine under the then-incumbent president who lost to Volodymyr Zelensky in April 2019. Although he would later recant many of his allegations, Mr. Lutsenko falsely accused Ambassador Yovanovitch of speaking negatively about President Trump and giving Mr. Lutsenko a "do-not-prosecute list."

The attacks against Ambassador Yovanovitch were amplified by prominent, close allies of President Trump, including Mr. Giuliani and his associates, Sean Hannity, and Donald Trump Jr. President Trump tweeted the smears himself just a month before he recalled the Ambassador from Ukraine. In the face of attacks driven by Mr. Lutsenko and the President's allies, Ambassador Yovanovitch and other senior State Department officials asked Secretary of State Mike Pompeo to issue a statement of support for her and for the U.S. Embassy in Ukraine. The Secretary declined, fearing that President Trump might publicly undermine those efforts, possibly through a tweet.

Following a ceremony in which she presented an award of courage to the family of a young female anti-corruption activist killed in Ukraine for her work, Ambassador Yovanovitch received an urgent call from the State Department regarding her "security," and imploring her to take the first plane back to Washington. When she arrived, she was informed that she had done nothing wrong, but that the President had lost confidence in her. She was told to leave her post as soon as possible.

In her place, the President would designate three new agents to spearhead Ukraine policy, political appointees far more willing to engage in an improper "domestic political errand" than an ambassador known for her efforts to fight corruption.

The President's Hand-Picked Agents Began the Scheme

Just three days before Ambassador Yovanovitch's abrupt recall to Washington, President Trump had his first telephone call with President-elect Zelensky. During that conversation, President Trump congratulated the Ukrainian leader on his victory, complimented him on his country's Miss Universe Pageant contestants, and invited him to visit the White House. A White House meeting would help demonstrate the United States' strong support for Ukraine as it fought a hot war with Russia and attempted to negotiate an end to the conflict with Russian President Vladimir Putin, as well as to bolster President-elect Zelensky's standing with his own people as he sought to deliver on his promised anti-corruption agenda. Although the White House's public summary of the call included some discussion of a commitment to "root out corruption," President Trump did not mention corruption at all.

Shortly after the conversation, President Trump asked Vice President Mike Pence to attend President Zelensky's inauguration. Vice President Pence confirmed directly to President Zelensky his intention to attend during a phone conversation on April 23, and Vice President Pence's staff and the U.S. Embassy in Kyiv began preparations for the trip.

At the same time, President Trump's personal attorney, Mr. Giuliani, intensified his campaign to pressure Ukraine's newly-elected President to initiate investigations into Joe Biden, who had officially entered the race for the Democratic nomination on April 25, and the baseless conspiracy theory about Ukrainian interference in the 2016 election. On May 9, the *New York Times* published an article in which Mr. Giuliani declared that he intended to travel to Ukraine on behalf of his client, President Trump, in order to meddle in an investigation. After public backlash, Mr. Giuliani canceled the trip, blaming "some bad people" around President Zelensky. Days later, President Trump rescinded the plans for Vice President Pence to attend President

Zelensky's inauguration, which had not yet been scheduled. The staff member planning the trip was not provided an explanation for the about-face, but staff in the U.S. Embassy in Kyiv were disappointed that President Zelensky would not receive a "high level" show of support from the United States.

In Vice President Pence's stead, Secretary of Energy Rick Perry led the American delegation to the Ukrainian President's inauguration. Ambassador Sondland, Special Representative for Ukraine Negotiations Ambassador Kurt Volker, and Lt. Col. Vindman also attended. In comments that would foreshadow troubling events to come, Lt. Col. Vindman warned President Zelensky to stay out of U.S. domestic politics to avoid jeopardizing the bipartisan support Ukraine enjoyed in Congress.

The delegation returned to the United States impressed with President Zelensky, especially his focus on anti-corruption reforms. Ambassador Sondland quickly organized a meeting with President Trump in the Oval Office on May 23, attended by most of the other members of the delegation. The three political appointees, who would describe themselves as the "Three Amigos," relayed their positive impression of President Zelensky to President Trump and encouraged him to schedule the Oval Office meeting he promised in his April 21 phone call with the new leader.

President Trump reacted poorly to the suggestion, claiming that Ukraine "tried to take me down" in 2016. In order to schedule a White House visit for President Zelensky, President Trump told the delegation that they would have to "talk to Rudy." Ambassador Sondland testified that he understood the President's instruction to be a directive to work with Mr. Giuliani if they hoped to advance relations with Ukraine. President Trump directed the three senior U.S. government officials to assist Mr. Giuliani's efforts, which, it would soon become clear, were exclusively for the benefit of the President's reelection campaign.

As the Three Amigos were given responsibility over the U.S. government's Ukraine portfolio, Bill Taylor, a former Ambassador to Ukraine, was considering whether to come out of retirement to accept a request to succeed Ambassador Yovanovitch in Kyiv. As of May 26, Ambassador Taylor was "still struggling with the decision," and, in particular, whether anyone can "hope to succeed with the Giuliani-Biden issue swirling." After receiving assurances from Secretary Pompeo that U.S. policy toward Ukraine would not change, Ambassador Taylor accepted the position and arrived in Kyiv on June 17. Ambassador Taylor would quickly come to observe an "irregular channel" led by Mr. Giuliani that, over time, began to undermine the official channel of diplomatic relations with Ukraine. Mr. Giuliani would prove to be, as the President's National Security Advisor Ambassador John Bolton would tell a colleague, a "hand grenade that was going to blow everyone up."

The President Froze Vital Military Assistance

For fiscal year 2019, Congress appropriated and authorized $391 million in security assistance to Ukraine: $250 million in funds administered by DOD and $141 million in funds administered by the State Department. On June 18, DOD issued a press release announcing its intention to provide $250 million in taxpayer-funded security assistance to Ukraine following the certification that all legitimate conditions on the aid, including anti-corruption reforms, had been met. Shortly after this announcement, however, both the Office of Management and Budget (OMB) and DOD received inquiries from the President related to the funds. At that time, and throughout the next few months, support for Ukraine security assistance was overwhelming and unanimous among all of the relevant agencies and within Congress.

By July 3, OMB blocked a Congressional notification which would have cleared the way for the release of $141 million in State Department security assistance funds. By July 12, President Trump had placed a hold on all military support funding for Ukraine. On July 18, OMB announced the hold to all of the relevant agencies and indicated that it was directed by the President. No other reason was provided.

During a series of policy meetings involving increasingly senior officials, the uniform and consistent position of all policymaking agencies supported the release of funding. Ukraine experts at DOD, the State Department, and the NSC argued that it was in the national security interest of the United States to continue to support Ukraine. As Mr. Morrison testified, "The United States aids Ukraine and her people so that they can fight Russia over there, and we don't have to fight Russia here."

Agency officials also expressed concerns about the legality of President Trump's direction to withhold assistance to Ukraine that Congress had already appropriated for this express purpose. Two OMB career officials, including one of its legal counsels, would resign, in part, over concerns regarding the hold.

By July 25, the date of President Trump's call with President Zelensky, DOD was also receiving inquiries from Ukrainian officials about the status of the security assistance. Nevertheless, President Trump continued to withhold the funding to Ukraine without explanation, against the interests of U.S. national security, and over the objections of these career experts.

The President Conditioned a White House Meeting on Investigations

By the time Ukrainian officials were first learning about an issue with the anticipated military assistance, the President's hand-picked representatives to Ukraine had already informed their Ukrainian counterparts that President Zelensky's coveted White House meeting would only happen after Ukraine committed to pursuing the two political investigations that President Trump and Mr. Giuliani demanded.

Ambassador Sondland was unequivocal in describing this conditionality, testifying, "I know that members of this committee frequently frame these complicated issues in the form of a simple question: Was there a quid pro quo? As I testified previously with regard to the requested White House call and the White House meeting, the answer is yes." Ambassadors Sondland and Volker worked to obtain the necessary assurance from President Zelensky that he would personally commit to initiate the investigations in order to secure both.

On July 2, in Toronto, Canada, Ambassador Volker conveyed the message directly to President Zelensky, specifically referencing the "Giuliani factor" in President Zelensky's engagement with the United States. For his part, Mr. Giuliani made clear to Ambassadors Sondland and Volker, who were directly communicating with the Ukrainians, that a White House meeting would not occur until Ukraine announced its pursuit of the two political investigations. After observing Mr. Giuliani's role in the ouster of a U.S. Ambassador and learning of his influence with the President, Ukrainian officials soon understood that "the key for many things is Rudi [sic]."

On July 10, Ambassador Bolton hosted a meeting in the White House with two senior Ukrainian officials, several American officials, including Ambassadors Sondland and Volker, Secretary Perry, Dr. Fiona Hill, Senior Director for Europe and Russia at the NSC, and Lt. Col. Vindman. As had become customary each time Ukrainian officials met with their American counterparts, the Ukrainians asked about the long-delayed White House meeting. Ambassador Bolton demurred, but Ambassador Sondland spoke up, revealing that he had worked out an arrangement with Acting Chief of Staff Mick Mulvaney to schedule the White House visit after Ukraine initiated the "investigations." Ambassador Bolton "stiffened" and quickly ended the meeting.

Undaunted, Ambassador Sondland ushered many of the attendees to the Ward Room downstairs to continue their discussion. In the second meeting, Ambassador Sondland explained that he had an agreement with Mr. Mulvaney that the White House visit would come only after Ukraine announced the Burisma/Biden and 2016 Ukraine election interference investigations. At this second meeting, both Lt. Col. Vindman and Dr. Hill objected to intertwining a "domestic political errand" with official foreign policy, and they indicated that a White House meeting would have to go through proper channels.

Following these discussions, Dr. Hill reported back to Ambassador Bolton, who told her to "go and tell [the NSC Legal Advisor] that I am not part of whatever drug deal Sondland and Mulvaney are cooking up on this." Both Dr. Hill and Lt. Col. Vindman separately reported the incident to the NSC Legal Advisor.

The President's Agents Pursued a "Drug Deal"

Over the next two weeks, Ambassadors Sondland and Volker worked closely with Mr. Giuliani and senior Ukrainian and American officials to arrange a telephone call between President Trump and President Zelensky and to ensure that the Ukrainian President explicitly promised to undertake the political investigations required by President Trump to schedule the White House meeting. As Ambassador Sondland would later testify: "Mr. Giuliani was expressing the desires of the President of the United States, and we knew these investigations were important to the President."

On July 19, Ambassador Volker had breakfast with Mr. Giuliani and his associate, Lev Parnas, at the Trump Hotel in Washington, D.C. Mr. Parnas would subsequently be indicted for campaign finance violations as part of an investigation that remains ongoing. During the conversation, Ambassador Volker stressed his belief that the attacks being leveled publicly against Vice President Biden related to Ukraine were false and that the former Vice President was "a person of integrity." He counseled Mr. Giuliani that the Ukrainian prosecutor pushing the false narrative, Mr. Lutsenko, was promoting "a self-serving narrative to preserve himself in power." Mr. Giuliani agreed, but his promotion of Mr. Lutsenko's false accusations for the benefit of President Trump did not cease. Ambassador Volker also offered to help arrange an in-person meeting between Mr. Giuliani and Andriy Yermak, one of President Zelensky's most trusted advisors, which would later take place in Madrid, Spain in early August.

After the breakfast meeting at the Trump Hotel, Ambassador Volker reported back to Ambassadors Sondland and Taylor about his conversation with Mr. Giuliani, writing in a text message that, "Most impt [sic] is for Zelensky to say that he will help investigation—and address any specific personnel issues—if there are any," likely referencing President Zelensky's decision to remove Mr. Lutsenko as prosecutor general, a decision with which Mr. Giuliani disagreed. The same day, Ambassador Sondland spoke with President Zelensky and recommended that the Ukrainian leader tell President Trump that he "will leave no stone unturned" regarding the political investigations during the upcoming presidential phone call.

Ambassador Sondland emailed several top Administration officials, including Secretary of State Pompeo, Acting Chief of Staff Mulvaney, and Secretary Perry, stating that President Zelensky confirmed that he would "assure" President Trump that "he intends to run a fully transparent investigation and will 'turn over every stone.'" According to Ambassador Sondland, he was referring in the email to the Burisma/Biden and 2016 election interference investigations. Secretary Perry and Mr. Mulvaney responded affirmatively that the call would soon take place, and Ambassador Sondland testified later that "everyone was in the loop" on plans to condition the White House meeting on the announcement of political investigations beneficial to President Trump. The arrangement troubled the Ukrainian President, who "did not want to be used as a pawn in a U.S. reelection campaign."

The President Pressed President Zelensky to Do a Political Favor

On the morning of July 25, Ambassador Volker sent a text message to President Zelensky's top aide, Mr. Yermak, less than 30 minutes before the presidential call. He stated: "Heard from White House—assuming President Z convinces trump he will investigate / 'get to the bottom of what happened' in 2016, we will nail down date for visit to Washington. Good luck!" Shortly before the call, Ambassador Sondland spoke directly with President Trump.

President Zelensky followed this advice during his conversation with President Trump. President Zelensky assured that he would pursue the investigations that President Trump had discussed—into the Bidens and 2016 election interference—and, in turn, pressed for the White House meeting that remained outstanding.

The following day, Ambassadors Volker, Sondland, and Taylor met with President Zelensky in Kyiv. The Ukrainian President told them that President Trump had mentioned "sensitive issues" three times during the previous day's phone call. Following the meeting with the Ukrainian leader, Ambassador Sondland had a private, one-on-one conversation with Mr. Yermak in which they discussed "the issue of investigations." He then retired to lunch at an outdoor restaurant terrace with State Department aides where he called President Trump directly from his cellphone. The White House confirmed that the conversation lasted five minutes.

At the outset of the call, President Trump asked Ambassador Sondland whether President Zelensky "was going to do the investigation" that President Trump had raised with President Zelensky the day before. Ambassador Sondland stated that President Zelensky was "going to do it" and "would do anything you ask him to." According to David Holmes, the State Department aide sitting closest to Ambassador Sondland and who overheard the President's voice on the phone, Ambassador Sondland and President Trump spoke only about the investigation in their discussion about Ukraine. The President made no mention of other major issues of importance in Ukraine, including President Zelensky's aggressive anti-corruption reforms and the ongoing war it was fighting against Russian-led forces in eastern Ukraine.

After hanging up the phone, Ambassador Sondland explained to Mr. Holmes that President Trump "did not give a shit about Ukraine." Rather, the President cared only about "big stuff" that benefitted him personally, like "the Biden investigation that Mr. Giuliani was pitching," and that President Trump had pushed for in his July 25 call with the Ukrainian leader. Ambassador Sondland did not recall referencing Biden specifically, but he did not dispute Mr. Holmes' recollection of the call with the President or Ambassador Sondland's subsequent discussion with Mr. Holmes.

The President's Representatives Ratcheted up Pressure on the Ukrainian President

In the weeks following the July 25 call, the President's hand-picked representatives increased the President's pressure campaign on Ukrainian government officials—in person, over the phone, and by text message—to secure a public announcement of the investigations beneficial to President Trump's reelection campaign.

In discussions with Ukrainian officials, Ambassador Sondland understood that President Trump did not require that Ukraine *conduct* investigations as a prerequisite for the White House meeting so much as publicly *announce* the investigations—making clear that the goal was not the investigations, but the political benefit Trump would derive from their announcement and the cloud they might put over a political opponent.

On August 2, President Zelensky's advisor, Mr. Yermak, traveled to Madrid to meet Mr. Giuliani in person. There, they agreed that Ukraine would issue a public statement, and they discussed potential dates for a White House meeting. A few days later, Ambassador Volker told Mr. Giuliani that it "would be good" if Mr. Giuliani would report to "the boss," President Trump, about "the results" of his Madrid discussion so that President Trump would finally agree to a White House visit by President Zelensky.

On August 9, Ambassador Volker and Mr. Giuliani spoke twice by phone, and Ambassador Sondland spoke twice to the White House for a total of about 20 minutes. In a text message to Ambassador Volker later that day, Ambassador Sondland wrote, "I think potus [sic] really wants the deliverable," which Ambassador Sondland acknowledged was the public statement announcing the two political investigations sought by President Trump and Mr. Giuliani.

The following day, Ambassador Sondland briefed State Department Counselor Ulrich Brechbuhl, a top advisor to Secretary Pompeo, on these discussions about President Zelensky issuing a statement that would include an announcement of the two political investigations. Ambassador Sondland also emailed Secretary Pompeo directly, copying the State Department's executive secretary and Mr. Brechbuhl, to inform them about the agreement for President Zelensky to give the press conference. He expected to see a draft of the statement, which would be "delivered for our review in a day or two." Ambassador Sondland noted his hope that the draft statement would "make the boss happy enough to authorize an invitation."

On August 12, Mr. Yermak sent the proposed statement to Ambassador Volker, but it lacked specific references to the two investigations politically beneficial to President Trump's reelection campaign. The following morning, Ambassadors Sondland and Volker spoke with Mr. Giuliani, who made clear that if the statement "doesn't say Burisma and 2016, it's not credible." Ambassador Volker revised the statement following this direction to include those references and returned it to the Ukrainian President's aide.

Mr. Yermak balked at getting drawn into U.S. politics and asked Ambassador Volker whether the United States had inquired about investigations through any appropriate Department of Justice channels. The answer was no, and several witnesses testified that a request to a foreign country to investigate a U.S. citizen "for political reasons" goes "against everything" the United States sought to promote in eastern Europe, specifically the rule of law. Ambassador Volker eventually agreed with Mr. Yermak that the announcement of the Biden/Burisma and 2016 elections investigations would "look like it would play into our domestic politics," so the statement was temporarily "shelved."

Nevertheless, Ambassador Sondland, in accordance with President Trump's wishes, continued to pursue the statement into early September 2019.

Ukrainians Inquired about the President's Hold on Security Assistance

Once President Trump placed security assistance on hold in July, "it was inevitable that it was eventually going to come out." On July 25, DOD officials learned that diplomats at the Ukrainian Embassy in Washington had made multiple overtures to DOD and the State Department "asking about security assistance." Separately, two different contacts at the Ukrainian Embassy approached Ambassador Volker's special advisor, Catherine Croft, to ask her in confidence about the hold. Ms. Croft was surprised at the effectiveness of their "diplomatic tradecraft," noting that they "found out very early on" that the United States was withholding critical military aid to Ukraine. By mid-August, before the freeze on aid became public, Lt. Col. Vindman had also received inquiries from an official at the Ukrainian Embassy.

The hold remained in place throughout August against the unanimous judgment of American officials focused on Ukraine policy. Without an explanation for the hold, which ran contrary to the recommendation of all relevant agencies, and with President Trump already

22

conditioning a White House visit on the announcement of the political investigations, it became increasingly apparent to multiple witnesses that the military aid was also being withheld in exchange for the announcement of those. As both Ambassador Sondland and Mr. Holmes would later testify, it became as clear as "two plus two equals four."

On August 22, Ambassador Sondland emailed Secretary Pompeo again, recommending a plan for a potential meeting between President Trump and President Zelensky in Warsaw, Poland on September 1. Ambassador Sondland noted that President Zelensky should "look him in the eye" and tell President Trump that once new prosecutorial officials were in place in Ukraine, "Zelensky should be able to move forward publicly and with confidence on those issues of importance to Potus and the U.S." Ambassador Sondland testified that this was a reference to the political investigations that President Trump discussed on the July 25 call, that Secretary Pompeo had listened to. Ambassador Sondland hoped this would "break the logjam"—the hold on critical security assistance to Ukraine. Secretary Pompeo replied three minutes later: "Yes."

The President's Security Assistance Hold Became Public

On August 28, *Politico* published a story revealing President Trump's weeks-long hold on U.S. military assistance to Ukraine. Senior Ukrainian officials expressed grave concern, deeply worried about the practical impact on their efforts to fight Russian aggression, but also about the public message it sent to the Russian government, which would almost certainly seek to exploit any real or perceived crack in U.S. resolve toward Ukraine.

On August 29, at the urging of National Security Advisor Bolton, Ambassador Taylor wrote a first-person cable to Secretary Pompeo. This was the only first-person cable the Ambassador had ever sent in his decades of government service. He explained the "folly" of withholding security assistance to Ukraine as it fought a hot war against Russia on its borders. He wrote that he "could not and would not defend such a policy." Ambassador Taylor stated that Secretary Pompeo may have carried the cable with him to a meeting at the White House.

The same day that Ambassador Taylor sent his cable, President Trump cancelled his planned trip to Warsaw for a World War II commemoration event, where he was scheduled to meet with President Zelensky. Vice President Pence traveled in his place. Ambassador Sondland also traveled to Warsaw and, at a pre-briefing discussion with the Vice President before he met President Zelensky, Ambassador Sondland raised the issue of the hold on security assistance. He told Vice President Pence that he was concerned that the security assistance "had become tied to the issue of investigations" and that "everything is being held up until these statements get made." Vice President Pence nodded in response, apparently expressing neither surprise nor dismay at the linkage between the two.

At the meeting, President Zelensky expressed concern that even an appearance of wavering support from the United States for Ukraine could embolden Russia. Vice President Pence reiterated U.S. support for Ukraine, but could not promise that the hold would be lifted. Vice President Pence said he would relay his support for lifting the hold to President Trump so a decision could be made on security assistance as soon as possible. Vice President Pence spoke with President Trump that evening, but the hold was not lifted.

Following this meeting, Ambassador Sondland pulled aside President Zelensky's advisor, Mr. Yermak, to explain that the hold on security assistance was conditioned on the public announcement of the Burisma/Biden and the 2016 election interference investigations. After learning of the conversation, Ambassador Taylor texted Ambassador Sondland: "Are we now saying that security assistance and WH meeting are conditioned on investigations?"

The two then spoke by phone. Ambassador Sondland explained that he had previously made a "mistake" in telling Ukrainian officials that only the White House meeting was conditioned on a public announcement of the political investigations beneficial to President Trump. He clarified that "everything"—the White House meeting and hundreds of millions of dollars of security assistance to Ukraine—was now conditioned on the announcement. President Trump wanted President Zelensky in a "public box," which Ambassador Taylor understood to mean that President Trump required that President Zelensky make a public announcement about the investigations and that a private commitment would not do.

On September 7, President Trump and Ambassador Sondland spoke. Ambassador Sondland stated to his colleagues that the President said, "there was no quid pro quo," but that President Zelensky would be required to announce the investigations in order for the hold on security assistance to be lifted, "and he should want to do it." Ambassador Sondland passed on a similar message directly to President Zelensky and Mr. Yermak that, "although this was not a quid pro quo, if President Zelensky did not clear things up in public, we would be at a stalemate," referring to the hold on security assistance. Arrangements were made for the Ukrainian President to make a public statement during an interview on CNN.

After speaking with Ambassador Sondland, Ambassador Taylor texted Ambassadors Sondland and Volker: "As I said on the phone, I think it's crazy to withhold security assistance for help with a political campaign." Notwithstanding his long-held understanding that the White House meeting was conditioned on the public announcement of two political investigations desired by President Trump—and not broader anti-corruption concerns—Ambassador Sondland responded hours later:

> Bill, I believe you are incorrect about President Trump's intentions. The President has been crystal clear: no quid pro quo's of any kind. The President is trying to evaluate whether Ukraine is truly going to adopt the transparency and reforms that President Zelensky promised during his campaign. I suggest we stop the back and forth by text. If you still have concerns, I recommend you give Lisa Kenna or [Secretary Pompeo] a call to discuss with them directly. Thanks.

Ambassador Sondland's subsequent testimony revealed this text to be a false exculpatory—an untruthful statement that can later be used to conceal incriminating information. In his public testimony, Ambassador Sondland testified that the President's direction to withhold a presidential telephone call and a White House meeting for President Zelensky were both quid pro quos designed to pressure Ukraine to announce the investigations. He also testified that he developed a clear understanding that the military aid was also conditioned on the investigations, that it was as simple as 2+2=4. Sondland confirmed that his clear understanding was unchanged after speaking with President Trump, which he then communicated to the Ukrainians—President Zelensky had to publicly announce the two investigations if he wanted to get the meeting or the military aid.

In Ambassador Sondland's testimony, he was not clear on whether he had one conversation with the President in which the subject of a quid pro quo came up, or two, or on precisely which date the conversation took place during the period of September 6 through 9. In one version of the conversation which Ambassador Sondland suggested may have taken place on September 9, he claimed that the President answered an open question about what he wanted from Ukraine with an immediate denial—"no quid pro quo." In another, he admitted that the President told him that President Zelensky should go to a microphone and announce the investigations, and that he should want to do so—effectively confirming a quid pro quo.

Both Ambassador Taylor and Mr. Morrison, relying on their contemporaneous notes, testified that the call between Ambassador Sondland and President Trump occurred on September 7, which is further confirmed by Ambassador Sondland's own text message on September 8 in which he wrote that he had "multiple convos" with President Zelensky and President Trump. A call on September 9, which would have occurred in the middle of the night, is at odds with the weight of the evidence and not backed up by any records the White House was willing to provide Ambassador Sondland. Regardless of the date, Ambassador Sondland did not contest telling both Mr. Morrison and Ambassador Taylor of a conversation he had with the President in which the President reaffirmed Ambassador Sondland's understanding of the quid pro quo for the military aid.

As Ambassador Sondland acknowledged bluntly in his conversation with Mr. Holmes, President Trump's sole interest with respect to Ukraine was the "big stuff" that benefited him personally, such as the investigations into former Vice President Biden, and not President Zelensky's promises of transparency and reform.

The President's Scheme Unraveled

By early September, President Zelensky was ready to make a public announcement of the two investigations to secure a White House meeting and the military assistance his country desperately needed. He proceeded to book an interview on CNN during which he could make such an announcement, but other events soon intervened.

On September 9, the House Permanent Select Committee on Intelligence, the Committees on Oversight and Reform, and the Committee on Foreign Affairs announced an investigation into the scheme by President Trump and his personal attorney, Mr. Giuliani "to improperly pressure the Ukrainian government to assist the President's bid for reelection." The Committees sent document production and preservation requests to the White House and the State Department related to the investigation. NSC staff members believed this investigation might have had "the effect of releasing the hold" on Ukraine military assistance because it would have been "potentially politically challenging" to "justify that hold."

Later that day, the Inspector General of the Intelligence Community (ICIG) sent a letter to Chairman Schiff and Ranking Member Nunes notifying the Committee that a whistleblower had filed a complaint on August 12 that the ICIG had determined to be both an "urgent concern" and "credible." Nevertheless, the Acting Director of National Intelligence (DNI) took the unprecedented step of withholding the complaint from the Congressional Intelligence Committees, in coordination with the White House and the Department of Justice.

The White House had been aware of the whistleblower complaint for several weeks, and press reports indicate that the President was briefed on it in late August. The ICIG's notification to Congress of the complaint's existence, and the announcement of a separate investigation into the same subject matter, telegraphed to the White House that attempts to condition the security assistance on the announcement of the political investigations beneficial to President Trump—and efforts to cover up that misconduct—would not last.

On September 11, in the face of growing public and Congressional scrutiny, President Trump lifted the hold on security assistance to Ukraine. As with the implementation of the hold, no clear reason was given. By the time the President ordered the release of security assistance to Ukraine, DOD was unable to spend approximately 14 percent of the funds appropriated by Congress for Fiscal Year 2019. Congress had to pass a new law to extend the funding in order to ensure the full amount could be used by Ukraine to defend itself.

Even after the hold was lifted, President Zelensky still intended to sit for an interview with CNN in order to announce the investigations—indeed, he still wanted the White House meeting. At the urging of Ambassador Taylor, President Zelensky cancelled the CNN interview on September 18 or 19. The White House meeting, however, still has not occurred.

The President's Chief of Staff Confirmed Aid was Conditioned on Investigations

The conditioning of military aid to Ukraine on the investigations sought by the President was as clear to Ambassador Sondland as "two plus two equals four." In fact, the President's own Acting Chief of Staff, someone who meets with him daily, admitted that he had discussed security assistance with the President and that his decision to withhold it was directly tied to his desire to get Ukraine to conduct a political investigation.

On October 17, at a press briefing in the White House, Acting Chief of Staff Mick Mulvaney confirmed that President Trump withheld the essential military aid for Ukraine as leverage to pressure Ukraine to investigate the conspiracy theory that Ukraine had interfered in the 2016 U.S. election. As Dr. Hill made clear in her testimony, this false narrative has been promoted by President Putin to deflect away from Russia's systemic interference in our election and to drive a wedge between the United States and a key partner.

According to Mr. Mulvaney, President Trump "[a]bsolutely" mentioned "corruption related to the DNC server" in connection with the security assistance during his July 25 call. Mr. Mulvaney also stated that the server was part of "why we held up the money." After a reporter attempted to clarify this explicit acknowledgement of a quid pro quo, Mr. Mulvaney replied:

"We do that all the time with foreign policy." He added, "I have news for everybody: get over it. There is going to be political influence in foreign policy."

Ambassador Taylor testified that in his decades of military and diplomatic service, he had never seen another example of foreign aid conditioned on the personal or political interests of the President. Rather, "we condition assistance on issues that will improve our foreign policy, serve our foreign policy, ensure that taxpayers' money is well-spent," not specific investigations designed to benefit the political interests of the President of the United States.

In contrast, President Trump does not appear to believe there is any such limitation on his power to use White House meetings, military aid or other official acts to procure foreign help in his reelection. When asked by a reporter on October 3 what he had hoped President Zelensky would do following their July 25 call, President Trump responded: "Well, I would think that, if they were honest about it, they'd start a major investigation into the Bidens. It's a very simple answer."

SECTION II—THE PRESIDENT'S OBSTRUCTION OF THE HOUSE OF REPRESENTATIVES' IMPEACHMENT INQUIRY

The President Obstructed the Impeachment Inquiry by Instructing Witnesses and Agencies to Ignore Subpoenas for Documents and Testimony

An Unprecedented Effort to Obstruct an Impeachment Inquiry

Donald Trump is the first President in the history of the United States to seek to completely obstruct an impeachment inquiry undertaken by the House of Representatives under Article I of the Constitution, which vests the House with the "sole Power of Impeachment." He has publicly and repeatedly rejected the authority of Congress to conduct oversight of his actions and has directly challenged the authority of the House to conduct an impeachment inquiry into his actions regarding Ukraine.

President Trump ordered federal agencies and officials to disregard all voluntary requests for documents and defy all duly authorized subpoenas for records. He also directed all federal officials in the Executive Branch not to testify—even when compelled.

No other President has flouted the Constitution and power of Congress to conduct oversight to this extent. No President has claimed for himself the right to deny the House's authority to conduct an impeachment proceeding, control the scope of a power exclusively vested in the House, and forbid any and all cooperation from the Executive Branch. Even President Richard Nixon—who obstructed Congress by refusing to turn over key evidence—accepted the authority of Congress to conduct an impeachment inquiry and permitted his aides and advisors to produce documents and testify to Congressional committees.

Despite President Trump's unprecedented and categorical commands, the House gathered overwhelming evidence of his misconduct from courageous individuals who were willing to follow the law, comply with duly authorized subpoenas, and tell the truth. In response, the President engaged in a brazen effort to publicly attack and intimidate these witnesses.

If left unanswered, President Trump's ongoing effort to thwart Congress' impeachment power risks doing grave harm to the institution of Congress, the balance of power between our branches of government, and the Constitutional order that the President and every Member of Congress have sworn to protect and defend.

Constitutional Authority for Congressional Oversight and Impeachment

The House's Constitutional and legal authority to conduct an impeachment inquiry is clear, as is the duty of the President to cooperate with the House's exercise of this authority.

Article I of the U.S. Constitution gives the House of Representatives the "sole Power of Impeachment." The Framers intended the impeachment power to be an essential check on a President who might engage in corruption or abuse of power. Congress is empowered to conduct oversight and investigations to carry out its authorities under Article I. Because the impeachment power is a core component of the nation's Constitutional system of checks and balances, Congress' investigative authority is at its zenith during an impeachment inquiry.

The Supreme Court has made clear that Congress' authority to investigate includes the authority to compel the production of information by issuing subpoenas, a power the House has delegated to its committees pursuant to its Constitutional authority to "determine the Rules of its Proceedings."

Congress has also enacted statutes to support its power to investigate and oversee the Executive Branch. These laws impose criminal and other penalties on those who fail to comply with inquiries from Congress or block others from doing so, and they reflect the broader Constitutional requirement to cooperate with Congressional investigations.

Unlike President Trump, past Presidents who were the subject of impeachment inquiries—including Presidents Andrew Johnson, Richard Nixon, and Bill Clinton—recognized and, to varying degrees, complied with information requests and subpoenas.

President Nixon, for example, agreed to let his staff testify voluntarily in the Senate Watergate investigation, stating: "All members of the White House Staff will appear voluntarily when requested by the committee. They will testify under oath, and they will answer fully all proper questions." President Nixon also produced documents in response to the House's subpoenas as part of its impeachment inquiry, including more than 30 transcripts of White House recordings and notes from meetings with the President. When President Nixon withheld tape recordings and produced heavily edited and inaccurate records, the House Judiciary Committee approved an article of impeachment for obstruction.

The President's Categorical Refusal to Comply

Even before the House of Representatives launched its investigation regarding Ukraine, President Trump rejected the authority of Congress to investigate his actions, proclaiming, "We're fighting all the subpoenas," and "I have an Article II, where I have the right to do whatever I want as president."

When the Intelligence, Oversight and Reform, and Foreign Affairs Committees began reviewing the President's actions as part of the House's impeachment inquiry, the President repeatedly challenged the legitimacy of the investigation in word and deed. His rhetorical attacks appeared intended not only to dispute reports of his misconduct, but to persuade the American people that the House lacks authority to investigate the President.

On September 26, President Trump argued that Congress should not be "allowed" to impeach him under the Constitution and that there "should be a way of stopping it—maybe legally, through the courts." A common theme of his defiance has been his claims that Congress is acting in an unprecedented way and using unprecedented rules. However, the House has been following the same investigative rules that Republicans championed when they were in control.

On October 8, White House Counsel Pat Cipollone sent a letter to House Speaker Nancy Pelosi and the Chairmen of the investigating Committees confirming that President Trump directed his entire Administration not to cooperate with the House's impeachment inquiry. Mr. Cipollone wrote: "President Trump cannot permit his Administration to participate in this partisan inquiry under these circumstances."

Mr. Cipollone's letter advanced remarkably politicized arguments and legal theories unsupported by the Constitution, judicial precedent, and more than 200 years of history. If allowed to stand, the President's defiance, as justified by Mr. Cipollone, would represent an existential threat to the nation's Constitutional system of checks and balances, separation of powers, and rule of law.

The President's Refusal to Produce Any and All Subpoenaed Documents

Following President Trump's categorical order, not a single document has been produced by the White House, the Office of the Vice President, the Office of Management and Budget, the Department of State, the Department of Defense, or the Department of Energy in response to 71 specific, individualized requests or demands for records in their possession, custody, or control. These subpoenas remain in full force and effect. These agencies and offices also blocked many current and former officials from producing records directly to the Committees.

Certain witnesses defied the President's sweeping, categorical, and baseless order and identified the substance of key documents. For example, Ambassador Gordon Sondland attached ten exhibits to his written hearing testimony reflecting reproductions of certain communications with high-level Administration officials, including Acting White House Chief of Staff Mick Mulvaney, former National Security Advisor John Bolton, Secretary of State Mike Pompeo, and Secretary of Energy Rick Perry. Other witnesses identified numerous additional documents that the President and various agencies are withholding that are directly relevant to the impeachment inquiry.

Like the White House, the Department of State refused to produce a single document in response to its subpoena, even though there is no legal basis for the Department's actions. In fact, on November 22, the Department was forced to produce 99 pages of emails, letters, notes, timelines, and news articles to a non-partisan, nonprofit ethics watchdog organization pursuant to a court order in a lawsuit filed under the Freedom of Information Act (FOIA). Although limited in scope, this production affirms that the Department is withholding responsive documents from Congress without any valid legal basis.

The President's Refusal to Allow Top Aides to Testify

No other President in history has issued an order categorically directing the entire Executive Branch not to testify before Congress, including in the context of an impeachment inquiry. President Trump issued just such an order.

As reflected in Mr. Cipollone's letter, President Trump directed government witnesses to violate their legal obligations and defy House subpoenas—regardless of their offices or

30

positions. President Trump even extended his order to former officials no longer employed by the federal government. This Administration-wide effort to prevent all witnesses from providing testimony was coordinated and comprehensive.

At President Trump's direction, twelve current or former Administration officials refused to testify as part of the House's impeachment inquiry, ten of whom did so in defiance of duly authorized subpoenas:

- Mick Mulvaney, Acting White House Chief of Staff
- Robert B. Blair, Assistant to the President and Senior Advisor to the Chief of Staff
- Ambassador John Bolton, Former National Security Advisor
- John A. Eisenberg, Deputy Counsel to the President for National Security Affairs and Legal Advisor, National Security Council
- Michael Ellis, Senior Associate Counsel to the President and Deputy Legal Advisor, National Security Council
- Preston Wells Griffith, Senior Director for International Energy and Environment, National Security Council
- Dr. Charles M. Kupperman, Former Deputy Assistant to the President for National Security Affairs, National Security Council
- Russell T. Vought, Acting Director, Office of Management and Budget
- Michael Duffey, Associate Director for National Security Programs, Office of Management and Budget
- Brian McCormack, Associate Director for Natural Resources, Energy, and Science, Office of Management and Budget
- T. Ulrich Brechbuhl, Counselor, Department of State
- Secretary Rick Perry, Department of Energy

These witnesses were warned that their refusal to testify "shall constitute evidence that may be used against you in a contempt proceeding" and "may be used as an adverse inference against you and the President."

The President's Unsuccessful Attempts to Block Other Key Witnesses

Despite President Trump's orders that no Executive Branch employees should cooperate with the House's impeachment inquiry, multiple key officials complied with duly authorized subpoenas and provided critical testimony at depositions and public hearings. These officials not only served their nation honorably, but they fulfilled their oath to support and defend the Constitution of the United States.

In addition to the President's broad orders seeking to prohibit all Executive Branch employees from testifying, many of these witnesses were personally directed by senior political appointees not to cooperate with the House's impeachment inquiry. These directives frequently cited or enclosed copies of Mr. Cipollone's October 8 letter conveying the President's order not to comply.

For example, the State Department, relying on President Trump's order, attempted to block Ambassador Marie Yovanovitch from testifying, but she fulfilled her legal obligations by appearing at a deposition on October 11 and a hearing on November 15. More than a dozen current and former officials followed her courageous example by testifying at depositions and public hearings over the course of the last two months. The testimony from these witnesses produced overwhelming and clear evidence of President Trump's misconduct, which is described in detail in the first section of this report.

The President's Intimidation of Witnesses

President Trump publicly attacked and intimidated witnesses who came forward to comply with duly authorized subpoenas and testify about his misconduct, raising grave concerns about potential violations of criminal laws intended to protect witnesses appearing before Congressional proceedings. For example, the President attacked:

- Ambassador Marie Yovanovitch, who served the United States honorably for decades as a U.S. diplomat and anti-corruption advocate in posts around the world under six different Presidents;

- Ambassador Bill Taylor, who graduated at the top of his class at West Point, served as an infantry commander in Vietnam, and earned a Bronze Star and an Air Medal with a V device for valor;

- Lieutenant Colonel Alexander Vindman, an active-duty Army officer for more than 20 years who earned a Purple Heart for wounds he sustained in an improvised explosive device attack in Iraq, as well as the Combat Infantryman Badge; and

- Jennifer Williams, who is Vice President Mike Pence's top advisor on Europe and Russia and has a distinguished record of public service under the Bush, Obama, and Trump Administrations.

The President engaged in this effort to intimidate these public servants to prevent them from cooperating with Congress' impeachment inquiry. He issued threats, openly discussed possible retaliation, made insinuations about their character and patriotism, and subjected them to mockery and derision—when they deserved the opposite. The President's attacks were broadcast to millions of Americans—including witnesses' families, friends, and coworkers.

It is a federal crime to intimidate or seek to intimidate any witness appearing before Congress. This prohibition applies to anyone who knowingly "uses intimidation, threatens, or corruptly persuades" another person in order to "influence, delay, or prevent the testimony of any person in an official proceeding." Violations of this law can carry a criminal sentence of up to 20 years in prison.

In addition to his relentless attacks on witnesses who testified in connection with the House's impeachment inquiry, the President also repeatedly threatened and attacked a member of the Intelligence Community who filed an anonymous whistleblower complaint raising an "urgent concern" that "appeared credible" regarding the President's conduct. The whistleblower filed the complaint confidentially with the Inspector General of the Intelligence Community, as authorized by the relevant whistleblower law. Federal law prohibits the Inspector General from revealing the whistleblower's identity. Federal law also protects the whistleblower from retaliation.

In more than 100 public statements about the whistleblower over a period of just two months, the President publicly questioned the whistleblower's motives, disputed the accuracy of the whistleblower's account, and encouraged others to reveal the whistleblower's identity. Most chillingly, the President issued a threat against the whistleblower and those who provided information to the whistleblower regarding the President's misconduct, suggesting that they could face the death penalty for treason.

The President's campaign of intimidation risks discouraging witnesses from coming forward voluntarily, complying with mandatory subpoenas for documents and testimony, and disclosing potentially incriminating evidence in this inquiry and future Congressional investigations.

KEY FINDINGS OF FACT

Based on witness testimony and evidence collected during the impeachment inquiry, the Intelligence Committee has found that:

I. Donald J. Trump, the 45th President of the United States—acting personally and through his agents within and outside of the U.S. government—solicited the interference of a foreign government, Ukraine, in the 2020 U.S. presidential election. The President engaged in this course of conduct for the benefit of his reelection, to harm the election prospects of a political opponent, and to influence our nation's upcoming presidential election to his advantage. In so doing, the President placed his personal political interests above the national interests of the United States, sought to undermine the integrity of the U.S. presidential election process, and endangered U.S. national security.

II. In furtherance of this scheme, President Trump—directly and acting through his agents within and outside the U.S. government—sought to pressure and induce Ukraine's newly-elected president, Volodymyr Zelensky, to publicly announce unfounded investigations that would benefit President Trump's personal political interests and reelection effort. To advance his personal political objectives, President Trump encouraged the President of Ukraine to work with his personal attorney, Rudy Giuliani.

III. As part of this scheme, President Trump, acting in his official capacity and using his position of public trust, personally and directly requested from the President of Ukraine that the government of Ukraine publicly announce investigations into (1) the President's political opponent, former Vice President Joseph R. Biden, Jr. and his son, Hunter Biden, and (2) a baseless theory promoted by Russia alleging that Ukraine—rather than Russia—interfered in the 2016 U.S. election. These investigations were intended to harm a potential political opponent of President Trump and benefit the President's domestic political standing.

IV. President Trump ordered the suspension of $391 million in vital military assistance urgently needed by Ukraine, a strategic partner, to resist Russian aggression. Because the aid was appropriated by Congress, on a bipartisan basis, and signed into law by the President, its expenditure was required by law. Acting directly and through his subordinates within the U.S. government, the President withheld from Ukraine this military assistance without any legitimate foreign policy, national security, or anti-corruption justification. The President did so despite the longstanding bipartisan support of Congress, uniform support across federal departments and agencies for the provision to Ukraine of the military assistance, and his obligations under the Impoundment Control Act.

V. President Trump used the power of the Office of the President and exercised his authority over the Executive Branch, including his control of the instruments of the federal government, to apply increasing pressure on the President of Ukraine and the Ukrainian government to announce the politically-motivated investigations desired by President Trump. Specifically, to advance and promote his scheme, the President withheld official acts of value to Ukraine and conditioned their fulfillment on actions by Ukraine that would benefit his personal political interests:

A.   President Trump—acting through agents within and outside the U.S. government—conditioned a head of state meeting at the White House, which the President of Ukraine desperately sought to demonstrate continued United States support for Ukraine in the face of Russian aggression, on Ukraine publicly announcing the investigations that President Trump believed would aid his reelection campaign.

B.   To increase leverage over the President of Ukraine, President Trump, acting through his agents and subordinates, conditioned release of the vital military assistance he had suspended to Ukraine on the President of Ukraine's public announcement of the investigations that President Trump sought.

C.   President Trump's closest subordinates and advisors within the Executive Branch, including Acting Chief of Staff Mick Mulvaney, Secretary of State Mike Pompeo, Secretary of Energy J. Richard Perry, and other senior White House and Executive Branch officials had knowledge of, in some cases facilitated and furthered the President's scheme, and withheld information about the scheme from the Congress and the American public.

VI.   In directing and orchestrating this scheme to advance his personal political interests, President Trump did not implement, promote, or advance U.S. anti-corruption policies. In fact, the President sought to pressure and induce the government of Ukraine to announce politically-motivated investigations lacking legitimate predication that the U.S. government otherwise discourages and opposes as a matter of policy in that country and around the world. In so doing, the President undermined U.S. policy supporting anti-corruption reform and the rule of law in Ukraine, and undermined U.S. national security.

VII.   By withholding vital military assistance and diplomatic support from a strategic foreign partner government engaged in an ongoing military conflict illegally instigated by Russia, President Trump compromised national security to advance his personal political interests.

VIII.   Faced with the revelation of his actions, President Trump publicly and repeatedly persisted in urging foreign governments, including Ukraine and China, to investigate his political opponent. This continued solicitation of foreign interference in a U.S. election presents a clear and present danger that the President will continue to use the power of his office for his personal political gain.

IX.   Using the power of the Office of the President, and exercising his authority over the Executive Branch, President Trump ordered and implemented a campaign to conceal his conduct from the public and frustrate and obstruct the House of Representatives' impeachment inquiry by:

A.   refusing to produce to the impeachment inquiry's investigating Committees information and records in the possession of the White House, in defiance of a lawful subpoena;

B.   directing Executive Branch agencies to defy lawful subpoenas and withhold the production of all documents and records from the investigating Committees;

C.   directing current and former Executive Branch officials not to cooperate with the Committees, including in defiance of lawful subpoenas for testimony; and

D.   intimidating, threatening, and tampering with prospective and actual witnesses in the impeachment inquiry in an effort to prevent, delay, or influence the testimony of those witnesses.

In so doing, and despite the fact that the Constitution vests in the House of Representatives the "sole Power of Impeachment," the President sought to arrogate to himself the right to determine the propriety, scope, and nature of an impeachment inquiry into his own misconduct, and the right to deny any and all information to the Congress in the conduct of its constitutional responsibilities.

SECTION I.

THE PRESIDENT'S MISCONDUCT

1.   The President Forced Out the U.S. Ambassador to Ukraine

> *The President forced out the United States Ambassador to Ukraine, Marie Yovanovitch,*
> *following a baseless smear campaign promoted by President Trump's personal attorney,*
> *Rudy Giuliani, and others. The campaign publicized conspiracy theories that benefited the*
> *President's personal political interests and undermined official U.S. policy, some of which*
> *the President raised during his July 25 call with the President of Ukraine.*

Overview

On April 24, 2019, President Donald J. Trump abruptly recalled the U.S. Ambassador to Ukraine, Marie Yovanovitch. Ambassador Yovanovitch, an award-winning 33-year veteran Foreign Service officer, aggressively advocated for anti-corruption reforms in Ukraine consistent with U.S. foreign policy. President Trump forced her out following a baseless smear campaign promoted by his personal attorney, Rudy Giuliani, associates of Mr. Giuliani, and corrupt Ukrainians.

Ambassador Yovanovitch was told by the State Department that President Trump had lost confidence in her, but she was never provided a substantive justification for her removal. Her ouster set the stage for other U.S. officials appointed by President Trump to work in cooperation with Mr. Giuliani to advance a scheme in support of the President's reelection.

Mr. Giuliani and his associates promoted false conspiracy theories about Ukraine colluding with Democrats to interfere in the 2016 U.S. election. This false claim was promoted by Russian President Vladimir Putin in February 2017—less than a month after the unanimous U.S. Intelligence Community assessment that Russia alone was responsible for a covert influence campaign aimed at helping President Trump during the 2016 election. Mr. Giuliani also made discredited public allegations about former Vice President Joe Biden and his son, Hunter, in an apparent effort to hurt President Trump's political rival in the 2020 presidential election. Mr. Giuliani's associates, with their own ties to President Trump, also worked to enter into arrangements with current and former corrupt Ukrainian officials to promote these false allegations—the same unfounded allegations President Trump requested that Ukraine investigate on his July 25 call with Ukrainian President Volodymyr Zelensky.

President Trump amplified these baseless allegations by tweeting them just a month before he recalled Ambassador Yovanovitch. Despite requests from Ambassador Yovanovitch and other senior State Department officials, Secretary of State Mike Pompeo refused to issue a statement of support for the Ambassador or the U.S. Embassy in Ukraine for fear of being undermined by a tweet by President Trump.

The removal of Ambassador Yovanovitch left a vacuum in the leadership of the U.S. Embassy in Ukraine at an important time. A new president had just been elected on an anti-corruption platform, and the country was in a period of transition as it continued to defend itself against Russia-led military aggression in the east.

Anti-Corruption Ceremony Interrupted to Recall Anti-Corruption Ambassador

Ambassador Yovanovitch represented the United States of America as the U.S. Ambassador to Ukraine from 2016 to 2019. She is a non-partisan career public servant, first selected for the American Foreign Service in 1986. President George W. Bush named her as his Ambassador twice, to the Kyrgyz Republic and Armenia, and President Barack Obama nominated her for the posting in Kyiv.[1]

On the evening of April 24, Ambassador Yovanovitch approached a podium in front of gold drapes at the U.S. Ambassador's residence in Ukraine's capital city. She was hosting an event to present an award of courage to the father of Kateryna Handziuk, who was brutally murdered by people who opposed her efforts to expose and root out public corruption in Ukraine. In 2018, attackers threw sulfuric acid at Ms. Handziuk, burning more than 30 percent of her body. After months of suffering and nearly a dozen surgeries, she died at the age of 33.[2] Her attackers have still not been held to account.[3]

Ambassador Yovanovitch began her speech by noting that Ms. Handziuk "was a woman of courage who committed herself to speaking out against wrongdoing." She lamented how Ms. Handziuk had "paid the ultimate price for her fearlessness in fighting against corruption and for her determined efforts to build a democratic Ukraine." She pledged that the United States would "continue to stand with those engaged in the fight for a democratic Ukraine free of corruption, where people are held accountable" and commended Ukrainians who "have demonstrated to the world that they are willing to fight for a better system."[4]

Ambassador Yovanovitch concluded her remarks by holding Ms. Handziuk's story up as an inspiration to the many Ukrainians striving to chart a new course for their country in the face of Russian interference and aggression:

> I think we can all see what a remarkable woman Kateryna Handziuk was, but she continues to inspire all of us to fight for justice. She was a courageous woman, who wanted to make Ukraine a better place. And she is continuing to do so. And I'll just leave you with one thought that was expressed in Washington at the ceremony—that courage is contagious. I think we saw that on the Maidan in 2014, we see that on the front lines every day in the Donbas, we see it in the work that Kateryna Handziuk did here in Ukraine. And we see it in the work of all of you—day in, day out—fighting for Ukraine and the future of Ukraine.[5]

Ambassador Yovanovitch's evening was interrupted around 10:00 p.m. by a telephone call from the State Department's headquarters in Washington, D.C.

Director General of the Foreign Service and Director of Human Resources Ambassador Carol Perez warned that the Department's leaders had "great concern" and "were worried" about her. Ambassador Yovanovitch testified that it is "hard to know how to react to something like that." Ambassador Perez said she did not know what the concerns were but pledged she would "try to find out more" and would try to call back "by midnight."[6]

Finally, at 1:00 a.m. in Kyiv, Ambassador Perez called again: The "concerns" were from "up the street" at the White House. Ambassador Perez said that Ambassador Yovanovitch needed to "come home immediately, get on the next plane to the U.S." She warned that there were concerns about Ambassador Yovanovitch's "security." When Ambassador Yovanovitch asked if Ambassador Perez was referring to her physical safety, Ambassador Perez relayed that she "hadn't gotten that impression that it was a physical security issue," but that Ambassador Yovanovitch "needed to come home right away."[7]

Ambassador Yovanovitch asked Ambassador Perez specifically whether this order had anything to do with President Trump's personal attorney, Rudy Giuliani, who had been making unfounded allegations against her in the media. Ambassador Perez said she "didn't know."[8] Ambassador Yovanovitch argued that this order to return to Washington, D.C. was "extremely irregular" and that no one had provided her a reason.[9] In the end, however, Ambassador Yovanovitch swiftly returned to Washington.[10]

Rudy Giuliani, on Behalf of President Trump, Led a Smear Campaign to Oust Ambassador Yovanovitch

Ambassador Yovanovitch's recall followed a concerted smear campaign by Mr. Giuliani and his associates, promoted by President Trump. The campaign was largely directed by Rudy Giuliani, President Trump's personal attorney since early 2018.[11] A cast of supporting characters, which included corrupt Ukrainian prosecutors, now-indicted middlemen, conservative media pundits, and attorneys close to President Trump, assisted Mr. Giuliani. Among those associates were two U.S. citizens, Lev Parnas and Igor Fruman. Mr. Parnas and Mr. Fruman were Florida-based businessmen who were represented by Mr. Giuliani "in connection with their personal and business affairs" and who also "assisted Mr. Giuliani in connection with his representation of President Trump."[12] Both Mr. Parnas and Mr. Fruman were criminally indicted in the Southern District of New York in October and face charges of conspiring to violate the federal ban on foreign donations and contributions in connection with federal and state elections.[13] Dr. Fiona Hill, former Deputy Assistant to the President and Senior Director for Europe and Russian Affairs, National Security Council (NSC), learned from her colleagues that "these guys were notorious in Florida and that they were bad news."[14]

The campaign was also propelled by individuals in Ukraine, including two prosecutors general. Yuriy Lutsenko served as the Prosecutor General of Ukraine under former Ukrainian President Petro Poroshenko—the incumbent who lost to President Zelensky in April 2019—and previously was the head of President Poroshenko's faction in the Ukrainian parliament.[15] Viktor Shokin was Mr. Lutsenko's predecessor and was removed from office in 2016.[16] Mr. Shokin has been described as "a typical Ukraine prosecutor who lived a lifestyle far in excess of his government salary, who never prosecuted anybody known for having committed a crime," and "covered up crimes that were known to have been committed."[17]

In late 2018, Ukrainian officials informed Ambassador Yovanovitch about Mr. Giuliani's and Mr. Lutsenko's plans to target her. They told her that Mr. Lutsenko "was in communication with Mayor Giuliani" and that "they were going to, you know, do things, including to me."[18]

Soon thereafter, Ambassador Yovanovitch learned that "there had been a number of meetings" between Mr. Giuliani and Mr. Lutsenko, who was looking to "hurt" her "in the U.S."[19]

The allegations against Ambassador Yovanovitch, which later surfaced publicly, concerned false claims that she had provided a "do-not-prosecute list" to Mr. Lutsenko and made disparaging comments about President Trump.[20]

Ambassador Yovanovitch inferred that Mr. Lutsenko was spreading "falsehoods" about her because she was "effective at helping Ukrainians who wanted reform, Ukrainians who wanted to fight against corruption, and ... that was not in his interest."[21] Anti-corruption reform was not in Mr. Lutsenko's interest because he himself was known to be corrupt.[22] David Holmes, Counselor for Political Affairs at the U.S. Embassy in Kyiv, Ukraine, explained that:

> In mid-March 2019, an Embassy colleague learned from a Ukrainian contact that Mr. Lutsenko had complained that Ambassador Yovanovitch had, quote, unquote, destroyed him, with her refusal to support him until he followed through with his reform commitments and ceased using his position for personal gain.[23]

Deputy Assistant Secretary of State George Kent similarly summarized Mr. Lutsenko's smear campaign against Ambassador Yovanovitch, which was facilitated by Mr. Giuliani and his associates, as motivated by revenge:

> Over the course of 2018 and 2019, I became increasingly aware of an effort by Rudy Giuliani and others, including his associates Lev Parnas and Igor Fruman, to run a campaign to smear Ambassador Yovanovitch and other officials at the U.S. Embassy in Kyiv. The chief agitators on the Ukrainian side of this effort were some of those same corrupt former prosecutors I had encountered, particularly Yuriy Lutsenko and Viktor Shokin. They were now peddling false information in order to extract revenge against those who had exposed their misconduct, including U.S. diplomats, Ukrainian anticorruption officials, and reform-minded civil society groups in Ukraine.[24]

Mr. Kent succinctly summarized, "[y]ou can't promote principled anti-corruption efforts without pissing off corrupt people."[25] By doing her job, Ambassador Yovanovitch drew Mr. Lutsenko's ire.

In late 2018 and early 2019, Mr. Lutsenko also risked losing his job as Prosecutor General and possible criminal investigation, if then-candidate Volodymyr Zelensky won the presidency. Special Representative for Ukraine Negotiations, Ambassador Kurt Volker, explained:

> As is often the case in Ukraine, a change in power would mean change in prosecutorial powers as well, and there have been efforts in the past at prosecuting the previous government. I think Mr. Lutsenko, in my estimation, and I said this to Mayor Giuliani when I met with him, was interested in preserving his own position. He wanted to avoid being fired by a new government in order to prevent prosecution of himself, possible prosecution of himself.[26]

Officials in Ukraine have also speculated that Mr. Lutsenko cultivated his relationship with Mr. Giuliani in an effort to hold on to his position.[27] Ambassador Yovanovitch described Mr. Lutsenko as an "opportunist" who "will ally himself, sometimes simultaneously … with whatever political or economic forces he believes will suit his interests best at the time."[28]

Mr. Lutsenko promoted debunked conspiracy theories that had gained traction with President Trump and Mr. Giuliani. Those debunked conspiracy theories alleged that the Ukrainian government—not Russia—was behind the hack of the Democratic National Committee (DNC) server in 2016, and that former Vice President Biden had petitioned for the removal of Mr. Shokin to prevent an investigation into Burisma Holdings, a Ukrainian energy company for which Vice President Biden's son, Hunter, served as a board member.

Both conspiracy theories served the personal political interests of President Trump because they would help him in his campaign for reelection in 2020. The first would serve to undercut Special Counsel Robert Mueller's investigation, which was still underway when Mr. Giuliani began his activities in Ukraine and was denounced as a "witch hunt" by the President and his supporters.[29] The second would serve to damage Democratic presidential candidate Vice President Biden.

These conspiracies lacked any basis in fact. The Intelligence Community, the Senate Select Committee on Intelligence, both the Majority and Minority of the House Permanent Select Committee on Intelligence, and the investigation undertaken by Special Counsel Robert Mueller concluded that Russia was responsible for interfering in the 2016 election.[30] President Trump's former Homeland Security Advisor, Tom Bossert, said that the idea of Ukraine hacking the DNC server was "not only a conspiracy theory, it is completely debunked."[31]

Russia has pushed the false theory that Ukraine was involved in the 2016 election to distract from its own involvement.[32] Mr. Holmes testified that it was to President Putin's advantage to promote the theory of Ukrainian interference in the 2016 U.S. elections for several reasons:

> First of all, to deflect from the allegations of Russian interference. Second of all, to drive a wedge between the United States and Ukraine which Russia wants to essentially get back into its sphere of influence. Thirdly, to besmirch Ukraine and its political leadership, [and] to degrade and erode support for Ukraine from other key partners in Europe and elsewhere.[33]

The allegations that Vice President Biden inappropriately pressured the Ukrainians to remove Mr. Shokin also are without merit. Mr. Shokin was widely considered to be ineffective and corrupt.[34] When he urged the Ukrainian government to remove Mr. Shokin, Vice President Biden was advocating for anti-corruption reform and pursuing official U.S. policy.[35] Moreover, Mr. Shokin's removal was supported by other countries, the International Monetary Fund, and the World Bank, and was "widely understood internationally to be the right policy."[36] In May 2019, even Mr. Lutsenko himself admitted that there was no credible evidence of wrongdoing by Hunter Biden or Vice President Biden.[37]

Nevertheless, Mr. Giuliani engaged with both Mr. Lutsenko and Mr. Shokin regarding these baseless allegations. According to documents provided to the State Department Office of Inspector General, in January 23, 2019, Mr. Giuliani, Mr. Parnas, and Mr. Fruman participated in a conference call with Mr. Shokin. According to notes of the call, Mr. Shokin made allegations about Vice President Biden and Burisma. Mr. Shokin also claimed that Ambassador Yovanovitch had improperly denied him a U.S. visa and that she was close to Vice President Biden.[38]

Mr. Giuliani separately met with Mr. Lutsenko in New York.[39] Over the course of two days, on January 25 and 26, Mr. Giuliani, Mr. Lutsenko, Mr. Parnas, and Mr. Fruman, reportedly discussed whether Ambassador Yovanovitch was "loyal to President Trump," as well as investigations into Burisma and the Bidens.[40] For his part, Mr. Lutsenko later said he "understood very well" that Mr. Giuliani wanted Mr. Lutsenko to investigate former Vice President Biden and his son, Hunter. "I have 23 years in politics," Lutsenko said. "I knew. … I'm a political animal."[41]

Mr. Giuliani later publicly acknowledged that he was seeking information from Ukrainians on behalf of his client, President Trump. On October 23, Mr. Giuliani tweeted "everything I did was to discover evidence to defend my client against false charges."[42] Then, in a series of tweets on October 30, Mr. Giuliani stated:

> All of the information I obtained came from interviews conducted as … private defense counsel to POTUS, to defend him against false allegations. I began obtaining this information while Mueller was still investigating his witch hunt and a full 5 months before Biden even announced his run for Pres.[43]

President Trump and Mr. Giuliani's efforts to investigate alleged Ukrainian interference in the 2016 U.S. election and Vice President Biden negatively impacted the U.S. Embassy in Kyiv. Mr. Holmes testified:

> Beginning in March 2019, the situation at the Embassy and in Ukraine changed dramatically. Specifically, the three priorities of security, economy, and justice and our support for Ukrainian democratic resistance to Russian aggression became overshadowed by a political agenda promoted by former New York City Mayor Rudy Giuliani and a cadre of officials operating with a direct channel to the White House.[44]

U.S. national interests in Ukraine were undermined and subordinated to the personal, political interests of President Trump.

The Smear Campaign Accelerated in Late March 2019

The smear campaign entered a more public phase in the United States in late March 2019 with the publication of a series of opinion pieces in *The Hill*.

On March 20, 2019, John Solomon penned an opinion piece quoting a false claim by Mr. Lutsenko that Ambassador Yovanovitch had given him a do-not-prosecute list.[45] Mr. Lutsenko later retracted the claim.[46] Mr. Solomon's work also included false allegations that Ambassador Yovanovitch had "made disparaging statements about President Trump."[47] Ambassador Yovanovitch called this allegation "fictitious," and the State Department issued a statement describing the allegations as a "fabrication."[48]

The Committees uncovered evidence of close ties and frequent contacts between Mr. Solomon and Mr. Parnas, who was assisting Mr. Giuliani in connection with his representation of the President. Phone records show that in the 48 hours before publication of *The Hill* opinion piece, Mr. Parnas spoke with Mr. Solomon at least six times.[49] In addition, *The Hill* piece cited a letter dated May 9, 2018, from Representative Pete Sessions (R-Texas) to Secretary Pompeo, in which Rep. Sessions accused Ambassador Yovanovitch of speaking "privately and repeatedly about her disdain for the current administration."[50] A federal criminal indictment alleges that in or about May 2018, Mr. Parnas sought a congressman's assistance to remove Ambassador Yovanovitch, at the request of one or more Ukrainian government officials.[51]

On March 20, 2019, the day *The Hill* opinion piece was published, Mr. Parnas again spoke with Mr. Solomon for 11 minutes.[52] Shortly after that phone call, President Trump promoted Mr. Solomon's article in a tweet.[53]

Following President Trump's tweet, the public attacks against Ambassador Yovanovitch were further amplified on social media and were merged with the conspiracy theories regarding both Ukrainian interference in the 2016 U.S. election and the Bidens. On March 22, 2019, Mr. Giuliani tweeted: "Hillary, Kerry, and Biden people colluding with Ukrainian operatives to make money and affect 2016 election." He also gave an interview to *Fox News* in which he raised Hunter Biden and called for an investigation.[54] Then, on March 24, Donald Trump Jr. called Ambassador Yovanovitch a "joker" on Twitter and called for her removal.[55]

This campaign reverberated in Ukraine. Mr. Kent testified that "starting in mid-March" Mr. Giuliani was "almost unmissable" during this "campaign of slander" against Ambassador Yovanovitch.[56] According to Mr. Kent, Mr. Lutsenko's press spokeswoman retweeted Donald Trump, Jr.'s tweet attacking the Ambassador.[57]

Concerns About President Trump Kept State Department from Issuing Statement of Support

At the end of March, as this smear campaign intensified, Ambassador Yovanovitch sent Under Secretary of State for Political Affairs David Hale an email identifying her concerns with the false allegations about her and asking for a strong statement of support from the State Department. She explained that, otherwise, "it makes it hard to be a credible ambassador in a country."[58] Ambassador Hale had been briefed on the smears in a series of emails from Mr. Kent.[59] Ambassador Hale agreed that the allegations were without merit.[60]

Ambassador Yovanovitch was told that State Department officials were concerned that if they issued a public statement supporting her, "it could be undermined" by "[t]he President."[61] Ambassador Hale explained that a statement of support "would only fuel further negative reaction" and that "it might even provoke a public reaction from the President himself about the

Ambassador."[62] In short, State Department officials were concerned "that the rug would be pulled out from underneath the State Department."[63]

Ambassador Yovanovitch turned to the U.S. Ambassador to the European Union, Gordon Sondland, for advice. According to Ambassador Yovanovitch, Ambassador Sondland suggested that, in response to the smear campaign, she make a public statement in support of President Trump. She said Ambassador Sondland told her, "you need to go big or go home" and "tweet out there that you support the President, and that all these are lies and everything else."[64] Ambassador Yovanovitch said she felt that this "was advice that I did not see how I could implement in my role as an Ambassador, and as a Foreign Service officer."[65]

Ultimately, Secretary Pompeo refused to issue a public statement of support for Ambassador Yovanovitch. At the same time Secretary Pompeo was refusing to issue a statement, he was communicating with one of the individuals involved in the smear campaign against her. State Department records show that Secretary Pompeo spoke to Mr. Giuliani on March 26 and 28, not long after Mr. Solomon's first article in *The Hill*.[66]

The Smear Campaign was a Coordinated Effort by Mr. Giuliani, His Associates, and One or More Individuals at the White House

In April, Mr. Solomon continued to publish opinion pieces about Ambassador Yovanovitch and other conspiracy theories being pursued by Mr. Giuliani on behalf of President Trump. Mr. Solomon was not working alone. As further described below, there was a coordinated effort by associates of President Trump to push these false narratives publicly, as evidenced by public statements, phone records, and contractual agreements.

On April 1, Mr. Solomon published an opinion piece in *The Hill* alleging that Vice President Biden had inappropriately petitioned for the removal of Mr. Shokin to protect his son, Hunter.[67] The opinion piece was entitled, "Joe Biden's 2020 Ukrainian Nightmare: A Closed Probe is Revived." Many of the allegations in the piece were based on information provided by Mr. Lutsenko. The following day, Donald Trump, Jr. retweeted the article.[68]

Phone records obtained by the Committees show frequent communication between key players during this phase of the scheme. Between April 1 and April 7, Mr. Parnas exchanged approximately 16 calls with Mr. Giuliani (longest duration approximately seven minutes) and approximately 10 calls with Mr. Solomon (longest duration approximately nine minutes).[69]

On April 7, Mr. Solomon followed up with another opinion piece. The piece accused Ambassador Yovanovitch of preventing the issuance of U.S. visas for Ukrainian officials who wished to travel to the United States to provide purported evidence of wrongdoing by "American Democrats and their allies in Kiev."[70] One of those Ukrainian officials allegedly denied a visa was Konstiantyn Kulyk, a deputy to Mr. Lutesenko. Mr. Kulyk participated in a "wide-ranging interview" with Mr. Solomon and was extensively quoted.[71]

These Ukrainian officials claimed to have evidence of wrongdoing about Vice President Biden's efforts in 2015 to remove Mr. Shokin, Hunter Biden's role as a Burisma board member,

Ukrainian interference in the 2016 U.S. election in favor of Hillary Clinton, and the misappropriation and transfer of Ukrainian funds abroad.[72] The opinion piece also made clear that Mr. Giuliani was pursuing these very same theories on behalf of the President:

> More recently, President Trump's private attorney Rudy Giuliani—former mayor and former U.S. attorney in New York City—learned about some of the allegations while, on behalf of the Trump legal team, he looked into Ukrainian involvement in the 2016 election.

According to Mr. Solomon's piece, Mr. Lutsenko was reported to have sufficient evidence, "particularly involving Biden, his family and money spirited out of Ukraine—to warrant a meeting with U.S. Attorney General William Barr."[73]

On the same day that Mr. Solomon published these allegations, Mr. Giuliani appeared on *Fox News*. Mr. Giuliani discussed how he learned about alleged Ukrainian interference in the 2016 U.S. elections and the Bidens' purported misconduct in Ukraine:

> Let me tell you my interest in that. I got information about three or four months ago that a lot of the explanations for how this whole phony investigation started will be in the Ukraine, that there were a group of people in the Ukraine that were working to help Hillary Clinton and were colluding really—[LAUGHTER]—with the Clinton campaign. And it stems around the ambassador and the embassy, being used for political purposes. So I began getting some people that were coming forward and telling me about that. And then all of a sudden, they revealed the story about Burisma and Biden's son ... [Vice President Biden] bragged about pressuring Ukraine's president to firing [sic] a top prosecutor who was being criticized on a whole bunch of areas but was conducting investigation of this gas company which Hunter Biden served as a director.[74]

The next day, April 8, Mr. Giuliani tweeted about Mr. Solomon's opinion piece.[75]

Over the course of the four days following the April 7 article, phone records show contacts between Mr. Giuliani, Mr. Parnas, Representative Devin Nunes, and Mr. Solomon. Specifically, Mr. Giuliani and Mr. Parnas were in contact with one another, as well as with Mr. Solomon.[76] Phone records also show contacts on April 10 between Mr. Giuliani and Rep. Nunes, consisting of three short calls in rapid succession, followed by a text message, and ending with a nearly three minute call.[77] Later that same day, Mr. Parnas and Mr. Solomon had a four minute, 39 second call.[78]

Victoria Toensing, a lawyer who, along with her partner Joseph diGenova, once briefly represented President Trump in connection with Special Counsel Robert Mueller's investigation,[79] also was in phone contact with Mr. Giuliani and Mr. Parnas at the beginning of April.[80]

Beginning in mid-April, Ms. Toensing signed retainer agreements between diGenova & Toensing LLP and Mr. Lutsenko, Mr. Kulyk, and Mr. Shokin—all of whom feature in Mr. Solomon's opinion pieces.[81] In these retainer agreements, the firm agreed to represent Mr.

Lutsenko and Mr. Kulyk in meetings with U.S. officials regarding alleged "evidence" of Ukrainian interference in the 2016 U.S. elections, and to represent Mr. Shokin "for the purpose of collecting evidence regarding his March 2016 firing as Prosecutor General of Ukraine and the role of Vice President Biden in such firing, and presenting such evidence to U.S. and foreign authorities."[82] On July 25, President Trump would personally press President Zelensky to investigate these very same matters.

On April 23, Mr. Parnas had a call with Mr. Solomon, and multiple phone contacts with Mr. Giuliani.[83] On that same day, Mr. Giuliani had a series of short phone calls (ranging from 11 to 18 seconds) with a phone number associated with the White House, followed shortly thereafter by an eight minute, 28 second call with an unidentified number that called him.[84] Approximately half an hour later, Mr. Giuliani had a 48 second call with a phone number associated with Ambassador John Bolton, National Security Advisor to the President.[85]

That same day, Mr. Giuliani tweeted:

Hillary is correct the report is the end of the beginning for the second time...NO COLLUSION. Now Ukraine is investigating Hillary campaign and DNC conspiracy with foreign operatives including Ukrainian and others to affect 2016 election. And there's no Comey to fix the result.[86]

The next day, on the morning of April 24, Mr. Giuliani appeared on *Fox and Friends*, lambasting the Mueller investigation. Mr. Giuliani also promoted the false conspiracy theories about Ukraine and Vice President Biden:

And I ask you to keep your eye on Ukraine, because in Ukraine, a lot of the dirty work was done in digging up the information. American officials were used, Ukrainian officials were used. That's like collusion with the Ukrainians. And, or actually in this case, conspiracy with the Ukrainians. I think you'd get some interesting information about Joe Biden from Ukraine. About his son, Hunter Biden. About a company he was on the board of for years, which may be one of the most crooked companies in Ukraine. … And Biden bragged about the fact that he got the prosecutor general fired. The prosecutor general was investigating his son and then the investigation went south.[87]

Later that day, Mr. Giuliani had three phone calls with a number associated with OMB, and eight calls with a White House number.[88] One of the calls with the White House was four minutes, 53 seconds, and another was three minutes, 15 seconds.

Later that evening, the State Department phoned Ambassador Yovanovitch and abruptly called her home because of "concerns" from "up the street" at the White House.[89]

Ambassador Yovanovitch Was Informed That the President "Lost Confidence" in Her

When Ambassador Yovanovitch returned to the United States at the end of April, Deputy Secretary of State John Sullivan informed her that she had "done nothing wrong," but "there had been a concerted campaign" against her and that President Trump had "lost confidence" in her leadership.[90] He also told her that "the President no longer wished me to serve as Ambassador to Ukraine, and that, in fact, the President had been pushing for my removal since the prior summer."[91] Ambassador Philip T. Reeker, Acting Assistant Secretary of State for the Bureau of European and Eurasian Affairs, offered a similar assessment. He explained to Ambassador Yovanovitch that Secretary Pompeo had tried to "protect" her, but "was no longer able to do that."[92]

Counselor of the Department of State T. Ulrich Brechbuhl, who had been handling Ambassador Yovanovitch's recall, refused to meet with her.[93]

Ambassador Yovanovitch's final day as U.S. Ambassador to Ukraine was May 20, 2019. This was the same day as President Zelensky's inauguration, which was attended by Secretary of Energy Rick Perry, Ambassador Sondland, and Ambassador Volker.[94] Rather than joining the official delegation at the inaugural festivities, she finished packing her personal belongings and boarded an airplane for her final flight home. Three days later, President Trump met in the Oval Office with his hand-picked delegation and gave them the "directive" to "talk with Rudy [Giuliani]" about Ukraine.[95]

The President Provided No Rationale for the Recall of Ambassador Yovanovitch

Ambassador Yovanovitch testified that she was never provided a justification for why President Trump recalled her.[96] Only two months earlier, in early March 2019, Ambassador Yovanovitch had been asked by Ambassador Hale to extend her assignment as Ambassador to Ukraine until 2020.[97]

Ambassador Hale testified that Ambassador Yovanovitch was "an exceptional officer doing exceptional work at a very critical embassy in Kyiv."[98] He added, "I believe that she should've been able to stay at post and continue to do the outstanding work that she was doing."[99]

During her more than three-decade career, Ambassador Yovanovitch received a number of awards, including: the Presidential Distinguished Service Award, the Secretary's Diplomacy in Human Rights Award, the Senior Foreign Service Performance Award six times, and the State Department's Superior Honor Award five times.[100]

Career foreign service officer Ambassador P. Michael McKinley, former Senior Advisor to Secretary Pompeo, testified that Ambassador Yovanovitch's reputation was "excellent, serious, committed."[101] Ambassador Reeker described her as an "[o]utstanding diplomat," "very precise, very—very professional," "an excellent mentor," and "a good leader."[102]

Ambassador Yovanovitch Strongly Advocated for the U.S. Policy to Combat Corruption

Throughout the course of her career, and while posted to Kyiv, Ambassador Yovanovitch was a champion of the United States' longstanding priority of combatting corruption.

Mr. Kent described U.S. foreign policy in Ukraine as encompassing the priorities of "promoting the rule of law, energy independence, defense sector reform, and the ability to stand up to Russia."[103] Ambassador Yovanovitch testified that it "was—and remains—a top U.S. priority to help Ukraine fight corruption" because corruption makes Ukraine more "vulnerable to Russia."[104] Additionally, she testified that an honest and accountable Ukrainian leadership makes a U.S.-Ukrainian partnership more reliable and more valuable to the United States.[105]

Mr. Holmes testified that Ambassador Yovanovitch was successful in implementing anti-corruption reforms in Ukraine by achieving, for example, "the hard-fought passage of a law establishing an independent court to try corruption cases."[106] Mr. Holmes said Ambassador Yovanovitch was "[a]s good as anyone known for" combatting corruption.[107] The reforms achieved by Ambassador Yovanovitch helped reduce the problem faced by many post-Soviet countries of selective corruption prosecutions to target political opponents.[108]

There was a broad consensus that Ambassador Yovanovitch was successful in helping Ukraine combat pervasive and endemic corruption.

President's Authority Does Not Explain Removal of Yovanovitch

While ambassadors serve at the pleasure of the president, the manner and circumstances of Ambassador Yovanovitch's removal were unusual and raise questions of motive.[109]

Ambassador Yovanovitch queried "why it was necessary to smear my reputation falsely."[110] She found it difficult to comprehend how individuals "who apparently felt stymied by our efforts to promote stated U.S. policy against corruption" were "able to successfully conduct a campaign of disinformation against a sitting ambassador using unofficial back channels." [111]

Dr. Hill similarly testified that while the President has the authority to remove an ambassador, she was concerned "about the circumstances in which [Ambassador Yovanovitch's] reputation had been maligned, repeatedly, on television and in all kinds of exchanges." Dr. Hill "felt that that was completely unnecessary."[112]

Recall of Yovanovitch Threatened U.S.-Ukraine Policy

The smear campaign questioning Ambassador Yovanovitch's loyalty undermined U.S. diplomatic efforts in Ukraine, a key U.S. partner and a bulwark against Russia's expansion into Europe. As Ambassador Yovanovitch explained:

Ukrainians were wondering whether I was going to be leaving, whether we really represented the President, U.S. policy, et cetera. And so I think it was—you know, it really kind of cut the ground out from underneath us.[113]

Summarizing the cumulative impact of the attacks, she emphasized: "If our chief representative is kneecapped it limits our effectiveness to safeguard the vital national security interests of the United States."[114]

President Trump's recall of Ambassador Yovanovitch left the U.S. Embassy in Ukraine without an ambassador at a time of electoral change in Ukraine and when the Embassy was also without a deputy chief of mission. Mr. Kent explained:

> During the late spring and summer of 2019, I became alarmed as those efforts bore fruit. They led to the outer [ouster] of Ambassador Yovanovitch and hampered U.S. efforts to establish rapport with the new Zelensky administration in Ukraine.[115]
> ...
> One of the unfortunate elements of the timing was that we were also undergoing a transition in my old job as deputy chief of mission. The person who replaced me had already been moved early to be our DCM and Charge in Sweden, and so we had a temporary acting deputy chief of mission. So that left the embassy not only without—the early withdrawal of Ambassador Yovanovitch left us not only without an Ambassador but without somebody who had been selected to be deputy chief of mission.[116]

It was not until late May that Secretary Pompeo asked Ambassador Bill Taylor, who had previously served as Ambassador to Ukraine, to return to Kyiv as Chargé d'Affaires to lead the embassy while it awaited a confirmed Ambassador. Ambassador Taylor did not arrive in Kyiv until June 17, more than a month after Ambassador Yovanovitch officially left Kyiv.[117] His mission to carry out U.S. objectives there would prove challenging in the face of ongoing efforts by Mr. Giuliani and others—at the direction of the President—to secure investigations demanded by the President to help his reelection.

2.   The President Put Giuliani and the Three Amigos in Charge of Ukraine Issues

After President Trump recalled Ambassador Yovanovitch, his personal agent, Rudy Giuliani, intensified the President's campaign to pressure Ukraine's newly-elected president to interfere in the 2020 U.S. election. President Trump directed his own political appointees to coordinate with Mr. Giuliani on Ukraine, while National Security Council officials expressed alarm over the efforts to pursue a "domestic political errand" for the political benefit of the President. Officials at the highest levels of the White House and Trump Administration were aware of the President's scheme.

Overview

On April 21, 2019, the day that Ukrainian President Volodymyr Zelensky was elected as president of Ukraine, President Trump called to congratulate him. After a positive call—in which Mr. Zelensky complimented President Trump and requested that President Trump attend his inauguration—President Trump instructed Vice President Mike Pence to lead the U.S. delegation to the inauguration. However, on May 13—before the inauguration date was even set—President Trump instructed Vice President Pence not to attend.

Rudy Giuliani also announced a plan to visit Ukraine in mid-May 2019—not on official U.S. government business, but instead to pursue on behalf of his client, President Trump, the debunked conspiracy theories about alleged Ukrainian interference in the 2016 election and discredited claims about the Bidens. After public scrutiny in response to his announced visit, Mr. Giuliani cancelled his trip and alleged that President-elect Zelensky was surrounded by "enemies of the President."

Secretary of Energy Rick Perry, Ambassador to the European Union Gordon Sondland, and Ambassador Kurt Volker, Special Representative for Ukraine Negotiations, ultimately led the U.S. delegation to President Zelensky's inauguration. Upon returning to Washington, D.C., the three U.S. officials—who dubbed themselves the "Three Amigos"—debriefed the President in the Oval Office and encouraged him to engage with President Zelensky. Instead of accepting their advice, President Trump complained that Ukraine is "a terrible place, all corrupt, terrible people," and asserted that Ukraine "tried to take me down in 2016." The President instructed the "Three Amigos" to "talk to Rudy" and coordinate with him on Ukraine matters. They followed the President's orders.

Dr. Fiona Hill, Deputy Assistant to the President and Senior Director for Europe and Russian Affairs at the National Security Council, would later observe that Ambassador Sondland "was being involved in a domestic political errand, and we [the NSC staff] were being involved in national security foreign policy, and those two things had just diverged."

A Political Newcomer Won Ukraine's Presidential Election on an Anti-Corruption Platform

On April 21, popular comedian and television actor, Volodymyr Zelensky, won a landslide victory in Ukraine's presidential election, earning the support of 73 percent of voters and unseating the incumbent Petro Poroshenko. Mr. Zelensky, who had no prior political experience, told voters a week before his victory: "I'm not a politician. I'm just a simple person who came to break the system."[118] Five years earlier, in late 2013, Ukrainians had gathered in Kyiv and rallied against the corrupt government of former President Viktor Yanukovych, eventually forcing him to flee to the safety of Vladimir Putin's Russia. Mr. Zelensky's victory in April 2019 reaffirmed the Ukrainian people's strong desire to overcome an entrenched system of corruption and pursue closer partnership with the West.[119]

Following the election results, at 4:29 p.m. Eastern Time, President Trump was connected by telephone to President-elect Zelensky and congratulated him "on a job well done … a fantastic election." He declared, "I have no doubt you will be a fantastic president."[120]

According to a call record released publicly by the White House, President Trump did not openly express doubts about the newly-elected leader.[121] And contrary to a public readout of the call originally issued by the White House, President Trump did not mention corruption in Ukraine, despite the NSC staff preparing talking points on that topic.[122] Indeed, "corruption" was not mentioned once during the April 21 conversation, according to the official call record.[123]

In the call, President-elect Zelensky lauded President Trump as "a great example" and invited him to visit Ukraine for his upcoming inauguration—a gesture that President Trump called "very nice."[124] President Trump told Mr. Zelensky:

> I'll look into that, and well—give us the date and, at a very minimum, we'll have a great representative. Or more than one from the United States will be with you on that great day. So, we will have somebody, at a minimum, at a very, very high level, and they will be with you.[125]

Mr. Zelensky persisted. "Words cannot describe our country," he went on, "so it would be best for you to see it yourself. So, if you can come, that would be great. So again, I invite you to come."[126] President Trump responded, "Well, I agree with you about your country and I look forward to it."[127] In a nod to his past experience working with Ukraine as a businessman, President Trump added, "When I owned Miss Universe … Ukraine was always very well represented."[128]

President Trump then invited Mr. Zelensky to the White House to meet, saying: "When you're settled in and ready, I'd like to invite you to the White House. We'll have a lot of things to talk about, but we're with you all the way." Mr. Zelensky promptly accepted the President's invitation, adding that the "whole team and I are looking forward to that visit."[129]

Mr. Zelensky then reiterated his interest in President Trump attending his inauguration, saying, "it will be absolutely fantastic if you could come and be with us." President Trump promised to let the Ukrainian leader know "very soon" and added that he would see Mr. Zelensky "very soon, regardless."[130]

Shortly after the April 21 call, Jennifer Williams, Special Advisor to the Vice President for Europe and Russia, learned that President Trump asked Vice President Pence to attend Mr. Zelensky's inauguration.[131] Ms. Williams testified that in a separate phone call between Vice President Pence and President-elect Zelensky two days later, "the Vice President accepted that invitation from President Zelensky, and looked forward to being able to attend ... if the dates worked out."[132] Ms. Williams and her colleagues began planning for the Vice President's trip to Kyiv.[133]

Rudy Giuliani and his Associates Coordinated Efforts to Secure and Promote the Investigations with Ukrainian President Zelensky

As previously explained in Chapter 1, Mr. Giuliani, acting on behalf of President Trump, had for months engaged corrupt current and former Ukrainian officials, including Ukrainian Prosecutor General Yuriy Lutsenko. The April election of Mr. Zelensky, however, raised the possibility that Mr. Lutsenko might lose his job as Prosecutor General once Mr. Zelensky took power.

In the immediate aftermath of President-elect Zelensky's election, Mr. Giuliani continued publicly to project confidence that Ukraine would deliver on investigations related to the Bidens. On April 24—before Ambassador Yovanovitch received calls abruptly summoning her back to Washington—Mr. Giuliani stated in an interview on *Fox and Friends* that viewers should,

> [K]eep your eye on Ukraine... I think you'd get some interesting information about Joe Biden from Ukraine. About his son, Hunter Biden. About a company he was on the board of for years, which may be one of the most crooked companies in Ukraine.[134]

Behind the scenes, however, Mr. Giuliani was taking steps to engage the new Ukrainian leader and his aides.

The day before, on April 23, the same day that Vice President Pence confirmed his plans to attend President-elect Zelensky's inauguration, Mr. Giuliani dispatched his own delegation— consisting of Lev Parnas and Igor Fruman—to meet with Ihor Kolomoisky, a wealthy Ukrainian with ties to President-elect Zelensky. Instead of going to Kyiv, they booked tickets to Israel, where they met with Mr. Kolomoisky.[135] Mr. Kolomoisky owned Ukraine's largest bank until 2016, when Ukrainian authorities nationalized the failing financial institution. Although he denied allegations of committing any crimes, Mr. Kolomoisky subsequently left Ukraine for Israel, where he remained until President Zelensky assumed power.[136]

Mr. Kolomoisky confirmed to *The New York Times* that he met with Mr. Parnas and Mr. Fruman in late April 2019. He claimed they sought his assistance in facilitating a meeting between Mr. Giuliani and President-elect Zelensky, and he told them, "you've ended up in the wrong place," and declined to arrange the requested meeting.[137]

Mr. Giuliani was not deterred.

During the time surrounding Ambassador Yovanovitch's recall, Mr. Giuliani and Mr. Parnas connected over a flurry of calls around a planned trip to Ukraine by Mr. Giuliani, which he would eventually cancel after growing public scrutiny. As previously described in Chapter 1, call records obtained by the Committees show a series of contacts on April 23 and 24 between Mr. Giuliani, the White House, Mr. Parnas, and John Solomon, among others.[138]

On April 25, 2019, former Vice President Biden publicly announced his campaign for the Democratic nomination for President of the United States and launched his effort to unseat President Trump in the 2020 election.[139]

That evening, Mr. Solomon published a new opinion piece in *The Hill* entitled, "How the Obama White House Engaged Ukraine to Give Russia Collusion Narrative an Early Boost." Like Mr. Solomon's previous work, this April 25 piece repeated unsubstantiated conspiracy theories about alleged Ukrainian interference in the 2016 U.S. presidential election.[140]

Meanwhile, in Kyiv, David Holmes, Counselor for Political Affairs at U.S. Embassy Kyiv, learned on April 25 that Mr. Giuliani had reached out to Mr. Zelensky's campaign chair, Ivan Bakanov, seeking a channel to the newly-elected leader. Mr. Bakanov told Mr. Holmes "that he had been contacted by, quote, someone named Giuliani, who said he was an advisor to the Vice President, unquote."[141] Mr. Holmes clarified that Mr. Bakanov was "speaking in Russian" and that he did not "know what he [Bakanov] meant" by his reference to the Vice President, "but that's what he [Bakanov] said."[142] Regardless of Mr. Bakanov's apparent confusion as to who Mr. Giuliani represented, Mr. Holmes explained that by this point in time, Ukrainian officials seemed to think that Mr. Giuliani "was a significant person in terms of managing their relationship with the United States."[143]

At 7:14 p.m. Eastern Time on April 25, Mr. Giuliani once again received a call from an unknown "-1" number, which lasted four minutes and 40 seconds.[144] Minutes later, Mr. Giuliani held a brief 36 second call with Sean Hannity, a *Fox News* opinion host.[145]

On the night of April 25, President Trump called into Mr. Hannity's prime time *Fox News* show. In response to a question about Mr. Solomon's recent publication, President Trump said:

> It sounds like big stuff. It sounds very interesting with Ukraine. I just spoke to the new president a little while ago, two days ago, and congratulated him on an incredible race. Incredible run. A big surprise victory. That's 75 percent of the vote. But that sounds like big, big stuff. I'm not surprised.[146]

As Mr. Holmes later learned on July 26 from Ambassador Sondland, President Trump did not care about Ukraine, he cared about this "big stuff"—such as the investigation into Vice President Biden.[147]

In the same *Fox News* interview, Mr. Hannity asked President Trump whether America needed to see the purported evidence possessed by the unnamed Ukrainians noted in Mr. Solomon's piece. The President replied, invoking Attorney General William P. Barr:

> Well, I think we do. And, frankly, we have a great new attorney general who has done an unbelievable job in a very short period of time. And he is very smart and tough and I would certainly defer to him. I would imagine he would want to see this. People have been saying this whole—the concept of Ukraine, they have been talking about it actually for a long time. You know that, and I would certainly defer to the attorney general. And we'll see what he says about it. He calls them straight. That's one thing I can tell you.[148]

Ukraine's current Prosecutor General Ruslan Ryaboshapka, who assumed his new position in late August 2019, told *The Financial Times* in late November 2019 that Attorney General Barr had made no contact regarding a potential investigation into allegations of wrongdoing by former Vice President Biden.[149] In an apparent reference to President Trump's demand for Ukrainian interference in U.S. elections, Mr. Ryaboshapka stated: "It's critically important for the west not to pull us into some conflicts between their ruling elites, but to continue to support so that we can cross the point of no return."[150]

President Trump Promoted False Information About Former Vice President Joe Biden

In early May, Mr. Giuliani continued his outreach to President-elect Zelensky and promoted the need for Ukrainian investigations into former Vice President Biden that served President Trump's political needs.

On May 2, at 6:21 a.m. Eastern Time, President Trump retweeted a link to an article in *The New York Times,* which assessed that Mr. Giuliani's efforts underscored "the Trump campaign's concern about the electoral threat from the former vice president's presidential campaign" and noted that "Mr. Giuliani's involvement raises questions about whether Mr. Trump is endorsing an effort to push a foreign government to proceed with a case that could hurt a political opponent at home."[151]

Later that evening, in an interview with *Fox News* at the White House, President Trump referenced the false allegations about the firing of a corrupt former Ukrainian prosecutor, Viktor Shokin, that Mr. Giuliani had been promoting. He was asked, "Should the former vice president explain himself on his feeling in Ukraine and whether there was a conflict … with his son's business interests?"[152] President Trump replied:

> I'm hearing it's a major scandal, major problem. Very bad things happened, and we'll see what that is. They even have him on tape, talking about it. They have Joe Biden on tape talking about the prosecutor. And I've seen that tape. A lot of people are talking about that tape, but that's up to them. They have to solve that problem.[153]

"The tape" President Trump referenced in his interview was a publicly available video of former Vice President Biden speaking in January 2018 at an event hosted by the Council on Foreign Relations (CFR), a nonpartisan think-tank focused on foreign policy matters. During an interview with the CFR president, Vice President Biden detailed how the United States—consistent with the policy of its European allies and the International Monetary Fund (IMF)—withheld $1 billion in loan guarantees until the Ukrainian government acceded to uniform American and international demands to fire the corrupt prosecutor.[154]

By late 2015, Ukrainians were agitating for Mr. Shokin's removal, and in March 2016, Ukraine's parliament voted to dismiss the prosecutor general.[155] Multiple witnesses testified that Mr. Shokin's dismissal in 2016 made it *more*—not less—likely that Ukrainian authorities might investigate any allegations or wrongdoing at Burisma or other allegedly corrupt companies.[156] Nonetheless, President Trump and his supporters sought to perpetuate the false narrative that Mr. Shokin should not have been removed from office and that Vice President Biden had acted corruptly in carrying out U.S. policy.

Rudy Giuliani Was "Meddling in an Investigation" on Behalf of President Trump

On May 7, 2019, Christopher Wray, the Director of the Federal Bureau of Investigation, testified before the U.S. Senate Appropriations Subcommittee on Commerce, Justice, Science, and Related Agencies regarding foreign interference in U.S. elections:

> My view is that, if any public official or member of any campaign is contacted by any nation-state or anybody acting on behalf of a nation-state about influencing or interfering with our election, then that is something that the FBI would want to know about.[157]

Mr. Giuliani nonetheless pressed forward with his plan to personally convey to President-elect Zelensky, on behalf of his client President Trump, the importance of opening investigations that would assist President Trump's reelection campaign.

On the morning of May 8, Mr. Giuliani called the White House Switchboard and connected for six minutes and 26 seconds with someone at the White House.[158] That same day, Mr. Giuliani also connected with Mr. Solomon for almost six minutes, with Mr. Parnas, and with Derek Harvey, a member of Representative Nunes' staff on the Intelligence Committee.[159]

During a meeting that same day, Ukraine Minister of Interior Arsen Avakov disclosed to Deputy Assistant Secretary of State George Kent that Mr. Parnas and Mr. Fruman would soon visit Kyiv "and that they were coming with their associate, the Mayor Giuliani."[160] Minister Avakov confided to Mr. Kent that "Mayor Giuliani had reached out to him and invited him to come and meet the group of them in Florida" in February 2019.[161] Although he declined that offer, Minister Avakov indicated that he intended to accept their new invitation to meet in Kyiv.[162]

The next day, on May 9, *The New York Times* publicized Mr. Giuliani's plan to visit Ukraine.[163] Mr. Giuliani confirmed that he planned to meet with President Zelensky and press the Ukrainians to pursue investigations that President Trump promoted only days earlier on *Fox News*.[164] *The New York Times* described Mr. Giuliani's planned trip as:

[P]art of a monthslong effort by the former New York mayor and a small group of Trump allies working to build interest in the Ukrainian inquiries. Their motivation is to…undermine the case against Paul Manafort, Mr. Trump's imprisoned former campaign chairman; and potentially to damage Mr. Biden, the early front-runner for the 2020 Democratic presidential nomination.[165]

Mr. Giuliani claimed, "We're not meddling in an election, we're meddling in an investigation, which we have a right to do."[166]

Only a few days after Director Wray's public comments about foreign interference in U.S. elections, Mr. Giuliani acknowledged that "[s]omebody could say it's improper" to pressure Ukraine to open investigations that would benefit President Trump. But, Mr. Giuliani argued:

[T]his isn't foreign policy—I'm asking them to do an investigation that they're doing already, and that other people are telling them to stop. And I'm going to give them reasons why they shouldn't stop it because that information will be very, very helpful to my client, and may turn out to be helpful to my government.[167]

Mr. Giuliani's "client" was President Trump, as Mr. Giuliani repeatedly stated publicly. According to Mr. Giuliani, the President fully supported putting pressure on Ukraine to open investigations that would benefit his 2020 reelection campaign.[168] Mr. Giuliani emphasized that President Trump "basically knows what I'm doing, sure, as his lawyer."[169] Underscoring his commitment to pressuring Ukraine until it opened the investigations President Trump promoted on *Fox News*, Mr. Giuliani told *The Washington Post* that he would "make sure that nothing scuttles the investigation that I want."[170]

On May 9, following public revelation of his trip by the *New York Times*, Mr. Giuliani connected in quick succession with Mr. Solomon and then Mr. Parnas for several minutes at a time.[171] Mr. Giuliani then made brief connections with the White House Switchboard and Situation Room several times, before connecting at 1:43 p.m. Eastern Time with someone at the White House for over four minutes.[172] He connected, separately, thereafter with Mr. Parnas several times in the afternoon and into the evening.[173]

That evening, Mr. Giuliani tweeted:

If you doubt there is media bias and corruption then when Democrats conspiring with Ukrainian officials comes out remember much of the press, except for Fox, the Hill, and NYT, has suppressed it. If it involved @realDonaldTrump or his son it would have been front page news for weeks.[174]

Shortly thereafter, on the night of May 9, he made an appearance on *Fox News* and reiterated that his trip to Ukraine was intended to further the President's personal and political interests by pressuring the Ukrainian government to investigate the Bidens:

It's a big story. It's a dramatic story. And I guarantee you, Joe Biden will not get to election day without this being investigated, not because I want to see him investigated. This is collateral to what I was doing.[175]

The next morning, on May 10, amidst the press coverage of his trip, Mr. Giuliani tweeted:

Explain to me why Biden shouldn't be investigated if his son got millions from a Russian loving crooked Ukrainian oligarch while He was VP and point man for Ukraine. Ukrainians are investigating and your fellow Dems are interfering. Election is 17 months away. Let's answer it now[176]

He then had another flurry of calls with Mr. Parnas. Shortly after 2:00 p.m., Eastern Time, Mr. Giuliani also spoke with Ambassador Volker on the phone. [177] Ambassador Volker had learned that Mr. Giuliani intended to travel to Ukraine "to pursue these allegations that Lutsenko had made, and he was going to investigate these things"—specifically, the debunked story that Vice President Biden had improperly pressured Ukraine to fire a corrupt prosecutor general, as well as the Russian-backed conspiracy that the Ukrainians interfered in the 2016 U.S. election.[178] Ambassador Volker testified that he had a simple warning for Mr. Giuliani: Prosecutor General Lutsenko "is not credible. Don't listen to what he is saying."[179] Call records obtained by the Committees reveal that their call lasted more than 30 minutes.[180]

Call records also show that around midday on May 10, Mr. Giuliani began trading aborted calls with Kashyap "Kash" Patel, an official at the National Security Council who previously served on Ranking Member Devin Nunes' staff on the Intelligence Committee. Mr. Patel successfully connected with Mr. Giuliani less than an hour after Mr. Giuliani's call with Ambassador Volker. Beginning at 3:23 p.m., Eastern Time, Mr. Patel and Mr. Giuliani spoke for over 25 minutes.[181] Five minutes after Mr. Patel and Mr. Giuliani disconnected, an unidentified "-1" number connected with Mr. Giuliani for over 17 minutes.[182] Shortly thereafter, Mr. Giuliani spoke with Mr. Parnas for approximately 12 minutes.[183]

That same afternoon, President Trump conducted a 15-minute long phone interview with *Politico*. In response to a question about Mr. Giuliani's upcoming visit to Kyiv, the President replied, "I have not spoken to him at any great length, but I will … I will speak to him about it before he leaves."[184]

Recently, when asked what Mr. Giuliani was doing in Ukraine on his behalf, the President responded: "Well, you have to ask that to Rudy, but Rudy, I don't, I don't even know. I know he was going to go to Ukraine, and I think he canceled a trip."[185] Prior to that, on October 2, the President publicly stated; "And just so you know, we've been investigating, on a personal basis—through Rudy and others, lawyers—corruption in the 2016 election."[186] On October 4, the President publicly stated: "If we feel there's corruption, like I feel there was in the 2016 campaign—there was tremendous corruption against me—if we feel there's corruption, we have a right to go to a foreign country."[187]

By the evening of May 10, Mr. Giuliani appeared to have concerns about the incoming Ukrainian president. He appeared on *Fox News* and announced, "I'm not going to go" to Ukraine "because I think I'm walking into a group of people that are enemies of the President."[188] In a text message to *Politico*, Mr. Giuliani alleged the original offer for a meeting with Mr. Zelensky was a "set up" orchestrated by "several vocal critics" of President Trump who were advising President-elect Zelensky.[189] Mr. Giuliani declared that President-elect Zelensky "is in [the] hands of avowed enemies of Pres[ident] Trump."[190]

Like Mr. Giuliani, President Trump would express hostility toward Ukraine in the days and weeks to come.

Russian President Putin and Hungarian Prime Minister Orban Counseled President Trump on Ukraine

In early May, Mr. Giuliani was not the only person who conveyed his skepticism of Ukraine to President Trump. The President reportedly discussed Ukraine with Russian President Vladimir Putin when they spoke by phone on May 3. President Trump posted on Twitter that he "[h]ad a long and very good conversation with President Putin of Russia" and discussed "even the 'Russian Hoax'"—an apparent reference to the unanimous finding by the U.S. Intelligence Community that Russia interfered in the 2016 election with the aim of assisting President Trump's candidacy.[191] Mr. Kent subsequently heard from Dr. Hill, the NSC's Senior Director for Europe and Russia, that President Putin also expressed negative views about Ukraine to President Trump. He testified that President Putin's motivation in undercutting President-elect Zelensky was "very clear":

> He denies the existence of Ukraine as a nation and a country, as he told President Bush in Bucharest in 2008. He invaded and occupied 7 percent of Ukraine's territory and he's led to the death of 13,000 Ukrainians on Ukrainian territory since 2014 as a result of aggression. So that's his agenda, the agenda of creating a greater Russia and ensuring that Ukraine does not survive independently.[192]

On May 13, President Trump met one-on-one for an hour with Hungarian Prime Minister Viktor Orban. President Trump offered the leader a warm reception in the Oval Office and claimed Prime Minister Orban had "done a tremendous job in so many different ways. Highly respected. Respected all over Europe."[193] The European Union and many European leaders, however, have widely condemned Mr. Orban for undermining Hungary's democratic institutions and promoting anti-Semitism and xenophobia.[194]

Mr. Kent explained to the Committees that Prime Minister Orban's "animus towards Ukraine is well-known, documented, and has lasted now two years." Due to a dispute over the rights of 130,000 ethnic Hungarians who live in Ukraine, Kent noted that Prime Minister Orban "blocked all meetings in NATO with Ukraine at the ministerial level or above," undercutting U.S. and European efforts to support Ukraine in its war against Russia.[195] Nonetheless, President Trump told reporters prior to his meeting with Prime Minister Orban to not "forget they're a member of NATO, and a very good member of NATO."[196]

Commenting on what Dr. Hill shared with him following the May 3 call and May 13 meeting, Mr. Kent said he understood President Trump's discussions about Ukraine with President Putin and Prime Minister Orban "as being similar in tone and approach." He explained that "both leaders" had "extensively talked Ukraine down, said it was corrupt, said Zelensky was in the thrall of oligarchs" the effect of which was "negatively shaping a picture of Ukraine, and even President Zelensky personally."[197] The veteran State Department diplomat concluded, "[T]hose two world leaders [Putin and Orban], along with former Mayor Giuliani, their communications with President Trump shaped the President's view of Ukraine and Zelensky, and would account for the change from a very positive first call on April 21 to his negative assessment of Ukraine."[198]

President Trump Instructs Vice President Pence Not to Attend President Zelensky's Inauguration

On Monday, May 13, at approximately 11:00 a.m. Eastern Time, Ms. Williams received a call from an assistant to the Vice President's chief of staff.[199] President Trump, the assistant relayed, had "decided that the Vice President would not attend the inauguration in Ukraine," despite the fact that Vice President Pence previously had accepted the invitation.[200] Ms. Williams was never given a reason for the change in President Trump's decision.[201]

Mr. Holmes later testified that:

[The U.S. Embassy in Kyiv had] gone back and forth with NSC staff about proposing a list of potential members of the delegation. It was initially quite a long list. We had asked who would be the senior [U.S.] member of that delegation. We were told that Vice President Pence was likely to be that senior member, it was not yet fully agreed to. And so we were anticipating that to be the case. And then the Giuliani event happened, and then we heard that he was not going to play that role.[202]

Asked to clarify what he meant by "the Giuliani event," Mr. Holmes replied, "the interview basically saying that he had planned to travel to Ukraine, but he canceled his trip because there were, quote, unquote, enemies of the U.S. President in Zelensky's orbit."[203]

One of the individuals around President-elect Zelensky whom Mr. Giuliani publicly criticized was the oligarch Mr. Kolomoisky, who had refused to set up a meeting between Mr. Giuliani and President Zelensky. On May 18, Mr. Giuliani complained on Twitter that the oligarch "returned from a long exile and immediately threatened and defamed two Americans, Lev Parnas and Igor Fruman. They are my clients and I have advised them to press charges."[204]

Mr. Kolomoisky responded to Mr. Giuliani in a televised interview and declared, "Look, there is Giuliani, and two clowns, Lev Parnas and Igor Fruman, who were engaging in nonsense. They are Giuliani's clients." He added: "They came here and told us that they would organize a meeting with Zelensky. They allegedly struck a deal with [Prosecutor-General Yuriy] Lutsenko about the fate of this criminal case—Burisma, [former Vice President] Biden, meddling in the U.S. election and so on."[205] He warned that a "big scandal may break out, and not only in

Ukraine, but in the United States. That is, it may turn out to be a clear conspiracy against Biden."[206]

Despite Ukraine's significance to U.S. national security as a bulwark against Russian aggression and the renewed opportunity that President Zelensky's administration offered for bringing Ukraine closer to the United States and Europe, President Trump did not ask Secretary of State Michael Pompeo, Acting Secretary of Defense Patrick Shanahan, or National Security Advisor John Bolton to lead the delegation to President Zelensky's inauguration. Instead, according to Mr. Holmes, the White House "ultimately whittled back an initial proposed list for the official delegation to the inauguration from over a dozen individuals to just five."[207]

Topping that list was Secretary Perry. Accompanying him were Ambassador Sondland, U.S. Special Representative for Ukraine Negotiations Ambassador Volker, and NSC Director for Ukraine Lt. Col. Alexander Vindman.[208] Acting Deputy Chief of Mission (Chargé d'Affaires) of U.S. Embassy Kyiv Joseph Pennington joined the delegation, in place of outgoing U.S. Ambassador to Ukraine Marie Yovanovitch. U.S. Senator Ron Johnson also attended the inauguration and joined several meetings with the presidential delegation. When asked if this delegation was "a good group," Mr. Holmes replied that it "was not as senior a delegation as we [the U.S. embassy] might have expected."[209]

Secretary Perry, Ambassador Volker, and Ambassador Sondland subsequently began to refer to themselves as the "Three Amigos." During the delegation's meeting with President Zelensky, Mr. Holmes recounted that "Secretary Perry passed President Zelensky a list of, quote, 'people he trusts' from whom Zelensky could seek advice on energy sector reform, which was the topic of subsequent meetings between Secretary Perry and key Ukrainian energy sector contacts, from which Embassy personnel were excluded by Secretary Perry's staff."[210]

Mr. Holmes assessed that the delegation's visit proceeded smoothly, although "at one point during a preliminary meeting of the inaugural delegation, someone in the group wondered aloud about why Mr. Giuliani was so active in the media with respect to Ukraine."[211] Ambassador Sondland responded: "Dammit, Rudy. Every time Rudy gets involved he goes and effs everything up."[212] Mr. Holmes added: "He used the 'F' word."[213]

By the time of the inauguration, Mr. Holmes assessed that President Zelensky and the Ukrainians were already starting to feel pressure to conduct political investigations related to former Vice President Biden.[214] Lt. Col. Vindman also was concerned about the potentially negative consequences of Mr. Giuliani's political efforts on behalf of President Trump—both for U.S. national security and also Ukraine's longstanding history of bipartisan support in the U.S. Congress.[215]

During the U.S. delegation's meeting with President Zelensky on the margins of the inauguration, Lt. Col. Vindman was the last person to speak.[216] He "offered two pieces of advice" to President Zelensky. First, he advised the new leader, "be particularly cautious with regards to Russia, and its desire to provoke Ukraine."[217] And second, Lt. Col. Vindman warned, "stay out of U.S. domestic ... politics."[218] Referencing the activities of Mr. Giuliani, Lt. Col Vindman explained:

[I]n the March and April timeframe, it became clear that there were—there were actors in the U.S., public actors, nongovernmental actors that were promoting the idea of investigations and 2016 Ukrainian interference. And it was consistent with U.S. policy to advise any country, all the countries in my portfolio, any country in the world, to not participate in U.S. domestic politics. So I was passing the same advice consistent with U.S. policy.[219]

U.S. Officials Briefed President Trump About their Positive Impressions of Ukraine

Ambassadors Volker and Sondland left Kyiv with "a very favorable impression" of the new Ukrainian leader.[220] They believed it was important that President Trump "personally engage with the President of Ukraine in order to demonstrate full U.S. support for him," including by inviting him to Washington for a meeting in the Oval Office.[221] It was agreed that the delegation would request a meeting with President Trump and personally convey their advice. They were granted time with President Trump on May 23.

According to Mr. Kent, the delegation was able to secure the Oval Office meeting shortly after the return from Kyiv because of Ambassador Sondland's "connections" to Acting White House Chief of Staff Mick Mulvaney and President Trump.[222] Christopher Anderson, Special Advisor to Ambassador Kurt Volker, also attributed the delegation's ability to quickly confirm a meeting with President Trump to Ambassador Sondland's "connections to the White House."[223]

At the May 23 meeting, Ambassadors Sondland and Volker were joined by Secretary Perry, Senator Johnson, and Dr. Charles M. Kupperman, the Deputy National Security Advisor. Mr. Mulvaney may have also participated.[224]

Lt. Col. Vindman, who had represented the White House at President Zelensky's inauguration, did not participate in the meeting. Dr. Hill directed him not to join, because she had learned that "there was some confusion" from the President "over who the director for Ukraine is."[225] Specifically, Dr. Hill testified that around the time of the May 23 debriefing in the Oval Office, she "became aware by chance and accident" that President Trump had requested to speak with the NSC's Ukraine director about unspecified "materials."[226] A member of the NSC executive secretary's staff stated that in response to the President's request, "we might be reaching out to Kash."[227]

Dr. Hill testified that she understood the staff to be referring to Mr. Patel, who then served as a director in the NSC's directorate of International Organizations and Alliances, not the directorate of Europe and Russia.[228] She subsequently consulted with Dr. Kupperman and sought to clarify if Mr. Patel "had some special ... Ambassador Sondland-like representational role on Ukraine" that she had not been informed about, but "couldn't elicit any information about that."[229] All Dr. Kupperman said was that he would look into the matter.[230] Dr. Hill also testified that she never saw or learned more about the Ukraine-related "materials" that the President believed he had received from Mr. Patel, who maintained a close relationship with Ranking Member Nunes after leaving his staff to join the NSC.[231]

*President Trump Put the Three Amigos in Charge of the United States' Ukraine Relationship
and Directed Them to "Talk to Rudy" About Ukraine*

According to witness testimony, the May 23 debriefing with the President in the Oval Office proved consequential for two reasons. President Trump authorized Ambassador Sondland, Secretary Perry, and Ambassador Volker to lead engagement with the President Zelensky's new administration in Ukraine. He instructed them, however, to talk to and coordinate with his personal attorney, Mr. Giuliani.

Ambassador Sondland, Ambassador Volker, Secretary Perry, and Senator Johnson "took turns" making their case "that this is a new crowd, it's a new President" in Ukraine who was "committed to doing the right things," including fighting corruption.[232] According to Ambassador Sondland, the group "emphasized the strategic importance of Ukraine" and the value to the United States of strengthening the relationship with President Zelensky.[233] They recommended that President Trump once again call President Zelensky and follow through on his April 21 invitation for President Zelensky to meet with him in the Oval Office.[234]

President Trump reacted negatively to the positive assessment of Ukraine. Ambassador Volker recalled that President Trump said Ukraine is "a terrible place, all corrupt, terrible people" and was "just dumping on Ukraine."[235] This echoed Mr. Giuliani's public statements about Ukraine during early May.

According to both Ambassadors Volker and Sondland, President Trump also alleged, without offering any evidence, that Ukraine "tried to take me down" in the 2016 election.[236] The President emphasized that he "didn't believe" the delegation's positive assessment of the new Ukrainian president, and added "that's not what I hear" from Mr. Giuliani.[237] President Trump said that Mr. Giuliani "knows all of these things" and knows that President Zelensky has "some bad people around him."[238] Rather than committing to an Oval Office meeting with the Ukrainian leader, President Trump directed the delegation to "[t]alk to Rudy, talk to Rudy."[239]

Ambassador Sondland testified that the "Three Amigos" saw the writing on the wall and concluded "that if we did not talk to Rudy, nothing would move forward on Ukraine."[240] He continued:

> [B]ased on the President's direction we were faced with a choice. We could abandon the goal of a White House meeting for President Zelensky, which we all believed was crucial to strengthening U.S.-Ukrainian ties ... or we could do as President Trump directed and talk to Mr. Giuliani to address the President's concerns. We chose the latter path.[241]

Ambassador Volker reached a similar conclusion. He believed "that the messages being conveyed by Mr. Giuliani were a problem, because they were at variance with what our official message to the President was, and not conveying that positive assessment that we all had. And so, I thought it was important to try to step in and fix the problem."[242] Ultimately, however, the "problem" posed by the President's instruction to coordinate regarding Ukraine with his personal attorney persisted and would become more acute.

After the May 23 meeting, Ambassador Sondland stayed behind with President Trump and personally confirmed that the Three Amigos "would be working on the Ukraine file."[243]

Multiple witnesses testified about this shift in personnel in charge of the Ukraine relationship.[244] Mr. Kent recalled that, after the Oval Office meeting, Secretary Perry, Ambassador Sondland, and Ambassador Volker began "asserting that, going forward, they would be the drivers of the relationship with Ukraine."[245] Catherine Croft, Special Advisor to Ambassador Kurt Volker, recalled that "Sondland, Volker, and sort of Perry, as a troika, or as the Three Amigos, had been sort of tasked with Ukraine policy" by President Trump.[246] Under Secretary of State for Political Affairs David Hale testified about his understanding of the meeting, "[I]t was clear that the President, from the readout I had received, the President had tasked that group, members of that delegation to pursue these objectives: the meeting, and the policy goals that I outlined earlier. So I was, you know, knowing I was aware that Ambassador Volker and Ambassador Sondland would be doing that."[247]

On a June 10 conference call with the Three Amigos, "Secretary Perry laid out for Ambassador Bolton the notion that" they "would assist Ambassador Taylor on Ukraine and be there to support" him as the U.S.-Ukraine relationship "move[ed] forward."[248]

This *de facto* change in authority was never officially communicated to other officials, including Dr. Hill, who had responsibility for Ukraine at the National Security Council.[249]

U.S. Officials Collaborated with Rudy Giuliani to Advance the President's Political Agenda

Ambassador Sondland testified that in the weeks and months after the May 23 Oval Office meeting, "everyone was in the loop" regarding Mr. Giuliani's role in advancing the President's scheme regarding Ukraine.[250] The "Three Amigos" did as the President ordered and began communicating with Mr. Giuliani. E-mail messages described to the Committees by Ambassador Sondland showed that he informed Mr. Mulvaney, Ambassador Bolton, and Secretaries Pompeo and Perry, as well as their immediate staffs, of his Ukraine-related efforts on behalf of the President.[251]

According to Ambassador Sondland, Secretary Perry agreed to reach out to Mr. Giuliani first "given their prior relationship."[252] Secretary Perry discussed with Mr. Giuliani the political concerns that President Trump articulated in the May 23 meeting.[253]

Dr. Hill testified that Ambassador Volker, Ambassador Sondland, and Secretary Perry "gave us every impression that they were meeting with Rudy Giuliani at this point, and Rudy Giuliani was also saying on the television, and indeed has said subsequently, that he was closely coordinating with the State Department."[254] These meetings ran counter to Ambassador Bolton's repeated declarations that "nobody should be meeting with Giuliani"[255]

Like Dr. Hill, Ambassador Bolton also closely tracked Mr. Giuliani's activities on behalf of the President. According to Dr. Hill, Ambassador Bolton closely monitored Mr. Giuliani's public statements and repeatedly referred to Mr. Giuliani as a "hand grenade that was going to blow everyone up."[256] During a meeting on June 13, Ambassador Bolton made clear that he supported more engagement with Ukraine by senior White House officials but warned that "Mr. Giuliani was a key voice with the President on Ukraine."[257] According to Ambassador Bolton, Mr. Giuliani's influence "could be an obstacle to increased White House engagement."[258] Ambassador Bolton joked that "every time Ukraine is mentioned, Giuliani pops up."[259]

Ambassador Bolton also reportedly joined Dr. Hill in warning Ambassador Volker against contacting Mr. Giuliani.[260] Dr. Hill was particularly concerned about engagement with Mr. Giuliani because "the more you engage with someone who is spreading untruths, the more validity you give to those untruths."[261] She further testified that she also discussed Mr. Giuliani's activities with Dr. Kupperman, specifically her concern that "Ukraine was going to be played by Giuliani in some way as part of the campaign."[262]

On June 18, Ambassador Volker, Acting Assistant Secretary of State Ambassador Philip T. Reeker, Secretary Perry, Ambassador Sondland, and State Department Counselor T. Ulrich Brechbuhl participated in a meeting at the Department of Energy to follow up to the May 23 Oval Office meeting.[263] Ambassador Bill Taylor, Chargé d'Affaires for U.S. Embassy in Kyiv, who had arrived in Ukraine just the day before, participated by phone from Kyiv.[264] The group agreed that a meeting between President Trump and President Zelensky would be valuable.[265] However, Ambassadors Volker and Sondland subsequently relayed to Ambassador Taylor that President Trump "wanted to hear from Zelensky before scheduling the meeting in the Oval Office."[266] Ambassador Taylor testified that he did not understand, at that time, what the President wanted to hear from his Ukrainian counterpart.[267] However, Ambassador Volker's assistant, Mr. Anderson, recalled "vague discussions" about addressing "Mr. Giuliani's continued calls for a corruption investigation."[268]

The quid pro quo—conditioning the Oval Office meeting that President Trump first offered the Ukrainian leader during their April 21 call on the Ukrainians' pursuit of investigations that would benefit President Trump politically—was beginning to take shape. As Ambassador Sondland testified, the conditions put on the White House meeting and on Ukraine's continued engagement with the White House would get "more insidious" with the passage of time.[269]

President Trump Invited Foreign Interference in the 2020 Election

As U.S. officials debated how to meet the President's demands as articulated by Mr. Giuliani, President Trump publicly disclosed on June 12 in an Oval Office interview with ABC News' anchor George Stephanopoulos that there was "nothing wrong with listening" to a foreign power who offered political dirt on an opponent. The President added, "I think I'd want to hear it."

Mr. Stephanopoulos then pressed the President directly, "You want that kind of interference in our elections?" to which President Trump replied, "It's not an interference, they have information. I think I'd take it."[270] President Trump also made clear that he did not think a foreign power offering damaging information on an opponent was necessarily wrong, and said only that he would "maybe" contact the FBI "*if* I thought there was something wrong."[271]

President Trump's willingness to accept foreign interference in a U.S. election during his interview with Mr. Stephanopoulos was consistent with tweets and interviews by Mr. Giuliani at this time. For example, on June 21, Mr. Giuliani tweeted:

New Pres of Ukraine still silent on investigation of Ukrainian interference in 2016 election and alleged Biden bribery of Pres Poroshenko. Time for leadership and investigate both if you want to purge how Ukraine was abused by Hillary and Obama people.[272]

On June 18, Dr. Hill met with Ambassador Sondland at the White House. She "asked him quite bluntly" what his role was in Ukraine. Ambassador Sondland replied that "he was in charge of Ukraine."[273] Dr. Hill was taken aback and a bit irritated. She prodded Ambassador Sondland again and asked, "Who put you in charge of Ukraine?" Dr. Hill testified: "And, you know, I'll admit, I was a bit rude. And that's when he told me the President, which shut me up."[274]

Dr. Hill tried to impress upon Ambassador Sondland the "importance of coordinating" with other national security officials in the conduct of Ukraine policy, including the NSC staff and the State Department. Ambassador Sondland "retorted" that he was "coordinating with the President" and Mr. Mulvaney, "filling in" Ambassador Bolton, and talking to State Department Counselor Ulrich Brechbuhl. Ambassador Sondland asked: "Who else did he have to inform?"[275]

Dr. Hill stated that, in hindsight, with the benefit of the sworn testimony by others during the impeachment inquiry and seeing documents displayed by witnesses, she realized that she and Ambassador Sondland were working on two fundamentally different tasks. Dr. Hill testified:

But it struck me when yesterday, when you put up on the screen Ambassador Sondland's emails and who was on these emails, and he said, These are the people who need to know, that he was absolutely right. Because he was being involved in a domestic political errand, and we were being involved in national security foreign policy, and those two things had just diverged. So he was correct. And I had not put my finger on that at the moment, but I was irritated with him and angry with him that he wasn't fully coordinating. And I did say to him, Ambassador Sondland, Gordon, I think this is all going to blow up. And here we are. [276]

Reflecting on her June 18 conversation with Ambassador Sondland, Dr. Hill concluded:

Ambassador Sondland is not wrong that he had been given a different remit than we had been. And it was at that moment that I started to realize how those things had diverged. And I realized, in fact, that I wasn't really being fair to Ambassador Sondland, because he was carrying out what he thought he had been instructed to carry out, and we were doing something that we thought was just as—or perhaps even more important, but it wasn't in the same channel.[277]

3.   **The President Froze Military Assistance to Ukraine**

> *The President froze military assistance to Ukraine against U.S. national security interests and over the objections of career experts.*

Overview

Since 2014, the United States has maintained a bipartisan policy of delivering hundreds of millions of dollars in security assistance to Ukraine each year. These funds benefit the security of the United States and Europe by ensuring that Ukraine is equipped to defend itself against Russian aggression. In 2019, that bipartisan policy was undermined when President Trump ordered, without justification, a freeze on military assistance to Ukraine.

For fiscal year 2019, Congress authorized and appropriated $391 million in security assistance: $250 million through the Department of Defense's (DOD) Ukraine Security Assistance Initiative and $141 million through the State Department's Foreign Military Financing program. In July 2019, however, President Trump ordered the Office of Management and Budget (OMB) to put a hold on all $391 million in security assistance to Ukraine.

The hold surprised experts from DOD and the State Department. DOD had already announced its intent to deliver security assistance to Ukraine after certifying that the country had implemented sufficient anti-corruption reforms, and the State Department was in the process of notifying Congress of its intent to deliver foreign military financing to Ukraine. In a series of interagency meetings, every represented agency other than OMB (which is headed by Mick Mulvaney, who is also the President's Acting Chief of Staff) supported the provision of assistance to Ukraine and objected to President Trump's hold. Ukraine experts at DOD, the State Department, and the National Security Council (NSC) argued that it was in the national security interest of the United States to continue to support Ukraine. Agency experts also expressed concerns about the legality of President Trump withholding assistance to Ukraine that Congress had already appropriated for this express purpose.

Despite these concerns, OMB devised a plan to implement President Trump's hold on the assistance. On July 25, 2019, OMB began using a series of footnotes in funding documents to notify DOD that the assistance funds were temporarily on hold to allow for interagency review. Throughout August and September, OMB continued to use this method and rationale to maintain the hold, long after the final interagency meeting on Ukraine assistance occurred on July 31. The hold continued despite concerns from DOD that the hold would threaten its ability to fully spend the money before the end of the fiscal year, as legally required.

On July 25—the same day as President Trump's call with President Zelensky—officials at Ukraine's embassy emailed DOD to ask about the status of the hold. By mid-August, officials at DOD, the State Department, and the NSC received numerous questions from Ukrainian officials about the hold. President Trump's hold on the Ukraine assistance was publicly reported on August 28, 2019.

Security Assistance to Ukraine is Important to U.S. National Security Interests

The United States has an interest in providing security assistance to Ukraine to support the country in its longstanding battle against Russian aggression and to shore it up as an independent and democratic country that can deter Kremlin influence in both Ukraine and other European countries. In early 2014, in what became known as the Revolution of Dignity, Ukrainian citizens demanded democratic reforms and an end to corruption, thereby forcing the ouster of pro-Kremlin Viktor Yanukovych as Ukraine's president. Shortly thereafter, Russian military forces and their proxies began an incursion into Ukraine that led to Russia's illegal annexation of the Crimean Peninsula of Ukraine, as well as the ongoing, Russian-led armed conflict in the Donbass region of eastern Ukraine. Approximately 13,000 people have been killed as a result of the conflict and over 1.4 million people have been displaced.[278]

Former U.S. Ambassador to the United Nations, Nikki Haley, noted that "militants in eastern Ukraine report directly to the Russian military, which arms them, trains them, leads them, and fights alongside them."[279] Similarly, then-Secretary of Defense James Mattis, during a visit to Ukraine in 2017, chided Russia, stating that "despite Russia's denials, we know they are seeking to redraw international borders by force, undermining the sovereign and free nations of Europe."[280]

In response to Russia's aggression, the international community imposed financial and visa sanctions on Russian individuals and entities, and committed to providing billions of dollars in economic, humanitarian, and security assistance to Ukraine to continue to support its sovereignty and democratic development.

The European Union is the single largest contributor of total foreign assistance to Ukraine, having provided €15 billion in grants and loans since 2014.[281] In addition to economic and humanitarian assistance, the United States has contributed a substantial amount of security assistance, mostly lethal and non-lethal military equipment and training, to Ukraine. In fact, the United States is the largest contributor of security assistance to Ukraine. Since 2014, the United States has delivered approximately $1.5 billion in security assistance to Ukraine.[282]

Multiple witnesses—including Ambassador William Taylor, Deputy Assistant Secretary of State George Kent, Lt. Col. Alexander Vindman, and Deputy Assistant Secretary of Defense Laura Cooper—testified that this security assistance to Ukraine is vital to the national security of the United States and Europe.[283] As Ambassador Taylor noted:

> [R]adar and weapons and sniper rifles, communication, that saves lives. It makes the Ukrainians more effective. It might even shorten the war. That's what our hope is, to show that the Ukrainians can defend themselves and the Russians, in the end, will say "Okay, we're going to stop."[284]

State Department Special Advisor for Ukraine, Catherine Croft, further emphasized that Ukrainians currently "face casualties nearly every day in defense of their own territory against Russian aggression."[285] Ambassador Taylor testified that American aid is a concrete demonstration of the United States' "commitment to resist aggression and defend freedom."[286]

Witnesses also testified that it is in the interest of the United States for Russian aggression to be halted in Ukraine. In the 20th century, the United States fought two bloody wars to resist the aggression of a hostile power that tried to change the borders of Europe by force. As Ambassador Taylor put it, Russian aggression in Ukraine "dismissed all the principles that have kept the peace and contributed to prosperity in Europe since World War II."[287]

Timothy Morrison, former Senior Director for Europe and Russia at the NSC, put the importance of U.S. assistance in stark terms:

> Russia is a failing power, but it is still a dangerous one. The United States aids Ukraine and her people so that they can fight Russia over there, and we don't have to fight Russia here.[288]

Bipartisan Support for Security Assistance to Ukraine

Congressional support for security assistance to Ukraine has been overwhelming and bipartisan. Congress provided $391 million in security assistance to Ukraine for fiscal year 2019: $250 million through the DOD-administered Ukraine Security Assistance Initiative (USAI) and $141 million through the State Department-administered Foreign Military Financing program.

On September 26, 2018, Congress appropriated $250 million for the Ukraine Security Assistance Initiative, which is funded through DOD. The funding law made clear that the funding was only "available until September 30, 2019." President Trump signed the bill into law on September 28, 2018.[289]

The Ukraine Security Assistance Initiative—a Congressionally-mandated program codifying portions of the European Reassurance Initiative, which was originally launched by the Obama Administration in 2015—authorizes DOD to provide "security assistance and intelligence support, including training, equipment, and logistics support, supplies and services, to military and other security forces of the Government of Ukraine."[290] Recognizing that strengthening Ukraine's institutions, in addition to its military, is vital to helping it break free of Russia's influence, Congress imposed conditions upon DOD before it could spend a portion of the security assistance funds. Half of the money was held in reserve until the Secretary of Defense, in coordination with the Secretary of State, certified to Congress that Ukraine had undertaken sufficient anti-corruption reforms, such as in civilian control of the military and increased transparency and accountability.[291]

On February 28, 2019, John C. Rood, Under Secretary of Defense for Policy, notified Congress that DOD intended to deliver the first half ($125 million) of assistance appropriated in September 2018 to Ukraine, including "more than $50 million of assistance to deliver counter-artillery radars and defensive lethal assistance."[292] Congress cleared the Congressional notification, which enabled DOD to begin obligating (spending) funds.[293]

For Ukraine to qualify to receive the remaining $125 million of assistance, Congress required that the Secretary of Defense, in coordination with the Secretary of State, certify that the

Government of Ukraine had taken substantial anticorruption reform actions.[294] Ms. Cooper and others at DOD conducted a review to evaluate whether Ukraine had met the required benchmarks.[295] Ms. Cooper explained that the review involved "pulling in all the views of the key experts on Ukraine defense, and coming up with a consensus view," which was then run "up the chain in the Defense Department, to ensure we have approval."[296]

On May 23, 2019, Under Secretary Rood certified to Congress that Ukraine had completed the requisite defense institutional reforms to qualify for the remaining $125 million in funds. He wrote:

> On behalf of the Secretary of Defense, and in coordination with the Secretary of State, I have certified that the Government of Ukraine has taken substantial actions to make defense institutional reforms for the purposes of decreasing corruption, increasing accountability, and sustaining improvements of combat capability enabled by U.S. assistance.[297]

Congress then cleared the related Congressional notification, which enabled DOD to begin obligating the remaining $125 million in funds.[298]

On June 18, 2019, DOD issued a press release announcing its intention to provide $250 million in security assistance funds to Ukraine "for additional training, equipment, and advisory efforts to build the capacity of Ukraine's armed forces." DOD announced that the security assistance would provide Ukraine with sniper rifles, rocket-propelled grenade launchers, and counter-artillery radars, command and control, electronic warfare detection and secure communications, military mobility, night vision, and military medical treatment.[299]

On February 15, 2019, Congress also appropriated $115 million for Ukraine through the State Department-administered Foreign Military Financing Program (FMF).[300] The Foreign Military Financing Program is administered by the State Department and provides grants or loans to foreign countries to help them purchase military services or equipment manufactured by U.S. companies in the United States. In addition to the $115 million appropriated for fiscal year 2019, approximately $26 million carried over from fiscal year 2018.[301] Thus, the total amount of foreign military financing available for Ukraine was approximately $141 million.

Before a country receives foreign military financing, the State Department must first seek Congressional approval through a notification to Congress.[302] The State Department never sent the required Congressional notification to Congress in the spring or summer of 2019. As described below, OMB blocked the notification.[303]

President Trump Had Questions About Ukraine Security Assistance

The day after DOD issued its June 18 press release announcing $250 million in security assistance funds for Ukraine, President Trump started asking OMB questions about the funding for Ukraine. On June 19, Mark Sandy, Deputy Associate Director for National Security Programs at OMB, was copied on an email from his boss, Michael Duffey, Associate Director for National Security Programs at OMB, to Elaine McCusker, Deputy Under Secretary of

Defense (Comptroller) that said that "the President had questions about the press report and that he was seeking additional information."[304] Notably, the same day, President Trump gave an interview on *Fox News* where he raised the so-called "Crowdstrike" conspiracy theory that Ukraine, rather than Russia, had interfered in the 2016 election, a line he would repeat during his July 25 call with the Ukrainian president.[305]

On June 20, in response to the President's inquiry, Ms. McCusker responded to President Trump's inquiry by providing Mr. Sandy information on the security assistance program.[306] Mr. Sandy shared the document with Mr. Duffey, who had follow-up questions about the "financial resources associated with the program, in particular," the "history of the appropriations, [and] any more details about the intent of the program."[307] Mr. Sandy said that his staff provided the relevant information to Mr. Duffey, but he did not know whether Mr. Duffey shared the information with the White House.[308]

Ms. Cooper also recalled receiving an email inquiring about DOD-administered Ukraine security assistance a "few days" after DOD's June 18, 2019 press release.[309] The email was from the Secretary of Defense's Chief of Staff, "asking for follow-up on a meeting with the President." The email contained three questions:

> And the one question was related to U.S. industry. Did U.S—is U.S. industry providing any of this equipment? The second question that I recall was related to international contributions. It asked, what are other countries doing, something to that effect. And then the third question, I don't recall—I mean, with any of these I don't recall the exact wording, but it was something to the effect of, you know, who gave this money, or who gave this funding?[310]

Like Mr. Sandy, Ms. Cooper believed that the President's inquiries were spurred by DOD's June 18 press release. She testified, "we did get that series of questions just within a few days after the press release and after that one article that had the headline."[311] Ms. Cooper noted that it was "relatively unusual" to receive questions from the President, and that she and her staff at the DOD responded "as quickly" as they could.[312] According to Ms. Cooper, DOD officials included in their answers that security assistance funding "has strong bipartisan support," but never received a response.[313]

President Trump Froze Military Assistance

Despite the fact that DOD experts demonstrated that the security assistance was crucial for both Ukraine and U.S. national security and had strong bipartisan support in Congress, President Trump ordered OMB to freeze the funds in July.

On July 3, the State Department notified DOD and NSC staff that OMB was blocking the State Department from transmitting a Congressional notification for the provision of State Department-administered security assistance to Ukraine (i.e., the $141 million in foreign military financing).[314] Because the State Department is legally required to transmit such a notification to Congress before spending funds, blocking the Congressional notification effectively barred the State Department from spending the funding.[315] Ms. Williams testified that she saw the news in a draft email that was being prepared as part of the nightly update for the National Security Advisor.[316] She agreed that the hold came "out of the blue" because it had not been discussed previously by OMB or the NSC.[317]

On or about July 12, 2019, President Trump directed that a hold be placed on security assistance funding for Ukraine. That day, Robert Blair, Assistant to the President and Senior Advisor to the Chief of Staff, sent an email to Mr. Duffey at OMB about Ukraine security assistance.[318] Mr. Sandy, who was on personal leave at the time but later received a copy of the email from Mr. Duffey, testified that in the July 12 email, Mr. Blair communicated "that the President is directing a hold on military support funding for Ukraine."[319] The email mentioned no concerns about any other country, security assistance package, or aid of any sort.[320]

On or about July 15, Mr. Morrison learned from Deputy National Security Advisor Charles Kupperman "that it was the President's direction to hold the assistance."[321] On or about July 17 or 18, 2019, Mr. Duffey and Mr. Blair again exchanged emails about Ukraine security assistance.[322] Mr. Sandy later received a copy of the emails, which showed that when Mr. Duffey asked Mr. Blair about the reason for the hold, Mr. Blair provided no explanation and instead said, "we need to let the hold take place" and then "revisit" the issue with the President.[323]

On July 18 or 19, when he returned from two weeks of personal leave, Mr. Sandy learned for the first time that the President had placed a hold on Ukraine security assistance from Mr. Duffey.[324] According to Mr. Sandy, Mr. Duffey was not aware of the reason but "there was certainly a desire to learn more about the rationale" for the hold.[325]

Agency Experts Repeatedly Objected to the Hold on Security Assistance

Between July 18 and July 31, 2019, the NSC staff convened a series of interagency meetings, at which the hold on security assistance was discussed in varying degrees of detail. Over the course of these meetings, it became evident that:

- the President directed the hold through OMB;

- no justification was provided for the hold;

- with the exception of OMB, all represented agencies supported Ukraine security assistance because it was in the national security interests of the United States; and

- there were concerns about the legality of the hold.

The first interagency meeting was held on July 18 at the Deputy Assistant Secretary level (i.e., a "sub-Policy Coordination Committee"). It was supposed to be a "routine Ukraine policy meeting." [326] Ambassador Taylor, Lt. Col. Vindman, Ms. Croft, and Mr. Kent were among the attendees. Witnesses testified that OMB announced at the meeting that President Trump had directed a hold on Ukraine security assistance. Mr. Kent testified that at the meeting, an OMB staff person announced that Acting White House Chief of Staff Mick Mulvaney "at the direction of the President had put a hold on all security assistance to the Ukraine."[327] Ambassador Taylor testified that the "directive had come from the President to the Chief of Staff to OMB" and that when he learned of the hold on military assistance, he "realized that one of the key pillars of our strong support for Ukraine was threatened."[328]

According to Ms. Croft, when Mr. Kent raised the issue of security assistance, it "blew up the meeting."[329] Ambassador Taylor testified that he and others on the call "sat in astonishment" when they learned about the hold.[330] David Holmes, Political Counselor at the U.S. Embassy in Kyiv, was also on the call. He testified he was "shocked" and thought the hold was "extremely significant."[331] He thought the hold undermined what he had understood to be longstanding U.S. policy in Ukraine.[332]

Ms. Croft testified that "the only reason given was that the order came at the direction of the President."[333] Ms. Cooper, who did not participate but received a readout of the meeting, testified that the fact that the hold was announced without explanation was "unusual."[334] Mr. Kent testified that "[t]here was great confusion among the rest of us because we didn't understand why that had happened."[335] He explained that "[s]ince there was unanimity that this [security assistance to Ukraine] was in our national interest, it just surprised all of us."[336]

With the exception of OMB, all agencies present at the July 18 meeting advocated for the lifting of the hold.[337]

There was also a lack of clarity as to whether the hold applied only to the State Department-administered Foreign Military Financing to Ukraine or whether it also applied to the DOD-administered Ukraine Security Assistance Initiative funding.[338] Ms. Cooper and her colleagues at the DOD were "concerned" about the hold.[339] After the meeting, DOD sought further clarification from the NSC and State Department about its impact on the DOD-administered funding.[340] However, there was no "specific guidance for DOD at the time."[341]

The second interagency meeting to discuss the hold on Ukraine security assistance was held at the Assistant Secretary level (i.e., a "Policy Coordination Committee") on July 23, 2019.[342] The meeting was chaired by Mr. Morrison.[343] Ms. Cooper, who participated via secure video teleconference, testified that "the White House chief of staff ha[d] conveyed that the President has concerns about Ukraine and Ukraine security assistance."[344] Jennifer Williams, Special Advisor to Vice President Pence for Europe and Eurasia, who also attended the meeting on behalf of the Vice President, testified that the "OMB representative conveyed that they had been directed by the Chief of Staff, the White House Chief of Staff, to continue holding it [the Ukraine security assistance] until further notice."[345] Similar to the July 18 meeting, the July 23 meeting did not provide clarity about whether the President's hold applied to the DOD-administered funding or only to the funds administered by the State Department.[346]

Again, no reason was provided for the hold.[347] Mr. Sandy did not attend the July 23 meeting as the representative for OMB, but he received a readout that other agencies expressed concerns about the hold. Specifically, the concerns related to the lack of rationale for the hold, the hold's implications on U.S. assistance and "overall policy toward Ukraine" and "similar legal questions."[348]

Mr. Morrison also testified that there was a discussion at the July 23 meeting about the legality of the hold, and specifically whether it is "actually legally permissible for the President to not allow for the disbursement of the funding."[349] Mr. Morrison recalled that DOD raised concerns about possible violations of the Impoundment Control Act.[350] The Impoundment Control Act gives the President the authority to delay spending, or not spend, funds *only* if Congress is notified of those intentions and approves the proposed action (see below for further discussion of the act).[351]

With the exception of OMB, all agencies present at the July 23rd meeting advocated for the lifting of the hold.[352] Ambassador Taylor explained that the State Department "made a strong statement about the importance of this assistance" and that Ms. Cooper, on behalf of DOD, "made a very strong case and continued to make a very strong case for the effectiveness" of the security assistance.[353] Lt. Col. Vindman, who also attended the meeting, testified that there was agreement that the issue should be elevated to the Agency deputies "as quickly as possible to recommend a release of security assistance."[354]

The third interagency meeting, a Deputies Small Group meeting at the Cabinet Deputies level, was held on July 26, 2019. Mr. Duffey was the OMB representative, and Mr. Sandy prepared Mr. Duffey for the meeting.[355] Mr. Sandy explained that he prepared Mr. Duffey to get policy guidance on six critical issues: (1) the reason for the hold; (2) the extent of the hold; (3) the duration of the hold; (4) the Congressional affairs approach; (5) the public affairs approach; and (6) and the diplomatic approach.[356] Mr. Sandy testified that on July 26, OMB still did not have an understanding of the reason for the hold.[357] According to Mr. Sandy, at that time, there was no discussion within OMB about the amount of money that was being contributed to Ukraine by other countries, or whether that topic was the reason for the President's hold.[358]

Mr. Morrison, Lt. Col. Vindman, Ms. Cooper, Under Secretary of State for Political Affairs David Hale, and Mr. Duffey attended the July 26 meeting. At the meeting, OMB stated that "they had guidance from the President and from Acting Chief of Staff Mulvaney to freeze the assistance."[359] It also was "stated very clearly" that the hold applied to both the State Department and Defense Department security assistance funds.[360] Ambassador Hale, as the representative for the Department of State, "advocated strongly for resuming the assistance," as did representatives from all agencies other than OMB.[361]

Mr. Morrison testified that, at the meeting, "OMB represented that—and the Chief of Staff's Office was present—that the President was concerned about corruption in Ukraine, and he wanted to make sure that Ukraine was doing enough to manage that corruption."[362] Ms. Cooper had a similar recollection but received no further understanding of what OMB meant by "corruption."[363] Ms. Cooper recalled that the deputies did not consider corruption to be a legitimate reason for the hold because they unanimously agreed that Ukraine was making sufficient progress on anti-corruption reforms, as had been certified by DOD on May 23.[364]

President Trump Continued the Hold Despite Agency Concerns About Legality

Prior to the passage of the Impoundment Control Act, presidents had frequently impounded—i.e., refused to spend—Congressionally-appropriated funds to enforce their policy priorities when they diverged from Congress'. However, most of these impoundments were small (i.e., no more than a few percent of the total program budget) or temporary (i.e., funds were released in time for them to be spent before the end of the fiscal year) and rooted in policy, rather than political interests of the President. It was not until President Nixon that presidential impoundment of funds would prompt Congress to take action citing constitutional concerns.[365]

Unlike his predecessors, Nixon undertook impoundments that were both substantial and, in some cases, permanent, which raised concerns for Congress over its Article I powers. In fact, between 1969 and 1972, Nixon impounded between 15% and 20% of Congressionally-appropriated funds in various accounts.[366]

To reassert Congressional authority over the budget, in 1973, Congress established the Joint Study Committee on Budget Control, which held a series of hearings and produced more than 4,600 pages of testimony and reports. The Joint Study Committee's findings ultimately led to the overwhelmingly bipartisan passage—over President Nixon's veto—of the Impoundment Control Act of 1974, one of a series of reform bills designed to reign in presidential power. Looking back at that moment in history, Rep. Bill Archer (R-TX), a fiscal conservative who served 30 years in the House of Representatives, including as the Chairman of the Ways and Means Committee, remarked, "the culture then was that the president had too much power…the president is abusing his power."[367]

In addition to establishing the Congressional Budget Committees and the independent Congressional Budget Office, the Impoundment Control Act also limits the circumstances under which a president can *legally* impound Congressionally-appropriated funds. According to the Act, although the President may request authority from Congress to withhold or permanently cancel the availability of budget authority, such an action is not allowed without Congressional approval. Any amount of budget authority proposed to be deferred (i.e., temporarily withheld) or rescinded (i.e., permanently withheld) must be made available for obligation unless Congress, within 45 legislative days, completes action on a bill rescinding all or part of the amount proposed for rescission.[368] The Impoundment Control Act does not permit the withholding of funds through their date of expiration, which would be a de facto rescission without Congressional approval.[369]

At the July 26 interagency meeting, senior agency officials raised serious concerns about the legality of the hold under the Impoundment Control Act. Ms. Cooper testified:

A: Well, I'm not an expert on the law, but in that meeting immediately deputies began to raise concerns about how this could be done in a legal fashion because there was broad understanding in the meeting that the funding—the State Department funding related to an earmark for Ukraine and that the DOD funding was specific to Ukraine security assistance. So the comments in the room at the deputies' level reflected a sense that there was not an understanding of how this could legally play out. And at that meeting the deputies agreed to look into the legalities and to look at what was possible.

Q: Okay. So is it fair to say the deputies thought the President was not authorized to place a hold on these funds?

A: They did not use that term, but the expression in the room that I recall was a sense that there was not an available mechanism to simply not spend money that has been in the case of USAI [DOD security assistance] already notified to Congress.[370]

Lt. Col. Vindman testified that the issue needed to be "elevated to a PC [Principals Committee] as quickly as possible to release the hold on security assistance" so that the funds could be obligated before the end of the fiscal year.[371]

A Principals Committee meeting was never convened.[372] According to Mr. Morrison, National Security Advisor John Bolton "believed that it was unnecessary, that he already had a reasonable idea of where the principals were, and he wanted to get directly to the President as early as possible in the most effective way."[373] Ambassador Bolton understood that the principals "were all supportive of the continued disbursement of the aid." [374] As had been clear since the very first interagency meeting on July 18, the lifting of the hold was "the unanimous position of the entire interagency."[375] At this point, it remained unclear to many officials why the President continued to hold the funds.

On July 31, 2019, a fourth and final interagency meeting was held at the Policy Coordination Committee level. Ms. Cooper attended the meeting on behalf of DOD. According to Ms. Cooper, the agenda "was largely focused on just routine Ukraine business, postelection follow up," and "security assistance was not actually an explicit agenda item."[376] Ms. Cooper nevertheless raised security assistance and expressed her understanding, after consulting with DOD counsel, that there were only two legally available options to implement the hold: a Presidential rescission notice to Congress (i.e., requesting that Congress "take back" funds it had already appropriated) or for the Defense Department to do a reprogramming action (i.e., use Congressionally-appropriated funds for a different purpose).[377] In either case, the law requires that the Executive Branch notify, and seek approval from, Congress before taking any action.[378]

At the July 31 meeting, Ms. Cooper emphasized to the participants that because "there are only two legally available options and we do not have direction to pursue either," DOD would have to start obligating the funds on or about August 6.[379] She explained at her deposition that DOD would have had to begin obligating the funds by that date or risk violation of the Impoundment Control Act.[380]

The Administration, however, never proposed a rescission or reprogramming of funds for Ukraine security assistance and never notified Congress of its intent to withhold funds.[381]

OMB Used Unusual Process to Implement President's Hold, Skirting Legal Concerns

OMB plays a critical role in the release of security assistance funding. The Antideficiency Act requires that, before any department or agency may spend Congressionally-appropriated funding, the Director of OMB or his delegates must "apportion" (i.e., make available to spend) the funds in writing.[382] Through this mechanism, OMB has the ability to directly impact security assistance funding or funding of any kind that is appropriated by Congress.

In parallel with the interagency meetings that occurred during the latter half of July 2019, OMB devised a way to implement the President's hold on security assistance to Ukraine, notwithstanding DOD's Congressional notifications of February 28 and May 23. Over the course of his twelve-year career at OMB, Mr. Sandy could not recall any other time when a hold had been placed on security assistance after a Congressional notification had been sent.[383]

When speaking with Mr. Duffey on or about July 18 or 19, Mr. Sandy immediately raised concerns about how to implement the hold without violating the Impoundment Control Act, which required that the funds be obligated (i.e. spent) before they expired at the end of the fiscal year, on September 30.[384] In light of that legal requirement, the hold would have to be temporary.[385] An additional hurdle was the fact that OMB had already authorized DOD to spend the security assistance funds DOD administered for fiscal year 2019.[386] Therefore, when President Trump directed the hold in July, OMB scrambled to reverse that prior authorization.

From July 19 through July 24, Mr. Sandy consulted with the OMB Office of General Counsel as well as Ms. McCusker at DOD on how to legally implement a hold on the funds.[387] Mr. Sandy's staff at OMB also conferred with OMB's Budget Review Division.[388] Based on these consultations, OMB decided to implement the hold through a series of nine funding documents, known legally as "apportionments."[389] Apportionments typically are used to convey authority to an agency to spend funds, not to withhold funds; thus, in order to bar DOD from spending money, these particular apportionments included footnotes that would impose the holds while using creative language to skirt legal concerns. Mr. Sandy testified that "the purpose of the footnote was to preclude obligation for a limited period of time but enable planning and casework to continue."[390] He also testified that this use of footnotes was unusual and that in his 12 years of OMB experience, he could "not recall another event like it."[391]

On July 25, OMB issued the first funding document implementing the hold. In this document, the relevant footnote notified DOD that the Ukraine Security Assistance Initiative funds "are not available for obligation until August 5, 2019, to allow for an interagency process to determine the best use of such funds." The footnote also stated that:

> Based on OMB's communication with DOD on July 25, 2019, OMB understands from the Department that this brief pause in obligations will not preclude DOD's timely execution of the final policy direction. DOD may continue its planning and casework for the Initiative during this period.[392]

Mr. Sandy explained that the "interagency process" referenced in the footnote referred to the NSC-led interagency meetings convened during the latter half of July, and that the August 5 date provided a "reasonable timeframe for an interagency process" to produce "clear guidance" on the hold.[393] The August 5 date was determined in consultation with Mr. Duffey at OMB and Ms. McCusker at DOD.[394]

Mr. Sandy further testified that the second sentence in the footnote—which states, in relevant part, that "OMB understands from the Department that this brief pause in obligations will not preclude DOD's timely execution of the final policy direction"—was critical to the implementation of the hold:

Well, that gets to the heart of that issue about ensuring that we don't run afoul of the Impoundment Control Act, which means that you have to allow for the timely execution. And this reflects my conversation with—conversations plural with Elaine McCusker that they can confirm that, during this brief period, they would not foresee any problem fully executing the program by the end of the fiscal year.[395]

The sentence, in effect, affirmed that if the hold remained in place only until August 5, DOD would still have sufficient time to spend all security assistance funds by September 30, 2019. President Trump, however, would continue the hold long past August 5.

Trump Appointee Took Over Signing Authority from Career Budget Expert

Since becoming Deputy Associate Director for National Security in 2013, Mr. Sandy was responsible for approving release of the funding for programs within his portfolio, including the Ukraine Security Assistance Initiative.[396] Mr. Sandy approved and signed the July 25 funding document.[397] On July 29, however, Mr. Duffey—a political appointee of President Trump whose prior position had been as Executive Director of the Republican Party of Wisconsin—told Mr. Sandy—a career civil servant with decades of experience in this area—that he would no longer be responsible for approving the release of funding for Ukraine Security Assistance Initiative.[398] Mr. Duffey also revoked the authority for approving the release of funding for Foreign Military Financing from Mr. Sandy's colleague at OMB.[399] Instead, Mr. Duffey would himself assume authority for the $250 million in DOD-administered Ukraine security assistance and authority for approving the release of funding for the $141 million in State Department-administered Foreign Military Financing to Ukraine.[400]

Mr. Duffey did not tell Mr. Sandy whether he requested this change in authority but did say that "it was in essence a joint decision reflecting both guidance from the Acting Director and also his support."[401] Over the course of several days, Mr. Duffey explained to Mr. Sandy and others in the National Security Division that "there was interest among the leadership in tracking the uses of moneys [sic] closely."[402] Mr. Duffey expressed an "interest in being more involved in daily operations" and "regarded this responsibility as a way for him to learn more about specific accounts within his area."[403]

Mr. Sandy testified that prior to July 29, he had never heard Mr. Duffey state any interest in approving the release of funding.[404] Furthermore, when they learned that Mr. Duffey was taking on this new responsibility, Mr. Sandy and other staff relayed their concerns to Mr. Duffey that it was a substantial workload.[405] Mr. Sandy also testified that "people were curious what he thought he would learn from apportionments about the accounts as opposed to the other, you know, sources of information."[406] Mr. Sandy agreed that there are more efficient ways of learning about accounts and programs, and that "I can think of other ways—other materials that I personally would find more informative."[407]

Mr. Sandy was not aware of any prior instance when a political appointee assumed this kind of funding approval authority.[408]

After the July 31 interagency meeting at which Ms. Cooper announced that DOD would have to start obligating the funds on or about August 6, Mr. Duffey sought clarification. [409] Ms. Cooper explained to Mr. Duffey that at a certain point DOD would not have sufficient time to fully obligate the funds before they expired at the end of the fiscal year. In response, Mr. Duffey "wanted more information on the precise nature of how long does it take to obligate, and how many cases, and that sort of thing." [410] Ms. Cooper referred Mr. Duffey to the DOD comptroller and to the Defense Security Cooperation Agency. [411] During the month of August, Mr. Duffey and Ms. McCusker communicated about the implementation of the hold on the Ukraine Security Assistance Initiative funds. [412]

On August 6 and August 15, Mr. Duffey approved two more funding documents that contained footnotes with language nearly identical to the footnote in the July 25 funding document that initiated the hold; the only difference was that the date funds would become available for spending was changed from August 5 to August 12. [413]

The August 6 and 15 footnotes, and all subsequent footnotes through September 10, continued to state that the hold was in place "to allow for an interagency process to determine the best use of such funds," even though the final interagency meeting regarding Ukraine security assistance occurred on July 31. [414] Not only was there no active interagency process after July, but Ms. Cooper also was not aware of any review of the funding conducted by DOD in July, August, or September. [415] In fact, Ms. Cooper noted that months before, DOD had completed its review of whether Ukraine "had made sufficient progress in meeting defense reform and anticorruption goals consistent with the NDAA," and certified to Congress in May 2019 that Ukraine had met the requirements to receive funding. [416] Similarly, Mr. Kent testified that the State Department did not conduct, and was never asked to conduct, a review of the security assistance funding administered by the State Department. [417]

At the same time that OMB was implementing the President's hold through the funding footnotes, officials inside OMB were advocating for release of the funds. On August 7, the National Security Division, International Affairs Division, and Office of Legal Counsel of OMB drafted and transmitted a memo on Ukraine security assistance to OMB Acting Director Vought "in anticipation of a principals-level discussion to address the topic." [418] The National Security Division's portion of the memorandum recommended to remove the hold because (1) the assistance was consistent with the national security strategy in terms of supporting a stable, peaceful Europe; (2) the aid countered Russian aggression; and (3) there was bipartisan support for the program. [419] Mr. Duffey approved the memorandum and agreed with the policy recommendation. [420]

Sometime in mid-August, DOD raised concerns that it might not be able to fully obligate the Defense Department administered funds before the end of the fiscal year. [421] Ms. Cooper testified that the Defense Security Cooperation Agency estimated that $100 million of aid might not be obligated in time and was at risk. [422]

Because of this, DOD concluded that it could no longer support OMB's claim in the footnote that "this brief pause in obligations will not preclude DOD's timely execution of the final policy direction."[423] As mentioned above, Mr. Sandy testified that this sentence was at "the heart of that issue about ensuring that we don't run afoul of the Impoundment Control Act." [424]

As a result of DOD's concerns, all of the subsequent footnotes issued by OMB during the pendency of the hold—approved by Mr. Duffey on August 20, 27, and 31, and September 5, 6, and 10—removed the sentence regarding DOD's ability to fully obligate by the end of the fiscal year.[425] Each footnote extended the hold for a period of two to six days.[426]

Mr. Sandy and his staff "continued to express concerns [to Mr. Duffey] about the potential implications vis-à-vis the Impoundment Control Act,"[427] and advised Mr. Duffey to consult with OMB's Office of General Counsel "on every single footnote."[428] Mr. Sandy was copied on emails with the Office of General Counsel on these topics. [429] Although Mr. Sandy understood that the Office of General Counsel supported the footnotes, he noted that there were dissenting opinions within the Office of General Counsel.[430] Concerns about whether the Administration was bending, if not breaking, the law by holding back this vital assistance contributed to at least two OMB officials resigning, including one attorney in the Office of General Counsel.[431] Mr. Sandy testified that the resignation was motivated in part by concerns about the way OMB was handling the hold on Ukraine security assistance.[432] According to Mr. Sandy, the colleague disagreed with the Office of General Counsel about the application of the Impoundment Control Act to the hold on Ukraine security assistance.[433]

Nevertheless, at the direction of the President, OMB continued to implement the hold through September 11.

Senior Officials Failed to Convince President Trump to Release the Aid in August

Sometime prior to August 16, Ambassador Bolton had a one-on-one meeting with President Trump about the aid.[434] According to Mr. Morrison, at that meeting the President "was not yet ready to approve the release of the assistance."[435] Following the meeting, Ambassador Bolton instructed Mr. Morrison to look for opportunities to get the principals together "to have the direct, in-person conversation with the President about this topic." [436]

On or about August 13 or 14, Lt. Col. Vindman was directed to draft a Presidential Decision Memorandum for Ambassador Bolton and the other principals to present to President Trump for a decision on Ukraine security assistance.[437] The memorandum, finalized on August 15, recommended that the hold should be lifted, explained why, and included the consensus views from the July 26 meeting that the funds should be released.[438] Lt. Col. Vindman received conflicting accounts about whether the memorandum was presented to the President.[439]

Mr. Morrison, who was Lt. Col. Vindman's supervisor at the NSC and agreed with the recommendation to lift the hold, testified that the memorandum was never provided to the President.[440] Mr. Morrison explained that Ambassador Bolton intended to present the memorandum to the President during an unrelated meeting in Bedminster, New Jersey, on August 15, but the "other subject matter of that meeting consumed all the time."[441] However, while at Bedminster, the principals "all represented to Ambassador Bolton that they were prepared to tell the President they endorsed the swift release and disbursement of the funding."[442]

Mr. Morrison testified that he attempted to gather the "the right group of principals" to meet with the President but was unable to do so because of scheduling issues.[443] According to Mr. Morrison, the next possible opportunity was during a trip to Warsaw, Poland at the beginning of September, but President Trump did not end up making that trip.[444]

Ms. Cooper recalled receiving an email at the end of August from Secretary of Defense Esper referencing a meeting or discussion with the President, and that there was "no decision on Ukraine."[445]

Ukrainian Officials Learned About the Hold in July 2019

Witnesses testified that officials in the Ukraine government knew of President Trump's hold on security assistance before it was publicly reported in the press on August 28, 2019. Ms. Croft testified that after July 18—when the hold was announced by OMB at the interagency meeting—it was "inevitable that it was eventually going to come out."[446]

Two individuals from the Ukrainian Embassy in Washington, D.C., approached Ms. Croft approximately a week apart "quietly and in confidence to ask me about an OMB hold on Ukraine security assistance."[447] Ms. Croft could not precisely recall the dates of these conversations, but testified that she was "very surprised at the effectiveness of my Ukrainian counterparts' diplomatic tradecraft, as in to say they found out very early on or much earlier than I expected them to."[448]

Ms. Croft explained that the Ukrainian officials came to her quietly because they would not want the hold to become public:

> I think that if this were public in Ukraine it would be seen as a reversal of our policy and would, just to say sort of candidly and colloquially, this would be a really big deal, it would be a really big deal in Ukraine, and an expression of declining U.S. support for Ukraine.[449]

DOD also received questions from the Ukraine Embassy about the status of the military assistance. Ms. Cooper testified that those occurred on July 25, 2019—the same day as President Trump's call with President Zelensky:

> On July 25th, a member of my staff got a question from a Ukraine Embassy contact asking what was going on with Ukraine security assistance, because at that time, we did not know what the guidance was on USAI [DOD-administered funds]. The OMB notice of apportionment arrived that day, but this staff member did not find out about it until later. I was informed that the staff member told the Ukrainian official that we were moving forward on USAI, but recommended that the Ukraine Embassy check in with State regarding the FMF [State Department-administered funds].[450]

On July 25, Ms. Cooper's staff received two emails from the State Department revealing that the Ukrainian Embassy was "asking about security assistance" and that "the Hill knows about the FMF situation to an extent, and so does the Ukrainian Embassy."[451]

One of Ms. Cooper's staff members reported that sometime during the week of August 6, a Ukrainian Embassy officer stated that "a Ukrainian official might raise concerns about security assistance in an upcoming meeting," but that the issue was "not, in fact, raised."[452] Ms. Cooper's staff further reported that Ukrainian officials were aware of the hold on security assistance in August.[453]

Lt. Col. Vindman testified that, by mid-August, he too was getting questions from Ukrainians about the status of the hold on security assistance:

> So to the best of my knowledge, the Ukrainians, first of all, are in general pretty sophisticated, they have their network of, you know, Ukrainian interest groups and so forth. They have bipartisan support in Congress. And certainly there are—it was no secret, at least within government and official channels, that security assistance was on hold. And to the best of my recollection, I believe there were some of these light inquires in the mid-August timeframe.[454]

While numerous individuals, including Ukrainians, were aware of the hold, it did not become publicly known until a *Politico* report on August 28, 2019.[455]

4.   **The President's Meeting with the Ukrainian President Was Conditioned on An Announcement of Investigations**

> *President Trump demanded the public announcement by President Zelensky of investigations into President Trump's political rival and alleged Ukrainian interference in the 2016 U.S. election in exchange for an Oval Office meeting. The President's representatives made that quid pro quo clear to Ukrainian officials.*

Overview

After ordering the hold on security assistance to Ukraine against the unanimous advice of the relevant U.S. government agencies, President Trump used his hand-picked representatives to demand that Ukrainian leaders publicly announce investigations into his political rival, former Vice President Joe Biden, and into the debunked conspiracy theory that Ukraine, not Russia, interfered in the 2016 U.S. election. President Trump, through his agents, made clear that his demand needed to be met before a coveted White House meeting with Ukrainian President Volodymyr Zelensky would be scheduled. A face-to-face meeting with President Trump in the Oval Office would have conferred on the new Ukrainian leader much-sought prestige and would have signaled to Russia that Ukraine could continue to count on the support of the President of the United States, which was particularly important as Russia continued to wage war in eastern Ukraine.

To date, the White House meeting for President Zelensky has not occurred. Following the May 23 meeting in the Oval Office, President Trump's hand-picked representatives—the so-called "Three Amigos"—worked with the President's personal attorney, Rudy Giuliani, to pressure Ukrainian leaders to announce publicly investigations that would benefit the President's reelection campaign. Testimony of multiple witnesses and contemporaneous text messages exchanged between and among President Trump's representatives confirm that the White House meeting—and later the release of security assistance for Ukraine—was conditioned on Ukraine acquiescing to the President's demands.

In the weeks leading up to the July 25 call between President Trump and President Zelensky, President Trump's representatives repeatedly relayed the message of conditionality to Ukrainian government officials—including to President Zelensky himself—in meetings in Kyiv, Toronto, and Washington, D.C. President Zelensky and his advisors struggled to navigate these demands, recognizing that President Trump's desire that Ukraine announce these political investigations threatened to render Ukraine a "pawn" in U.S. domestic reelection politics.

An Oval Office Meeting for President Zelensky Was Important to Ukraine and U.S. National Security

A face-to-face meeting with the President of the United States in the Oval Office was critical to President Zelensky as the newly-elected Ukrainian leader sought U.S. support for his ambitious anti-corruption agenda and to repel Russian aggression. A White House meeting was also important for U.S. national security because it would have served to bolster Ukraine's negotiating position in peace talks with Russia. It also would have supported Ukraine as a bulwark against further Russian advances in Europe.

Multiple witnesses unanimously attested to the importance of a White House meeting for Ukraine and the United States. For example, David Holmes, the Political Counselor at the U.S. Embassy in Kyiv, testified that a White House meeting was "critical" to President Zelensky's ability to "encourage Russian President Putin to take seriously President Zelensky's peace efforts."[456] Likewise, Deputy Assistant Secretary George Kent explained that a White House meeting was "very important" for Ukrainians to demonstrate the strength of their relationship with "Ukraine's strongest supporter." He also said that it "makes sense" for the United States to meet with the Ukrainians as they were on "the front lines of Russian malign influence and aggression."[457]

Dr. Fiona Hill, Deputy Assistant to the President and Senior Director of European and Russian Affairs at the NSC, explained that a White House meeting would supply the new Ukrainian Government with "the legitimacy that it needed, especially vis-à-vis the Russians,"— and that the Ukrainians viewed a White House meeting as "a recognition of their legitimacy as a sovereign state."[458] Lt. Col. Alexander Vindman, the NSC Director for Ukraine, testified that a White House meeting would provide a "show of support" from "the most powerful country in the world and Ukraine's most significant benefactor," which would help the Ukrainian President "establish his bona fides" and "implement his agenda."[459]

Ambassador Kurt Volker, Special Representative for Ukraine Negotiations, also recognized that it was "a tremendous symbol of support" to have President Zelensky visit the White House.[460] He explained that a meeting "enhances [President Zelensky's] stature, that he is accepted, that he is seen at the highest level. The imagery you get from being at the White House is the best in the world, in terms of how it enhances someone's image."[461]

President Trump "Wanted to Hear from Zelensky" Before Scheduling Oval Office Meeting

Ambassador William B. Taylor, Jr. arrived in Ukraine as the new Chargé d'Affaires at the U.S. Embassy in Kyiv on June 17, 2019. After arriving, Ambassador Taylor worked to secure an Oval Office meeting between President Trump and President Zelensky. This was "an agreed-upon goal" of policymakers in both Ukraine and the United States.[462]

Ambassador Taylor worked with Ambassador Volker and Ambassador to the European Union Gordon Sondland—two of the Three Amigos—to try to schedule this meeting. Just days after beginning his new position, Ambassador Taylor learned that President Trump "wanted to hear from Zelensky" before scheduling the Oval Office meeting, but Ambassador Taylor did not understand what that meant at the time.[463] On June 27, Ambassador Sondland informed Ambassador Taylor that President Zelensky needed to "make clear" to President Trump that he, President Zelensky, was not "standing in the way of 'investigations.'"[464] Ambassador Taylor relayed this conversation to Mr. Holmes, who testified that he understood "investigations" in that context to mean the "Burisma-Biden investigations that Mr. Giuliani and his associates had been speaking about" publicly.[465]

On June 28, Secretary of Energy Rick Perry—the third of the Three Amigos—and Ambassadors Sondland, Volker, and Taylor participated in a conference call to prepare for a discussion later that day with President Zelensky. During this preparatory call, Ambassador Volker explained that he planned to be "explicit" with President Zelensky in an upcoming one-on-one meeting in Toronto, Canada. Specifically, Ambassador Volker intended to inform President Zelensky that President Trump would require Ukraine to address "rule of law, transparency, but also, specifically, cooperation on investigations to get to the bottom of things" in order to "get the meeting in the White House."[466]

For the subsequent call with President Zelensky on June 28, Ambassador Sondland sought to limit the number of U.S. government personnel listening in. According to Ambassador Taylor, Ambassador Sondland stated that he did not want to include "most of the regular interagency participants" and that "he wanted to make sure no one was transcribing or monitoring" the call when President Zelensky was patched in. Ambassador Taylor testified that he considered Ambassador Sondland's requests to be "odd."[467] During that call, President Zelensky and the U.S. officials discussed energy policy and the conflict with Russia in eastern Ukraine. The Ukrainian president also noted that he looked forward to the White House visit that President Trump had offered in a letter dated May 29.[468]

The exclusion of State Department staff and notetakers from the June 28 call was an early indication to Ambassador Taylor that separate channels of diplomacy related to Ukraine policy—an official channel and an irregular channel—were "diverging." Ambassador Taylor testified:

> This suggested to me that there were the two channels. This suggested to me that the normal channel, where you would have staff on the phone call, was being cut out, and the other channel, of people who were working, again, toward a goal which I supported, which was having a meeting to further U.S.-Ukrainian relations, I supported, but that irregular channel didn't have a respect for or an interest in having the normal staff participate in this call with the head of state.[469]

Given Ambassador Sondland's efforts to exclude staff on the June 28 call with President Zelensky, Ambassador Taylor asked Ambassadors Sondland and Volker by text message how they planned to handle informing other U.S. officials about the contents of the call. Ambassador Volker responded: "I think we just keep it among ourselves to try to build working relationship and just get the d*** date for the meeting!"[470] Ambassador Sondland then texted: "Agree with KV. Very close hold."[471] Nevertheless, Ambassador Taylor informed Mr. Kent about the call and wrote a memo for the record dated June 30 that summarized the conversation with President Zelensky.[472]

Ambassador Volker Pressed "Investigations" with President Zelensky in Toronto

On July 2, Ambassador Volker met with President Zelensky and his chief of staff on the sidelines of the Ukraine Reform Conference in Toronto. As he later texted to Ambassador Taylor, Ambassador Volker "pulled the two of them aside at the end and explained the Giuliani factor."[473] Ambassador Volker clarified that by "the Giuliani factor," he meant "a negative narrative about Ukraine" that was "being amplified by Rudy Giuliani" and was unfavorably impacting "Ukraine's image in the United States and our ability to advance the bilateral relationship."[474] Ambassador Volker later informed Ukraine's incoming Minister of Foreign Affairs, Vadym Prystaiko, about his pull-aside with President Zelensky in Toronto via text message: "I talked to him privately about Giuliani and impact on president T[rump]."[475]

On July 3, the day after his pull-aside with President Zelensky in Toronto, Ambassador Volker sent a message to Ambassador Taylor emphasizing that "The key thing is to tee up a phone call w potus and then get visit nailed down."[476] Ambassador Volker told Ambassador Taylor that during the Toronto conference, he counseled the Ukrainian president about how he could "prepare for the phone call with President Trump." Specifically, Ambassador Volker told the Ukrainian leader that President Trump "would like to hear about the investigations." [477] In his public testimony, Ambassador Volker confirmed that he mentioned "investigations" to President Zelensky in Toronto, explaining that he was "thinking of Burisma and 2016" in raising the subject, and that his "assumption" was that Ukrainian officials also understood his reference to "investigations" to be "Burisma/2016."[478]

Ambassador Volker's efforts to prepare President Zelensky for his phone call with President Trump appear to have borne fruit. As discussed further in Chapter 5, during the July 25 call, President Zelensky expressed his openness to pursuing investigations into President Trump's political rival, former Vice President Biden, and the conspiracy theory that Ukraine, rather than Russia, interfered in the 2016 U.S. election. President Zelensky also specifically referenced "Burisma" during the call.

Ambassadors Volker and Sondland Worked to Get Mr. Giuliani What He Needed

According to Ambassador Sondland, President Zelensky's commitment to make a public announcement about investigations into Burisma and the 2016 election was a "prerequisite[]" for the White House meeting.[479] In fact, Ambassador Sondland testified that the *announcement* of the investigations—and not the investigations themselves—was the price President Trump sought in exchange for a White House meeting with Ukrainian President Zelensky:

Q: But he had to get those two investigations if that official act was going to take place, correct?

A: He had to announce the investigations. He didn't actually have to do them, as I understood it.

Q: Okay. President Zelensky had to announce the two investigations the President wanted, make a public announcement, correct?

A: Correct.[480]

Ambassadors Sondland and Volker understood that they needed to work with Mr. Giuliani, who was publicly pressing for the announcement of investigations that would benefit President Trump politically. As discussed in Chapter 2, Ambassador Sondland testified that the key to overcoming President Trump's skepticism about Ukraine was satisfying the President's personal attorney. Sondland said, "Nonetheless, based on the President's direction, we were faced with a choice: We could abandon the efforts to schedule the White House phone call and a

White House visit" or "do as President Trump had directed and 'talk with Rudy'" because "it was the only constructive path open to us."[481]

Ambassador Volker discussed his intention to contact Mr. Giuliani with Mr. Kent. Ambassador Volker explained that he intended to reach out to Mr. Giuliani because it was clear that the former mayor "had influence" with President Trump "in terms of the way the President thought of Ukraine."[482] Ukrainian officials also understood the importance of working through Mr. Giuliani, something that was underscored by his successful effort to smear and remove Ambassador Marie Yovanovitch from Kyiv in late April.[483]

In response to Ambassador Volker's stated intention to reach out to Mr. Giuliani, Mr. Kent raised concerns about Mr. Giuliani's "track record," including "asking for a visa for a corrupt former prosecutor," attacking Ambassador Yovanovitch, and "tweeting that the new President needs to investigate Biden and the 2016 campaign." Mr. Kent also warned Ambassador Volker that "asking another country to investigate a prosecution for political reasons undermines our advocacy of the rule of law."[484]

On July 10, Ambassador Taylor met with Ukrainian officials in Kyiv, before their Ukrainian colleagues were scheduled to meet with National Security Advisor John Bolton at the White House later that day. At the meeting in Kyiv, the Ukrainian officials expressed that they were "very concerned" because they had heard from former Prosecutor General Yuriy Lutsenko, who had learned from Mr. Giuliani, that President Trump had decided not to meet with President Zelensky.[485]

Ambassador Taylor texted Ambassador Volker to explain the situation and advised that he had also informed T. Ulrich Brechbuhl, Counselor of the Department of State:

Volker:	Good grief. Please tell Vadym to let the official USG representatives speak for the U.S. lutsenko has his own self-Interest here…
Taylor:	Exactly what I told them.
Taylor:	And I said that RG is a private citizen.
Taylor:	I briefed Ulrich this afternoon on this.[486]

Despite his text message to Ambassador Taylor that official U.S. government representatives should be allowed to "speak for the U.S.," and notwithstanding Mr. Kent's warnings about engaging with Mr. Giuliani, Ambassador Volker almost immediately reached out to Mr. Giuliani. Four minutes after sending the text message above, Ambassador Volker texted Mr. Giuliani to request a meeting to "update you on my conversations about Ukraine." He told Mr. Giuliani that he believed he had "an opportunity to get you what you need."[487]

One hour later, around 9:00 a.m. Eastern Time, Ambassador Volker met Ukrainian presidential aide Andriy Yermak for coffee at the Trump Hotel before they traveled down Pennsylvania Avenue to their afternoon meetings at the White House.[488] Over coffee, Mr. Yermak asked Ambassador Volker to connect him to Mr. Giuliani, thus further demonstrating the Ukrainians' understanding that satisfying Mr. Giuliani's demands was a key to getting what they wanted from President Trump, namely the Oval Office meeting.[489]

July 10 White House Meetings: Ambassador Sondland
Explicitly Communicated the "Prerequisite of Investigations" to Ukrainians

On July 10, during two separate meetings at the White House, Ambassador Sondland informed senior Ukrainian officials that there was a "prerequisite of investigations" before an Oval Office meeting between President Trump and President Zelensky would be scheduled.[490]

The first meeting took place in Ambassador Bolton's office. NSC officials, including Ambassador Bolton's staff responsible for Ukraine—Dr. Hill and Lt. Col. Vindman—attended, as did the Three Amigos: Secretary Perry, Ambassador Sondland, and Ambassador Volker. The Ukrainian delegation included Mr. Yermak, a senior aide to President Zelensky, and Oleksandr "Sasha" Danyliuk, the incoming Ukrainian National Security Advisor.[491] The purpose of the meeting was twofold. The Ukrainians were seeking advice and assistance from Ambassador Bolton about how to "revamp" the Ukrainian National Security Council, and they were also "very anxious to set up a meeting, a first meeting between President Zelensky and our President."[492]

Near the end of the meeting, the Ukrainian officials raised the scheduling of the Oval Office meeting for President Zelensky. According to Dr. Hill, Ambassador Sondland, who is "a fairly big guy, kind of leaned over" and then "blurted out: Well, we have an agreement with the [White House] Chief of Staff for a meeting if these investigations in the energy sector start." Dr. Hill described that others in the room looked up from their notes, thinking the comment was "somewhat odd." Ambassador Bolton "immediately stiffened" and ended the meeting. Dr. Hill recounted that Ambassador Bolton was polite but was "very abrupt. I mean, he looked at the clock as if he had, you know, suddenly another meeting and his time was up, but it was obvious he ended the meeting," she added.[493]

Lt. Col. Vindman similarly testified that the meeting in Ambassador Bolton's office "proceeded well" until Ukrainian officials raised the meeting between President Trump and President Zelensky. The Ukrainians stated that they considered the Oval Office meeting to be "critically important in order to solidify the support for their most important international partner." When Ambassador Sondland mentioned Ukraine "delivering specific investigations in order to secure the meeting with the President," Ambassador Bolton cut the meeting short.[494]

Although Ambassador Volker did not recall any mention of "investigations" during the July 10 meeting at his deposition,[495] he later testified at his public hearing, "As I remember, the meeting [in Ambassador Bolton's office] was essentially over when Ambassador Sondland made a general comment about investigations. I think all of us thought it was inappropriate" and "not what we should be talking about."[496]

After Ambassador Bolton ended the meeting in his office, Ambassador Sondland "went out into the office in front of Ambassador Bolton" and made "unusual" arrangements for the Ukrainians, Ambassador Volker, Secretary Perry, and others to go to a second meeting in the Ward Room of the White House, located near the secure spaces of the White House Situation Room. As Dr. Hill described it, the purpose of the Ward Room meeting was "to talk to the

Ukrainians about next steps" regarding the Oval Office meeting for President Zelensky.[497] As Dr. Hill was leaving Ambassador Bolton's office, he pulled her aside and directed her to attend the Ward Room meeting to "find out what they're talking about and come back" and report to him. Dr. Hill followed his instruction.[498]

During the Ward Room meeting, which occurred after a brief photo opportunity outside the West Wing, Ambassador Sondland was more explicit in pressing the Ukrainians to undertake the investigations in order to secure an Oval Office meeting for President Zelensky. Lt. Col. Vindman testified that when the group entered the Ward Room, Ambassador Sondland began to "review what the deliverable would be in order to get the meeting," and that "to the best of my recollection, he did specifically say 'investigation of the Bidens.'" Lt. Col. Vindman said the request "was explicit. There was no ambiguity" and that Ambassador Sondland also mentioned "Burisma."[499]

Dr. Hill entered the Ward Room as the discussion was underway. She testified that "Ambassador Sondland, in front of the Ukrainians, as I came in, was talking about how he had an agreement with Chief of Staff Mulvaney for a meeting with the Ukrainians if they were going to go forward with investigations. And my director for Ukraine [Lt. Col. Vindman] was looking completely alarmed."[500] Dr. Hill recalled that Ambassador Sondland mentioned "Burisma" in the presence of the Ukrainians, in response to which Mr. Danyliuk also appeared "very alarmed" and as if he did not know what was happening.[501]

Dr. Hill confronted Ambassador Sondland, informing him that Ambassador Bolton had sent her there to ensure that the U.S. officials did not commit "at this particular juncture" to a meeting between President Trump and President Zelensky. Ambassador Sondland responded that he and the Ukrainians already had an agreement that the meeting would go forward.[502] At Dr. Hill's urging, however, Ambassador Sondland excused the Ukrainian officials, who moved into the corridor near the White House Situation Room.

Dr. Hill then told Ambassador Sondland: "Look, I don't know what's going on here, but Ambassador Bolton wants to make it very clear that we have to talk about, you know, how are we going to set up this meeting. It has to go through proper procedures." Lt. Col. Vindman relayed his own concerns to Ambassador Sondland in the Ward Room.[503] He explained that "the request to investigate the Bidens and his son had nothing to do with national security, and that such investigations were not something that the NSC was going to get involved in or push."[504]

Ambassador Sondland responded that he had had conversations with Mr. Mulvaney and he also mentioned Mr. Giuliani. Lt. Col. Vindman confirmed that Ambassador Sondland described an agreement he had with Mr. Mulvaney about the Oval Office meeting: "I heard him say that this had been coordinated with White House Chief of Staff Mr. Mick Mulvaney ... He just said that he had had a conversation with Mr. Mulvaney, and this is what was required in order to get a meeting."[505] Dr. Hill then cut the conversation short because she "didn't want to get further into this discussion at all." She testified that Ambassador Sondland "was clearly annoyed with this, but then, you know, he moved off. He said he had other meetings."[506]

Later on July 10, when Ambassador Taylor asked Ambassador Volker how the meetings went with the Ukrainian officials and whether they had resulted in a decision on a presidential call, Ambassador Volker replied: "Not good—lets talk."[507]

Following the July 10 White House meetings, Mr. Yermak followed up with Ambassador Volker by text message: "Thank you for meeting and your clear and very logical position. Will be great meet with you before my departure and discuss. I feel that the key for many things is Rudi and I ready to talk with him at any time."[508]

Concerned Officials Reported Details of This "Drug Deal" to White House Lawyers

After the Ward Room meeting, Dr. Hill returned to Ambassador Bolton's office and relayed what she had just witnessed. Ambassador Bolton was "very angry" and instructed her to report the conversation to John Eisenberg, Deputy Counsel to the President for National Security Affairs and the Legal Advisor to the National Security Council:

> And he told me, and this is a direct quote from Ambassador Bolton: You go and tell Eisenberg that I am not part of whatever drug deal Sondland and Mulvaney are cooking up on this, and you go and tell him what you've heard and what I've said.[509]

Dr. Hill explained that "drug deal" referred to Ambassador Sondland's and Mr. Mulvaney's conditioning of a White House meeting on investigations.[510] By this point, Dr. Hill explained, it was clear that investigations were "code, at least, for Burisma. Because that had been mentioned, you know, in the course of Mr. Giuliani's appearances on television."[511] Numerous U.S. officials, including Ambassadors Sondland, Volker, and Bolton, as well as Lt. Col. Vindman and others, were well aware of Mr. Giuliani's efforts to push Ukraine to pursue these political investigations.

Following the meeting with Ambassador Bolton, Dr. Hill reported what had occurred to Mr. Eisenberg. She conveyed to Mr. Eisenberg the details of the two meetings, including Ambassador Sondland's agreement with Mr. Mulvaney to provide the White House meeting if Ukraine agreed to pursue the investigations.[512] The initial conversation between Dr. Hill and Mr. Eisenberg was brief, and they scheduled a longer discussion for the next day.[513]

On July 11, Dr. Hill enlisted another NSC official who attended the July 10 meetings, Senior Director for International Energy and Environment P. Wells Griffith, to attend the longer discussion with Mr. Eisenberg.[514] Dr. Hill and Mr. Griffith went over the events of July 10 and further explained that Ambassador Sondland said that he had been communicating with Mr. Giuliani. Mr. Eisenberg was "very concerned" and stated that he would follow up. Dr. Hill understood that Mr. Eisenberg later discussed the issue with his "reporting authority," specifically, White House Counsel Pat Cipollone.[515]

Lt. Col. Vindman separately reported his concerns about the July 10 meetings to Mr. Eisenberg. He told Mr. Eisenberg that Ambassador Sondland had asked for investigations into "Bidens and Burisma," which he thought was "inappropriate."[516] Lt. Col. Vindman also reported that the investigation "Mr. Giuliani was pushing was now being pulled into a, you know, national security dialogue."[517] Mr. Eisenberg said that he would look into it and invited Lt. Col. Vindman to return if any further concerns arose. No one from the of the White House Counsel's Office, however, followed up with Lt. Col. Vindman on this issue.[518]

Dr. Hill and Lt. Col. Vindman discussed their reactions and alarm about the July 10 discussions with each other. They both believed that Ambassador Sondland's statements were inappropriate and "had nothing to do with national security," and that they would not get involved with the scheme.[519] On July 19, they also shared their concerns about Ambassador Sondland's comments during the July 10 meetings with Ambassador Taylor.[520]

Ambassador Sondland Coached President Zelensky on Investigations and Kept Senior White House and State Department Officials "In the Loop"

In mid-July, Dr. Hill was preparing to depart the NSC and transitioning her role to Timothy Morrison, who had been serving in another role at the NSC.[521] On July 13, Ambassador Sondland emailed Mr. Morrison, explaining that the "[s]ole purpose" of a presidential call was for President Zelensky to assure President Trump that, "Corruption ending, unbundling moving forward and any hampered investigations will be allowed to move forward transparently." In exchange, Ambassador Sondland wrote, the "Goal is for Potus to invite him to Oval. Volker, Perry, Bolton and I strongly recommend."[522] Later that evening, Mr. Morrison responded, "Thank you. Tracking."[523]

On July 19, a little over a week after the July 10 meetings at the White House, Ambassador Sondland spoke directly to President Zelensky about the upcoming call between the two presidents: "It was a short call. I think I said: It looks like your call is finally on, and I think it's important that you, you know, give President Trump—he wanted this—some kind of a statement about corruption."[524]

Following his call with President Zelensky, Ambassador Sondland emailed several senior Trump Administration officials, including Mr. Mulvaney, Secretary of State Michael Pompeo, Secretary Perry, and their staffs. The subject line of the July 19 email read: "I Talked to Zelensky just now." Ambassador Sondland wrote:

> He is prepared to receive Potus' call. Will assure him that he intends to run a fully transparent investigation and will "turn over every stone". He would greatly appreciate a call prior to Sunday so that he can put out some media about a "friendly and productive call" (no details) prior to Ukraine election on Sunday.[525]

Secretary Perry responded that Mr. Mulvaney had confirmed a call would be set up "for tomorrow by NSC,"[526] and Mr. Mulvaney also responded to confirm that he had asked the NSC to set up the call between the presidents for the following day, July 20.[527]

Ambassador Sondland explained that this email chain showed that "[e]veryone was in the loop" regarding his discussions with Ukrainian officials about the need for the Ukrainian leader to confirm to President Trump that he would announce the investigations. As Ambassador Sondland further testified:

It was no secret. Everyone was informed via email on July 19th, days before the Presidential call. As I communicated to the team, I told President Zelensky in advance that assurances to run a fully transparent investigation and turn over every stone were necessary in his call with President Trump.[528]

Call records reviewed by the Committees show repeated contact between Ambassador Sondland and the White House around this time. For example, on July 19, at 10:43 a.m. Eastern Time, a number associated with the White House dialed Ambassador Sondland. Four minutes later, at 10:47 a.m., Ambassador Sondland called a White House phone number and connected for approximately seven minutes.[529]

Later in the afternoon of July 19, Ambassador Sondland texted Ambassadors Volker and Taylor: "Looks like Potus call tomorrow. I spike [sic] directly to Zelensky and gave him a full briefing. He's got it."[530] Ambassador Volker replied: "Good. Had breakfast with Rudy this morning—teeing up call w Yermak Monday. Must have helped. Most impt is for Zelensky to say that he will help investigation—and address any specific personnel issues—if there are any."[531]

Mr. Giuliani Met with State Department Officials and Ukrainian Government Officials

As Ambassador Volker informed Ambassador Sondland in the above text message, on July 19, Ambassador Volker met Mr. Giuliani and his now-indicted associate Lev Parnas for breakfast at the Trump Hotel in Washington, D.C.[532] Ambassador Volker also texted Mr. Yermak to inform him that he and Mr. Giuliani were meeting that day: "Having our long anticipated breakfast today—will let you know and try to connect you directly."[533]

During the breakfast, Mr. Giuliani and Ambassador Volker discussed the discredited allegations against former Vice President Biden relating to Ukraine. Ambassador Volker testified that he pushed back against the allegations during his breakfast with Mr. Giuliani:

> One of the things that I said in that breakfast that I had with Mr. Giuliani, the only time Vice President Biden was ever discussed with me, and he was repeating—he wasn't making an accusation and he wasn't seeking an investigation—but he was repeating all of the things that were in the media that we talked about earlier about, you know, firing the prosecutor general and his son being on the company and all that.

> And I said to Rudy in that breakfast the first time we sat down to talk that it is simply not credible to me that Joe Biden would be influenced in his duties as Vice President by money or things for his son or anything like that. I've known him a long time, he's a person of integrity, and that's not credible.[534]

Ambassador Volker further advised Mr. Giuliani during the breakfast that the then-Ukrainian Prosecutor General, Yuriy Lutsenko, was promoting a "self-serving narrative to preserve himself in power." Mr. Giuliani agreed with Ambassador Volker and stated that he had come to that conclusion as well.[535]

Following the breakfast, Ambassador Volker connected Mr. Giuliani with Mr. Yermak by text message:

Volker: Mr Mayor — really enjoyed breakfast this morning. As discussed, connecting you here with Andrey Yermak, who is very close to President Zelensky. I suggest we schedule a call together on Monday — maybe 10am or 11am Washington time? Kurt

Giuliani: Monday 10 to 11

Yermak: Ok, thank you

Volker: I will set up call — 10 am — thanks – Kurt

Yermak: 👍[536]

On the morning of July 22, Mr. Yermak texted Ambassador Volker about the upcoming call with Mr. Giuliani, writing that it was "very good" that their discussion would take place before the call between President Trump and President Zelensky.[537] Later that day, the three men spoke by phone. Ambassador Volker described the July 22 discussion as merely an "introductory phone call,"[538] although phone records indicate that the call lasted for approximately 38 minutes.[539]

Ambassador Volker testified that during the call, Mr. Giuliani and Mr. Yermak discussed plans for an in-person meeting in Madrid in early August.[540] Afterward, Ambassador Volker texted Mr. Yermak that he thought the call had been "very useful" and recommended that Mr. Yermak send Mr. Giuliani a text message to schedule a date for the Madrid meeting.[541] Mr. Yermak texted Mr. Giuliani later that day about a plan to "take this relationship to a new level" and to meet in person as soon as possible.[542]

Later on July 22, Ambassador Volker updated Ambassador Sondland on the "great call" he "[o]rchestrated" between Mr. Giuliani and Mr. Yermak, noting that "Rudy is now advocating for phone call," an apparent reference to the call between President Trump and President Zelensky that would occur on July 25. Ambassador Volker also recommended that Ambassador Sondland inform Mr. Mulvaney that "Rudy agrees," and that he planned to convey the same information to Ambassador Bolton. Ambassador Sondland replied that Mr. Morrison of the White House NSC was also in support of the call.[543] Ambassador Volker also told Ambassador Sondland that Mr. Giuliani and Mr. Yermak would meet in person in Madrid within a couple of weeks.[544]

President Zelensky Feared Becoming "A Pawn" in U.S. Reelection Campaign

Around this time, senior Ukrainian officials informed U.S. officials that the new Ukrainian president did not want Ukraine to become enmeshed in U.S. domestic reelection politics.

On July 20, Ambassador Taylor spoke with Mr. Danyliuk, the Ukrainian national security advisor, who conveyed that President Zelensky "did not want to be used as a pawn in a U.S. reelection campaign."[545] Ambassador Taylor discussed President Zelensky's concern with Ambassador Volker and, the next day, texted Ambassador Sondland:

Taylor: Gordon, one thing Kurt and I talked about yesterday was Sasha Danyliuk's point that President Zelenskyy is sensitive about Ukraine being taken seriously, not merely as an instrument in Washington domestic, reelection politics.

Sondland: Absolutely, but we need to get the conversation started and the relationship built, irrespective of the pretext. I am worried about the alternative.[546]

Ambassador Taylor explained that his reference to "Washington domestic reelection politics" was "a reference to the investigations that Mr. Giuliani wanted to pursue."[547] According to Ambassador Taylor, President Zelensky understood what President Trump and Mr. Giuliani meant by "investigations," and "he did not want to get involved." Specifically, the Ukrainians understood that the "investigations were pursuant to Mr. Giuliani's request to develop information, to find information about Burisma and the Bidens. This was very well known in public. Mr. Giuliani had made this point clear in several instances in the beginning— in the springtime."[548] Ambassador Taylor also testified that the "whole thrust" of the activities undertaken by Mr. Giuliani and Ambassador Sondland "was to get these investigations, which Danyliuk and presumably Zelensky were resisting because they didn't want to be seen to be interfering but also to be a pawn."[549]

Despite the Ukrainian resistance, Ambassador Sondland said he believed that the public announcement of investigations would "fix" an impasse between the Ukrainian government and President Trump. When asked what he meant by "irrespective of the pretext" in his July 21 text message to Ambassador Taylor, Ambassador Sondland explained, "Well, the pretext being the agreed-upon interview or the agreed-upon press statement. We just need to get by it so that the two can meet, because, again, it was back to once they meet, all of this will be fixed."[550]

Witnesses Confirmed the President Conditioned an Oval Office Meeting on Investigations

Multiple witnesses testified that the conditioning of an Oval Office meeting on President Zelensky's announcement of investigations to benefit the President's reelection campaign came from the very top: President Trump.

Ambassador Sondland testified that he, Secretary Perry, and Ambassador Volker worked with Mr. Giuliani "at the express direction of the President of the United States."[551] Ambassador Sondland stated that "Mr. Giuliani was expressing the desires of the President of the United States, and we knew these investigations were important to the President."[552] Ambassador Sondland explained that he "followed the directions of the President" and that "we followed the President's orders."[553]

94

Ambassador Sondland further testified that President Trump expressed—both directly and through Mr. Giuliani—that he wanted "a public statement from President Zelensky committing to the investigations of Burisma and the 2016 election" as "prerequisites for the White House call and the White House meeting."[554] Ambassador Sondland explained:

> I know that members of this committee frequently frame these complicated issues in the form of a simple question: Was there a quid pro quo? As I testified previously with regard to the requested White House call and the White House meeting, the answer is yes.[555]

Ambassador Sondland also testified that knowledge of this quid pro quo was widespread among the President's advisers: "Everyone was in the loop" about the President's expectation that President Zelensky had to announce these specific investigations to secure an Oval Office meeting. As an example, Ambassador Sondland cited an email—copying Senior Advisor to the White House Chief of Staff Robert Blair, State Department Executive Secretary Lisa Kenna, Chief of Staff to the Secretary of Energy Brian McCormack, Mr. Mulvaney, Secretary Perry, and Secretary Pompeo—where "[e]veryone was informed."[556]

Other U.S. government officials also understood this scheme as a quid pro quo. Ambassador Taylor testified that as early as mid-July, it was "becoming clear" to him that "the meeting President Zelensky wanted was conditioned on investigations of Burisma and alleged Ukrainian influence in the 2016 elections" and that "this condition was driven by the irregular policy channel I had come to understand was guided by Mr. Giuliani."[557] Mr. Holmes similarly understood that by July, "it was made clear that some action on a Burisma/Biden investigation was a precondition for an Oval Office visit."[558] Dr. Hill testified that this quid pro quo was readily apparent after reading the July 25 call summary, explaining that it revealed that the White House meeting was used as "some kind of asset" that was "dangled out to the Ukrainian Government" to secure a political benefit.[559]

Final Preparation for Trump-Zelensky Call: Ambassador Volker Counseled Ukrainians and Ambassador Sondland Prepped President Trump

Ambassador Taylor testified that the call between President Trump and President Zelensky that ultimately occurred on July 25 was not confirmed until the last minute: "We were trying to schedule it for about a week in advance, that whole week. As I say, back and forth, yes, no, this time, that time. … it may have been about the day before that it was actually locked down, so about the 24th."[560] According to Ambassador Taylor, at least one person had prescient concerns about the call before it occurred: "Ambassador Bolton was not interested in having—did not want to have the call because he thought it was going to be a disaster. He thought that there could be some talk of investigations or worse on the call."[561]

Before the call took place on July 25, Ambassador Volker had lunch with Mr. Yermak in Kyiv. Ambassador Volker followed up with a text message to Mr. Yermak approximately 30 minutes before the call, noting that a White House visit was still on the table if, during the call, President Zelensky convinced President Trump that Ukraine would "investigate" and "get to the bottom of what happened" in 2016:

Volker: Good lunch – thanks. Heard from White House—assuming President Z
               convinces trump he will investigate / "get to the bottom of what
               happened" in 2016, we will nail down date for visit to Washington. Good
               luck! See you tomorrow - kurt

Ambassador Volker later informed Ambassador Sondland that he had relayed this
"message" to Mr. Yermak, which Ambassador Sondland had conveyed to Ambassador Volker
earlier that day:

Volker: Hi Gordon - got your message. Had a great lunch w Yermak and then
               passed your message to him. He will see you tomorrow. Think
               everything in place[562]

Ambassador Sondland testified that the "message" that Ambassador Volker conveyed to
Mr. Yermak in advance of the July 25 call likely originated from an earlier conversation that
Ambassador Sondland had with President Trump:

Q: So is it fair to say that this message is what you received from President Trump on
       that phone call that morning?
A: Again, if he testified to that, to refresh my own memory, then, yes, likely I would
       have received that from President Trump.
Q: But the sequence certainly makes sense, right?
A: Yeah, it does.
Q: You talked to President Trump.
A: Yeah.
Q: You told Kurt Volker to call you. You left a message for Kurt Volker. Kurt
       Volker sent this text message to Andriy Yermak to prepare President Zelensky
       and then President Trump had a phone call where President Zelensky spoke very
       similar to what was in this text message, right?
A: Right.
Q: And you would agree that the message in this–that is expressed here is that
       President Zelensky needs to convince Trump that he will do the investigations in
       order to nail down the date for a visit to Washington, D.C. Is that correct?
A: That's correct.[563]

Ambassador Sondland testified that he spoke with President Trump before the call with
President Zelensky.[564] Mr. Morrison also confirmed that President Trump and Ambassador
Sondland spoke before President Trump's call with President Zelensky.[565] Mr. Morrison stated
that Ambassador Sondland emailed him on the morning of the call and listed "three topics that he
was working on, the first of which was 'I spoke to the President this morning to brief him on the
call.'"[566] According to Mr. Morrison, Ambassador Sondland "believed" that he helped to
facilitate the July 25 call between President Trump and President Zelensky.[567]

On July 26, the day after the call between President Trump and President Zelensky,
Ambassador Volker acknowledged his role in prepping President Zelensky for the call with

President Trump in a text to Mr. Giuliani: "Hi Mr Mayor – you may have heard—the President has [sic] a great phone call with the Ukrainian President yesterday. Exactly the right messages as we discussed."[568]

5. The President Asked the Ukrainian President to Interfere in the 2020 U.S. Election by Investigating the Bidens and 2016 Election Interference

> *During a call on July 25, President Trump asked President Zelensky of Ukraine to "do us a favor though" and investigate his political opponent, former Vice President Joe Biden, and a debunked conspiracy theory that Ukraine interfered in the 2016 U.S. election. The next day, Ambassador Gordon Sondland informed President Trump that President Zelensky "was gonna do the investigation" and "anything" President Trump asked of him.*

Overview

During a telephone call on July 25, 2019, President Donald J. Trump asked Ukrainian President Volodymyr Zelensky to investigate his political rival, former Vice President Joseph Biden, and a debunked conspiracy theory that Ukraine interfered in the 2016 U.S. election. President Trump also discussed the removal of Ambassador Marie Yovanovitch, former U.S. Ambassador to Ukraine, said that she was "bad news," and warned that she would "go through some things." Two witnesses who listened to the call testified that they immediately reported the details of the call to senior White House lawyers.

When asked by a reporter on October 3, 2019, what he had hoped President Zelensky would do following the call, President Trump responded: "Well, I would think that, if they were honest about it, they'd start a major investigation into the Bidens. It's a very simple answer."

Witnesses unanimously testified that President Trump's claims about former Vice President Biden and alleged Ukrainian interference in the 2016 U.S. election have been discredited. The witnesses reaffirmed that in late 2015 and early 2016, when former Vice President Biden advocated for the removal of a corrupt Ukrainian prosecutor, he acted in accordance with a "broad-based consensus" and the official policy of the United States, the European Union, and major international financial institutions. Witnesses also unanimously testified that the removal of that prosecutor made it more likely that Ukraine would investigate corruption, not less likely.

Dr. Fiona Hill, former Deputy Assistant to the President and Senior Director for European and Russian Affairs at the National Security Council, testified that the conspiracy theories about Ukrainian interference in the 2016 U.S. election touted by President Trump are a "fictional narrative that is being perpetrated and propagated by the Russian security services." She noted that President Trump's former Homeland Security Advisor Tom Bossert and former National Security Advisor H.R. McMaster repeatedly advised the President that the so-called "CrowdStrike" conspiracy theory that President Trump raised in the July 25 call is completely "debunked," and that allegations Ukraine interfered in the 2016 U.S. election are false.

Nonetheless, on July 26, 2019, U.S. Ambassador to the European Union Gordon Sondland met with senior Ukrainian officials in Kyiv and then informed President Trump that President Zelensky "was gonna do the investigation" into former Vice President Biden and alleged Ukrainian interference in the 2016 U.S. election. Ambassador Sondland added that President Zelensky would "do anything" President Trump asked of him. After the call, Ambassador Sondland told David Holmes, Counselor for Political Affairs at the U.S. Embassy in Kyiv, that President Trump "did not give a shit about Ukraine" and that he only cared about the "big stuff" that benefits his personal interests, like the "Biden investigation."

President Trump's Call with President Zelensky on July 25, 2019

On July 25, 2019, President Zelensky finally had a long-awaited phone call with Ukraine's most important international partner: The President of the United States.

It had been over three months since the two leaders first spoke. Despite a warm but largely non-substantive call on April 21, President Trump had since declined President Zelensky's invitation to attend his inauguration and directed Vice President Mike Pence not to attend either.[569] Ukrainian efforts to set a date for a promised Oval Office meeting with President Trump were stalled. As Mr. Holmes explained, following the April 21 call:

> President Zelensky's team immediately began pressing to set a date for that visit. President Zelensky and senior members of his team made clear that they wanted President Zelensky's first overseas trip to be to Washington, to send a strong signal of American support, and requested a call with President Trump as soon as possible.[570]

Before scheduling the July 25 call or a White House visit, President Trump met on June 28 with Russian President Vladimir Putin—whose armed forces were engaged in a war of attrition against U.S.-backed Ukrainian forces—on the sidelines of the G20 summit in Osaka, Japan.[571] During their meeting, President Trump and President Putin shared a joke about Russia's meddling in the 2016 U.S. election.[572]

On July 25, President Trump joined the call with President Zelensky from the Executive Residence at the White House, away from a small group of senior national security aides who would normally join him in the Oval Office for a conversation with a foreign head of state. President Trump and President Zelensky began to speak at 9:03 a.m. Washington time—4:03 p.m. in Kyiv. According to Tim Morrison, the newly-installed Senior Director for Europe and Russia on the NSC, President Zelensky spoke in Ukrainian and occasionally in "chopped English."[573] Translators interpreted the call on both sides.[574] American aides listening to the call from the White House Situation Room hoped that what was said over the next 30 minutes would provide President Zelensky with the strong U.S. endorsement he needed in order to successfully negotiate an end to the five-year-old war with Russia that had killed over 13,000 Ukrainian soldiers and to advance President Zelensky's ambitious anti-corruption initiatives in Ukraine.[575]

The Trump Administration's subject-matter experts, NSC Director for Ukraine Lt. Col. Alexander Vindman and Mr. Morrison, were both on the call.[576] They had prepared talking points for President Trump and were taking detailed notes of what both leaders said, so that they could promptly implement any agreed-upon actions.[577] They were joined by Lt. Gen. Keith Kellogg, National Security Advisor to the Vice President, and Jennifer Williams, Special Advisor to the Vice President for Europe and Russia. Assistant to the President Robert Blair, a senior aide to Acting Chief of Staff Mick Mulvaney, was also present, along with an NSC press officer.[578] Secretary of State Mike Pompeo listened from a different location, as did Dr. Charles M. Kupperman, the Deputy National Security Advisor.[579]

Notably, Secretary Pompeo did not reveal that he listened to the July 25 call when asked directly about it on *This Week* on September 22.[580] Neither Secretary Pompeo nor the State Department corrected the record until September 30, when "a senior State Department official" disclosed the Secretary of State's participation in the July 25 call.[581]

The two presidents first exchanged pleasantries. President Trump congratulated the Ukrainian leader on his party's parliamentary victory. In a nod to their shared experience as political outsiders, President Zelensky called President Trump "a great teacher" who informed his own efforts to involve "many many new people" in Ukraine's politics and "drain the swamp here in our country."[582]

The discussion turned to U.S. support for Ukraine. President Trump contrasted U.S. assistance to that of America's closest European allies, stating: "We spend a lot of effort and a lot of time. Much more than the European countries are doing and they should be helping you more than they are." The call then took a more ominous turn. President Trump stated that with respect to U.S. support for Ukraine, "I wouldn't say that it's reciprocal necessarily because things are happening that are not good but the United States has been very very good to Ukraine."[583]

President Zelensky, whose government receives billions of dollars in financial support from the European Union and its member states, responded that European nations were "not working as much as they should work for Ukraine," including in the area of enforcing sanctions against Russia.[584] He noted that "the United States is a much bigger partner than the European Union" and stated that he was "very grateful" because "the United States is doing quite a lot for Ukraine."[585]

President Zelensky then raised the issue of U.S. military assistance for Ukraine with President Trump: "I also would like to thank you for your great support in the area of defense"—an area where U.S. support is vital.[586] President Zelensky continued: "We are ready to continue to cooperate for the next steps specifically we are almost ready to buy more Javelins from the United States for defense purposes."[587] The Javelin anti-tank missiles, first transferred to Ukraine by the United States in 2018, were widely viewed by U.S. officials as a deterrent against further Russian encroachment into Ukrainian territory.[588]

Immediately after the Ukrainian leader raised the issue of U.S. military assistance to Ukraine, President Trump replied: "I would like you to do us a favor though because our country has been through a lot and Ukraine knows a lot about it."[589]

President Trump then explained the "favor" he wanted President Zelensky to do. He first requested that Ukraine investigate a discredited conspiracy theory aimed at undercutting the U.S. Intelligence Community's unanimous conclusion that the Russian government interfered in the 2016 U.S. election.[590] Specifically, President Trump stated:

> I would like you to find out what happened with this whole situation with Ukraine, they say Crowdstrike... I guess you have one of your wealthy people... The server, they say Ukraine has it. There are a lot of things that went on, the whole situation. I think you're surrounding yourself with some of the same people. I would like to have the Attorney General call you or your people and I would like you to get to the bottom of it. As you saw yesterday, that whole nonsense ended with a very poor performance by a man named Robert Mueller, an incompetent performance, but they say a lot of it started with Ukraine. Whatever you can do, it's very important that you do it if that's possible.[591]

President Trump was referencing the widely debunked conspiracy theory that the Ukrainian government—and not Russia—was behind the hack of Democratic National Committee (DNC) servers in 2016, and that the American cybersecurity firm CrowdStrike moved the DNC's servers to Ukraine to prevent U.S. law enforcement from examining them. This theory is often referred to in shorthand as "CrowdStrike" and has been promoted by the Russian government.[592]

For example, during a press conference in February 2017, just weeks after the U.S. Intelligence Community unanimously assessed in a public report that Russia interfered in the 2016 U.S. election to benefit the candidacy of Donald J. Trump, President Putin falsely asserted that "the Ukrainian government adopted a unilateral position in favour of one candidate. More than that, certain oligarchs, certainly with the approval of the political leadership, funded this candidate, or female candidate, to be more precise."[593] President Trump's reference in his July 25 telephone call to "one of your wealthy people" tracked closely with President Putin's accusations that "certain oligarchs" in Ukraine meddled in the 2016 U.S. election to support Democratic candidate Hillary Clinton.

Dr. Hill, an expert on Russia and President Putin, testified that the claim that "Russia and its security services did not conduct a campaign against our country and that perhaps, somehow for some reason, Ukraine did" is "a fictional narrative that is being perpetrated and propagated by the Russian security services themselves." Dr. Hill reaffirmed that the U.S. Intelligence Community's January 2017 conclusion that Russia interfered in the 2016 U.S. election is "beyond dispute, even if some of the underlying details must remain classified."[594]

Tom Bossert, President Trump's former Homeland Security Advisor, stated publicly that the CrowdStrike theory is "not only a conspiracy theory, it is completely debunked."[595] Dr. Hill testified that White House officials—including Mr. Bossert and former National Security Advisor H.R. McMaster—"spent a lot of time" refuting the CrowdStrike conspiracy theory to President Trump. Dr. Hill explained that Mr. Bossert and others "who were working on cybersecurity laid out to the President the facts about the interference." She affirmed that

President Trump was advised that "the alternative theory that Ukraine had interfered in the election was false."[596]

President Zelensky did not directly address President Trump's reference to CrowdStrike during the July 25 call, but he tried to assure President Trump that "it is very important for me and everything that you just mentioned earlier."[597] President Zelensky committed to proceed with an investigation, telling President Trump that he had "nobody but friends" in the new Ukrainian presidential administration, possibly attempting to rebut Rudy Giuliani's earlier claims that President Zelensky was surrounded by "enemies" of President Trump. President Zelensky then specifically noted that one of his assistants "spoke with Mr. Giuliani just recently and we are hoping very much that Mr. Giuliani will be able to travel to Ukraine and we will meet once he comes to Ukraine."[598]

Significantly, President Zelensky referenced Mr. Giuliani even before President Trump had mentioned him, demonstrating the Ukrainian leader's understanding that Mr. Giuliani represented President Trump's interests in Ukraine. The Ukrainian leader then reassured President Trump, "I also plan to surround myself with great people and in addition to that investigation" into the CrowdStrike conspiracy theory. He said, "I guarantee as the President of Ukraine that all the investigations will be done openly and candidly. That I can assure you."[599] President Trump replied, "Rudy very much knows what's happening and he is a very capable guy. If you could speak to him that would be great."[600]

Request to Investigate Bidens

President Trump then returned to his requested "favor," asking President Zelensky about the "[t]he other thing": that Ukraine investigate President Trump's U.S. political rival, former Vice President Biden, for allegedly ending an investigation into the Ukrainian energy company Burisma Holdings. Vice President Biden's son, Hunter Biden, served as a member of Burisma's board of directors. President Trump told President Zelensky:

> The other thing, There's a lot of talk about Biden's son, that Biden stopped the prosecution and a lot of people want to find out about that so whatever you can do with the Attorney General would be great. Biden went around bragging that he stopped the prosecution so if you can look into it... It sounds horrible to me.[601]

President Trump later continued, "I will have Mr. Giuliani give you a call and I am also going to have Attorney General Barr call and we will get to the bottom of it. I'm sure you will figure it out."[602]

In public remarks on October 3, 2019, a reporter asked President Trump, "what exactly did you hope Zelensky would do about the Bidens after your phone call? Exactly." President Trump responded: "Well, I would think that, if they were honest about it, they'd start a major investigation into the Bidens. It's a very simple answer."[603]

When President Trump asserted to President Zelensky during the July 25 call that former Vice President "Biden went around bragging that he stopped the prosecution," President Trump was apparently referring to Vice President Biden's involvement in the removal of the corrupt former Ukrainian prosecutor general, Viktor Shokin.

Multiple witnesses—including Dr. Hill, former U.S. Ambassador to Ukraine Marie Yovanovitch, Mr. Holmes, and Deputy Assistant Secretary of State George Kent—testified that they were not aware of any credible evidence to support the claim that former Vice President Biden acted inappropriately when he advocated for the removal of Mr. Shokin.[604] To the contrary, those witnesses confirmed that it was the official policy of the United States, the European Union, and major international financial institutions, to demand Mr. Shokin's dismissal. As Mr. Kent testified, there was "a broad-based consensus" that Mr. Shokin was "a typical Ukraine prosecutor who lived a lifestyle far in excess of his government salary, who never prosecuted anybody known for having committed a crime" and who "covered up crimes that were known to have been committed."[605] Mr. Kent further explained:

> What former Vice President Biden requested of former President of Ukraine Poroshenko was the removal of a corrupt prosecutor general, Viktor Shokin, who had undermined a program of assistance that we had spent, again, U.S. taxpayer money to try to build an independent investigator unit to go after corrupt prosecutors.[606]

As Ambassador Yovanovitch testified, the removal of a corrupt Ukrainian prosecutor general, who was not prosecuting enough corruption, increased the chance that alleged corruption in companies in Ukraine could be investigated.[607]

Mr. Shokin was a known associate of Mr. Giuliani. As described in Chapter 1, Mr. Giuliani had been communicating with Mr. Shokin since at least 2018.[608] Mr. Giuliani also lobbied the White House on behalf of Mr. Shokin to intervene earlier in 2019 when the State Department rejected a visa application for Mr. Shokin to visit the United States based upon Mr. Shokin's notorious corrupt conduct.[609] Ambassador Kurt Volker, U.S. Special Representative for Ukraine Negotiations, testified that he explicitly warned Mr. Giuliani—to no avail—against pursuing "the conspiracy theory that Vice President Biden would have been influenced in his duties as Vice President by money paid to his son."[610] Ambassador Volker affirmed that former Vice President Biden is "an honorable man, and I hold him in the highest regard."[611]

Attacks Against Ambassador Yovanovitch

During the July 25 call, President Trump also attacked Ambassador Yovanovitch, whom he had ousted as the U.S. Ambassador to Ukraine three months earlier after a concerted smear campaign perpetuated by Mr. Giuliani. As described in Chapter 1, Mr. Giuliani viewed Ambassador Yovanovitch—a decorated diplomat who had championed Ukrainian anti-corruption officials and activists—as an impediment to his activities in Ukraine.[612] President Trump told President Zelensky: "The former ambassador from the United States, the woman, was bad news and the people she was dealing with in the Ukraine were bad news so I just want to let you know that." He later added: "Well, she's going to go through some things."[613]

Ambassador Yovanovitch described her visceral reaction when she first read the call record, after the White House released it publicly on September 25, 2019. She testified, "I was shocked. I mean, I was very surprised that President Trump would—first of all, that I would feature repeatedly in a Presidential phone call, but secondly, that the President would speak about me or any ambassador in that way to a foreign counterpart."[614] When asked whether she felt "threatened" by President Trump's statement that "she's going to go through some things," Ambassador Yovanovitch answered that she did.[615]

Praise of Corrupt Former Ukrainian Prosecutor

After disparaging Ambassador Yovanovitch, who had an extensive record of combatting corruption, President Trump praised an unnamed former Ukrainian prosecutor general—referring to Yuriy Lutsenko—who was widely considered to be corrupt and had promoted false allegations against Ambassador Yovanovitch.[616] President Trump told President Zelensky: "Good because I heard you had a prosecutor who was very good and he was shut down and that's really unfair. A lot of people are talking about that, the way they shut your very good prosecutor down and you had some very bad people involved."[617] He later added, "I heard the prosecutor was treated very badly and he was a very fair prosecutor so good luck with everything."[618]

At the time of the July 25 call, Mr. Lutsenko—who was collaborating with Mr. Giuliani to smear Ambassador Yovanovitch and the Bidens—was still the Ukrainian prosecutor general. Mr. Holmes testified that Mr. Lutsenko "was not a good partner. He had failed to deliver on the promised reforms that he had committed to when he took office, and he was using his office to insulate and protect political allies while presumably enriching himself."[619] By July 2019, Mr. Holmes assessed that Mr. Lutsenko was "trying to angle to keep his job" under the new Zelensky Administration and that part of his strategy was "appealing to Rudy Giuliani and Donald Trump by pushing out these false theories about the Bidens and the 2016 election."[620]

Multiple witnesses testified that another former Ukrainian prosecutor, Mr. Shokin, was also considered to be corrupt. For example, Mr. Kent testified during his deposition that Mr. Lutsenko and Mr. Shokin were "corrupt former prosecutors" who were "peddling false information in order to extract revenge against those who had exposed their misconduct, including U.S. diplomats, Ukrainian anticorruption officials, and reform-minded civil society groups in Ukraine."[621] Ambassador Volker testified at his public hearing that Mr. Lutsenko was "not credible, and was acting in a self-serving capacity."[622] Mr. Holmes further noted that Mr. Lutsenko "resisted fully empowering truly independent anticorruption institutions that would help ensure that no Ukrainians, however powerful, were above the law."[623]

After the call, the White House press office issued a short and incomplete summary of the call, omitting major elements of the conversation. The press statement read:

> Today, President Donald J. Trump spoke by telephone with President Volodymyr Zelenskyy of Ukraine to congratulate him on his recent election. President Trump and President Zelenskyy discussed ways to strengthen the relationship between the United States and Ukraine, including energy and economic cooperation. Both leaders also expressed that they look forward to the opportunity to meet.[624]

Concerns Raised by Lieutenant Colonel Alexander Vindman

Prior to President Trump's July 25 call with President Zelensky, Lt. Col. Vindman had prepared—with Mr. Morrison's review and approval—a call briefing package, including talking points for President Trump's use. This was consistent with the NSC's regular process of preparing for the President's phone calls with foreign leaders.[625] The NSC-drafted talking points did not include any reference to Biden, Burisma, CrowdStrike, or alleged Ukrainian interference in the 2016 U.S. election.[626]

Lt. Col. Vindman testified during his deposition that, prior to the July 25 call, he was aware of concerns from former National Security Advisor John Bolton and other U.S. officials that President Trump might raise these discredited issues with President Zelensky.[627] Indeed, Ambassador Bolton had resisted scheduling the call because he believed it might be a "disaster."[628]

As he sat in the White House Situation Room listening to the leaders, Lt. Col. Vindman quickly recognized that the President's conversation was diverging from the talking points he helped prepare based on the interagency policy process, and "straying" into an "unproductive narrative" promoted by Mr. Giuliani and other "external and nongovernmental influencers"[629]— topics that Lt. Col. Vindman dubbed "stray voltage."[630]

Lt. Col. Vindman knew immediately that he had a duty to report the contents of the call to the White House lawyers. He explained, "I had concerns, and it was my duty to report my concerns to the proper—proper people in the chain of command."[631] Lt. Col. Vindman testified that President Trump's request that a foreign leader dependent on the United States open an investigation into his U.S. political opponent constituted a "demand" that President Zelensky had to meet in order to secure a White House meeting:

> So, Congressman, the power disparity between the President of the United States and the President of Ukraine is vast, and, you know, in the President asking for something, it became—there was—in return for a White House meeting, because that's what this was about. This was about getting a White House meeting. It was a demand for him to fulfill his—fulfill this particular prerequisite in order to get the meeting.[632]

Lt. Col. Vindman further testified that President Trump's demand of the Ukrainian leader was "inappropriate" and "improper," and that it would undermine U.S. national security:

> Chairman, as I said in my statement, it was inappropriate. It was improper for the President to request—to demand an investigation into a political opponent, especially a foreign power where there's, at best, dubious belief that this would be a completely impartial investigation, and that this would have significant implications if it became public knowledge, and it would be perceived as a partisan play. It would undermine our Ukraine policy, and it would undermine our national security.[633]

Within an hour of the call ending, Lt. Col. Vindman reported his concerns to John A. Eisenberg, the Deputy Counsel to the President for National Security Affairs and the Legal

Advisor to the NSC , and Michael Ellis, a Senior Associate Counsel to the President and the Deputy Legal Advisor to the NSC.[634] Lt. Col. Vindman recounted the content of the call based on his handwritten notes and told the lawyers that he believed it was "wrong" for President Trump to ask President Zelensky to investigate Vice President Biden.[635]

Concerns Raised by Timothy Morrison

After 17 years as a Republican Congressional staffer and approximately a year serving elsewhere on the NSC staff, Mr. Morrison assumed his position as the NSC's Senior Director for Europe and Russia on July 15, 2019, only 10 days before President Trump's call with President Zelensky.[636]

Before he transitioned into his new role, Mr. Morrison met with his predecessor, Dr. Hill. She advised him to stay away from efforts orchestrated by Mr. Giuliani and Ambassador Sondland to pressure Ukraine into investigating a "bucket of issues" that included "Burisma the company," and "Hunter Biden on the board."[637] Dr. Hill also warned Mr. Morrison before the July 25 call about the President's interest in alleged Ukrainian interference in the 2016 U.S. election related to the DNC server.[638]

Mr. Morrison testified that he had no knowledge of any investigations at the time, but after performing a Google search of "what is Burisma?" and seeing the name Hunter Biden, Mr. Morrison decided to "stay away."[639] Even though he was new to the portfolio, Mr. Morrison promptly concluded that because "Burisma" involved Hunter Biden, and because former Vice President Biden was running for President, such investigations could be a "problematic" area.[640] Mr. Morrison further explained that he tried to stay away from requests related to Burisma and the 2016 U.S. election because these investigations were not related to "the proper policy process that I was involved in on Ukraine," and "had nothing to do with the issues that the interagency was working on."[641]

With that background in mind, Mr. Morrison admitted he was "concerned" when, while listening to the call on July 25, he heard President Trump raise "issues related to the [DNC] server." Ultimately, Mr. Morrison said, "the call was not the full-throated endorsement of the Ukraine reform agenda that I was hoping to hear."[642]

In "fairly short order," Mr. Morrison reported the contents of the call to Mr. Eisenberg and Mr. Ellis, the NSC lawyers. He asked them to review the call, which he feared would be "damaging" if leaked.[643] Mr. Morrison stated that at the time of the call, he "did not have a view" on whether the call was "appropriate and proper."[644] He also stated that he "was not concerned that anything illegal was discussed." [645] During his deposition, however, Mr. Morrison clarified, "I did not then and I do not now opine ... as to the legality" of what happened on the call.[646]

In a second meeting with Mr. Eisenberg, Mr. Morrison requested that access to the electronic files of the call record be restricted. This was an unusual request. Mr. Morrison confirmed to the Committee that he had never before asked the NSC Legal Advisor to restrict access to a presidential call record.[647] It was also unusual because Mr. Morrison raised restricting access with Mr. Eisenberg despite the fact that Mr. Morrison himself had the authority, as an NSC senior director, to recommend restrictions on the relevant files to the NSC's Executive Secretariat.

Lt. Col. Vindman also discussed restricting access to the July 25 call summary with Mr. Eisenberg and Mr. Ellis. At some point after the call, Lt. Col. Vindman discussed with the NSC lawyers the "sensitivity" of the matters raised on the call and "the fact that … there are constant leaks."[648] Lt. Col. Vindman explained that "[f]rom a foreign policy professional perspective, all of these types of calls would inherently be sensitive."[649] But the July 25 call was particularly sensitive because it could "undermine our relationship with the Ukrainians" given that it "would implicate a partisan play."[650] The NSC lawyers, therefore, believed that it was "appropriate to restrict access for the purpose of the leaks" and "to preserv[e] the integrity" of the transcript.[651] Lt. Col. Vindman recalled that Mr. Ellis raised the idea of placing the call summary on the NSC's server for highly classified information and Mr. Eisenberg "gave the go-ahead."[652]

Some weeks after his discussions with the NSC attorneys, Mr. Morrison could not locate the call record. He contacted the staff of the NSC's Executive Secretariat in search of an explanation and was informed that "John Eisenberg had directed it to be moved to a different server" utilized by the NSC staff for highly classified information.[653] This transfer occurred despite Mr. Morrison's view that the call record did not meet the requirements to be placed on the highly classified system.[654]

Mr. Eisenberg later told Mr. Morrison that the call record had been placed on the highly classified system by "mistake."[655] Even after Mr. Eisenberg stated that the call record was moved to the highly classified system by "mistake," it nevertheless remained on that system until at least the third week of September 2019, shortly before its declassification and public release by the White House.[656]

Concerns Raised by Jennifer Williams

Vice President Pence's advisor, Ms. Williams, had listened to nearly a dozen phone calls between President Trump and other heads of state prior to July 25, 2019, as well as Vice President Pence's April 23 call with President Zelensky.[657] As she sat listening to President Trump's July 25 call, she was struck by his requests relating to Vice President Biden. She stated that she believed that President Trump's comments were "unusual and inappropriate."[658]

Ms. Williams testified that she thought that "references to specific individuals and investigations, such as former Vice President Biden and his son" were "political in nature, given that the former Vice President is a political opponent of the President."[659] The comments struck her as "more specific to the President in nature, to his personal political agenda," as opposed to "a broader foreign policy objective of the United States."[660] She added, "it was the first time I had heard internally the President reference particular investigations that previously I had only heard about through Mr. Giuliani's press interviews and press reporting."[661]

Significantly, Ms. Williams, who had learned about the hold on security assistance for Ukraine on July 3, also said that the Trump-Zelensky call "shed some light on possible other motivations behind a security assistance hold."[662]

"Burisma" Omitted from Call Record

Mr. Morrison, Lt. Col. Vindman, and Ms. Williams all agreed that the publicly released record of the call was substantially accurate, but Lt. Col. Vindman and Ms. Williams both testified that President Zelensky made an explicit reference to "Burisma" that was not included in the call record. Specifically, Lt. Col. Vindman testified that his notes indicated President Zelensky used the word "Burisma"—instead of generically referring to "the company"—when discussing President Trump's request to investigate the Bidens.[663] Ms. Williams' notes also reflected that President Zelensky had said "Burisma" later in the call when referring to a "case."[664]

Lt. Col. Vindman indicated that President Zelensky's mention of "Burisma" was notable because it suggested that the Ukrainian leader was "prepped for this call." He explained that "frankly, the President of Ukraine would not necessarily know anything about this company Burisma." Lt. Col. Vindman continued, "he would certainly understand some of this—some of these elements because the story had been developing for some time, but the fact that he mentioned specifically Burisma seemed to suggest to me that he was prepped for this call."[665]

The Substance of the Call Remained Tightly Controlled

Ms. Williams testified that staff in the Office of the Vice President placed the draft call record in the Vice President's nightly briefing book on July 25.[666]

Separately, and following established protocols for coordinating U.S. government activities toward Ukraine, Lt. Col. Vindman provided Mr. Kent at the State Department with a readout. Because Mr. Kent had worked on Ukraine policy for many years, Lt. Col. Vindman sought Mr. Kent's "expert view" on the investigations requested by the President. Mr. Kent informed him that "there was no substance" behind the CrowdStrike conspiracy theory and "took note of the fact that there was a call to investigate the Bidens."[667] Recalling this conversation, Mr. Kent testified that Lt. Col. Vindman said "he could not share the majority of what was discussed [on the July 25 call] because of the very sensitive nature of what was discussed," but that Lt. Col. Vindman noted that the call "went into the direction of some of the most extreme narratives that have been discussed publicly."[668]

Ambassador Sondland Followed Up on President Trump's Request for Investigations

Soon after arriving in Kyiv from Brussels on July 25, Ambassador Sondland asked the U.S. Embassy to arrange a meeting the next day with Ukrainian presidential aide Andriy Yermak.[669]

On the morning of July 26, Ambassadors Sondland, Volker and Taylor—accompanied by Mr. Holmes, who acted as their official notetaker—went to the Presidential Administration

Building in central Kyiv for meetings with Ukrainian officials.[670] Contrary to standard procedure, Mr. Holmes and Ambassador Taylor did not receive readouts of the July 25 call, so they were unaware of what President Trump and President Zelensky had discussed.[671] Ambassador Volker also did not receive an official readout of the July 25 call from the NSC staff. He testified that Andriy Yermak, a senior aide to President Zelensky, simply characterized it as a "good call" in which "President Zelensky did reiterate his commitment to reform and fighting corruption in Ukraine."[672]

The first meeting on July 26 was with Chief of Staff to President Zelensky Andriy Bohdan.[673] Regarding the July 25 call, Mr. Holmes recalled Mr. Bohdan sharing that "President Trump had expressed interest … in President Zelensky's personnel decisions related to the Prosecutor General's office [PGO]."[674] Mr. Holmes further testified that Mr. Bohdan then "started asking … about individuals I've since come to understand they were considering appointing to different roles in the PGO."[675] Mr. Holmes explained that he "didn't understand it," and that "[i]t wasn't until I read the July 25th phone call transcript that I realized that the President [Trump] had mentioned Mr. Lutsenko in the call."[676]

Subsequently, Ambassadors Sondland, Taylor, and Volker met with President Zelensky and other senior officials. Mr. Holmes once again took notes.[677] He testified "During the meeting, President Zelensky stated that, during the July 25th call, President Trump had, quote, 'three times raised some very sensitive issues' and that he would have to follow up—he, Zelensky—would have to follow up on those issues when he and President Trump met in person."[678] After he read the transcript of the July 25 call, Mr. Holmes determined that President Zelensky's mention of "sensitive issues" was a reference to President Trump's demands for a "Burisma Biden investigation."[679]

Catherine Croft, Special Advisor to Ambassador Kurt Volker, was also in Kyiv on July 26. Although she did not attend the meeting with President Zelensky, she received a readout from Ambassadors Volker and Taylor later that day, as they were traveling in an embassy vehicle. Ms. Croft testified that her handwritten notes from that readout indicate "the President [Trump] had raised investigations multiple times" in his July 25 call with President Zelensky.[680] Ambassadors Sondland and Taylor told the Committee that they did not recall President Zelensky's comments about investigations.[681] Ambassador Volker similarly did not recall that the issue of investigations was discussed, but testified that he did not dispute the validity of "notes taken contemporaneously at the meeting."[682]

Ambassador Sondland Met One-on-One with Ukrainian Presidential Aide

The meeting with President Zelensky ended around noon.[683] After the meeting, Ambassadors Taylor and Volker departed the Presidential Administration building for a visit to the front lines of the war with Russia in eastern Ukraine.[684] Ambassador Sondland separately headed for Mr. Yermak's office. Mr. Holmes testified that, at the last minute, he received instruction from his leadership at the U.S. Embassy to join Ambassador Sondland.[685] By that point, Mr. Holmes recalled, he "was a flight of stairs behind Ambassador Sondland as he headed to meet with Mr. Yermak."[686] Mr. Holmes continued, "When I reached Mr. Yermak's office, Ambassador Sondland had already gone in to the meeting."[687] Mr. Holmes then "explained to

Mr. Yermak's assistant that I was supposed to join the meeting as the Embassy's representative and strongly urged her to let me in, but she told me that Ambassador Sondland and Mr. Yermak had insisted that the meeting be one on one with no note taker."[688] Mr. Holmes "then waited in the anteroom until the meeting ended, along with a member of Ambassador Sondland's staff and a member of the U.S. Embassy Kyiv staff."[689]

Ambassador Sondland's meeting with Mr. Yermak lasted approximately 30 minutes.[690] When it ended, Ambassador Sondland did not provide Mr. Holmes an explanation of what they discussed.[691] Ambassador Sondland later testified that he did not "recall the specifics" of his conversation with Mr. Yermak, but he believed "the issue of investigations was probably a part of that agenda or meeting."[692]

Call Between President Trump and Ambassador Sondland on July 26, 2019

After a busy morning of meetings with Ukrainian officials on July 26, Ambassador Sondland indicated that he wanted to get lunch. Mr. Holmes interjected that he would "be happy to join" Ambassador Sondland and two other State Department colleagues accompanying him "if he wanted to brief me out on his meeting with Mr. Yermak or discuss other issues."[693] Ambassador Sondland accepted the offer. The diplomats proceeded "to a nearby restaurant and sat on an outdoor terrace."[694] Mr. Holmes "sat directly across from Ambassador Sondland," close enough that they could "share an appetizer."[695]

Mr. Holmes recounted that "at first, the lunch was largely social. Ambassador Sondland selected a bottle of wine that he shared among the four of us, and we discussed topics such as marketing strategies for his hotel business."[696] Later during the meal, Ambassador Sondland "said that he was going to call President Trump to give him an update."[697] Ambassador Sondland then placed a call on his unsecure mobile phone. Mr. Holmes was taken aback. He told the Committee, "it was, like, a really extraordinary thing, it doesn't happen very often"—a U.S. Ambassador picking up his mobile phone at an outdoor cafe and dialing the President of the United States.[698]

Mr. Holmes, who was sitting directly opposite from Ambassador Sondland, said he "heard him announce himself several times, along the lines of, 'Gordon Sondland, holding for the President.' It appeared that he was being transferred through several layers of switchboards and assistants, and I then noticed Ambassador Sondland's demeanor changed and understood that he had been connected to President Trump."[699]

Mr. Holmes stated he was able to hear the first part of Ambassador Sondland's conversation with President Trump because it was "quite loud" and "quite distinctive" when the President began speaking. When President Trump started speaking, Ambassador Sondland "sort of winced and held the phone away from his ear," and "did that for the first couple exchanges."[700]

Recounting the conversation that followed, Mr. Holmes testified:

I heard Ambassador Sondland greet the President and explain he was calling from Kyiv. I heard President Trump then clarify that Ambassador Sondland was in Ukraine. Ambassador Sondland replied, yes, he was in Ukraine, and went on to state that President Zelensky, quote, "loves your ass." I then heard President Trump ask, "So he's going to do the investigation?" Ambassador Sondland replied that he is going to do it, adding that President Zelensky will do "anything you ask him to do."[701]

President Trump has denied that he spoke to Ambassador Sondland on July 26 and told reporters, "I know nothing about that."[702] But in his public testimony before the Committee, Ambassador Sondland noted that White House call records made available to his legal counsel confirmed that the July 26 call in fact occurred.[703] Ambassador Sondland further explained that Mr. Holmes's testimony—specifically, a "reference to A$AP Rocky"—refreshed his recollection about the July 26 call, which Ambassador Sondland had not originally disclosed to the Committee.[704]

Although Ambassador Sondland did not believe he mentioned the Bidens by name, he testified that with regard to the substance of his July 26 conversation with President Trump: "I have no reason to doubt that this conversation included the subject of investigations."[705] He added that he had "no reason" to doubt Mr. Holmes' testimony about the contents of the call, and that he would "have been more surprised if President Trump had not mentioned investigations, particularly given what we were hearing from Mr. Giuliani about the President's concerns."[706] Asked about his statement to President Trump that President Zelensky "loves your ass," Ambassador Sondland replied: "That sounds like something I would say. That's how President Trump and I communicate, a lot of four-letter words, in this case three letter."[707]

After the call between Ambassador Sondland and President Trump ended, Ambassador Sondland remarked to Mr. Holmes that "the President was in a bad mood," as "was often the case early in the morning."[708] Mr. Holmes, who had learned about the freeze on U.S. security assistance days earlier, was attempting to clarify the President's thinking, and said he "took the opportunity to ask Ambassador Sondland for his candid impression of the President's views on Ukraine":

> In particular, I asked Ambassador Sondland if it was true that the President did not give a shit about Ukraine. Ambassador Sondland agreed that the President did not give a shit about Ukraine. I asked, why not, and Ambassador Sondland stated, the President only cares about, quote, unquote, "big stuff." I noted there was, quote, unquote, big stuff going on in Ukraine, like a war with Russia. And Ambassador Sondland replied that he meant, quote, unquote, "big stuff" that benefits the President, like the, quote, unquote, "Biden investigation" that Mr. Giuliani was pushing. The conversation then moved on to other topics.[709]

Ambassador Sondland did not dispute the substance of Mr. Holmes' recollection of this discussion. He stated, "I don't recall my exact words, but clearly the President, beginning on May 23, when we met with him in the Oval Office, was not a big fan" of Ukraine. Asked whether President Trump "was a big fan of the investigations," Ambassador Sondland replied: "Apparently so."[710] Asked to clarify if, during his July 26 conversation with Mr. Holmes, he recalled "at least referring to an investigation that Rudy Giuliani was pushing," Ambassador Sondland replied, "I would have, yes."[711]

Mr. Holmes Informed U.S. Embassy Leadership about President Trump's Call with Ambassador Sondland

After the lunch, Mr. Holmes dropped off Ambassador Sondland at his hotel, the Hyatt Regency Kyiv. Mr. Holmes then returned to the U.S. Embassy.[712] Ambassador Taylor, the acting Ambassador in Kyiv, was still visiting the front line. So when he arrived at the Embassy, Mr. Holmes briefed his immediate supervisor, Kristina Kvien, Deputy Chief of Mission at U.S. Embassy Kyiv, about the President's call with Ambassador Sondland and Ambassador Sondland's subsequent description of President Trump's priorities for Ukraine.[713]

After taking a long-planned vacation from July 27 to August 5, Mr. Holmes told Ambassador Taylor about his lunch with Ambassador Sondland on the first day he returned to work, August 6.[714] Mr. Holmes told the Committee that he did not brief the call in detail to Ambassador Taylor because "it was obvious what the President was pressing for":

> Of course that's what's going on. Of course the President is pressing for a Biden investigation before he'll do these things the Ukrainians want. There was nodding agreement. So did I go through every single word in the call? No, because everyone by that point agreed, it was obvious what the President was pressing for.[715]

In October 2019, following the public release of testimony by several witnesses pursuant to the Committee's impeachment inquiry, Mr. Holmes reminded Ambassador Taylor about Ambassador Sondland's July 26 conversation with President Trump. Ambassador Taylor was preparing to return to Washington and testify publicly before the Committee. Mr. Holmes had been following news coverage of the inquiry and realized he had unique, firsthand evidence that "potentially bore on the question of whether the President did, in fact, have knowledge" of efforts to press the Ukrainian President to publicly announce investigations:

> I came to realize that I had firsthand knowledge regarding certain events on July 26 that had not otherwise been reported and that those events potentially bore on the question of whether the President did, in fact, have knowledge that those senior officials were using the levers of diplomatic power to influence the new Ukrainian President to announce the opening of a criminal investigation against President Trump's political opponent. It is at that point that I made the observation to Ambassador Taylor that the incident I had witnessed on July 26th had acquired greater significance, which is what he reported in his testimony last week and is what led to the subpoena for me to appear here today.[716]

Mr. Holmes testified that the July 26 call became "sort of a touchstone piece of information" for diplomats at the U.S. Embassy in Kyiv who "were trying to understand why we weren't able to get the meeting" between President Trump and President Zelensky and "what was going on with the security hold."[717] He elaborated:

I would refer back to it repeatedly in our, you know, morning staff meetings. We'd talk about what we're trying to do. We're trying to achieve this, that. Maybe it will convince the President to have the meeting. And I would say, 'Well, as we know, he doesn't really care about Ukraine. He cares about some other things. And we're trying to keep Ukraine out of our politics and so, you know, that's what we're up against.' And I would refer— use that repeatedly as a refrain.[718]

6. The President Wanted Ukraine to Announce the Investigations Publicly

> *In the weeks following the July 25 call, President Trump's hand-picked representatives carried out his wishes to condition a coveted White House meeting for the Ukrainian President on the public announcement of investigations beneficial to President Trump. Top U.S. officials, including the Secretary of State and Secretary of Energy, were "in the loop."*

Overview

In the weeks following the July 25 call, during which President Trump had pressed Ukrainian President Volodymyr Zelensky to "do us a favor though," the President's representatives worked to secure from the Ukrainian President a public announcement about the requested investigations as a condition for the White House meeting.

That meeting would have conferred vital support on a new president who relied on the United States to help defend his nation militarily, diplomatically, and politically against Russian aggression. U.S. Ambassador to the European Union Gordon Sondland provided testimony and quoted from documents demonstrating that he kept everyone "in the loop" about the plan, including the Secretaries of State and Energy.

Ambassadors Sondland and Volker worked closely with Mr. Giuliani, the President's personal lawyer, to help draft Ukraine's public statement. They sought to ensure that President Zelensky explicitly used the words "Burisma"—a reference to allegations about former Vice President Biden and his son—and "2016 elections."

Ukrainian officials were "very uncomfortable" with the provision of this statement, which they understood to be a requirement and a "deliverable" demanded by President Trump. The Ukrainian President was elected on a platform of rooting out public corruption, and so he resisted issuing the statement. Instead, President Zelensky's aides asked whether an official request for legal assistance with investigations had been made through appropriate channels at the U.S. Department of Justice. No such formal request was ever made. Consequently, Ukrainian officials made clear to Ambassador Volker that they did not support issuing a public statement because it could "play into" U.S. domestic politics. Nevertheless, U.S. efforts to secure a public statement continued.

Giuliani Met with Ukrainian Presidential Aide Andriy Yermak in Madrid and Discussed a White House Meeting

On July 26, the day after the call between President Trump and President Zelensky, Ambassador Volker wrote to Mr. Giuliani to confirm that he would soon be meeting with Andriy Yermak, a Ukrainian presidential aide, to "help" efforts.[719]

Ambassador Volker texted: "Please send dates when you will be in Madrid. I am seeing Yermak tomorrow morning. He will come to you in Madrid. Thanks for your help! Kurt."[720]

Mr. Giuliani replied that he would travel to Spain from August 1 to 5, and Ambassador Volker affirmed that he would tell the Ukrainian presidential aide to "visit with you there."[721] Ambassador Volker kept himself apprised of plans, texting Mr. Yermak on August 1 to ensure that everything was "on track" for the meeting in Spain's capital. He also asked whether Mr. Yermak planned to visit Washington.[722]

On August 2, Mr. Yermak and Mr. Giuliani met in Madrid.[723] Ambassador Volker received a meeting summary from Mr. Yermak the same day: "My meeting with Mr. Mayor was very good." Mr. Yermak added: "We asked for White House meeting during week start [sic] 16 Sept. Waiting for confirmation. Maybe you know the date?"[724]

The Madrid meeting set off a "series of discussions" among Mr. Giuliani, Ambassador Volker, and Ambassador Sondland about the need for President Zelensky to issue a public statement about the investigations into Burisma and the 2016 election conspiracy theory in order to secure a White House meeting with President Trump.[725] Ambassador Volker first spoke to Mr. Giuliani, who said that he thought Ukraine "should issue a statement."[726] Ambassador Volker then spoke to Mr. Yermak, who affirmed that the Ukrainian leader was "prepared to make a statement" that "would reference Burisma and 2016 in a wider context of bilateral relations and rooting out corruption anyway."[727]

Mr. Giuliani, acting as President Trump's personal attorney, exerted significant influence in the process. On August 4, Mr. Yermak inquired again about the presidential meeting. Ambassador Volker replied that he would speak with Mr. Giuliani later that day and would call the Ukrainian aide afterward.[728] Ambassador Volker texted the former mayor about the Madrid meeting and asked for a phone call. Mr. Giuliani replied: "It was excellent I can call a little later."[729]

Phone records obtained by the Committees show a 16 minute call on August 5 between Ambassador Volker and Mr. Giuliani.[730] Ambassador Volker texted Mr. Yermak: "Hi Andrey—had a good long talk w Rudy—call anytime—Kurt."[731] During the same period, Ambassador Volker informed Ambassador Sondland that "Giuliani was happy with that meeting," and "it looks like things are turning around."[732]

"Potus Really Wants the Deliverable" Before Scheduling a White House Visit for President Zelensky

Things had not turned around by August 7. Ambassador Volker texted Mr. Giuliani to recommend that he report to "the boss"—President Trump—about his meeting with Mr. Yermak in Madrid. He wrote:

Hi Rudy—hope you made it back safely. Let's meet if you are coming to DC. And would be good if you could convey results of your meeting in Madrid to the boss so we can get a firm date for a visit.[733]

The Committees did not find evidence that Mr. Giuliani responded to Ambassador Volker's text message.

However, call records show that the next day, on August 8, Mr. Giuliani connected with the White House Situation Room switchboard in the early afternoon, Eastern Time, for 42 seconds, and then again for one minute, 25 seconds.[734]

The same day, Mr. Giuliani texted several times with a number associated with the White House. The Committees were unable to identify the official associated with the phone number. In the mid-afternoon, someone using a telephone number associated with the Office of Management and Budget (OMB) called Mr. Giuliani, and the call lasted for nearly 13 minutes. Mr. Giuliani called the OMB number and the White House Situation Room several more times that evening, but each time connected for only a few seconds or not at all.

Rudy Giuliani Call History, August 8

Date	Connect-ing Time (EDT)	Duration of Call	Caller	Recipient
08/08/19	12:44:56	0:42	Giuliani, Rudy	White House Switchboard (Situation Room)[735]
08/08/19	12:45:38	1:25	Giuliani, Rudy	White House Switchboard (Situation Room)[736]
08/08/19	13:02:37	TEXT	Giuliani, Rudy	White House Number[737]
08/08/19	13:02:37	TEXT	Giuliani, Rudy	White House Number[738]
08/08/19	13:02:57	TEXT	Giuliani, Rudy	White House Number[739]
08/08/19	14:14:53	TEXT	White House Number	Giuliani, Rudy[740]
08/08/19	14:15:17	TEXT	Giuliani, Rudy	White House Number[741]
08/08/19	14:21:13	TEXT	Giuliani, Rudy	White House Number[742]
08/08/19	15:13:05	12:56	OMB Number	Giuliani, Rudy[743]
08/08/19	15:56:44	0:00	Giuliani, Rudy	OMB Number[744]
08/08/19	15:56:51	0:00	Giuliani, Rudy	OMB Number[745]
08/08/19	15:57:05	0:00	Giuliani, Rudy	OMB Number[746]
08/08/19	15:57:21	0:22	Giuliani, Rudy	White House Switchboard (Situation Room)[747]
08/08/19	17:20:33	0:17	Giuliani, Rudy	White House Switchboard (Situation Room)[748]
08/08/19	19:14:48	0:00	Giuliani, Rudy	White House Switchboard (Situation Room)[749]

Approximately 30 minutes after his text to Mr. Giuliani on August 7, Ambassador Volker received a text message from Mr. Yermak: "Do you have some news about White House meeting date?"[750] Ambassador Volker responded that he had asked Mr. Giuliani to "weigh in," presumably with the President, "following your meeting," and that Ambassador Sondland would be speaking with President Trump on Friday, August 9. Ambassador Volker added: "We are pressing this."[751] The next day, on August 8, Mr. Yermak texted Ambassador Volker to report that he had "some news."[752] Ambassador Volker replied that he was available to speak at that time.[753]

Later on the evening of August 8, Eastern Time, Mr. Giuliani sent a text message to a phone number associated with the White House. Approximately one hour 15 minutes later, someone using an unidentified number ("-1") dialed Mr. Giuliani three times in rapid succession. Less than three minutes later, Mr. Giuliani dialed the White House switchboard for the White House Situation Room. When the call did not connect, Mr. Giuliani immediately dialed another general number for the White House switchboard and connected for 47 seconds. Approximately 16 minutes later, someone using the "-1" number called Mr. Giuliani and connected for just over four minutes.[754]

Rudy Giuliani Call History, August 8, cont.

Date	Connect-ing Time (EDT)	Duration of Call	Caller	Recipient
08/08/19	20:53:13	TEXT	Giuliani, Rudy	White House Number[755]
08/08/19	22:09:31	0:00	"-1"	Giuliani, Rudy[756]
08/08/19	22:09:32	0:05	"-1"	Giuliani, Rudy[757]
08/08/19	22:09:46	0:00	"-1"	Giuliani, Rudy (Cell 2)[758]
08/08/19	22:09:47	0:02	"-1"	Giuliani, Rudy (Cell 2)[759]
08/08/19	22:10:08	0:05	"-1"	Giuliani, Rudy[760]
08/08/19	22:11:52	0:00	Giuliani, Rudy	OMB Number[761]
08/08/19	22:12:16	0:00	Giuliani, Rudy	White House Switchboard (Situation Room)[762]
08/08/19	22:12:25	0:47	Giuliani, Rudy	White House Switchboard[763]
08/08/19	22:28:51	4:06	"-1"	Giuliani, Rudy[764]

Late the next morning Washington time, on August 9, Ambassador Volker texted Mr. Giuliani and Ambassador Sondland:

Hi Mr. Mayor! Had a good chat with Yermak last night. He was pleased with your phone call. Mentioned Z [President Zelensky] making a statement. Can we all get on the phone to make sure I advise Z [President

Zelensky] correctly as to what he should be saying? Want to make sure we get this done right. Thanks![765]

It is unclear which "phone call" Ambassador Volker was referencing.

Text messages and call records obtained by the Committees show that Ambassador Volker and Mr. Giuliani connected by phone twice around noon Eastern Time on August 9 for several minutes each.[766] Following the calls with Mr. Giuliani, Ambassador Volker created a three-way group chat using WhatsApp that included Ambassador Volker, Ambassador Sondland, and Mr. Yermak.[767]

At 2:24 p.m. Eastern Time on August 9, Ambassador Volker texted the group: "Hi Andrey—we have all consulted here, including with Rudy. Can you do a call later today or tomorrow your afternoon time?"[768] Ambassador Sondland texted that he had a call scheduled for 3 p.m. Eastern Time "for the three of us. [State Department] Ops will call."[769]

Call records obtained by the Committees show that on August 9, Ambassador Sondland twice called numbers associated with the White House, once in early afternoon for approximately 18 minutes, and once in late afternoon for two minutes, 25 seconds with a number associated with OMB.[770]

By early evening, minutes after his second call with OMB number, Ambassador Volker and Ambassador Sondland discussed a breakthrough they had reached in obtaining a date for a White House visit, noting that President Trump really wanted "the deliverable":

Sondland:	[Tim] Morrison ready to get dates as soon as Yermak confirms.
Volker:	Excellent!! How did you sway him? :)
Sondland:	Not sure i did. I think potus really wants the deliverable
Volker:	But does he know that?
Sondland:	Yep
Sondland:	Clearly lots of convos going on
Volker:	Ok—then that's good it's coming from two separate sources[771]

Ambassador Sondland told the Committees that the "deliverable" required by President Trump was a press statement from President Zelensky committing to "do the investigations" pushed by President Trump and Mr. Giuliani.[772]

To ensure progress, immediately after their text exchange, Ambassador Sondland recommended to Ambassador Volker that Mr. Yermak share a draft of the press statement to "avoid misunderstandings" and so they would know "exactly what they propose to cover." Ambassador Sondland explained: "Even though Ze [President Zelensky] does a live presser [press event] they can still summarize in a brief statement." Ambassador Volker agreed.[773]

As they were negotiating the language that would appear in a press statement, "there was talk about having a live interview or a live broadcast" during which President Zelensky would make the agreed-upon statement.[774] Ambassador Sondland suggested reviewing a written summary of the statement because he was "concerned" that President Zelensky would "say whatever he would say on live television and it still wouldn't be good enough for Rudy, slash, the President [Trump]."[775]

"Everyone Was in the Loop" About Plan for Ukrainians to Deliver a Public Statement about Investigations in Exchange for a White House Visit

As negotiations continued, on August 10, Mr. Yermak texted Ambassador Volker in an attempt to schedule a White House meeting *before* the Ukrainian president made a public statement in support of investigations into Burisma and the 2016 election. He wrote:

> I think it's possible to make this declaration and mention all these things. Which we discussed yesterday. But it will be logic [sic] to do after we receive a confirmation of date. We inform about date of visit about our expectations and our guarantees for future visit. Let [sic] discuss it[776]

Ambassador Volker responded that he agreed, but that first they would have to "iron out [a] statement and use that to get [a] date," after which point President Zelensky would go forward with making the statement.[777] They agreed to have a call the next day, and to include Ambassador Sondland. Mr. Yermak texted:

> Excellent. Once we have a date, will call for a press briefing, announcing upcoming visit and outlining vision for the reboot of the US-UKRAINE relationship, including, among other things, Burisma and election meddling in investigations.[778]

Ambassador Volker forwarded the message to Ambassador Sondland, and they agreed to speak with Mr. Yermak the next day.[779]

Ambassador Sondland testified that "everyone was in the loop" regarding this plan.[780] Also on August 10, Ambassador Sondland informed Ambassador Volker that he briefed T. Ulrich Brechbuhl, Counselor of the Department of State, noting: "I briefed Ulrich. All good."[781] Ambassador Sondland testified that he "may have walked [Mr. Brechbuhl] through where we were."[782] When asked if Mr. Brechbuhl briefed Secretary Pompeo, Ambassador Sondland noted that it was Mr. Brechbuhl's "habit" to "consult with Secretary Pompeo frequently."[783]

Secretary of Energy Rick Perry was also made aware of efforts to pressure Ukraine to issue a public statement about political investigations in exchange for a White House meeting. Ambassador Sondland testified:

> Mr. Giuliani conveyed to Secretary Perry, Ambassador Volker, and others that President Trump wanted a public statement from President Zelensky committing to investigations of Burisma and the 2016 election. Mr. Giuliani expressed those requests directly to the Ukrainians. Mr. Giuliani also expressed those requests directly to us. We all understood that these prerequisites for the White House call and the White House meeting reflected President Trump's desires and requirements.[784]

On August 11, Ambassador Volker requested a phone call with Ambassador Sondland and Mr. Giuliani, noting that he had heard from Mr. Yermak that the Ukrainians were "writing the statement now and will send to us."[785] According to call records obtained by the Committees, Ambassador Volker and Mr. Giuliani connected for 34 seconds.[786]

The same day, Ambassador Sondland updated Mr. Brechbuhl and Lisa Kenna, Executive Secretary of the State Department, about efforts to secure a public statement and a "big presser" from President Zelensky, which he hoped might "make the boss happy enough to authorize an invitation." He addressed the email to Secretary Pompeo:

> Mike,
> Kurt [Volker] and I negotiated a statement from Zelensky to be delivered for our review in a day or two. The contents will hopefully make the boss happy enough to authorize an invitation. Zelensky plans to have a big presser on the openness subject (including specifics) next week.[787]

Ambassador Sondland made clear in his hearing testimony that by "specifics," he meant the "2016 and the Burisma" investigations; "the boss" referred to "President Trump;" and "the invitation" referred to "the White House meeting."[788] Ms. Kenna replied to Ambassador Sondland that she would "pass to S [Secretary Pompeo]. Thank you."[789] Ambassador Sondland cited the email as evidence that "everyone was in the loop" on plans to condition a White House meeting on a public statement about political investigations.[790]

President Trump's Agents Negotiated a Draft Statement about the Investigations

In the evening of the next day, August 12, Mr. Yermak texted Ambassador Volker an initial version of the draft statement, which read:

> Special attention should be paid to the problem of interference in the political processes of the United States, especially with the alleged involvement of some Ukrainian politicians. I want to declare that this is unacceptable. We intend to initiate and complete a transparent and unbiased investigation of all available facts and episodes, which in turn will prevent the recurrence of this problem in the future.[791]

The draft statement did not explicitly mention Burisma or 2016 election interference, as expected.

On August 13, around 10 a.m. Eastern Time, Ambassador Volker texted Mr. Giuliani: "Mr mayor—trying to set up call in 5 min via state Dept. If now is not convenient, is there a time later today?"[792] Phone records show that, shortly thereafter, someone using a State Department number called Mr. Giuliani and connected for more than nine minutes.[793] Ambassador Volker told the Committees that, during the call, Mr. Giuliani stated: "If [the statement] doesn't say Burisma and 2016, it's not credible, because what are they hiding?"[794] Ambassador Volker asked whether inserting references to "Burisma and 2016" at the end of the statement would make it "more credible." Mr. Giuliani confirmed that it would.[795]

Two minutes after the call ended, Ambassador Volker sent a WhatsApp message to Ambassador Sondland and Mr. Yermak: "Hi Andrey—we spoke with Rudy. When is good to call you?"[796] Ambassador Sondland replied that it was, "Important. Do you have 5 mins."[797] They agreed to a call approximately 10 minutes later.[798] When Ambassador Sondland suggested having his "operator" in Brussels dial in the group, Ambassador Volker asked if they could "do this one on what's App?"[799] Text messages and calls in the WhatsApp cell phone application are encrypted from end-to-end, ensuring that WhatsApp employees and third parties cannot listen in or retrieve deleted communications.[800]

Shortly before the call, Ambassador Volker sent a revised draft of the proposed statement to Ambassador Sondland. It had been edited to include reference to Burisma and the 2016 elections:

> Special attention should be paid to the problem of interference in the political processes of the United States, especially with the alleged involvement of some Ukrainian politicians. I want to declare that this is unacceptable. We intend to initiate and complete a transparent and unbiased investigation of all available facts and episodes **including those involving Burisma and the 2016 US elections**, which in turn will prevent the recurrence of this problem in the future.[801]

Ambassador Sondland replied: "Perfect. Lets send to Andrey after our call."[802]

Following the call, Ambassador Volker texted Ambassador Sondland and Mr. Yermak: "Andrey—good talking—following is text with insert at the end for the 2 key items."[803] Ambassador Volker then sent to them the revised statement that included the explicit references to "Burisma and 2016 elections."[804]

Comparison of Draft Statements

Yermak Draft August 12	Giuliani-Volker-Sondland Draft August 13
Special attention should be paid to the problem of interference in the political processes of the United States, especially with the alleged involvement of some Ukrainian politicians. I want to declare that this is unacceptable. We intend to initiate and complete a transparent and unbiased investigation of all available facts and episodes, which in turn will prevent the recurrence of this problem in the future.	Special attention should be paid to the problem of interference in the political processes of the United States, especially with the alleged involvement of some Ukrainian politicians. I want to declare that this is unacceptable. We intend to initiate and complete a transparent and unbiased investigation of all available facts and episodes, **including those involving Burisma and the 2016 US elections**, which in turn will prevent the recurrence of this problem in the future.

A "Quid Pro Quo" from "the President of the United States"

Ambassador Volker testified that the language reflected what Mr. Giuliani deemed necessary for the statement to be "credible."[805] Ambassador Sondland noted the language was "proposed by Giuliani."[806] Ambassador Sondland explained that the language was a clear quid pro quo that expressed "the desire of the President of the United States":

> Mr. Giuliani's requests were a quid pro quo for arranging a White House visit for President Zelensky. Mr. Giuliani demanded that Ukraine make a public statement announcing investigations of the 2016 election/DNC server and Burisma. Mr. Giuliani was expressing the desires of the President of the United States, and we knew that these investigations were important to the President.[807]

Shortly after Ambassador Volker sent the revised statement to Mr. Yermak on August 13, Ambassador Sondland called Mr. Giuliani and connected for nearly four minutes.

Ukrainian Officials and Career State Department Became Increasingly Concerned

On August 13—while Ambassador Volker, Ambassador Sondland, and Mr. Yermak were negotiating the draft statement about investigations—Mr. Yermak asked Ambassador Volker "whether any request had ever been made by the U.S. to investigate election interference in 2016." He appeared interested in knowing whether the U.S. Department of Justice had made an official request to Ukraine's law enforcement agency for legal assistance in such a matter.[808] When Ambassador Volker sent Mr. Giuliani's approved draft statement to Mr. Yermak, he stated that he would "work on official request."[809]

Ambassador Volker testified: "When I say official request, I mean law enforcement channels, Department of Justice to law enforcement in Ukraine, please investigate was there any effort to interfere in the U.S. elections."[810] Ambassador Volker explained:

> He [Yermak] said, and I think quite appropriately, that if they [Ukraine] are responding to an official request, that's one thing. If there's no official request, that's different. And I agree with that.[811]

According to Ambassador Volker, he was merely trying to "find out" if there was ever an official request made by the Department of Justice: "As I found out the answer that we had not, I said, well, let's just not go there."[812]

On September 25, within hours of the White House's public release of the record of the July 25 call between President Trump and President Zelensky, a Justice Department spokesperson issued a statement, apparently confirming that no such formal request had been made:

> The President has not spoken with the Attorney General about having Ukraine investigate anything relating to former Vice President Biden or his son. The President has not asked

122

the Attorney General to contact Ukraine—on this or any other matter. The Attorney General has not communicated with Ukraine—on this or any other subject.[813]

Ukraine's current Prosecutor General Ruslan Ryaboshapka, who assumed his new position in late August 2019, confirmed the Justice Department's account. He told *The Financial Times* in late November 2019 that Attorney General Barr had made no formal request regarding a potential investigation into allegations of wrongdoing by former Vice President Biden.[814] In an apparent reference to President Trump's demand that Ukraine interfere in U.S. elections, Mr. Ryaboshapka added: "It's critically important for the west not to pull us into some conflicts between their ruling elites, but to continue to support so that we can cross the point of no return."[815]

Neither Ambassador Taylor in Ukraine nor Deputy Assistant Secretary George Kent in Washington were aware of the efforts by Ambassadors Sondland and Volker, in coordination with Mr. Giuliani, to convince Ukrainian officials to issue a statement in real time. Ambassador Taylor told the Committees that, on August 16, in a text message exchange with Ambassador Volker, he "learned that Mr. Yermak had asked that the United States submit an official request for an investigation into Burisma's alleged violations of Ukrainian law, if that is what the United States desired."[816] Ambassador Taylor noted that "a formal U.S. request to the Ukrainians to conduct an investigation based on violations of their own law" was "improper" and advised Ambassador Volker to "stay clear."[817]

Nevertheless, Ambassador Volker requested Ambassador Taylor's help with the matter.[818] "To find out the legal aspects of the question," Ambassador Taylor gave Ambassador Volker the name of an official at the Department of Justice "whom I thought would be the proper point of contact for seeking a U.S. referral for a foreign investigation."[819]

On August 15, Ambassador Volker texted Ambassador Sondland that Mr. Yermak wanted to "know our status on asking them to investigate."[820] Two days later, Ambassador Volker wrote: "Bill [Taylor] had no info on requesting an investigation—calling a friend at DOJ." Ambassador Volker testified that he was not able to connect with his contact at the Department of Justice.[821]

Mr. Kent testified that on August 15, Catherine Croft, Ambassador Volker's special assistant, approached him to ask whether there was any precedent for the United States asking Ukraine to conduct investigations on its behalf. Mr. Kent advised Ms. Croft:

> [I]f you're asking me have we ever gone to the Ukrainians and asked them to investigate or prosecute individuals for political reasons, the answer is, I hope we haven't, and we shouldn't because that goes against everything that we are trying to promote in post-Soviet states for the last 28 years, which is the promotion of the rule of law.[822]

Mr. Kent testified that the day after his conversation with Ms. Croft, he spoke with Ambassador Taylor, who "amplified the same theme" and told Mr. Kent that "Yermak was very uncomfortable" with the idea of investigations and suggested that "it should be done officially and put in writing." As a result, it became clear to Mr. Kent in mid-August that Ukraine was being pressured to conduct politically-motivated investigations. Mr. Kent told Ambassador Taylor "that's wrong, and we shouldn't be doing that as a matter of U.S. policy."[823]

After speaking to Ms. Croft and Ambassador Taylor, Mr. Kent wrote a memo to file on August 16 documenting his "concerns that there was an effort to initiate politically motivated prosecutions that were injurious to the rule of law, both in Ukraine and U.S."[824] Mr. Kent testified:

> At the time, I had no knowledge of the specifics of the [July 25] call record, but based on Bill Taylor's account of the engagements with Andriy Yermak that were engagements of Yermak with Kurt Volker, at that point it was clear that the investigations that were being suggested were the ones that Rudy Giuliani had been tweeting about, meaning Biden, Burisma, and 2016.[825]

On August 17, Mr. Yermak reached out to both Ambassador Sondland and Ambassador Volker.[826] Ambassador Sondland texted Ambassador Volker that "Yermak just tapped on me about dates. Havent responded. Any updates?"[827] Ambassador Volker responded that "I've got nothing" and stated that he was contacting the Department of Justice to find out about requesting an investigation.[828]

Ambassador Sondland then asked: "Do we still want Ze [Zelensky] to give us an unequivocal draft with 2016 and Boresma [sic]?" Ambassador Volker replied: "That's the clear message so far ..." Ambassador Sondland said that he would ask that Mr. Yermak "send us a clean draft," to which Ambassador Volker replied that he had spoken to Mr. Yermak and suggested that he and Ambassador Sondland speak the following day, August 18, to discuss "all the latest."[829]

Ambassador Volker claimed that he "stopped pursuing" the statement from the Ukrainians around this time because of concerns raised by Mr. Yermak that Yuriy Lutsenko was still the Prosecutor General. Mr. Lutsenko was likely to be replaced by President Zelensky, and because Mr. Lutsenko was alleging the same false claims that President Trump and Mr. Giuliani were demanding of President Zelensky, Ukrainian officials "did not want to mention Burisma or 2016."[830] Ambassador Volker testified that he "agreed" and advised Mr. Yermak that "making those specific refences was not a good idea" because making those statements might "look like it would play into our domestic politics."[831]

Mr. Yermak agreed and, according to Ambassador Volker, plans to put out a statement were "shelved."[832] Ambassador Volker reasoned that the plan for a public statement did not materialize partly because of "the sense that Rudy was not going to be convinced that it meant anything, and, therefore, convey a positive message to the President if it didn't say Burisma and 2016."[833] He added:

> I agreed with the Ukrainians they shouldn't do it, and in fact told them just drop it, wait till you have your own prosecutor general in place. Let's work on substantive issues like this, security assistance and all. Let's just do that. So we dropped it.[834]

Ambassador Volker testified that, "From that point on, I didn't have any further conversations about this statement."[835] Nevertheless, efforts to secure a presidential statement announcing the two investigations into the Bidens and the 2016 U.S. election interference continued well into September.

On August 19, Ambassador Sondland told Ambassador Volker that he "drove the 'larger issue' home" with Mr. Yermak: that this was bigger than just a White House meeting and was about "the relationship per se."[836] Ambassador Volker told the Committees that he understood this referred to "the level of trust that the President has with President Zelensky. He has this general negative assumption about everything Ukraine, and that's the larger issue."[837] That negative assumption would prove difficult to overcome as Ukrainian and U.S. officials sought to finally obtain a White House meeting and shake free from the White House hundreds of millions of dollars in Congressionally-approved security assistance for Ukraine.

7. **The President's Conditioning of Military Assistance and a White House Meeting on Announcement of Investigations Raised Alarm**

> *Following the public disclosure in late August 2019 of a hold on U.S. security assistance to Ukraine, President Trump made clear that "everything"—an Oval Office meeting and the release of taxpayer-funded U.S. security assistance—was contingent on the Ukrainian president announcing investigations into former Vice President Joe Biden and a debunked conspiracy theory about Ukrainian interference in the 2016 U.S. election. President Trump wanted the Ukrainian leader "in a public box," even as Ambassador Bill Taylor warned that it was "crazy to withhold security assistance for help with a political campaign."*

Overview

On August 28, 2019, *Politico* first reported that President Trump was withholding hundreds of millions of dollars of Congressionally-appropriated U.S. security assistance from Ukraine, a fact that had been previously suspected by Ukrainian officials in July. Public revelations about the freeze raised questions about the U.S. commitment to Ukraine and harming efforts to deter Russian influence and aggression in Europe.

Around this time, American officials made clear to Ukrainians that a public announcement about investigations into Ukrainian interference in the 2016 election and former Vice President Joe Biden was a pre-condition—not only to obtain a White House meeting for President Zelensky, but also to end the freeze on military and other security assistance for Ukraine.

In early September, Ambassador Gordon Sondland conveyed President Trump's demands to both U.S. and Ukrainian officials. On September 1, he informed a senior Ukrainian official that the military aid would be released if the "prosecutor general would to go the mike [sic]" and announce the investigations. Later, on September 7, President Trump informed Ambassador Sondland that he wanted President Zelensky—not the Prosecutor General—in a "public box" and demanded that the Ukrainian president personally announce the investigations to "clear things up." Only then would Ukraine end the "stalemate" with the White House related to security assistance. President Zelensky proceeded to schedule an interview on CNN in order to announce the investigations and satisfy President Trump.

The President's efforts to withhold vital military and security assistance in exchange for political investigations troubled U.S. officials. NSC Senior Director for Europe and Russia Timothy Morrison twice reported what he understood to be the President's requirement of a quid pro quo to National Security Advisor John Bolton, who advised him to "make sure the lawyers are tracking." Ambassador Bill Taylor expressed his concerns to Ambassador Sondland, stating plainly that it was "crazy to withhold security assistance for help with a political campaign."

126

Secretary Pompeo and Ambassador Sondland Worked to "Break the Logjam"

President Trump's hold on security assistance persisted throughout August, without explanation to U.S. officials and contrary to the consensus recommendation of the President's national security team. At the same time, President Trump refused to schedule a coveted White House visit for President Zelensky until he announced two investigations that could benefit President Trump's reelection prospects. The confluence of those two circumstances led some American officials, including Ambassador Sondland and David Holmes, Counselor for Political Affairs at the U.S. Embassy in Kyiv, to conclude that the military assistance was conditioned on Ukraine's public announcement of the investigations.[838]

On August 20, Ambassador Kurt Volker met with Deputy Assistant Secretary of Defense Laura Cooper. Ms. Cooper and Ambassador Volker agreed that if the hold on security assistance was not lifted, "it would be very damaging to the relationship" between the U.S. and Ukraine.[839] During this meeting, Ambassador Volker mentioned that he was talking to an advisor to President Zelensky about making a statement "that would somehow disavow any interference in U.S. elections and would commit to the prosecution of any individuals involved in election interference."[840] Ambassador Volker indicated that if his efforts to get a statement were successful, the hold on security assistance might be lifted.[841]

Although he did not mention that conversation during his deposition, Ambassador Volker had a similar recollection, during his public testimony, of the meeting with Ms. Cooper. Ambassador Volker recalled discussing with Ms. Cooper the draft statement that had been coordinated with Ukrainian presidential aide Andriy Yermak—which included reference to the two investigations that President Trump demanded in the July 25 call—and that such a statement "could be helpful in getting a reset of the thinking of the President, the negative view of Ukraine that he had" which might, in turn, "unblock[] whatever hold there was on security assistance."[842]

Around this time, Ambassador Sondland sought to "break the logjam" on the security assistance and the White House meeting by coordinating a meeting between the two Presidents through Secretary of State Mike Pompeo. On August 22, Ambassador Sondland emailed Secretary Pompeo, copying the State Department's Executive Secretary, Lisa Kenna:

> Should we block time in Warsaw for a short pull-aside for POTUS to meet Zelensky? I would ask Zelensky to look him in the eye and tell him that once Ukraine's new justice folks are in place (mid-Sept) Ze should be able to move forward publicly and with confidence on those issues of importance to Potus and to the US. Hopefully, that will break the logjam.[843]

Secretary Pompeo replied, "Yes."[844]

Ambassador Sondland testified that when he referenced "issues of importance to Potus," he meant the investigation into the false allegations about Ukrainian interference in the 2016 election and the investigation into the Bidens.[845] He told the Committee that his goal was to "do what was necessary to get the aid released, to break the logjam."[846] Ambassador Sondland

127

believed that President Trump would not release the aid until Ukraine announced the two investigations the President wanted.[847]

Ambassador Sondland testified: "Secretary Pompeo essentially gave me the green light to brief President Zelensky about making those announcements."[848] He explained:

> This was a proposed briefing that I was going to give President Zelensky, and I was going to call President Zelensky and ask him to say what is in this email. And I was asking essentially ... [Secretary] Pompeo's permission to do that, which he said yes.[849]

He then forwarded the email to Ms. Kenna, seeking confirmation of "10-15 min on the Warsaw sched[ule]" for the pull-aside meeting. The Ambassador stated that he was seeking confirmation in order to brief President Zelensky. Ms. Kenna replied, "I will try for sure."[850]

On August 24, Ukraine celebrated its Independence Day. According to Mr. Holmes, Ukrainian Independence Day presented "another good opportunity to show support for Ukraine."[851] However, nobody senior to Ambassador Volker attended the festivities, even though Secretary of Defense James Mattis attended in 2017 and Ambassador Bolton attended in 2018.[852]

Two days later, on August 26, Ambassador Bolton's office requested Mr. Giuliani's contact information from Ambassador Sondland. Ambassador Sondland sent Ambassador Bolton the information directly.[853] Ambassador Sondland testified that he had "no idea" why Ambassador Bolton requested the contact information.[854]

Ambassador Bolton Visited Kyiv

On August 27, Ambassador Bolton arrived in Kyiv for an official visit. Ambassador Bolton emphasized to Andriy Bohdan, President Zelensky's chief of staff, that an upcoming meeting between Presidents Trump and Zelensky, scheduled for September 1 in Warsaw, Poland, would be "crucial to cementing their relationship."[855] Mr. Holmes, who accompanied Ambassador Bolton in Kyiv, testified that he also heard "Ambassador Bolton express to Ambassador Taylor and Mr. Morrison his frustration about Mr. Giuliani's influence with the President, making clear there was nothing he could do about it."[856]

Prior to Ambassador Bolton's departure from Kyiv, Ambassador Taylor asked to meet with him privately. Ambassador Taylor expressed his "serious concern about the withholding of military assistance to Ukraine while the Ukrainians were defending their country from Russian aggression."[857] During the conversation, Ambassador Bolton "indicated that he was very sympathetic" to Ambassador's Taylor's concerns.[858] He advised that Ambassador Taylor "send a first-person cable to Secretary Pompeo directly relaying my concerns" about the withholding of military assistance.[859]

Mr. Holmes testified that Ambassador Bolton advised during his trip that "the hold on security assistance would not be lifted prior to the upcoming meeting between President Trump and President Zelensky in Warsaw, where it would hang on whether Zelensky was able to favorably impress President Trump."[860]

Ukrainian Concern Over Military Aid Intensified After First Public Report of Hold

On August 28, 2019, *Politico* first reported that President Trump had implemented a hold on nearly $400 million of U.S. military assistance to Ukraine that had been appropriated by Congress.

Almost immediately after the news became public, Ukrainian officials expressed alarm to their American counterparts. Mr. Yermak sent Ambassador Volker a link to the *Politico* story and then texted: "Need to talk with you."[861] Other Ukrainian officials also expressed concerns to Ambassador Volker that the Ukrainian government was being "singled out and penalized for some reason."[862]

On August 29, Mr. Yermak also contacted Ambassador Taylor to express that he was "very concerned" about the hold on military assistance.[863] Mr. Yermak and other Ukrainian officials told Ambassador Taylor that they were "just desperate" and would be willing to travel to Washington to raise with U.S. officials the importance of the assistance. Ambassador Taylor described confusion among Ukrainian officials over the hold on military aid:

> I mean, the obvious question was, "Why?" So Mr. Yermak and others were trying to figure out why this was … They thought that there must be some rational reason for this being held up, and they just didn't—and maybe in Washington they didn't understand how important this assistance was to their fight and to their armed forces. And so maybe they could figure—so they were just desperate.[864]

Without any official explanation for the hold, American officials could provide little reassurance to their Ukrainian counterparts. Ambassador Taylor continued, "And I couldn't tell them. I didn't know and I didn't tell them, because we hadn't—we hadn't—there'd been no guidance that I could give them."[865]

Ambassador Taylor's First-Person Cable Described the "Folly" in Withholding Military Aid

The same day that Ambassador Taylor heard from Mr. Yermak about his concerns about the hold on military aid, Ambassador Taylor transmitted his classified, first-person cable to Washington. It was the first and only time in Ambassador Taylor's career that he sent such a cable to the Secretary of State.[866] The cable described "the folly I saw in withholding military aid to Ukraine at a time when hostilities were still active in the east and when Russia was watching closely to gauge the level of American support for the Ukrainian Government."[867]

Ambassador Taylor worried about the public message that such a hold on vital military assistance would send in the midst of Ukraine's hot war with Russia: "The Russians, as I said at my deposition, would love to see the humiliation of President Zelensky at the hands of the Americans. I told the Secretary that I could not and would not defend such a policy."[868]

The cable also sought to explain clearly "the importance of Ukraine and the security assistance to U.S. national security," according to Mr. Holmes.[869] However, Mr. Holmes worried that the national security argument might not achieve its purpose given the reasons he suspected for the hold on military aid. His "clear impression" at the time was that "the security assistance hold was likely intended by the President either as an expression of dissatisfaction with the Ukrainians, who had not yet agreed to the Burisma/Biden investigation, or as an effort to increase the pressure on them to do so."[870] Mr. Holmes viewed this as "the only logical conclusion."[871] He had "no other explanation for why there was disinterest in this [White House] meeting that the President had already offered" and there was a "hold of the security assistance with no explanation whatsoever."[872]

Ambassador Taylor never received a response to his cable, but was told that Secretary Pompeo carried it with him to a White House meeting about security assistance to Ukraine.[873]

Ambassador Sondland Told Senator Johnson That Ukraine Aid Was Conditioned on Investigations

The next day, on August 30, Republican Senator Ron Johnson spoke with Ambassador Sondland to express his concern about President Trump's decision to withhold military assistance to Ukraine. According to Senator Johnson, Ambassador Sondland told him that if Ukraine would commit to "get to the bottom of what happened in 2016—if President Trump has that confidence, then he'll release the military spending."[874]

On August 31, Senator Johnson spoke by phone with President Trump regarding the decision to withhold aid to Ukraine.[875] President Trump denied the quid pro quo that Senator Johnson had learned of from Ambassador Sondland.[876] At the same time, however, President Trump refused to authorize Senator Johnson to tell Ukrainian officials that the aid would be forthcoming.[877]

The message that Ambassador Sondland communicated to Senator Johnson mirrored that used by President Trump during his July 25 call with President Zelensky, in which President Trump twice asked that the Ukrainian leader "get to the bottom of it," including in connection to an investigation into the debunked conspiracy theory that Ukraine interfered in the 2016 election to help Hillary Clinton.[878] To the contrary, the U.S. Intelligence Community unanimously assessed that Russia interfered in the 2016 election to help Donald Trump, as did Special Counsel Robert Mueller.[879]

In a November 18 letter to House Republicans, Senator Johnson confirmed the accuracy of the *Wall Street Journal's* account of his August 30 call with Ambassador Sondland.[880]

Ambassador Sondland testified that he had "no reason to dispute" Senator Johnson's recollection of the August 30 call and testified that by late August 2019, he had concluded that "if Ukraine did something to demonstrate a serious intention to fight corruption, and specifically addressing Burisma and the 2016, then the hold on military aid would be lifted."[881]

Ambassador Sondland Raised the Link Between Investigations and Security Assistance to
Vice President Pence Before Meeting with President Zelensky

On September 1, President Trump was scheduled to meet President Zelensky in Warsaw, Poland during an event commemorating World War II. Citing the approach of Hurricane Dorian towards American soil, the President canceled his trip just days beforehand. Vice President Mike Pence traveled to Warsaw instead.[882]

Jennifer Williams, Special Advisor to the Vice President for Europe and Russia, learned of the change in the President's travel plans on August 29 and "relied heavily on the NSC briefing papers" originally prepared for President Trump. Ms. Williams recalled that "prior to leaving, [National Security Advisor to the Vice President] General Kellogg had asked, at the request of the Vice President, for an update on the status of the security assistance that was at that time still on hold." Given the public reporting about the hold on August 29, White House officials expected that President Zelensky would seek further information on the status of the funds.[883]

The delegation arrived in Warsaw and gathered in a hotel room to brief the Vice President shortly before his engagement with President Zelensky. Ambassador Bolton, who had just arrived from Kyiv, led the Ukraine briefing. He updated Vice President Pence on President Zelensky's efforts to combat corruption and explained "what the security assistance was for." Advisors in the room "agreed on the need to get a final decision on that security assistance as soon as possible so that it could be implemented before the end of the fiscal year."[884]

Before the bilateral meeting between Vice President Pence and President Zelensky, Ambassador Sondland attended a "general briefing" for the Vice President.[885] Ambassador Sondland testified that he raised concerns that the delay in security assistance had "become tied to the issue of investigations."[886] The Vice President "nodded like, you know, he heard what I said."[887]

During Ambassador Sondland's public testimony, Vice President Pence's office issued a carefully worded statement claiming that the Vice President "never had a conversation with Gordon Sondland about investigating the Bidens, Burisma, or the conditional release of financial aid to Ukraine based upon potential investigations," and that "Ambassador Gordon Sondland was never alone with the Vice President on the September 1 trip to Poland."[888] Ambassador Sondland did not testify that he specifically mentioned the Bidens, Burisma, or the conditional release of financial aid to Ukraine during his discussion with Vice President Pence, nor did he testify that he was alone with the Vice President.

Before Vice President Pence's meeting with President Zelensky, Ukrainian National Security Advisor Oleksandr "Sasha" Danyliuk wrote Ambassador Taylor, incorrectly describing the failure to provide security assistance as a "gradually increasing problem."[889] In the hours before Vice President Pence's meeting with President Zelensky, Ambassador Taylor replied, clarifying that "the delay of U.S. security assistance was an all-or-nothing proposition, in the sense that if the White House did not lift the hold prior to the end of the fiscal year, September 30th, the funds would expire and Ukraine would receive nothing."[890] Ambassador Taylor wanted to make sure Mr. Danyliuk understood that if the assistance was not provided "by the end of the fiscal year, then it goes away."[891]

President Zelensky Immediately Asked Vice President Pence About Security Assistance

As expected, at the outset of the bilateral meeting, President Zelensky immediately asked Vice President Pence about the status of U.S. security assistance. It was "the very first question" that he raised.[892] President Zelensky emphasized the multifold importance of American assistance, stating that "the symbolic value of U.S. support in terms of security assistance … was just as valuable to the Ukrainians as the actual dollars."[893] President Zelensky also expressed concern that "any hold or appearance of reconsideration of such assistance might embolden Russia to think that the United States was no longer committed to Ukraine."[894]

According to Ms. Williams, the Vice President "assured President Zelensky that there was no change in U.S. policy in terms of our … full-throated support for Ukraine and its sovereignty and territorial integrity."[895] Vice President Pence also assured the Ukrainian delegation that he would convey to President Trump the details of President Zelensky's "good progress on reforms, so that hopefully we could get a decision on the security assistance as soon as possible."[896]

The reassurance proved to be ineffective. *The Washington Post* later reported that one of President Zelensky's aides told Vice President Pence: "You're the only country providing us military assistance. You're punishing us."[897]

Mr. Holmes testified that President Trump's decision to cancel his Warsaw trip effectively meant that "the hold [on security assistance] remained in place, with no clear means to get it lifted."[898]

Ambassador Sondland Informed President Zelensky's Advisor that Military Aid Was Contingent on Ukraine Publicly Announcing the Investigations

After the bilateral meeting between Vice President Pence and President Zelensky, Ambassador Sondland briefly spoke to President Zelensky's aide, Mr. Yermak. Ambassador Sondland conveyed his belief that "the resumption of U.S. aid would likely not occur until Ukraine took some kind of action on the public statement that we had been discussing for many weeks" regarding the investigations that President Trump discussed during the July 25 call.[899]

Immediately following the conversation, Ambassador Sondland told Mr. Morrison what had transpired during his aside with Mr. Yermak. Mr. Morrison recounted to the Committees that Ambassador Sondland told Mr. Yermak "what could help them move the aid was if the prosecutor general would go to the mike [sic] and announce that he was opening the Burisma investigation."[900]

132

Mr. Morrison Reported Ambassador Sondland's Proposal to Get Ukrainians "Pulled Into Our Politics" to White House Officials and Ambassador Taylor

Mr. Morrison felt uncomfortable with "any idea that President Zelensky should allow himself to be involved in our politics."[901] He promptly reported the conversation between Ambassador Sondland and Mr. Yermak to Ambassador Bolton. Mr. Morrison had concerns with "what Gordon was proposing about getting the Ukrainians pulled into our politics."[902] Ambassador Bolton told Mr. Morrison—consistent with his own "instinct"—to "make sure the lawyers are tracking."[903] Upon his return to Washington, Mr. Morrison reported his concerns to NSC lawyers John Eisenberg and Michael Ellis.[904]

Mr. Morrison testified that, in speaking to the NSC legal advisors, he wanted to ensure "that there was a record of what Ambassador Sondland was doing, to protect the President."[905] At this point, Mr. Morrison was not certain that the President had authorized Ambassador Sondland's activities, but Mr. Morrison agreed that if the President had been aware of Ambassador Sondland's activities, the effect could be to create a paper trail that incriminated President Trump.[906]

Mr. Morrison also reported the conversation to Ambassador Taylor "because I wanted him to be in a position to advise the Ukrainians not to do it."[907] Ambassador Taylor said that he was "alarmed" to hear about the remarks to Mr. Yermak.[908] He explained that "this was the first time that I had heard that the security assistance, not just the White House meeting, was conditioned on the investigations."[909] To Ambassador Taylor, "It's one thing to try to leverage a meeting in the White House. It's another thing, I thought, to leverage security assistance … to a country at war, dependent on both the security assistance and the demonstration of support."[910]

President Trump Wanted President Zelensky in a "Public Box," and Said "Everything" Depended on Announcing the Investigations

Upon hearing from Mr. Morrison about the conditionality of the military aid on Ukraine publicly announcing the two investigations, Ambassador Taylor sent a text message to Ambassador Sondland: "Are we now saying that security assistance and WH meeting are conditioned on investigations?" Ambassador Sondland responded, "Call me."[911]

Ambassador Sondland confirmed over the phone to Ambassador Taylor that "everything"—the Oval Office meeting and the security assistance—was dependent on the Ukrainian government publicly announcing the political investigations President Trump requested on July 25. Informed by a review of contemporaneous notes that he took during his phone call, Ambassador Taylor testified:

> During that phone call, Ambassador Sondland told me that President Trump had told him that he wants President Zelensky to state publicly that Ukraine will investigate Burisma and alleged Ukrainian interference in the 2016 election. Ambassador Sondland also told me that he now recognized that he had made a mistake by earlier telling Ukrainian officials that only a White House meeting with President Zelensky was dependent on a public announcement of the investigations. In fact, Ambassador Sondland said,

everything was dependent on such an announcement, including security assistance. He said that President Trump wanted President Zelensky in a public box, by making a public statement about ordering such investigations.[912]

By this point, Ambassador Taylor's "clear understanding" was that President Trump would withhold security assistance until President Zelensky "committed to pursue the investigation."[913] He agreed that the U.S. position was "if they don't do this," referring to the investigations, "they are not going to get that," referring to the security assistance.[914] Ambassador Taylor also concurred with the statement that "if they don't do this, they are not going to get that" was the literal definition of a quid pro quo.[915]

Ambassador Taylor testified that his contemporaneous notes of the phone call with Ambassador Sondland reflect that Ambassador Sondland used the phrase "public box" to describe President Trump's desire to ensure that the initiation of his desired investigations was announced publicly.[916] Ambassador Sondland, who did not take contemporaneous notes of any of his conversations, did not dispute that he used those words.[917] He also testified that, when he spoke to Mr. Yermak, he believed that it would be sufficient to satisfy the requirements of President Trump and Mr. Giuliani if the new Ukrainian prosecutor general issued a statement about investigations, but his understanding soon changed.[918]

President Trump Informed Ambassador Sondland that President Zelensky Personally "Must Announce the Opening of the Investigations"

On September 7, Ambassador Sondland called Mr. Morrison to report that he had just concluded a call with President Trump. Mr. Morrison testified that Ambassador Sondland told him "that there was no quid pro quo, but President Zelensky must announce the opening of the investigations and he should want to do it."[919] This led Mr. Morrison to believe that a public announcement of investigations by the Ukrainian president—and not the prosecutor general—was a prerequisite for the release of the security assistance.[920] He reported the conversation to Ambassador Bolton, who once again instructed him to "tell the lawyers," which Mr. Morrison did.[921]

Later on September 7, Mr. Morrison relayed the substance of Ambassador Sondland's conversation with President Trump to Ambassador Taylor. Ambassador Taylor explained:

> I had a conversation with Mr. Morrison in which he described a phone conversation earlier that day between Ambassador Sondland and President Trump. Mr. Morrison said that he had a sinking feeling after learning about this conversation from Ambassador Sondland. According to Mr. Morrison, President Trump told Ambassador Sondland he was not asking for a quid pro quo, but President Trump did insist that President Zelensky go to a microphone and say he is opening investigations of Biden and 2016 election interference and that President Zelensky should want to do this himself. Mr. Morrison said that he told Ambassador Bolton and the NSC lawyers of this phone call between President Trump and Ambassador Sondland.[922]

134

The following day, on September 8, Ambassador Sondland texted Ambassadors Volker and Taylor: "Guys multiple convos with Ze, Potus. Lets talk." Ambassador Taylor responded one minute later, "Now is fine with me."[923] On the phone, Ambassador Sondland "confirmed that he had talked to President Trump" and that "President Trump was adamant that President Zelensky himself had to clear things up and do it in public. President Trump said it was not a quid pro quo."[924] Ambassador Sondland also shared that he told President Zelensky and Mr. Yermak that, "although this was not a quid pro quo, if President Zelensky did not clear things up in public, we would be at a stalemate."[925]

Ambassador Taylor testified that he understood "stalemate" to mean that "Ukraine would not receive the much-needed military assistance."[926] During his public testimony, Ambassador Sondland did not dispute Ambassador Taylor's recollection of events and agreed that the term "stalemate" referred to the hold on U.S. security assistance to Ukraine.[927]

Although Ambassador Sondland otherwise could not independently recall any details about his September 7 conversation with President Trump, he testified that he had no reason to dispute the testimony from Ambassador Taylor or Mr. Morrison—which was based on their contemporaneous notes—regarding this conversation.[928] Ambassador Sondland, however, did recall that President Zelensky agreed to make a public announcement about the investigations into Burisma and the Bidens and the 2016 election in an interview on CNN."[929]

According to Ambassador Taylor, Ambassador Sondland explained that President Trump was a "businessman," and that when "a businessman is about to sign a check to someone who owes him something, the businessman asks that person to pay up before signing the check."[930] Ambassador Taylor was concerned that President Trump believed Ukraine "owed him something" in exchange for the hundreds of millions of dollars in taxpayer-funded U.S. security assistance.[931] He argued to Ambassador Sondland that "the explanation made no sense. The Ukrainians did not owe President Trump anything. And holding up security assistance for domestic political gain was crazy."[932] Ambassador Sondland did not recall this exchange specifically, but did not dispute Ambassador Taylor's testimony.[933]

Ambassador Taylor Texted Ambassador Sondland that "It's Crazy to Withhold Security Assistance for Help with a Political Campaign"

Ambassador Taylor remained concerned by the President's directive that "everything" was conditioned on President Zelensky publicly announcing the investigations. He also worried that, even if the Ukrainian leader did as President Trump required, the President might continue to withhold the vital U.S. security assistance in any event. Ambassador Taylor texted his concerns to Ambassadors Volker and Sondland stating: "The nightmare is they give the interview and don't get the security assistance. The Russians love it. (And I quit.)"[934]

Ambassador Taylor testified:

"The nightmare" is the scenario where President Zelensky goes out in public, makes an announcement that he's going to investigate the Burisma and the ... interference in 2016 election, maybe among other things. He might put that in some series of investigations.

But ... the nightmare was he would mention those two, take all the heat from that, get himself in big trouble in this country and probably in his country as well, and the security assistance would not be released. That was the nightmare.[935]

Early in the morning in Europe on September 9, Ambassador Taylor reiterated his concerns about the President's "quid pro quo" in another series of text messages with Ambassadors Volker and Sondland:

Taylor: The message to the Ukrainians (and Russians) we send with the decision on security assistance is key. With the hold, we have already shaken their faith in us. Thus my nightmare scenario.
Taylor: Counting on you to be right about this interview, Gordon.
Sondland: Bill, I never said I was "right". I said we are where we are and believe we have identified the best pathway forward. Lets hope it works.
Taylor: As I said on the phone, I think it's crazy to withhold security assistance for help with a political campaign.[936]

By "help with a political campaign," Ambassador Taylor was referring to President Trump's 2020 reelection effort.[937] Ambassador Taylor testified: "The investigation of Burisma and the Bidens was clearly identified by Mr. Giuliani in public for months as a way to get information on the two Bidens."[938]

Ambassador Taylor framed the broader national security implications of President Trump's decision to withhold vital security assistance from Ukraine. He said:

[T]he United States was trying to support Ukraine as a frontline state against Russian attack. And, again, the whole notion of a rules-based order was being threatened by the Russians in Ukraine. So our security assistance was designed to support Ukraine. And it was not just the United States; it was all of our allies.[939]

Ambassador Taylor explained:

[S]ecurity assistance was so important for Ukraine as well as our own national interests, to withhold that assistance for no good reason other than help with a political campaign made no sense. It was counterproductive to all of what we had been trying to do. It was illogical. It could not be explained. It was crazy.[940]

Ambassador Sondland Repeated the President's Denial of a "Quid Pro Quo" to Ambassador Taylor, While He and President Trump Continued to Demand Public Investigations

In response to Ambassador Taylor's text message that it was "crazy to withhold security assistance for help with a political campaign," Ambassador Sondland denied that the President had demanded a "quid pro quo."

At approximately 5:17 a.m. Eastern Time, Ambassador Sondland responded to Ambassador Taylor:

> Bill, I believe you are incorrect about President Trump's intentions. The President has been crystal clear: no quid pro quo's of any kind. The President is trying to evaluate whether Ukraine is truly going to adopt the transparency and reforms that President Zelensky promised during his campaign. I suggest we stop the back and forth by text. If you still have concerns, I recommend you give Lisa Kenna or S [Secretary Pompeo] a call to discuss them directly. Thanks.[941]

Notably, Ambassador Sondland recalled that President Trump raised the possible existence of a quid pro quo entirely on his own, without any prompting. Ambassador Sondland asked President Trump what he affirmatively wanted from Ukraine, yet President Trump reportedly responded by asserting what was not the case:

> Q: Okay. During that telephone conversation with President Trump, you didn't ask the President directly if there was a quid pro quo, correct?
>
> A: No. As I testified, I asked the question open ended, what do you want from Ukraine?
>
> Q: President Trump was the first person to use the word "quid pro quo," correct?
>
> A: That is correct.[942]

In contrast, Ambassador Sondland testified unequivocally there was a quid pro quo in connection to a telephone call between President Trump and President Zelensky, as well as a White House meeting for President Zelensky.[943] He acknowledged that the reference to "transparency and reforms" in his text message to Ambassador Taylor "was my clumsy way of saying he wanted these announcement to be made."[944]

Ambassador Sondland also testified that President Trump immediately followed his stated denial of a quid pro quo by demanding that President Zelensky still make a public announcement, while the military assistance remained on an unexplained hold. Ambassador Sondland agreed that President Trump said that he wanted President Zelensky to "clear things up and do it in public," as Ambassador Taylor had testified.[945] Ambassador Sondland testified that nothing on his call with President Trump changed his understanding of a quid pro quo and, at least as of September 8, he was "absolutely convinced" the White House meeting and President Trump's release of the military assistance were conditioned on the public announcement of the investigations President Trump sought.[946]

After hearing from President Trump, Ambassador Sondland promptly told the Ukrainian leader and Mr. Yermak that "if President Zelensky did not clear things up in public, we would be at a stalemate."[947] President Zelensky responded to the demand relayed by Ambassador Sondland, by agreeing to make an announcement of investigations on CNN.[948]

Regardless of when the call between President Trump and Ambassador Sondland occurred, both that phone call and Ambassador's Sondland text message denying any quid pro quo occurred *after* the White House had been informed of the whistleblower complaint discussing the hold on security assistance. The White House first received notice of the whistleblower complaint alleging wrongdoing concerning the President's July 25 call with President Zelensky on August 26—over a week before the "no quid pro quo" denial.[949] In addition, Ambassador Sondland wrote his text message on September 9, the same day that the ICIG informed the Committee of the existence of a "credible" and "urgent" whistleblower complaint that was later revealed to be related to Ukraine.[950] The Administration received prior notice of the ICIG's intent to inform the Committee.[951]

Ambassador Sondland's Testimony is the Only Evidence the Committees Received Indicating That President Trump Denied Any "Quid Pro Quo" on the Phone on September 9

Ambassador Sondland testified in his deposition that he sent a text message to Ambassador Taylor after speaking directly with President Trump on September 9. However, testimony from other witnesses and documents available to the Committees do not confirm that Ambassador Sondland and President Trump spoke on that day.

Ambassador Sondland's own testimony indicated some ambiguity in his recollection of the timing of the call. At a public hearing on November 20, Ambassador Sondland testified that he "still cannot find a record of that call [on September 9] because the State Department and the White House cannot locate it."[952] While Ambassador Sondland testified that "I'm pretty sure I had the call on that day,"[953] he acknowledged that he might have misremembered the date of the September 9 call—"I may have even spoken to him on September 6th"—and that without his call records, he could not be certain about when he spoke to President Trump.[954]

After the deposition transcripts of Ambassador Taylor and Mr. Morrison were made public, including their detailed accounts of the September 7 conversation that Ambassador Sondland had with President Trump, Ambassador Sondland submitted a written addendum to his deposition based on his "refreshed" recollection.[955] In that addendum, Ambassador Sondland amended his testimony and stated, "I cannot specifically recall if I had one or two phone calls with President Trump in the September 6-9 time frame."[956]

Furthermore, the conversation recalled by Ambassador Sondland as having taken place on September 9 is consistent with a conversation that Ambassador Sondland relayed to Mr. Morrison and Ambassador Taylor during the previous two days. Both Mr. Morrison and Ambassador Taylor, after reviewing their contemporaneous written notes, provided detailed testimony about Ambassador Sondland's description of his call with President Trump. For example, Ambassador Sondland shared with Ambassador Taylor that even though President Trump asserted that "there is no quid pro quo," President Trump "did insist that President Zelensky go to a microphone and say he is opening investigations of Biden and 2016 election interference."[957] Mr. Morrison and Ambassador Taylor both testified that this conversation occurred on September 7.[958] Ambassador Sondland acknowledged that he had no basis to dispute the recollections of Mr. Morrison and Ambassador Taylor.[959] Ambassador Sondland, who testified that he does not take notes, stated: "If they have notes and they recall that, I don't have any reason to dispute it."[960]

Text messages produced to the Committees also indicate that Ambassador Sondland spoke to President Trump prior to September 8. On September 4, Ambassador Volker texted Mr. Yermak that Ambassador Sondland planned to speak to President Trump on September 6 or 7. Ambassador Volker wrote: "Hi Andrey. Reports are that pence liked meeting and will press trump on scheduling Ze visit. Gordon will follow up with pence and, if nothing moving, will have a chance to talk with President on Saturday [September 7]."[961] Ambassador Volker then corrected himself: "Sorry—on Friday [September 6]."[962]

On Sunday, September 8, at 11:20 a.m. Eastern Time, Ambassador Sondland texted Ambassadors Taylor and Volker: "Guys multiple convos with Ze, Potus. Lets talk."[963] Shortly after this text, Ambassador Taylor testified that he spoke to Ambassador Sondland, who recounted his conversation with President Trump on September 7, as well as a separate conversation that Ambassador Sondland had with President Zelensky.

The timing of the text messages also raises questions about Ambassador Sondland's recollection. If Ambassador Sondland spoke to President Trump after receiving Ambassador Taylor's text message on September 9, and before he responded, then the timing of the text messages would mean that President Trump took Ambassador Sondland's call in the middle of the night in Washington, D.C. Ambassador Taylor sent his message on September 9 at 12:47 a.m. Eastern Time, and Ambassador Sondland responded less than five hours later at 5:19 a.m. Eastern Time.[964]

In any event, President Trump's purported denial of the "quid pro quo" was also contradicted when Acting Chief of Staff Mick Mulvaney publicly admitted that security assistance was withheld in order to pressure Ukraine to conduct an investigation into the 2016 election.

On October 17, at a press briefing in the White House, Mr. Mulvaney confirmed that President Trump withheld the essential military aid for Ukraine as leverage to pressure Ukraine to investigate the conspiracy theory that Ukraine had interfered in the 2016 U.S. election, which was also promoted by Vladimir Putin.[965] Mr. Mulvaney confirmed that President Trump "absolutely" mentioned "corruption related to the DNC server. ... No question about that."[966] When the White House press corps attempted to clarify this acknowledgement of a quid pro quo related to security assistance, Mr. Mulvaney replied: "We do that all the time with foreign policy." He continued. "I have news for everybody: get over it."[967]

8.   The President's Scheme Was Exposed

President Trump lifted the hold on U.S. military assistance to Ukraine on September 11 after it became clear to the White House and President Trump that his scheme was exposed.

Overview

As news of the President's hold on military assistance to Ukraine became public on August 28, Congress, the press, and the public increased their scrutiny of President Trump's actions regarding Ukraine, which risked exposing President Trump's scheme. By this date, the White House had learned that the Inspector General of the Intelligence Community (ICIG), Michael Atkinson, had determined that a whistleblower complaint related to the same Ukraine matters was "credible" and an "urgent concern," and, pursuant to the applicable statute, recommended to the Acting Director of National Intelligence (DNI), Joseph Maguire, that the complaint should be transmitted to Congress.

In early September, bipartisan Members of both houses of Congress—publicly, and privately—expressed concerns to the White House about the hold on military assistance. On September 9, after months of internal discussion due to growing concern about the activity of President Trump's personal attorney, Rudy Giuliani, regarding Ukraine, the Chairs of the Permanent Select Committee on Intelligence, the Committee on Foreign Affairs, and the Committee on Oversight and Reform announced a joint investigation into efforts by President Trump and Mr. Giuliani, "to improperly pressure the Ukrainian government to assist the President's bid for reelection," including by withholding Congressionally-appropriated military assistance.

Later that same day, the ICIG notified Chairman Schiff and Ranking Member Nunes that, despite uniform past practice and a statutory requirement that credible, "urgent concern" complaints be provided to the intelligence committees, the Acting DNI was nevertheless withholding the whistleblower complaint from Congress. The Acting DNI later testified that his office initially withheld the complaint on the advice of the White House, with guidance from the Department of Justice.

Two days later, on September 11, the President lifted the hold on the military assistance to Ukraine. Numerous witnesses testified that they were never aware of any official reason for why the hold was either implemented or lifted.

Notwithstanding this ongoing inquiry, President Trump has continued to urge Ukraine to investigate his political rival, former Vice President Biden. For example, when asked by a journalist on October 3 what he hoped Ukraine's President would do about the Bidens in response to the July 25 call, President Trump responded: "Well, I would think that, if they were honest about it, they'd start a major investigation into the Bidens. It's a very simple answer." President Trump reiterated his affinity for the former Prosecutor General of Ukraine, Yuriy Lutsenko, whom numerous witnesses described as inept and corrupt: "And they got rid of a

140

prosecutor who was a very tough prosecutor. They got rid of him. Now they're trying to make it the opposite way."

Public Scrutiny of President Trump's Hold on Military Assistance for Ukraine

After news of the President's freeze on U.S. military assistance to Ukraine became public on August 28, both houses of Congress increased their ongoing scrutiny of President Trump's decision.[968] On September 3, a bipartisan group of Senators, including Senator Rob Portman and Senator Ron Johnson, sent a letter to Acting White House Chief of Staff Mick Mulvaney expressing "deep concerns" that the "Administration is considering not obligating the Ukraine Security Initiative funds for 2019."[969] The Senators' letter urged that the "vital" funds be obligated "immediately."[970] On September 5, the Chairman and Ranking Member of the House Foreign Affairs Committee sent a letter to Mr. Mulvaney and Acting Director of the OMB Russell Vought expressing "deep concern" about the continuing hold on security assistance funding for Ukraine.[971]

On September 5, the *Washington Post* editorial board reported concerns that President Trump was withholding military assistance for Ukraine and a White House meeting in order to force President Zelensky to announce investigations of Mr. Biden and purported Ukrainian interference in the 2016 U.S. election. The *Post* editorial board wrote:

> [W]e're reliably told that the president has a second and more venal agenda: He is attempting to force Mr. Zelensky to intervene in the 2020 U.S. presidential election by launching an investigation of the leading Democratic candidate, Joe Biden. Mr. Trump is not just soliciting Ukraine's help with his presidential campaign; he is using U.S. military aid the country desperately needs in an attempt to extort it.

It added:

> The White House claims Mr. Trump suspended Ukraine's military aid in order for it [sic] be reviewed. But, as CNN reported, the Pentagon has already completed the study and recommended that the hold be lifted. Yet Mr. Trump has not yet acted. If his recalcitrance has a rationale, other than seeking to compel a foreign government to aid his reelection, the president has yet to reveal it.[972]

On the same day that the *Washington Post* published its editorial, Senators Christopher Murphy and Ron Johnson visited Kyiv, and met with President Zelensky. They were accompanied by Ambassador Bill Taylor and Counselor for Political Affairs David Holmes of U.S. Embassy Kyiv. President Zelensky's "first question to the Senators was about the withheld security assistance."[973] Ambassador Taylor testified that both Senators "stressed that bipartisan support for Ukraine in Washington was Ukraine's most important strategic asset and that President Zelensky should not jeopardize that bipartisan support by getting drawn into U.S. domestic politics." [974]

As Senator Johnson and Senator Murphy later recounted, the Senators sought to reassure President Zelensky that there was bipartisan support in Congress for providing Ukraine with

141

military assistance for Ukraine and that they would continue to urge President Trump to lift the hold—as Senator Johnson had already tried, unsuccessfully, before traveling to Ukraine.[975]

Three Committees Announced Joint Investigation of President's Scheme

On September 9, the Chairs of the House Intelligence Committee, the Committee on Foreign Affairs, and the Committee on Oversight and Reform publicly announced a joint investigation of the scheme by President Trump and Mr. Giuliani "to improperly pressure the Ukrainian government to assist the President's bid for reelection."[976] The Committees had been planning and coordinating this investigation since early summer, after growing public scrutiny of Mr. Giuliani's activities in Ukraine and questions about Ambassador Yovanovitch's abrupt removal following a public smear campaign targeting her.

In a letter sent to White House Counsel Pat Cipollone the same day, the three Chairs stated that President Trump and Mr. Giuliani "appear to have acted outside legitimate law enforcement and diplomatic channels to coerce the Ukrainian government into pursuing two politically-motivated investigations under the guise of anti-corruption activity"—investigations into purported Ukrainian interference in the 2016 election and Vice President Biden and his son.[977]

With respect to the hold on Ukraine military assistance, the Chairs observed that "[i]f the President is trying to pressure Ukraine into choosing between defending itself from Russian aggression without U.S. assistance or leveraging its judicial system to serve the ends of the Trump campaign, this would represent a staggering abuse of power, a boon to Moscow, and a betrayal of the public trust."[978] The Chairs requested that the White House preserve all relevant records and produce them by September 16, including the transcript of the July 25 call between President Trump and President Zelensky.[979]

On the same day, the Chairs of the three Committees sent a similar letter to Secretary of State Mike Pompeo seeking the preservation and production of all relevant records at the Department of State by September 16.[980] To date, and as explained more fully in Section II, Secretary Pompeo has not produced a single document sought by the Committees pursuant to a lawful subpoena.

NSC Senior Director for Russia and Europe Timothy Morrison recalled seeing a copy of the letter that was sent by the three Chairs to the White House.[981] He also recalled that the three Committees' Ukraine investigation was discussed at meeting of senior-level NSC staff soon after it was publicly announced.[982] The NSC's legislative affairs staff issued a notice of the investigation to NSC staff members, although it is unclear exactly when.[983] NSC Director for Ukraine Alexander Vindman recalled discussions among NSC staff members, including Mr. Morrison's deputy, John Erath, that the investigation "might have the effect of releasing the hold" on Ukraine military assistance because it would be "potentially politically challenging" for the Administration to "justify that hold" to the Congress.[984]

Inspector General Notified Intelligence Committee that the Administration
Was Withholding Whistleblower Complaint

Later that same day, September 9, Inspector General Atkinson sent a letter to Chairman Adam Schiff and Ranking Member Devin Nunes notifying them that an Intelligence Community whistleblower had filed a complaint with the ICIG on August 12.[985] Pursuant to a statute governing whistleblower disclosures, the Inspector General—after a condensed, preliminary review—had determined that the complaint constituted an "urgent concern" and that its allegations appeared to be "credible."[986] The Inspector General's September 9 letter did not disclose the substance or topic of the whistleblower complaint.

Contrary to uniform past practice and the clear requirements of the whistleblower statute, Acting DNI Maguire withheld the whistleblower complaint based on advice from the White House.[987] Acting DNI Maguire also relied upon an unprecedented intervention by the Department of Justice into Intelligence Community whistleblower matters to overturn the ICIG's determination based on a preliminary investigation.[988]

The White House had been aware of the whistleblower complaint weeks prior to the ICIG's letter of September 9.[989] Acting DNI Maguire testified that, after receiving the whistleblower complaint from the Inspector General on August 26, his office contacted the White House Counsel's Office for guidance.[990]

Consistent with Acting DNI Maguire's testimony, the *New York Times* reported that in late August, Mr. Cipollone and National Security Council Legal Advisor John Eisenberg personally briefed President Trump about the complaint's existence—and explained to the President that they believed the complaint could be withheld on executive privilege grounds.[991] The report alleged that Mr. Cipollone and Mr. Eisenberg "told Mr. Trump they planned to ask the Justice Department's Office of Legal Counsel to determine whether they had to disclose the complaint to lawmakers."[992]

On September 10, Chairman Schiff wrote to Acting DNI Maguire to express his concern about the Acting DNI's "unprecedented departure from past practice" in withholding the whistleblower complaint from the Congressional intelligence committees notwithstanding his "express obligations under the law" and the Inspector General's determination.[993] Chairman Schiff observed that the "failure to transmit to the Committee an urgent and credible whistleblower complaint, as required by law, raises the prospect that an urgent matter of a serious nature is being purposefully concealed from the Committee."[994]

Also on September 10, Ambassador John Bolton resigned from his position as National Security Advisor. Ambassador Bolton's deputy, Dr. Charles Kupperman, became the Acting National Security Advisor. The Committee was unable to determine if Ambassador Bolton's departure related to the matters under investigation because neither he nor Dr. Kupperman agreed to appear for testimony as part of this inquiry.

On September 13, the Office of the Director of National Intelligence (ODNI) General Counsel informed the Committee that DOJ had overruled the ICIG's determination, and that the

ODNI could not transmit the complaint to the Committee at its discretion because it involved "potentially privileged communications by persons outside the Intelligence Community"—presumably presidential communications.[995] In response, Chairman Schiff issued a subpoena to the Acting DNI on September 13 and announced to the public that ODNI was withholding a "credible" whistleblower complaint of "urgent concern."[996] Following intense pressure from the public and Congress, on September 25, the White House released the complaint to the intelligence committees and the July 25 call record to the public.[997]

President Trump Lifted the Hold on Military Assistance for Ukraine

On September 11—two days after the three Committees launched their investigation into President Trump's scheme, and one day after Chairman Schiff requested that Acting DNI Maguire produce a copy of the whistleblower complaint—President Trump lifted the hold on military assistance for Ukraine.

On the evening of September 11, prior to lifting the hold, President Trump met with Vice President Mike Pence, Mr. Mulvaney, and Senator Portman to discuss the hold.[998] Around 8:00 p.m. on September 11, the Chief of Staff's office informed Dr. Kupperman that the hold had been lifted.[999]

Just like there was no official explanation for why the hold on Ukraine security assistance was implemented, numerous witnesses testified that they were not provided with a reason for why the hold was lifted on September 11.[1000] For example, Deputy Assistant Secretary of Defense Laura Cooper testified that President Trump's lifting of the hold "really came quite out of the blue... It was quite abrupt."[1001] Jennifer Williams, Special Advisor to the Vice President for Europe and Russia, testified that from the time when she first learned about the hold on July 3 until it was lifted on September 11, she never came to understand why President Trump ordered the hold.[1002]

OMB Deputy Associate Director of National Security Programs Mark Sandy, who was the senior career official overseeing the administration of some of the Ukraine military assistance, only learned of a possible rationale for the hold in early September—after the Acting DNI had informed the White House about the whistleblower complaint.[1003] Mr. Sandy testified that he could not recall another instance "where a significant amount of assistance was being held up" and he "didn't have a rationale for as long as I didn't have a rationale in this case."[1004] However, in "early September," approximately two months after President Trump had implemented the hold, and several weeks after the White House learned of the whistleblower complaint, Mr. Sandy received an email from OMB Associate Director of National Security Programs Michael Duffey. For the first time, it "attributed the hold to the President's concern about other countries not contributing more to Ukraine" and requested "information on what additional countries were contributing to Ukraine."[1005]

Mr. Sandy testified that he was not aware of any other countries committing to provide more financial assistance to Ukraine prior to the lifting of the hold on September 11.[1006] According to Lt. Col. Vindman, none of the "facts on the ground" changed before the President lifted the hold.[1007]

After the Hold was Lifted, Congress was Forced to Pass a Law to Ensure All of the Military Aid Could Be Distributed to Ukraine

The lengthy delay created by the hold on Ukraine military assistance prevented the Department of Defense from spending all of the Congressionally-appropriated funds by the end of the fiscal year, which meant that the funds would expire on September 30 because unused funds do not roll over to the next fiscal year.[1008] This confirmed the fears expressed by Ms. Cooper, Mr. Sandy, and others related to the illegal impoundment of Congressionally-mandated funding—concerns that were discussed in some depth within the relevant agencies in late July and throughout August.[1009]

Prior to the release of the funds, DOD's internal analysis raised concerns that up to $100 million of military assistance could go unspent as a result of the hold imposed by the President.[1010] Ultimately, approximately $35 million of Ukraine military assistance—14% of the total funds—remained unspent by the end of fiscal year 2019.[1011] Typically, DOD averages between 2 and 5 percent unspent funds for similar programs, substantially less than the 14 percent left unspent in this case.[1012]

In order to ensure that Ukraine did not permanently lose $35 million of the critical military assistance frozen by the White House,[1013] Congress passed a provision on September 27—three days before funds were set to expire—to ensure that the remaining $35 million in 2019 military assistance to Ukraine could be spent.[1014] Ms. Cooper testified that such an act of Congress was unusual—indeed, she had never heard of funding being extended in this manner.[1015]

As of November 2019, Pentagon officials confirmed that the $35 million in security assistance originally held by the President and extended by Congress had still yet to be disbursed. When asked for an explanation, the Pentagon only confirmed that the funds had not yet been spent but declined to say why.[1016]

Pressure to Announce Investigations Continued After the Hold was Lifted

Before President Trump lifted the hold on security assistance, Ukrainian officials had relented to the American pressure campaign to announce the investigations and had scheduled President Zelensky to appear on CNN.[1017] Even after President Trump lifted the hold on September 11, President Zelensky did not immediately cancel his planned CNN interview.[1018]

On September 12, Ambassador Taylor personally informed President Zelensky and the Ukrainian foreign minister that President Trump's hold on military assistance had been lifted.[1019] Ambassador Taylor remained concerned, however, that "there was some indication that there might still be a plan for the CNN interview in New York" during which President Zelensky would announce the investigations that President Trump wanted Ukraine to pursue.[1020] Ambassador Taylor testified that he "wanted to be sure that that didn't happen, so I addressed it with Zelensky's staff."[1021]

On September 13, a staff member at the U.S. Embassy in Kyiv texted Mr. Holmes to relay a message that "Sondland said the Zelensky interview is supposed to be today or Monday, and they plan to announce that a certain investigation that was 'on hold' will progress."[1022] The Embassy Kyiv staffer stated that he "did not know if this was decided or if Sondland was advocating for it. Apparently he's been discussing this with Yermak."[1023]

On September 13, during a meeting in President Zelensky's office, Ukrainian presidential aide Andriy Yermak "looked uncomfortable" when Ambassador Taylor sought to confirm that there were no plans for President Zelensky to announce the investigations during a CNN interview.[1024] Although President Zelensky's National Security Advisor Oleksandr Danyliuk indicated that there were no plans for President Zelensky to do the CNN interview, Ambassador Taylor was still concerned after he and Mr. Holmes saw Mr. Yermak following the meeting.[1025] According to Ambassador Taylor, Mr. Yermak's "body language was such that it looked to me like he was still thinking they were going to make that statement."[1026] Mr. Holmes also recalled that when he and Ambassador Taylor ran into Mr. Yermak following the meeting, Ambassador Taylor "stressed the importance of staying out of U.S. politics and said he hoped no interview was planned," but "Mr. Yermak shrugged in resignation and did not answer, as if to indicate he had no choice."[1027]

That same day, September 13, President Zelensky reportedly met with CNN's Fareed Zakaria, who was in Kyiv to moderate the Yalta European Strategy Conference.[1028] During the meeting with Mr. Zakaria, President Zelensky did not cancel his planned CNN interview.[1029]

Conflicting advice prompted the Ukrainian foreign minister to observe in a meeting with Ambassador Volker, Ambassador Taylor, and Deputy Assistant Secretary of State George Kent, "You guys are sending us different messages in different channels."[1030]

For example, at a September 14 meeting in Kyiv attended by Ambassador Volker, Mr. Yermak, and the Ukrainian foreign minister, Ambassador Volker stated that when the two Presidents finally meet, "it's important that President Zelensky give the messages that we discussed before," apparently referring to President Zelensky's "willingness to open investigations in the two areas of interest to the President and that had been pushed previously by Rudy Giuliani."[1031] Ambassador Taylor, however, replied: "Don't do that."[1032]

On September 18 or 19, President Zelensky cancelled his scheduled interview with CNN.[1033] Although President Zelensky did not publicly announce the investigations that President Trump wanted, he remains under pressure from President Trump, particularly because he requires diplomatic, financial, and military backing from the United States, the most powerful supporter of Ukraine. That pressure continues to this day. As Mr. Holmes testified:

[A]lthough the hold on the security assistance may have been lifted, there were still things they wanted that [the Ukrainians] weren't getting, including a meeting with the President in the Oval Office. Whether the hold—the security assistance hold continued or not, Ukrainians understood that that's something the President wanted, and they still wanted important things from the President.

And I think that continues to this day. I think they're being very careful. They still need us now going forward. In fact, right now, President Zelensky is trying to arrange a summit meeting with President Putin in the coming weeks, his first face to face meeting with him to try to advance the peace process. He needs our support. He needs President Putin to understand that America supports Zelensky at the highest levels. So this doesn't end with the lifting of the security assistance hold. Ukraine still needs us, and as I said, still fighting this war this very day.[1034]

Vice President Pence Spoke to President Zelensky

On September 18, approximately one week before President Trump was scheduled to meet with President Zelensky at the United Nations General Assembly in New York, Vice President Pence spoke with President Zelensky by telephone.[1035] According to Ms. Williams, during the call, Vice President Pence "reiterat[ed] the release of the funds" and "ask[ed] a bit more about … how Zelensky's efforts were going."[1036]

On November 26, Ms. Williams submitted a classified addendum to her hearing testimony on November 19 related to this telephone call. According to Ms. Williams' counsel, the Office of the Vice President informed Ms. Williams' counsel that certain portions of the September 18 call, including the additional information in Ms. Williams' addendum, are classified. The Committee has requested that the Office of the Vice President conduct a declassification review so that the Committee may share this additional information regarding the substance of the September 18 call publicly. On October 9, Vice President Pence told reporters, "I'd have no objection" to the White House releasing the transcript of his calls with President Zelensky and said that "we're discussing that with White House counsel as we speak."[1037] In a November 7 interview with *Fox Business*, Vice President Pence reiterated, "I have no objection at all" to releasing records of his calls.[1038]

President Trump and Rudy Giuliani, Undeterred, Continued to Solicit Foreign Interference in Our Elections

On September 19, Rudy Giuliani was interviewed by Chris Cuomo on CNN. During the interview, Mr. Giuliani confirmed that he had urged Ukraine to investigate "the allegations that there was interference in the election of 2016, by the Ukrainians, for the benefit of Hillary Clinton[.]" When asked specifically if he had asked Ukraine to look into Vice President Biden, Mr. Giuliani replied immediately, "of course I did."

Seconds later, Mr. Giuliani attempted to clarify his admission, insisting that he had not asked Ukraine to investigate Vice President Biden but instead "to look into the allegations that related to my client [President Trump], which tangentially involved Joe Biden in a massive bribery scheme." Mr. Giuliani insisted that his conduct was appropriate, telling Mr. Cuomo later in the interview that "it is perfectly appropriate for a President to say to a leader of a foreign country, investigate this massive bribe … that was paid by a former Vice President."[1039]

President Trump also has continued to publicly urge President Zelensky to launch an investigation of Vice President Biden and alleged 2016 election interference by Ukraine. On September 23, in a public press availability, President Trump stated:

> I put no pressure on them whatsoever. I could have. I think it would probably, possibly, have been okay if I did. But I didn't. I didn't put any pressure on them whatsoever. You know why? Because they want to do the right thing.[1040]

On September 24, in public remarks upon arriving at the opening session of the U.N. General Assembly, President Trump stated: "What Joe Biden did for his son, that's something they should be looking at."[1041]

On September 25—in a joint public press availability with President Zelensky—President Trump stated that "I want him to do whatever he can" in reference to the investigation of the Biden family. He added, "Now, when Biden's son walks away with millions of dollars from Ukraine, and he knows nothing, and they're paying him millions of dollars, that's corruption." President Trump added, "He [President Zelensky] was elected—I think, number one—on the basis of stopping corruption, which unfortunately has plagued Ukraine. And if he could do that, he's doing, really, the whole world a big favor. I know—and I think he's going to be successful."[1042]

On September 30, during his remarks at the swearing-in ceremony of Labor Secretary Eugene Scalia, President Trump stated:

> Now, the new President of Ukraine ran on the basis of no corruption. That's how he got elected. And I believe that he really means it. But there was a lot of corruption having to do with the 2016 election against us. And we want to get to the bottom of it, and it's very important that we do.[1043]

On October 2, in a public press availability, President Trump discussed the July 25 call with President Zelensky and stated that "the conversation was perfect; it couldn't have been nicer." He added:

> The only thing that matters is the transcript of the actual conversation that I had with the President of Ukraine. It was perfect. We're looking at congratulations. We're looking at doing things together. And what are we looking at? We're looking at corruption. And, in, I believe, 1999, there was a corruption act or a corruption bill passed between both— and signed—between both countries, where I have a duty to report corruption. And let me tell you something: Biden's son is corrupt, and Biden is corrupt.[1044]

On October 3, in remarks before he departed on Marine One, President Trump expressed his "hope" that Ukraine would investigate Mr. Biden and his son. Specifically, President Trump stated that he had hoped—after his July 25 conversation—that Ukraine would "start a major investigation into the Bidens." The President also stated that "by the way, likewise, China should start an investigation into the Bidens, because what happened in China is just about as bad as what happened with—with Ukraine." He addressed the corrupt prosecutor general, Yuriy

Lutsenko, who had recently been removed by Parliament: "And they got rid of a prosecutor who was a very tough prosecutor. They got rid of him. Now they're trying to make it the opposite way.[1045]

The next day, on October 4, in remarks before he departed on Marine One, the President again said:

When you look at what Biden and his son did, and when you look at other people — what they've done. And I believe there was tremendous corruption with Biden, but I think there was beyond—I mean, beyond corruption—having to do with the 2016 campaign, and what these lowlifes did to so many people, to hurt so many people in the Trump campaign—which was successful, despite all of the fighting us. I mean, despite all of the unfairness.[1046]

President Trump reiterated his willingness to solicit foreign assistance related to his personal interests: "Here's what's okay: If we feel there's corruption, like I feel there was in the 2016 campaign—there was tremendous corruption against me—if we feel there's corruption, we have a right to go to a foreign country."[1047] President Trump added that asking President Xi of China to investigate the Bidens "is certainly something we can start thinking about."[1048]

Consistent with the President's remarks after this inquiry began, Ambassador Volker understood that references to fighting "corruption" in Ukraine, when used by President Trump and Mr. Giuliani, in fact referred to the two investigations into "Burisma"—and former Vice President Biden—and the 2016 election interference that President Trump sought to benefit his reelection efforts.[1049]

The President's Scheme Undermined U.S. Anti-Corruption Efforts in Ukraine

Rather than combatting corruption in Ukraine, President Trump's ongoing efforts to urge Ukraine to pursue an investigation into former Vice President Biden undermine longstanding U.S. anti-corruption policy, which encourages countries to refrain from using the criminal justice system to investigate political opponents. When it became clear that President Trump was pressuring Ukraine to investigate his political rival, career public servants charged with implementing U.S. foreign policy in a non-partisan manner, such as Lt. Col. Vindman and Ambassador Taylor, communicated to President Zelensky and his advisors that Ukraine should avoid getting embroiled in U.S. domestic politics.[1050]

Mr. Kent, an anti-corruption and rule of law expert, explained that U.S. anti-corruption efforts prioritize "building institutional capacity so that the Ukrainian Government has the ability to go after corruption and effectively investigate, prosecute, and judge alleged criminal activities using appropriate institutional mechanisms, that is, to create and follow the rule of law. [1051]

Mr. Holmes concurred:

[O]ur longstanding policy is to encourage them [Ukraine] to establish and build rule of law institutions, that are capable and that are independent and that can actually pursue credible allegations. That's our policy. We've been doing that for quite some time with some success. So focusing on [particular] cases, including [] cases where there is an interest of the President, it's just not part of what we've done. It's hard to explain why we would do that.[1052]

Mr. Kent emphasized that when foreign government officials "hear diplomats on the ground saying one thing, and they hear other U.S. leaders saying something else," it raises concerns about the United States' credibility on anti-corruption efforts.[1053] Ambassador Taylor agreed, stating that "[o]ur credibility is based on a respect for the United States" and "if we damage that respect, then it hurts our credibility and makes it more difficult for us to do our jobs."[1054]

Mr. Kent, like many other witnesses, explained that urging Ukraine to engage in "selective politically associated investigations or prosecutions" undermined the rule of law more generally:

> As a general principle, I do not believe the United States should ask other countries to engage in selective politically associated investigations or prosecutions against opponents of those in power because such selective actions undermine the rule of law, regardless of the country.[1055]

Mr. Kent agreed that pressuring Ukraine to conduct political investigations is not a part of U.S. foreign policy to promote the rule of law in Ukraine and around the world.[1056] Mr. Kent concluded that the President's request for investigations "went against U.S. policy" and "would've undermined the rule of law and our longstanding policy goals in Ukraine, as in other countries, in the post-Soviet space."[1057]

These conflicting messages came to a head at a September 14 meeting between American and Ukrainian officials in Kyiv. During that meeting, Ambassador Volker advised Mr. Yermak about the "potential problems" with investigations that the Zelensky administration was contemplating into former Ukrainian President Petro Poroshenko.[1058] Mr. Yermak retorted, "what, you mean like asking us to investigate Clinton and Biden?"[1059] Ambassador Volker did not respond.[1060]

SECTION I ENDNOTES

[1] Yovanovitch Hearing Tr. at 16-17.

[2] *Kateryna Handziuk, Ukrainian Activist, Dies From Acid Attack*, New York Times (Nov. 5, 2018) (online at www.nytimes.com/2018/11/05/world/europe/kateryna-handziuk-dies-ukraine.html).

[3] Yovanovitch Hearing Tr. at 30-31.

[4] U.S. Embassy in Ukraine, Department of State, *Ambassador Yovanovitch's Remarks at a Women of Courage Reception in Honor of Kateryna Handziuk* (Apr. 24, 2019) (online at https://ua.usembassy.gov/ambassador-yovanovitchs-remarks-at-a-women-of-courage-reception-in-honor-of-kateryna-handziuk/).

[5] U.S. Embassy in Ukraine, Department of State, *Ambassador Yovanovitch's Remarks at a Women of Courage Reception in Honor of Kateryna Handziuk* (Apr. 24, 2019) (online at https://ua.usembassy.gov/ambassador-yovanovitchs-remarks-at-a-women-of-courage-reception-in-honor-of-kateryna-handziuk/).

[6] Yovanovitch Hearing Tr. at 31.

[7] Yovanovitch Hearing Tr. at 31-32.

[8] Yovanovitch Hearing Tr. at 32.

[9] Yovanovitch Hearing Tr. at 31.

[10] Yovanovitch Hearing Tr. at 31-32.

[11] *Giuliani to Join Trump's Legal Team*, New York Times (April 19, 2018) (online at https://www.nytimes.com/2018/04/19/us/politics/giuliani-trump.html).

[12] Letter from John M. Dowd, Counsel to Igor Fruman and Lev Parnas, to Committee Staff (Oct. 3, 2019).

[13] Department of Justice, *Lev Parnas and Igor Fruman Charged with Conspiring to Violate Straw and Foreign Donor Bans* (Oct. 10, 2019) (online at www.justice.gov/usao-sdny/pr/lev-parnas-and-igor-fruman-charged-conspiring-violate-straw-and-foreign-donor-bans).

[14] Hill Dep. Tr. at 59.

[15] Yovanovitch Dep. Tr. at 28-29.

[16] *Ukraine Ousts Victor Shokin, Top Prosecutor, and Political Stability Hangs in the Balance*, New York Times (Mar. 29, 2016) (online at www.nytimes.com/2016/03/30/world/europe/political-stability-in-the-balance-as-ukraine-ousts-top-prosecutor.html).

[17] Kent Dep. Tr. at 45.

[18] Yovanovitch Dep. Tr. at 27-28.

[19] Yovanovitch Dep. Tr. at 31-32.

[20] Yovanovitch Dep. Tr. at 21.

[21] Yovanovitch Dep. Tr. at 32-33, 38 ("I think that he felt that I and the embassy were effective at helping Ukrainians who wanted reform, Ukrainians who wanted to fight against corruption, and he did not – you know, that was not in his interest.").

[22] Yovanovitch Dep. Tr. at 30.

[23] Holmes Dep. Tr. at 14.

[24] Kent-Taylor Hearing Tr. at 25.

[25] Kent-Taylor Hearing Tr. at 132.

[26] Morrison-Volker Hearing Tr. at 27.

[27] Nickolay Kapitonenko, an advisor to the Ukrainian Parliament's Foreign Policy Committee, described Giuliani as a "mythical link to the U.S." who is viewed as "an extension of Trump." *Giuliani Sits at the Center of the Ukraine Controversy*, Wall Street Journal (Sep. 26, 2019) (online at www.wsj.com/articles/giuliani-sits-at-the-center-of-the-ukraine-controversy-11569546774); David Sakvarelidze, a former Ukrainian deputy prosecutor general, stated, "Lutsenko was trying to save his political skin by pretending to be Trumpist at the end of his career." *Meet the Ukrainian Ex-Prosecutor Behind the Impeachment Furor*, New York Times (Oct. 5, 2019) (online at www.nytimes.com/2019/10/05/world/europe/ukraine-prosecutor-trump.html).

[28] Yovanovitch Dep. Tr. at 30.

[29] Donald J. Trump, Twitter (Jan. 17, 2019) (online at https://twitter.com/realdonaldtrump/status/1086096691613323265) ("Gregg Jarrett: 'Mueller's prosecutors knew the 'Dossier' was the product of bias and deception.' It was a Fake, just like so much news coverage in our Country. Nothing but a Witch Hunt, from beginning to end!").

[30] Office of the Director of National Intelligence, *Background to "Assessing Russian Activities and Intentions in Recent US Elections": The Analytic Process and Cyber Incident Attribution* (Jan. 6, 2017) (online at www.dni.gov/files/documents/ICA_2017_01.pdf); Senate Select Committee on Intelligence, *Russian Active Measures Campaigns and Interference in the 2016 U.S. Election* (May 8, 2018) (online at www.intelligence.senate.gov/publications/report-select-committee-intelligence-united-states-senate-russian-active-measures); House Permanent Select Committee on Intelligence, *Report on Russian Active Measures* (Mar. 22, 2018) (online at https://docs.house.gov/meetings/IG/IG00/20180322/108023/HRPT-115-1_1-p1-U3.pdf); House Permanent Select Committee on Intelligence, *Minority Views* (Mar. 26, 2018) (online at https://intelligence.house.gov/uploadedfiles/20180411_-_final_-_hpsci_minority_views_on_majority_report.pdf).

[31] *President Trump's Former National Security Advisor 'Deeply Disturbed' by Ukraine Scandal: 'Whole World Is Watching,'* ABC News (Sept. 29, 2019) (online at https://abcnews.go.com/Politics/president-trumps-national-security-advisor-deeply-disturbed-ukraine/story?id=65925477).

[32] *Charges of Ukrainian Meddling? A Russian Operation, U.S. Intelligence Says*, New York Times (Nov. 22, 2019) (online at https://www.nytimes.com/2019/11/22/us/politics/ukraine-russia-interference.html).

[33] Hill-Holmes Hearing Tr. at 56-57.

[34] Kent Dep. Tr. at 45.

[35] Volker Transcribed Interview Tr. at 330.

[36] Volker Transcribed Interview Tr. at 330; *Explainer: Biden, Allies, Pushed Out Ukrainian Prosecutor Because He Didn't Pursue Corruption Cases,* USA Today (Oct. 3, 2019) (online at www.usatoday.com/story/news/politics/2019/10/03/what-really-happened-when-biden-forced-out-ukraines-top-prosecutor/3785620002/).

[37] *See, e.g., Ukraine Prosecutor Says No Evidence of Wrongdoing by Bidens*, Bloomberg (May 16, 2019) (online at www.bloomberg.com/news/articles/2019-05-16/ukraine-prosecutor-says-no-evidence-of-wrongdoing-by-bidens) ("Hunter Biden did not violate any Ukrainian laws -- at least as of now, we do not see any wrongdoing. A company can pay however much it wants to its board ... Biden was definitely not involved ... We do not have any grounds to think that there was any wrongdoing starting from 2014.").

[38] Notes of Call with Viktor Shokin (Jan. 23, 2019); *Ukraine Prosecutor Says No Evidence of Wrongdoing by Bidens*, Bloomberg (May 16, 2019) (online at www.bloomberg.com/news/articles/2019-05-16/ukraine-prosecutor-says-no-evidence-of-wrongdoing-by-bidens).

[39] *Giuliani Pursued Business in Ukraine While Pushing for Inquiries for Trump*, New York Times (Nov. 27, 2019) (online at www.nytimes.com/2019/11/27/nyregion/giuliani-ukraine-business-trump.html); *Ukraine Prosecutor Says No Evidence of Wrongdoing by Bidens*, Bloomberg (May 16, 2019) (online at www.bloomberg.com/news/articles/2019-05-16/ukraine-prosecutor-says-no-evidence-of-wrongdoing-by-bidens).

[40] Notes of Meeting with Yuriy Lutsenko (Jan. 25, 2019); *Ukraine Prosecutor Says No Evidence of Wrongdoing by Bidens*, Bloomberg (May 16, 2019) (online at www.bloomberg.com/news/articles/2019-05-16/ukraine-prosecutor-says-no-evidence-of-wrongdoing-by-bidens).

[41] *Giuliani Pursued Business in Ukraine While Pushing for Inquiries for Trump*, New York Times (Nov. 27, 2019) (online at www.nytimes.com/2019/11/27/nyregion/giuliani-ukraine-business-trump.html).

[42] Rudy Giuliani, Twitter (Oct. 23, 2019) (online at https://twitter.com/RudyGiuliani/status/1187168034835894272).

[43] Rudy Giuliani, Twitter (Oct. 30, 2019) (online at https://twitter.com/RudyGiuliani/status/1189667101079932928).

[44] Hill-Holmes Hearing Tr. at 19.

[45] *As Russia Collusion Fades, Ukrainian Plot to Help Clinton Emerges*, The Hill (Mar. 20, 2019) (online at https://thehill.com/opinion/campaign/435029-as-russia-collusion-fades-ukrainian-plot-to-help-clinton-emerges).

[46] *Ukraine Prosecutor General Lutsenko Admits U.S. Ambassador Didn't Give Him a Do Not Prosecute List*, The Ukrainian (Apr. 18, 2019) (online at www.unian.info/politics/10520715-ukraine-prosecutor-general-lutsenko-admits-u-s-ambassador-didn-t-give-him-a-do-not-prosecute-list.html).

[47] *As Russia Collusion Fades, Ukrainian Plot to Help Clinton Emerges*, The Hill (Mar. 20, 2019) (online at https://thehill.com/opinion/campaign/435029-as-russia-collusion-fades-ukrainian-plot-to-help-clinton-emerges).

[48] Yovanovitch Dep. Tr. at 21, 37.

[49] AT&T Document Production, Bates ATTHPSCI _20190930_00768, ATTHPSCI _20190930_00772, ATTHPSCI _20190930_00775.

[50] *As Russia Collusion Fades, Ukrainian Plot to Help Clinton Emerges*, The Hill (Mar. 20, 2019) (online at https://thehill.com/opinion/campaign/435029-as-russia-collusion-fades-ukrainian-plot-to-help-clinton-emerges).

[51] Department of Justice, *Lev Parnas and Igor Fruman Charged with Conspiring to Violate Straw and Foreign Donor Bans* (Oct. 10, 2019) (online at www.justice.gov/usao-sdny/pr/lev-parnas-and-igor-fruman-charged-conspiring-violate-straw-and-foreign-donor-bans) (alleging that in May and June 2018, Mr. Parnas sought the assistance of an unnamed congressman in causing the removal or recall of the then-U.S. ambassador to Ukraine).

[52] AT&T Document Production, Bates ATTHPSCI _20190930_00775.

[53] Donald J. Trump, Twitter (Mar. 20, 2019) (online at https://twitter.com/realdonaldtrump/status/1108559080204001280).

[54] Rudy Giuliani, Twitter (Mar. 22, 2019) (online at https://twitter.com/RudyGiuliani/status/1109117167176466432); *Giuliani Slams Mueller Leak*, Fox News (April 7, 2019) (online at https://www.foxnews.com/transcript/giuliani-slams-mueller-leak).

[55] Donald Trump, Jr., Twitter (Mar. 24, 2019) (online at https://twitter.com/donaldjtrumpjr/status/1109850575926108161).

[56] Kent Dep. Tr. at 57-58.

[57] Kent Dep. Tr. at 178.

[58] Yovanovitch Dep. Tr. at 62.

[59] Hale Dep. Tr. at 37-38.

[60] Hale Dep. Tr. at 99-100.

[61] Yovanovitch Dep. Tr. at 63-64.

[62] Hale Dep. Tr. at 27.

[63] Yovanovitch Dep. Tr. at 124.

[64] Yovanovitch Dep. Tr. at 267-268.

[65] Yovanovitch Dep. Tr. at 268.

[66] Email from [Redacted] to S_All (Mar. 26, 2019) (online at www.americanoversight.org/wp-content/uploads/2019/11/AO_State_Ukraine_Docs_11-22.pdf); Email from Operations Center to [Redacted] (Mar.

29, 2019) (online at www.americanoversight.org/wp-content/uploads/2019/11/AO_State_Ukraine_Docs_11-22.pdf). (The same State Department records show that Secretary Pompeo was scheduled to have a secure call with Rep. Nunes on April 1, 2019.); Email from Operations Center to [Redacted] (Mar. 29, 2019) (online at www.americanoversight.org/wp-content/uploads/2019/11/AO_State_Ukraine_Docs_11-22.pdf).

[67] *Joe Biden's 2020 Ukrainian Nightmare: A Closed Probe is Revived*, The Hill (Apr. 1, 2019) (online at https://thehill.com/opinion/white-house/436816-joe-bidens-2020-ukrainian-nightmare-a-closed-probe-is-revived).

[68] Donald Trump, Jr., Twitter (Apr. 2, 2019) (online at https://twitter.com/donaldjtrumpjr/status/1113046659456528385).

[69] AT&T Document Production, Bates ATTHPSCI_20190930_00848-ATTHPSCI_20190930_00884. Mr. Parnas also had an aborted call that lasted 5 seconds on April 5, 2019 with an aide to Rep. Devin Nunes on the Intelligence Committee, Derek Harvey. AT&T Document Production, Bates ATTHPSCI_20190930_00876. Call records obtained by the Committees show that Mr. Parnas and Mr. Harvey had connected previously, including a four minute 42 second call on February 1, 2019, a one minute 7 second call on February 4, and a one minute 37 second call on February 7, 2019. AT&T Document Production, Bates ATTHPSCI_20190930_00617, ATTHPSCI_20190930_00630, ATTHPSCI_20190930_00641. As explained later in this Chapter, Rep. Nunes would connect separately by phone on April 10, 11, and 12 with Mr. Parnas and Mr. Giuliani. AT&T Document Production, Bates ATTHPSCI_20190930_00913- ATTHPSCI_20190930_00914; ATTHPSCI_20190930-02125.

[70] *Ukrainian to US Prosecutors: Why Don't You Want Our Evidence on Democrats?*, The Hill (Apr. 7, 2019) (online at https://thehill.com/opinion/white-house/437719-ukrainian-to-us-prosecutors-why-dont-you-want-our-evidence-on-democrats).

[71] *Ukrainian to US Prosecutors: Why Don't You Want Our Evidence on Democrats?*, The Hill (Apr. 7, 2019) (online at https://thehill.com/opinion/white-house/437719-ukrainian-to-us-prosecutors-why-dont-you-want-our-evidence-on-democrats).

[72] *Ukrainian to US Prosecutors: Why Don't You Want Our Evidence on Democrats?*, The Hill (Apr. 7, 2019) (online at https://thehill.com/opinion/white-house/437719-ukrainian-to-us-prosecutors-why-dont-you-want-our-evidence-on-democrats).

[73] *Ukrainian to US Prosecutors: Why Don't You Want Our Evidence on Democrats?*, The Hill (Apr. 7, 2019) (online at https://thehill.com/opinion/white-house/437719-ukrainian-to-us-prosecutors-why-dont-you-want-our-evidence-on-democrats).

[74] *Giuliani Slams Mueller Leak*, Fox News (Apr. 7, 2019) (online at www.foxnews.com/transcript/giuliani-slams-mueller-leak).

[75] Rudy Giuliani, Twitter (Apr. 8, 2019) (online at https://twitter.com/RudyGiuliani/status/1115171828618731520).

[76] Specifically, between April 8 and April 11, phone records show the following phone contacts:

- six calls between Mr. Giuliani and Mr. Parnas (longest duration approximately five minutes), AT&T Document Production, Bates ATTHPSCI_20190930-02115-ATTHPSCI_20190930-02131;
- four calls between Mr. Giuliani and Mr. Solomon (all on April 8, longest duration approximately one minute, 30 seconds) AT&T Document Production, Bates ATTHPSCI_20190930-02114-ATTHPSCI_20190930-02115;
- nine calls between Mr. Parnas and Mr. Solomon (longest duration four minutes, 39 seconds) AT&T Document Production, Bates ATTHPSCI_20190930-00885- ATTHPSCI_20190930-00906; and
- three calls between Mr. Parnas and Ms. Toensing (longest duration approximately six minutes), AT&T Document Production, Bates ATTHPSCI_20190930-00885- ATTHPSCI_20190930-00905.

[77] AT&T Document Production, Bates ATTHPSCI_20190930-02125, ATTHPSCI_20190930-03236.

Date	Connecting Time (ET)	Duration of Call	Caller	Recipient
04/10/19	12:00:36	0:35	Giuliani, Rudy	Nunes, Devin
04/10/19	12:10:35	0:00	Nunes, Devin	Giuliani, Rudy
04/10/19	12:10:37	0:31	Nunes, Devin	Giuliani, Rudy
04/10/19	12:11:10	SMS	UNKNOWN	Giuliani, Rudy
04/10/19	12:12:35	2:50	Giuliani, Rudy	Nunes, Devin
04/10/19	12:15:38	0:00	Giuliani, Rudy	Nunes, Devin

[78] AT&T Document Production, Bates ATTHPSCI_20190930-00902.

[79] Jay Sekulow, personal counsel to President Trump, stated that the President was disappointed that Mr. diGenova and Ms. Toensing had to withdraw due to a conflict of interest, but noted that "those conflicts do not prevent them from assisting the President in other legal matters. The President looks forward to working with them." *Trump's Legal Team Remains in Disarray as New Lawyer Will No Longer Represent Him in Russia Probe*, Washington Post (Mar. 25, 2018) (online at www.washingtonpost.com/politics/in-another-blow-to-trumps-efforts-to-combat-russia-probe-digenova-will-no-longer-join-legal-team/2018/03/25/8ac8c8d2-3038-11e8-94fa-32d48460b955_story.html).

[80] For example, between April 1 and April 7, Ms. Toensing exchanged approximately five calls with Mr. Parnas and two calls with Mr. Giuliani. In addition, on April 10, Ms. Toensing and Mr. Giuliani spoke for approximately six minutes, 19 seconds. AT&T Document Production, Bates ATTHPSCI_20190930-02126. Mr. diGenova and Ms. Toensing were also very active on social media in promoting these conspiracy theories as well as the false accusations against Ambassador Yovanovitch. *See, e.g.*, Ryan Saavedra, Twitter (Mar. 23, 2019) (online at https://twitter.com/RealSaavedra/status/1109546629672009728); Victoria Toensing, Twitter (Mar. 21, 2019) (online at https://twitter.com/VicToensing/status/1108751525239762944); Victoria Toensing, Twitter (Mar. 24, 2019) (online at https://twitter.com/VicToensing/status/1109882728101625856).

[81] Retainer Letter, diGenova & Toensing, LLP, Yuriy Lutsenko, and Kostiantyn Kulyk (Apr. 12, 2019); Retainer Letter, diGenova & Toensing, LLP, Viktor Shokin (Apr. 15, 2019).

[82] On April 12, less than a week after the latest piece in *The Hill*, Ms. Toensing signed a retainer agreement between diGenova & Toensing, LLP, Mr. Lutsenko, and his former deputy Kostiantyn Kulyk, two of the primary sources for Mr. Solomon's articles. The Committees' obtained a copy of this document which is not signed by the Ukrainians, but a spokesman for Ms. Toensing and Mr. diGenova confirmed that the firm represented Mr. Lutsenko. *See Giuliani Weighed Doing Business with Ukrainian Government*, Wall Street Journal (Nov. 27, 2019) (online at www.wsj.com/articles/giuliani-weighed-doing-business-with-ukrainian-government-11574890951).

The first paragraph of the retainer agreement sets forth the services to be provided by diGenova & Toensing, LLP to their Ukrainian clients:

Yurii Lutsenko and Kostiantyn Kulyk ("Clients") hereby engage the firm of diGenova & Toensing, LLP ("Firm" or "Attorneys") to represent them in connection with recovery and return to the Ukraine government of funds illegally embezzeled from that country and providing assistance to meet and discuss with United States government officials the evidence of illegal conduct in Ukraine regarding the United States, for example, interference in the 2016 U.S. elections.

See Retainer Letter, diGenova & Toensing, LLP, Yuriy Lutsenko, and Kostiantyn Kulyk (Apr. 12, 2019).

The scope of representation—which includes representing Mr. Lutsenko and Mr. Kulyk in meetings with U.S. officials regarding Ukrainian interference in the 2016 U.S. elections—mirrors the allegations reported in *The*

Hill, pursued by Mr. Giuliani on behalf of President Trump, and pushed by the President on his July 25 call with President Zelensky. According to the retainer agreement, Mr. Lutsenko was to pay diGenova & Toensing, LLP $25,000 per month, plus costs, for four months for this work. *See* Retainer Letter, diGenova & Toensing, LLP, Yuriy Lutsenko, and Kostiantyn Kulyk (Apr. 12, 2019).

On April 12, the same day Ms. Toensing signed the retainer agreement with Mr. Lutsenko, phone records show contacts between Ms. Toensing, Mr. Giuliani, and Mr. Parnas, as well as contacts between Mr. Parnas and Mr. Solomon, and Mr. Parnas and Rep. Nunes. In addition, among these calls are contacts between Mr. Giuliani and a phone number associated with the Office of Management and Budget (OMB), an unidentified number ("-1"), and a phone number associated with the White House:

Date	Connecting Time (ET)	Duration of Call	Caller	Recipient	Source
04/12/19	9:48:57	0:24	Toensing, Victoria	Parnas, Lev	AT&T Document Production, Bates ATTHPSCI_20190930-00908
04/12/19	10:40:19	3:25	Parnas, Lev	Toensing, Victoria	AT&T Document Production, Bates ATTHPSCI_20190930-00909
04/12/19	11:05:25	0:03	OMB Phone Number	Giuliani, Rudy	AT&T Document Production, Bates ATTHPSCI_20190930-02134
04/12/19	11:05:39	12:10	"-1"	Giuliani, Rudy	AT&T Document Production, Bates ATTHPSCI_20190930-02134
04/12/19	13:13:49	0:12	Giuliani, Rudy	White House Phone Number	AT&T Document Production, Bates ATTHPSCI_20190930-02135
04/12/19	13:18:46	0:07	Toensing, Victoria	Giuliani, Rudy	AT&T Document Production, Bates ATTHPSCI_20190930-02135
04/12/19	13:26:54	0:24	Giuliani Partners	Parnas, Lev	AT&T Document Production, Bates ATTHPSCI_20190930-00911
04/12/19	14:11:22	0:03	"-1"	Giuliani, Rudy	AT&T Document Production, Bates ATTHPSCI_20190930-02136
04/12/19	14:11:27	0:03	OMB Phone Number	Giuliani, Rudy	AT&T Document Production, Bates ATTHPSCI_20190930-02136
04/12/19	14:17:46	0:07	Toensing, Victoria	Parnas, Lev	AT&T Document Production, Bates ATTHPSCI_20190930-00912

04/12/19	15:09:22	0:02	Parnas, Lev	Giuliani, Rudy	AT&T Document Production, Bates ATTHPSCI_20190930-00912
04/12/19	15:09:32	0:01	Parnas, Lev	Giuliani, Rudy	AT&T Document Production, Bates ATTHPSCI_20190930-00912
04/12/19	15:16:09	1:38	Parnas, Lev	Solomon, John	AT&T Document Production, Bates ATTHPSCI_20190930-00912
04/12/19	15:48:09	0:03	OMB Phone Number	Giuliani, Rudy	AT&T Document Production, Bates ATTHPSCI_20190930-02137
04/12/19	16:10:49	0:00	Parnas, Lev	Giuliani, Rudy	AT&T Document Production, Bates ATTHPSCI_20190930-00913
04/12/19	16:10:51	0:02	Parnas, Lev	Giuliani, Rudy	AT&T Document Production, Bates ATTHPSCI_20190930-00913
04/12/19	16:10:51	0:02	Parnas, Lev	Giuliani, Rudy	AT&T Document Production, Bates ATTHPSCI_20190930-00913
4/12/19	16:12:53	1:00	Parnas, Lev	Nunes, Devin	AT&T Document Production, Bates ATTHPSCI_20190930-00913
04/12/19	16:54:11	0:00	Nunes, Devin	Parnas, Lev	AT&T Document Production, Bates ATTHPSCI_20190930-00913
04/12/19	16:54:13	0:02	Nunes, Devin	Parnas, Lev	AT&T Document Production, Bates ATTHPSCI_20190930-00913
04/12/19	17:07:20	1:27	Parnas, Lev	Giuliani, Rudy	AT&T Document Production, Bates ATTHPSCI_20190930-00913
04/12/19	17:17:36	7:52	Sekulow, Jay	Giuliani, Rudy	AT&T Document Production, Bates ATTHPSCI_20190930-03565
04/12/19	17:24:05	1:49	Parnas, Lev	Solomon, John	AT&T Document Production, Bates ATTHPSCI_20190930-00914

04/12/19	17:26:48	0:28	Parnas, Lev	Solomon, John	AT&T Document Production, Bates ATTHPSCI_20190930-00914
04/12/19	17:30:19	8:34	Parnas, Lev	Nunes, Devin	AT&T Document Production, Bates ATTHPSCI_20190930-00914
04/12/19	17:39:25	0:53	Parnas, Lev	Solomon, John	AT&T Document Production, Bates ATTHPSCI_20190930-00914
04/12/19	19:56:43	5:03	Giuliani, Rudy	White House Phone Number	AT&T Document Production, Bates ATTHPSCI_20190930-02139

Mr. Lutsenko and Mr. Kulyk were not the only Ukrainians who appear to have engaged with diGenova & Toensing, LLP. On April 15, Ms. Toensing signed another retainer agreement between diGenova & Toensing, LLP and former Prosecutor General Viktor Shokin. Again, the Committees' copy is not signed by Mr. Shokin. A spokesman for Ms. Toensing and Mr. diGenova acknowledged that the firm represented "Ukrainian whistleblowers," but claimed that the identities of those clients (other that Mr. Lutsenko) are protected by attorney-client privilege. *See Giuliani Weighed Doing Business with Ukrainian Government*, Wall Street Journal (Nov. 27, 2019) (online at www.wsj.com/articles/giuliani-weighed-doing-business-with-ukrainian-government-11574890951).

The first paragraph of the retainer agreement outlined the services to be rendered:

Viktor Shokin ("Client") hereby engaged the firm diGenova & Toensing, LLP ("Firm" or "Attorneys") to represent him for the purpose of collecting evidence regarding his March 2016 firing as Prosecutor General of Ukraine and the role of then-Vice President Joe Biden in such firing, and presenting such evidence to U.S. and foreign authorities.

See Retainer Letter, diGenova & Toensing, LLP, Viktor Shokin (Apr. 15, 2019).

The subject matter of the agreement—the activities of Vice President Biden—again echo Mr. Solomon's pieces in *The Hill*, conspiracy theories spread by Mr. Giuliani on behalf of President Trump, and the President's statements about Vice President Biden on his July 25 call with President Zelensky.

[83] AT&T Document Production, Bates ATTHPSCI_20190930-00947-ATTHPSCI_20190930-00950.

[84] AT&T Document Production, Bates ATTHPSCI_20190930-02222-ATTHPSCI_20190930-02223.

Date	Connecting Time (ET)	Duration of Call	Caller	Recipient
04/23/19	14:00:56	1:50	Giuliani, Rudy	Parnas, Lev
04/23/19	14:15:18	0:18	Giuliani, Rudy	White House Phone Number
04/23/19	14:15:43	0:11	Giuliani, Rudy	White House Phone Number
04/23/19	15:20:17	0:11	Giuliani, Rudy	White House Phone Number
04/23/19	15:50:23	8:28	"-1"	Giuliani, Rudy

[85] AT&T Document Production, Bates ATTHPSCI_20190930-02224.

[86] Rudy Giuliani, Twitter (Apr. 23, 2019) (online at https://twitter.com/RudyGiuliani/status/1120798794692612097).

[87] *Giuliani Fires Back at Hillary Clinton's Remarks on Mueller Probe*, Fox News (Apr. 24, 2019) (online at www.youtube.com/watch?v=FDtg8z12Q7s&feature=youtu.be).

[88] AT&T Document Production, Bates ATTHPSCI_20190930-02229- ATTHPSCI_20190930-02237.

Date	Connecting Time (ET)	Duration of Call	Caller	Recipient
04/24/19	7:17:48	0:42	OMB Phone Number	Giuliani, Rudy
04/24/19	7:47:57	0:37	Giuliani, Rudy	White House Phone Number
04/24/19	7:48:39	0:21	Giuliani, Rudy	White House Phone Number
04/24/19	7:49:00	0:31	OMB Phone Number	Giuliani, Rudy
04/24/19	7:49:00	0:20	Giuliani, Rudy	White House Phone Number
04/24/19	7:49:35	4:53	Giuliani, Rudy	White House Phone Number
04/24/19	7:54:52	0:24	Giuliani, Rudy	White House Phone Number
04/24/19	13:03:50	13:44	OMB Phone Number	Giuliani, Rudy
04/24/19	16:42:52	8:00	Parnas, Lev	Giuliani, Rudy
04/24/19	18:38:57	0:44	Giuliani, Rudy	White House Phone Number
04/24/19	18:42:43	8:42	"-1"	Giuliani, Rudy
04/24/19	20:09:14	0:06	Giuliani, Rudy	White House Phone Number
04/24/19	20:12:08	3:15	White House #	Giuliani, Rudy

[89] Yovanovitch Hearing Tr. at 31-32.

[90] Yovanovitch Dep. Tr. at 22.

[91] Yovanovitch Hearing Tr. at 21-22.

[92] Yovanovitch Dep. Tr. at 129.

[93] Yovanovitch Dep. Tr. at 139.

[94] Yovanovitch Hearing Tr. at 28.

[95] Sondland Hearing Tr. at 21.

[96] Yovanovitch Hearing Tr. at 131-132.

[97] Hale Dep. Tr. at 16-17; Hale Dep. Tr. at 112-113; Yovanovitch Hearing Tr. at 21.

[98] "I only met her when I took this job, but immediately I understood that we had an exceptional officer doing exceptional work at a very critical embassy in Kyiv. And during my visits to Kyiv, I was very impressed by

what she was doing there, to the extent that I asked her if she'd be willing to stay, if that was a possibility, because we had a gap coming up." Cooper-Hale Hearing Tr. at 63.

[99] Cooper-Hale Hearing Tr. at 64.

[100] *Biography of Marie L. Yovanovitch*, Department of State (online at https://2009-2017.state.gov/r/pa/ei/biog/261588.htm).

[101] McKinley Transcribed Interview Tr. at 37.

[102] Reeker Dep. Tr. at 26.

[103] Kent Dep. Tr. at 188-189.

[104] Yovanovitch Hearing Tr. at 18-19.

[105] Yovanovitch Hearing Tr. at 18-19.

[106] Hill-Holmes Hearing Tr. at 18-19, 45-46.

[107] Holmes Dep. Tr. at 142.

[108] *What "Corruption" Means in the Impeachment Hearings*, New Yorker (Nov. 16, 2019) (online at www.newyorker.com/news/our-columnists/the-corruption-of-the-word-corruption-and-so-much-else-amid-the-impeachment-hearings).

[109] 22 U.S.C. § 3941.

[110] Yovanovitch Hearing Tr. at 110-111.

[111] Ambassador Yovanovitch said: "Although then and now I have always understood that I served at the pleasure of the President, I still find it difficult to comprehend that foreign and private interests were able to undermine U.S. interests in this way. Individuals who apparently felt stymied by our efforts to promote stated U.S. policy against corruption, that is, to do our mission, were able to successfully conduct a campaign of disinformation against a sitting ambassador using unofficial back channels. As various witnesses have recounted, they shared baseless allegations with the President and convinced him to remove his ambassador despite the fact that the State Department fully understood that the allegations were false and the sources highly suspect." Yovanovitch Hearing Tr. at 22.

[112] Hill-Holmes Hearing Tr. at 78-79.

[113] Yovanovitch Dep. Tr. at 313-314.

[114] Yovanovitch Hearing Tr. at 22.

[115] Kent-Taylor Hearing Tr. at 25.

[116] Kent. Dep. Tr. at 131-132.

[117] Kent-Taylor Hearing Tr. at 31-32.

[118] *Comedian Volodymyr Zelensky Unseats Incumbent in Ukraine's Presidential Election, Exit Polls Show*, Washington Post (Apr. 21, 2019) (online at www.washingtonpost.com/world/as-ukraine-votes-in-presidential-runoff-a-comedian-looks-to-unseat-the-incumbent/2019/04/21/b7d69a38-603f-11e9-bf24-db4b9fb62aa2_story.html).

[119] *Comedian Volodymyr Zelensky Unseats Incumbent in Ukraine's Presidential Election, Exit Polls Show*, The Washington Post (Apr. 21, 2019) (online at www.washingtonpost.com/world/as-ukraine-votes-in-presidential-runoff-a-comedian-looks-to-unseat-the-incumbent/2019/04/21/b7d69a38-603f-11e9-bf24-db4b9fb62aa2_story.html).

[120] The White House, *Memorandum of Telephone Conversation* (Apr. 21, 2019) (online at https://assets.documentcloud.org/documents/6550349/First-Trump-Ukraine-Call.pdf).

[121] The White House, *Memorandum of Telephone Conversation* (Apr. 21, 2019) (online at https://assets.documentcloud.org/documents/6550349/First-Trump-Ukraine-Call.pdf).

[122] *Conflicting White House accounts of 1ˢᵗ Trump-Zelenskiy call*, The Associated Press (Nov. 15, 2019) (online at https://apnews.com/2f3c9910e0a14ec08d6d76ed93148059).

[123] The White House, *Memorandum of Telephone Conversation* (Apr. 21, 2019) (online at https://assets.documentcloud.org/documents/6550349/First-Trump-Ukraine-Call.pdf).

[124] The White House, *Memorandum of Telephone Conversation* (Apr. 21, 2019) (online at https://assets.documentcloud.org/documents/6550349/First-Trump-Ukraine-Call.pdf).

[125] The White House, *Memorandum of Telephone Conversation* (Apr. 21, 2019) (online at https://assets.documentcloud.org/documents/6550349/First-Trump-Ukraine-Call.pdf).

[126] The White House, *Memorandum of Telephone Conversation* (Apr. 21, 2019) (online at https://assets.documentcloud.org/documents/6550349/First-Trump-Ukraine-Call.pdf).

[127] The White House, *Memorandum of Telephone Conversation* (Apr. 21, 2019) (online at https://assets.documentcloud.org/documents/6550349/First-Trump-Ukraine-Call.pdf).

[128] The White House, *Memorandum of Telephone Conversation* (Apr. 21, 2019) (online at https://assets.documentcloud.org/documents/6550349/First-Trump-Ukraine-Call.pdf).

[129] The White House, *Memorandum of Telephone Conversation* (Apr. 21, 2019) (online at https://assets.documentcloud.org/documents/6550349/First-Trump-Ukraine-Call.pdf).

[130] The White House, *Memorandum of Telephone Conversation* (Apr. 21, 2019) (online at https://assets.documentcloud.org/documents/6550349/First-Trump-Ukraine-Call.pdf).

[131] Williams Dep. Tr. at 36.

[132] Williams Dep. Tr. at 37.

[133] Williams Dep. Tr. at 36.

[134] *Fox & Friends*, Fox News (Apr. 24, 2019) (online at www.youtube.com/watch?v=FDtg8z12Q7s#action=share).

[135] *Why Giuliani Singled Out 2 Ukrainian Oligarchs to Help Look for Dirt*, New York Times (Nov. 25, 2019) (online at www.nytimes.com/2019/11/25/us/giuliani-ukraine-oligarchs.html).

[136] *Ukraine's Unlikely President, Promising a New Style of Politics, Gets a Taste of Trump's Swamp,* New Yorker (Oct. 25, 2019) (online at www.newyorker.com/magazine/2019/11/04/how-trumps-emissaries-put-pressure-on-ukraines-new-president).

[137] *Why Giuliani Singled Out 2 Ukrainian Oligarchs to Help Look for Dirt*, New York Times (Nov. 25, 2019) (online at www.nytimes.com/2019/11/25/us/giuliani-ukraine-oligarchs.html).

[138] AT&T Document Production, Bates ATTHPSCI_20190930_00947; ATTHPSCI_20190930_00949; ATTHPSCI_20190930_02222; ATTHPSCI_20190930_02223.

[139] *Joe Biden Announces 2020 Run for President, After Months of Hesitation*, New York Times (Apr. 25, 2019) (online at www.nytimes.com/2019/04/25/us/politics/joe-biden-2020-announcement.html).

[140] *How the Obama White House Engaged Ukraine to Give Russia Collusion Narrative an Early Boost*, The Hill (Apr. 25, 2019) (online at https://thehill.com/opinion/white-house/440730-how-the-obama-white-house-engaged-ukraine-to-give-russia-collusion).

[141] Holmes Dep. Tr. at 17.

[142] Holmes Dep. Tr. at 116.

[143] Holmes Dep. Tr. at 116.

[144] AT&T Document Production, Bates ATTHPSCI_20190930_02245.

[145] AT&T Document Production, Bates ATTHPSCI_20190930_02245.

[146] *Sean Hannity Interviews Trump on Biden, Russia Probe, FISA Abuse, Comey*, Fox News (Apr. 26, 2019) (online at www.realclearpolitics.com/video/2019/04/26/full_video_sean_hannity_interviews_trump_on_biden_russia_probe_fisa_abuse_comey.html).

[147] Holmes Dep. Tr. at 55-56.

[148] *Sean Hannity Interviews Trump on Biden, Russia Probe, FISA Abuse, Comey*, Fox News (Apr. 26, 2019) (online at www.realclearpolitics.com/video/2019/04/26/full_video_sean_hannity_interviews_trump_on_biden_russia_probe_fisa_abuse_comey.html). As discussed later in this report, on the morning of September 25, 2019, the Department of Justice would quickly issue a statement after President Trump released the record of his July 25 call with President Zelensky. The statement asserted that that Attorney General Barr had not engaged on Ukraine matters at the President's request:

> The President has not spoken with the Attorney General about having Ukraine investigate anything relating to former Vice President Biden or his son. The President has not asked the Attorney General to contact Ukraine—on this or any other matter. The Attorney General has not communicated with Ukraine—on this or any other subject.

[149] *Cleaning Up Ukraine in the Shadow of Trump*, The Financial Times (Nov. 28, 2019) (online at www.ft.com/content/eb8e4004-1059-11ea-a7e6-62bf4f9e548a).

[150] *Cleaning Up Ukraine in the Shadow of Trump*, The Financial Times (Nov. 28, 2019) (online at www.ft.com/content/eb8e4004-1059-11ea-a7e6-62bf4f9e548a).

[151] *Biden Faces Conflict of Interest Questions That Are Being Promoted by Trump and Allies*, New York Times (May 1, 2019) (online at www.nytimes.com/2019/05/01/us/politics/biden-son-ukraine.html).

[152] *Transcript: Fox News Interview with President Trump*, Fox News (May 7, 2019) (online at www.foxnews.com/politics/transcript-fox-news-interview-with-president-trump).

[153] *Transcript: Fox News Interview with President Trump*, Fox News (May 7, 2019) (online at www.foxnews.com/politics/transcript-fox-news-interview-with-president-trump).

[154] *Foreign Affairs Issue Launch with Former Vice President Joe Biden*, Council on Foreign Relations (Jan. 23, 2018) (online at: www.cfr.org/event/foreign-affairs-issue-launch-former-vice-president-joe-biden).

[155] *Ukraine Ousts Viktor Shokin, Top Prosecutor, and Political Stability Hangs in the Balance*, New York Times (Mar. 29, 2016) (online at www.nytimes.com/2016/03/30/world/europe/political-stability-in-the-balance-as-ukraine-ousts-top-prosecutor.html).

[156] Yovanovitch Hearing Tr. at 50; Kent-Taylor Hearing Tr. at 115.

[157] *Trump Says He'd Consider Accepting Information from Foreign Governments on His Opponents*, The Washington Post (June 12, 2019) (online at www.washingtonpost.com/politics/trump-says-hed-consider-accepting-dirt-from-foreign-governments-on-his-opponents/2019/06/12/b84ba860-8d5c-11e9-8f69-a2795fca3343_story.html).

[158] AT&T Document Production, Bates ATTHPSCI_20190930_02313.

[159] AT&T Document Production, Bates ATTHPSCI_20190930_02314; ATTHPSCI_20190930_02316; ATTHPSCI_20190930_02318; ATTHPSCI 20190930 01000.

[160] Kent Dep. Tr. at 137.

[161] Kent Dep. Tr. at 137.

[162] Kent Dep. Tr. at 137.

[163] *Rudy Giuliani Plans Ukraine Trip to Push for Inquiries That Could Help Trump*, New York Times (May 9, 2019) (online at www.nytimes.com/2019/05/09/us/politics/giuliani-ukraine-trump.html).

[164] *Rudy Giuliani Plans Ukraine Trip to Push for Inquiries That Could Help Trump*, New York Times (May 9, 2019) (online at www.nytimes.com/2019/05/09/us/politics/giuliani-ukraine-trump.html).

[165] *Rudy Giuliani Plans Ukraine Trip to Push for Inquiries That Could Help Trump*, New York Times (May 9, 2019) (online at www.nytimes.com/2019/05/09/us/politics/giuliani-ukraine-trump.html).

[166] *Rudy Giuliani Plans Ukraine Trip to Push for Inquiries That Could Help Trump*, New York Times (May 9, 2019) (online at www.nytimes.com/2019/05/09/us/politics/giuliani-ukraine-trump.html).

[167] *Rudy Giuliani Plans Ukraine Trip to Push for Inquiries That Could Help Trump*, New York Times (May 9, 2019) (online at www.nytimes.com/2019/05/09/us/politics/giuliani-ukraine-trump.html).

[168] *Rudy Giuliani Plans Ukraine Trip to Push for Inquiries That Could Help Trump*, New York Times (May 9, 2019) (online at www.nytimes.com/2019/05/09/us/politics/giuliani-ukraine-trump.html).

[169] *Rudy Giuliani Plans Ukraine Trip to Push for Inquiries That Could Help Trump*, New York Times (May 9, 2019) (online at www.nytimes.com/2019/05/09/us/politics/giuliani-ukraine-trump.html).

[170] *Trump's Interest in Stirring Ukraine Investigations Sows Confusion in Kiev*, Washington Post (May 11, 2019) (online at www.washingtonpost.com/world/europe/trumps-interest-stirring-ukraine-investigations-sows-confusion-in-kiev/2019/05/11/cb94f7f4-73ea-11e9-9331-30bc5836f48e_story.html).

[171] AT&T Document Production, Bates ATTHPSCI_20190930_02321; ATTHPSCI_20190930_02322.

[172] AT&T Document Production, Bates ATTHPSCI_20190930_02320, 02321, 02322, 02323, 03612.

[173] AT&T Document Production, Bates ATTHPSCI_20190930_03614; ATTHPSCI_20190930_02326; ATTHPSCI_20190930_02327; ATTHPSCI_20190930_03614.

[174] Rudy Giuliani, Twitter (May 9, 2019) (online at https://twitter.com/RudyGiuliani/status/1126701386224156673).

[175] *Giuliani: "Massive Collusion" Between DNC, Obama Admin, Clinton People & Ukraine To Create False Info About Trump*, Real Clear Politics (May 10, 2019) (online at www.realclearpolitics.com/video/2019/05/10/giuliani_massive_collusion_between_dnc_obama_admin_clinton_peo ple__ukraine_to_create_false_info_about_trump.html).

[176] Rudy Giuliani, Twitter (May 10, 2019) (online at https://twitter.com/rudygiuliani/status/1126858889209831424?lang=en).

[177] AT&T Document Production, Bates ATTHPSCI_20190930_02334.

[178] Volker Transcribed Interview Tr. at 227; *see also* Volker Transcribed Interview Tr. at 32-33, 36 (describing the allegations).

[179] Volker Transcribed Interview Tr. at 227.

[180] AT&T Document Production, Bates ATTHPSCI_20190930_02334.

[181] AT&T Document Production, Bates ATTHPSCI_20190930_02335.

[182] AT&T Document Production, Bates ATTHPSCI_20190930_02335.

[183] AT&T Document Production, Bates ATTHPSCI_20190930_02335.

[184] *Trump: Discussing a Biden Probe with Barr Would Be 'Appropriate,'* Politico (May 10, 2019) (online at www.politico.com/story/2019/05/10/trump-biden-ukraine-barr-1317601).

[185] *Trump Denies Sending Rudy Giuliani to Ukraine to Push Biden, Election Probes*, CNBC (Nov. 27, 2019) (online at www.cnbc.com/2019/11/27/trump-denies-sending-rudy-giuliani-to-ukraine-to-push-biden-election-probes.html).

[186] *Remarks by President Trump and President Niinisto of the Republic of Finland in Joint Press Conference*, The White House (Oct. 2, 2019) (online at www.whitehouse.gov/briefings-statements/remarks-president-trump-president-niinisto-republic-finland-joint-press-conference/).

[187] *Remarks by President Trump before Marine One Departure*, The White House (Oct. 4, 2019) (online at www.whitehouse.gov/briefings-statements/remarks-president-trump-marine-one-departure-68/).

[188] *Giuliani: I didn't go to Ukraine to start an investigation, there already was one*, Fox News (May 11, 2019) (online at https://video.foxnews.com/v/6035385372001/#sp=show-clips).

[189] *Trump: Discussing a Biden probe with Barr would be 'appropriate'*, Politico (May 10, 2019) (online at www.politico.com/story/2019/05/10/trump-biden-ukraine-barr-1317601) (documenting Giuliani text message).

[190] *Trump: Discussing a Biden probe with Barr would be 'appropriate'*, Politico (May 10, 2019) (online at www.politico.com/story/2019/05/10/trump-biden-ukraine-barr-1317601) (documenting Giuliani text message).

[191] Donald J. Trump, Twitter (May 3, 2019) (online at https://twitter.com/realDonaldTrump/status/1124359594418032640)

[192] Kent Dep. Tr. at 338-339.

[193] *Remarks by President Trump and Prime Minister Orban of Hungary Before Bilateral Meeting,* The White House (May 13, 2019) (online at www.whitehouse.gov/briefings-statements/remarks-president-trump-prime-minister-orban-hungary-bilateral-meeting/).

[194] *In Hungary, a Freewheeling Trump Ambassador Undermines U.S. Diplomat's*, New York Times (Oct. 22, 2019) (online at www.nytimes.com/2019/10/22/world/europe/david-cornstein-hungary-trump-orban.html); *Hungarian prime minister earns rare rebuke from European bloc that has long backed him*, The Washington Post (Mar. 20, 2019) (online at www.washingtonpost.com/world/europe/hungarys-orban-earns-rare-rebuke-from-european-bloc-that-has-long-backed-him/2019/03/20/83be110a-4b17-11e9-8cfc-2c5d0999c21e_story.html).

[195] Kent Dep. Tr. at 339.

[196] *Remarks by President Trump and Prime Minister Orban of Hungary Before Bilateral Meeting,* The White House (May 13, 2019) (online at www.whitehouse.gov/briefings-statements/remarks-president-trump-prime-minister-orban-hungary-bilateral-meeting/).

[197] Kent Dep. Tr. at 253.

[198] Kent Dep. Tr. at 254.

[199] Williams Dep. Tr. at 37-38.

[200] Vindman-Williams Hearing Tr. at 14. Other witnesses testified that Vice President Pence may not have been able to attend on account of scheduling issues. *See* Hill Dep. Tr. at 316 ("there was a lot of scheduling issues" regarding the attempts to schedule the Vice President's participation in the delegation); Kent Dep. Tr. at 189-191 (Vice President Pence was not available); Volker Transcribed Interview Tr. at 288-290, 293 (Volker "wasn't surprised" Pence could not make it and assumed it was a matter of scheduling). However, Ms. Williams was the only staff member in the Office of the Vice President to testify before the Committees, and the only witness to testify to having heard an explanation from Vice President Pence's staff about why Vice President Pence did not attend the inauguration.

[201] Williams Dep. Tr. at 39.

[202] Holmes Dep. Tr. at 37.

[203] Holmes Dep. Tr. at 37.

[204] Rudy Giuliani, Twitter (May 18, 2019) (online at https://twitter.com/RudyGiuliani/status/1129761193755910144)

[205] *Kolomoisky: We Called Varkuch and Asked: 'Do You Support Zelensky or No?'*, Pravda (May 27, 2019) (online at www.pravda.com.ua/rus/articles/2019/05/27/7216183/).

[206] *Kolomoisky: We Called Varkuch and Asked: 'Do You Support Zelensky or No?'*, Pravda (May 27, 2019) (online at www.pravda.com.ua/rus/articles/2019/05/27/7216183/).

[207] Holmes Dep. Tr. at 16.

[208] Volker Transcribed Interview Tr. at 288-290; Vindman Dep. Tr. at 125.

[209] Holmes Dep. Tr. at 101.

[210] Holmes Dep. Tr. at 18.

[211] Holmes Dep. Tr. 17-18.

[212] Holmes Dep. Tr. at 18.

[213] Holmes Dep. Tr. at 18.

[214] Hill-Holmes Hearing Tr. at 61.

[215] Vindman-Williams Hearing Tr. at 26.

[216] Hill-Holmes Hearing Tr. at 61.

[217] Vindman-Williams Hearing Tr. at 26

[218] Vindman-Williams Hearing Tr. at 26

[219] Vindman-Williams Hearing Tr. at 26; David Holmes separately testified that Lt. Col. Vindman "made a general point about the importance of Ukraine to our national security, and he said it's very important that the Zelensky administration stay out of U.S. domestic politics." Hill-Holmes Hearing Tr. at 61.

[220] Volker Transcribed Interview Tr. at 30.

[221] Volker Transcribed Interview Tr. at 29-30.

[222] Kent Dep. Tr. at 193.

[223] Anderson Dep. Tr. at 15, 54. Ambassador Sondland testified that he did not specifically recall who arranged the May 23 meeting and conjectured that "either Rick Perry or I reached out to someone at the NSC saying: Doesn't the President want a briefing about the inauguration. And I think—I think it was Perry, if I recall correctly, that got it nailed down." Sondland Dep. Tr. at 87.

[224] Volker Transcribed Interview Tr. at 29, 303; Vindman Dep. Tr. at 168.

[225] Hill Dep. Tr. at 311.

[226] Hill Dep. Tr. at 308.

[227] Hill Dep. Tr. at 308.

[228] Hill Dep. Tr. at 309-310.

[229] Hill Dep. Tr. at 309-310.

[230] Hill Dep. Tr. at 309-310.

[231] *Nunes Ally Kash Patel Who Fought Russia Probe Gets Senior White House National Security Job*, The Daily Beast (July 31, 2019) (online at www.thedailybeast.com/kash-patel-devin-nunes-ally-who-fought-russia-probe-gets-senior-white-house-national-security-job).

[232] Volker Transcribed Interview Tr. at 304.

[233] Sondland Dep. Tr. at 25.

[234] Sondland Dep. Tr. at 25.

[235] Volker Transcribed Interview Tr. at 304.

[236] Sondland Dep. Tr. at 337; Volker Transcribed Interview Tr. at 304; Hill Dep. Tr. at 320-321 (describing Volker's readout); Croft Dep. Tr. at 90 (describing Volker's readout); Anderson Dep. Tr. at 57 (describing Volker's readout).

[237] Volker Transcribed Interview Tr. at 305.

[238] Volker Transcribed Interview Tr. at 305.

[239] Sondland Dep. Tr. at 62; Volker Transcribed Interview Tr. 305; Morrison-Volker Hearing Tr. at 40.

[240] Sondland Hearing Tr. at 71.

[241] Sondland Dep. Tr. at 26. *See also* Sondland Dep. Tr. at 87-90.

[242] Morrison-Volker Hearing Tr. at 131.

[243] Sondland Hearing Tr. at 167.

[244] In addition to the testimony cited in this paragraph, *see also* Hill Dep. Tr. at 113; Hale Dep. Tr. at 90; Taylor Dep. Tr. at 58, 285; and Reeker Dep. Tr. at 148.

[245] Kent Dep. Tr. at 195.

[246] Croft Dep. Tr. at 91.

[247] Hale Dep. Tr. at 73.

[248] Sondland Dep. Tr. at 151-152.

[249] Hill Dep. Tr. at 59-60.

[250] Sondland Hearing Tr. at 24, 27, 123-124, 125-126.

[251] Sondland Hearing Tr. at 27-30.

[252] Sondland Hearing Tr. at 22.

[253] Sondland Dep. Tr. at 77-78.

[254] Hill-Holmes Hearing Tr. at 94.

[255] Hill Dep. Tr. at 127. According to call records obtained by the Committee, Mr. Giuliani connected with Ambassador Bolton's office three times for brief calls of under a minute between April 23 and May 10, 2019—a time period that corresponds with the recall of Ambassador Yovanovitch and the acceleration of Mr. Giuliani's efforts, on behalf of President Trump, to pressure Ukraine into opening investigations that would benefit his reelection campaign. AT&T Document Production, Bates ATTHPSCI_20190930_02224, 02322, 23330.

[256] Hill Dep. Tr. at 127.

[257] Anderson Dep. Tr. at 15.

[258] Anderson Dep. Tr. at 15.

[259] Anderson Dep. Tr. at 101.

[260] Hill Dep. Tr. at 127-128.

[261] Hill Dep. Tr. at 116-117.

[262] Hill Dep. Tr. at 130.

[263] Anderson Dep. Tr. at 16.

[264] Anderson Dep. Tr. at 16; Taylor Dep. Tr. at 24-25, 167.

[265] Taylor Dep. Tr. at 25.

[266] Taylor Dep. Tr. at 25.

[267] Taylor Dep. Tr. at 25.

[268] Anderson Dep. Tr. at 16-17.

[269] Sondland Dep. Tr. at 240.

[270] *ABC News' Oval Office Interview with President Trump*, ABC News (June 13, 2019) (online at https://abcnews.go.com/Politics/abc-news-oval-office-interview-president-donald-trump/story?id=63688943).

[271] *ABC News' Oval Office Interview with President Trump*, ABC News (June 13, 2019) (online at https://abcnews.go.com/Politics/abc-news-oval-office-interview-president-donald-trump/story?id=63688943) (emphasis added).

[272] Rudy Giuliani, Twitter (June 21, 2019) (online at https://twitter.com/RudyGiuliani/status/1142085975230898176)

[273] Hill-Holmes Hearing Tr. at 77.

[274] Hill-Holmes Hearing Tr. at 91.

[275] Hill Dep. Tr. at 222-223.

[276] Hill-Holmes Hearing Tr. at 92.

[277] Hill-Holmes Hearing Tr. at 93.

[278] Office of the United Nations High Commissioner for Human Rights, *Report on the Human Rights Situation in Ukraine: 16 November 2018 to 15 February 2019* (online at https://www.ohchr.org/Documents/Countries/UA/ReportUkraine16Nov2018-15Feb2019.pdf); Office of the United Nations High Commissioner for Human Rights, *Report on the Human Rights Situation in Ukraine: 16 August to 15 November 2017* (Dec. 12, 2017) (online at https://www.ohchr.org/Documents/Countries/UA/UAReport20th_EN.pdf); Office of the United Nations High Commissioner for Human Rights, *Conflict in Ukraine Enters its Fourth Year with No End in Sight* (June 13, 2017) (online at www.ohchr.org/EN/NewsEvents/Pages/DisplayNews.aspx?NewsID=21730&LangID=E). These figures do not include the 298 civilians of 13 different nationalities killed aboard Malaysia Airlines Flight 17, which a Dutch-led joint investigation found was shot down by a Russian missile system from a Russian military unit, a conclusion supported by U.S. intelligence. *See* Dutch Safety Board, *Report on the Crash of Malaysia Airlines Flight MH17* (Oct. 13, 2015) (online at www.onderzoeksraad.nl/en/page/3546/crash-mh17-17-july-2014); *U.S. Discloses Intelligence on Downing of Malaysian Jet*, Washington Post (July 22, 2014) (online at www.washingtonpost.com/world/national-security/us-discloses-intelligence-on-downing-of-malaysian-jet/2014/07/22/b178fe58-11e1-11e4-98ee-daea85133bc9_story.html).

[279] Ambassador Nikki Haley, United States Mission to the United Nations, *Remarks at a U.N. Security Council Briefing on Ukraine* (May 29, 2018) (online at https://usun.usmission.gov/remarks-at-a-un-security-council-briefing-on-ukraine-2/).

[280] Department of Defense, *Secretary of Defense James Mattis Remarks with President Petro Poroshenko* (Aug. 24, 2017) (online at www.defense.gov/Newsroom/Speeches/Speech/Article/1291430/secretary-of-defense-james-mattis-remarks-with-president-petro-poroshenko/).

[281] European Union External Action, *EU-Ukraine Relations Factsheet* (Sept. 30, 2019) (online at https://eeas.europa.eu/headquarters/headQuarters-homepage/4081/eu-ukraine-relations-factsheet_en); NATO, *Fact Sheet: NATO's Support to Ukraine* (Nov. 2018) (www.nato.int/nato_static_fl2014/assets/pdf/pdf_2018_11/20181106_1811-factsheet-nato-ukraine-support-eng.pdf).

[282] *DOD Announces $250M to Ukraine*, U.S. Department of Defense (June 18, 2019) (online at www.defense.gov/Newsroom/Releases/Release/Article/1879340/dod-announces-250m-to-ukraine/).

[283] Kent-Taylor Hearing Tr. at 21, 28-29, 50; Vindman Dep. Tr. at 40-41, 113; Cooper Dep. Tr. at 15-16.

[284] Taylor Dep. Tr. at 153.

[285] Croft Dep. Tr. at 16.

[286] Kent-Taylor Hearing Tr. at 30.

[287] Taylor Dep. Tr. at 20.

[288] Morrison-Volker Hearing Tr. at 11.

[289] Department of Defense and Labor, Health and Human Services, and Education Appropriations Act, 2019 and Continuing Appropriations Act, 2019, Pub. L. No. 115-245, § 9013 (2018).

[290] National Defense Authorization Act for Fiscal Year 2016, Pub. L. 114-92, § 1250 (2015), amended by the National Defense Act Authorization Act for Fiscal Year 2018, Pub. L. No. 115-91, § 1234 (2017) and most recently amended by the John S. McCain National Defense Authorization Act for Fiscal Year 2019, Pub. L. No. 115-232, § 1246 (2018).

[291] National Defense Authorization Act for Fiscal Year 2017, Pub. L. No. 114-328, § 1237 (2016); National Defense Authorization Act for Fiscal Year 2018, Pub. L. No. 115-91, § 1234 (2018); John S. McCain National Defense Authorization Act for Fiscal Year 2019, Pub. L. No. 115-232, § 1246 (2018).

[292] Letter from John C. Rood, Under Secretary of Defense for Policy, Department of Defense, to Chairman Eliot L. Engel, House Committee on Foreign Affairs (sent Feb. 28, 2019, received Mar. 5, 2019).

[293] Cooper Dep. Tr. at 27-28.

[294] National Defense Authorization Act for Fiscal Year 2016, Pub. L. No. 114-92, § 1250 (2015), as amended by the National Defense Act Authorization Act for Fiscal Year 2018, Pub. L. No. 115-91, § 1234 (2017), and most recently amended by the John S. McCain National Defense Authorization Act for Fiscal Year 2019, Pub. L. No. 115-232, § 1246 (2018).

[295] Cooper Dep. Tr. at 24.

[296] Cooper Dep. Tr. at 24.

[297] Letter from John C. Rood, Under Secretary of Defense for Policy, Department of Defense, to Chairman Eliot L. Engel, House Committee on Foreign Affairs (sent May 23, 2019, received May 28, 2019).

[298] Cooper Dep. Tr. at 31-32.

[299] *DOD Announces $250M to Ukraine*, Department of Defense (June 18, 2019) (online at www.defense.gov/Newsroom/Releases/Release/Article/1879340/dod-announces-250m-to-ukraine/).

[300] Consolidated Appropriations Act, 2019, Pub. L. No. 116-6, §7046(a)(2) (2019); Conference Report to Accompany Consolidated Appropriations Act, 2019, H.R. Rep. No. 116-9, p. 869 (2019).

[301] Consolidated Appropriations Act, 2018, Pub. L. No. 115-141, Title VIII (2017).

[302] Consolidated Appropriations Act, 2019, Pub. L. No. 116-6, §7015(c) (2019); Consolidated Appropriations Act, 2018, Pub. L. No. 115-141, § 7015(c) (2017).

[303] OMB Circular No. A-11, § 22.3 (2019) (requiring that the State Department receive clearance from OMB before notifying Congress).

[304] Sandy Dep. Tr. at 25; *DOD Announces $250M to Ukraine*, Department of Defense (June 18, 2019) (online at www.defense.gov/Newsroom/Releases/Release/Article/1879340/dod-announces-250m-to-ukraine/).

[305] *Sean Hannity Interviews Donald Trump via Telephone*, Fox News (June 19, 2019) (transcript at https://factba.se/transcript/donald-trump-interview-sean-hannity-fox-telephone-june-19-2019).

[306] Sandy Dep. Tr. at 26-27.

[307] Sandy Dep. Tr. at 27-28.

[308] Sandy Dep. Tr. at 29-30.

[309] Cooper Dep. Tr. at 33-34.

[310] Cooper Dep. Tr. at 33.

[311] Cooper Dep. Tr. at 34.

[312] Cooper Dep. Tr. at 38.

[313] Cooper Dep. Tr. at 37-38.

[314] Cooper-Hale Hearing Tr. at 14; Vindman Dep. Tr. at 178-179. *See also Stalled Ukraine Military Aid Concerned Members of Congress for Months,* CNN (Sept. 30, 2019) (online at www.cnn.com/2019/09/30/politics/ukraine-military-aid-congress/index.html) (suggesting that the State Department sought OMB's approval for $141 million in FMF funds on June 21, 2019).

[315] OMB Circular No. A-11, § 22.3 (2019) (requiring that the State Department receive clearance from OMB before notifying Congress).

[316] Williams Dep. Tr. at 54-55.

[317] Williams Dep. Tr. at 55.

[318] Blair previously served as Associate Director of National Security Programs at OMB (Blair was Duffey's predecessor), and left OMB for the White House Office of Chief of Staff with Mick Mulvaney. Sandy Dep. Tr. at 36-38.

[319] Sandy Dep. Tr. at 38-39.

[320] Sandy Dep. Tr. at 39.

[321] Morrison Dep. Tr. at 161.

[322] Sandy Dep. Tr. at 141-142.

[323] Sandy Dep. Tr. at 142.

[324] Sandy Dep. Tr. at 31-32.

[325] Sandy Dep. Tr. at 41-42.

[326] Cooper Dep. Tr. at 40; *see also* Croft Dep. Tr. at 83 ("very routine low-level business").

[327] Kent Dep. Tr. at 303-305.

[328] Taylor Dep. Tr. at 27-28.

[329] Croft Dep. Tr. at 83.

[330] Taylor Dep. Tr. at 27.

[331] Holmes Dep. Tr. at 154.

[332] Holmes Dep. Tr. at 154.

[333] Croft Dep. Tr. at 15.

[334] Cooper Dep. Tr. at 45.

[335] Kent Dep. Tr. at 304.

[336] Kent Dep. Tr. at 305.

[337] Sandy Dep. Tr. at 99; Vindman Dep. Tr. at 182.

[338] Cooper Dep. Tr. at 40. Morrison, who did not attend the sub-PCC meeting but received a readout, testified that he thought OMB announced at the July 18th meeting that the hold "covered all dollars, DOD and Department of State, and it was—it was beyond funds not yet obligated to include funds that had, in fact, been obligated but not yet expended." Morrison Dep. Tr. at 161.

[339] Cooper Dep. Tr. at 40.

[340] Cooper Dep. Tr. at 44-45.

[341] Cooper Dep. Tr. at 40.

[342] Kent Dep. Tr. at 307-308.

[343] Morrison Dep. Tr. at 162.

[344] Cooper Dep. Tr. at 46.

[345] Williams Dep. Tr. at 91-92; *see also* Morrison Dep. Tr. at 162 (testifying that representatives from OMB stated that the hold "had been imposed by the chief of staff's office" and that the hold "was at the direction of the President").

[346] Cooper Dep. Tr. at 46.

[347] Morrison Dep. Tr. at 162-163; Kent Dep. Tr. at 310; Sandy Dep. Tr. at 91.

[348] Sandy Dep. Tr. at 91.

[349] Morrison Dep. Tr. at 163.

[350] Morrison Dep. Tr. at 163.

[351] 2 U.S.C. § 601 et. seq.

[352] Williams Dep. Tr. at 91-92; Vindman Dep. Tr. at 182; Morrison Dep. Tr. at 162; Sandy Dep. Tr. at 99.

[353] Taylor Dep. Tr. at 195.

[354] Vindman Dep. Tr. at 182.

[355] Sandy Dep. Tr. at 54.

[356] Sandy Dep. Tr. at 54, 96-98.

[357] Sandy Dep. Tr. at 97.

[358] Sandy Dep. Tr. at 97.

[359] Hale Dep. Tr. at 81.

[360] Cooper Dep. Tr. at 47.

[361] Hale Dep. Tr. at 81; *see also* Vindman Dep. Tr. at 184 ("It was unanimous consensus on the approach that we had laid out in expanding engagement, the areas of cooperation that we wanted to focus on, and that this should be elevated to a PC as quickly as possible to release the hold on security assistance because we're talking about the end of July, and time these funds were set to expire September 30th, so there was some urgency to it."); Cooper Dep. Tr. at 49 ("Although each member went around to talk about how important it [security assistance] was and how they assessed the future in Ukraine based on the recent election results.").

[362] Morrison Dep. Tr. at 165.

[363] Cooper Dep. Tr. at 93.

[364] Cooper Dep. Tr. at 49, 93.

[365] *Nixon's Presidency: Crisis for Congress*, New York Times (Mar. 5, 1973) (online at www.nytimes.com/1973/03/05/archives/nixons-presidency-crisis-for-congress-this-is-the-second-of-a.html).

[366] Congressional Research Service, The Congressional Budget Act of 1974 (P.L. 93-344) Legislative History and Analysis (Feb. 26, 1975) (online at https://budgetcounsel.files.wordpress.com/2018/05/added-crs-the-congressional-budget-act-of-1974-p-l-93-344-legislative-history-and-analysis-order-code-75-94-s-february-26-1975.pdf).

[367] Calvin Coolidge Presidential Foundation, *The History of the 1921 and 1974 Budget Acts* (Nov. 26, 2014); *So... this is Nixon's Fault?*, Politico (Oct. 21, 2015) (online at www.politico.com/agenda/story/2015/10/richard-nixon-congressional-budget-control-act-history-000282).

[368] 2 U.S.C. § 683.

[369] U.S. Government Accountability Office, *Impoundment Control Act—Withholding of Funds through Their Date of Expiration* (Dec. 10, 2018) (online at www.gao.gov/assets/700/695889.pdf).

[370] Cooper Dep. Tr. at 47-48. With regard to interagency discussions about the legality of the hold, Vindman testified "[s]o I'm not a legal expert, but there was a sufficient amount of—a significant amount of work done to determine whether it was legal for OMB to be able to place the hold. ... I think at the—so my recollection in the [July 18th] sub-PCC was that the matter was raised; at the [July 23rd] PCC, it was tasked for further development; and I think by the time it got to our [July 26th] DSG it was determined that, you know, there was a legal basis to hold." Vindman Dep. Tr. at 185.

[371] Vindman Dep. Tr. at 184.

[372] Morrison Dep. Tr. at 165.

[373] Morrison Dep. Tr. at 264.

[374] Morrison Dep. Tr. at 264.

[375] Morrison Dep. Tr. at 264.

[376] Cooper Dep. Tr. at 51.

[377] Cooper Dep. Tr. at 51; *see also* Cooper Dep. Tr. at 113 (explaining that she relied on a conversation with DOD legal to form her understanding of the two proper legal mechanisms).

[378] 2 U.S.C. § 683.

[379] Cooper Dep. Tr. at 58-59.

[380] Cooper Dep. Tr. at 114.

[381] Cooper Dep. Tr. at 51, 57; Sandy Dep. Tr. at 147-148.

[382] 31 U.S.C. §§ 1511-1516.

[383] Sandy Dep. Tr. at 87, 163.

[384] Sandy Dep. Tr. at 34-35.

[385] Sandy Dep. Tr. at 51.

[386] Sandy Dep. Tr. at 23.

[387] Sandy Dep. Tr. at 33-35, 51-52.

[388] Sandy Dep. Tr. at 86.

[389] Sandy Dep. Tr. at 86-87.

[390] Sandy Dep. Tr. at 86.

[391] Sandy, Dep. Tr. at 87-88.

[392] SF-132 Apportionment Schedule FY 2019, OMB Footnote A4 (July 25, 2019).

[393] Sandy Dep. Tr. at 94.

[394] Sandy Dep. Tr. at 94.

[395] Sandy Dep. Tr. at 94-95; SF-132 Apportionment Schedule FY 2019, OMB Footnote A4 (July 25, 2019).

[396] Sandy Dep. Tr. at 87.

[397] SF-132 Apportionment Schedule FY 2019, OMB Footnote A4 (July 25, 2019); Sandy Dep. Tr. at 92.

[398] Sandy Dep. Tr. at 101.

[399] Sandy Dep. Tr. at 102.

[400] Sandy Dep. Tr. at 96-97, 102.

[401] Sandy Dep. Tr. at 101-102.

[402] Sandy Dep. Tr. at 63.

[403] Sandy Dep. Tr. at 63.

[404] Sandy Dep. Tr. at 102.

[405] Sandy Dep. Tr. at 64-65.

[406] Sandy Dep. Tr. at 65.

[407] Sandy Dep. Tr. at 108-109.

[408] Sandy Dep. Tr. at 104, 119-120.

[409] Cooper Dep. Tr. at 58-59.

[410] Cooper Dep. Tr. at 58-59.

[411] Cooper Dep. Tr. at 59.

[412] Sandy Dep. Tr. at 74-75, 127-128.

[413] SF-132 Apportionment Schedule FY 2019, OMB Footnote A4 (August 6, 2019); SF-132 Apportionment Schedule FY 2019, OMB Footnote A4 (August 15, 2019). Because of a drafting error in which OMB forgot to extend the date, the footnotes technically did not restrict DOD from spending funds between August 12 and August 20 (the date of the subsequent funding document reinstating the hold). However, Sandy testified that the hold was still in place and that the direction from the President remained unchanged. Sandy Dep. Tr. at 124-126.

[414] SF-132 Apportionment Schedule FY 2019, OMB Footnote A4 (August 6, 2019); SF-132 Apportionment Schedule FY 2019, OMB Footnote A4 (August 15, 2019); SF-132 Apportionment Schedule FY 2019, OMB Footnote A4 (August 20, 2019); SF-132 Apportionment Schedule FY 2019, OMB Footnote A4 (August 27, 2019); SF-132 Apportionment Schedule FY 2019, OMB Footnote A4 (August 31, 2019); SF-132 Apportionment Schedule FY 2019, OMB Footnote A4 (Sept. 5, 2019); SF-13; SF-132 Apportionment Schedule FY 2019, OMB Footnote A4 (Sept. 6, 2019); Apportionment Schedule FY 2019, OMB Footnote A4 (Sept. 10, 2019)

[415] Cooper Dep. Tr. at 91-92.

[416] Cooper Dep. Tr. at 92.

[417] Kent Dep. Tr. at 318-319.

[418] Sandy Dep. Tr. at 56-61.

[419] Sandy Dep. Tr. at 59-60.

[420] Sandy Dep. Tr. at 60-61.

[421] Sandy Dep. Tr. at 75, 127-128; Cooper Dep. Tr. at 57-58; *see also* Cooper Dep. Tr. at 59, ("And along the way, [the] Defense Security Cooperation Agency was expressing doubt that they could do it.").

[422] Cooper Dep. Tr. at 80-81. Ultimately, as described below, DOD was able to obligate all but approximately $35 million in USAI funds by September 30th. Sandy Dep. Tr. at 146-147.

[423] Sandy Dep. Tr. at 127-128.

[424] Sandy Dep. Tr. at 95.

[425] SF-132 Apportionment Schedule FY 2019 (August 20, 2019); SF-132 Apportionment Schedule FY 2019 (August 27, 2019); SF-132 Apportionment Schedule FY 2019 (August 31, 2019); SF-132 Apportionment Schedule FY 2019 (September 5, 2019); SF-132 Apportionment Schedule FY 2019 (September 6, 2019); SF-132 Apportionment Schedule FY 2019 (September 10, 2019).

[426] SF-132 Apportionment Schedule FY 2019 (August 20, 2019) (funds not available for obligation until August 26); SF-132 Apportionment Schedule FY 2019 (August 27, 2019) (funds not available for obligation until August 31); SF-132 Apportionment Schedule FY 2019 (August 31, 2019) (funds not available for obligation until September 5); SF-132 Apportionment Schedule FY 2019 (September 5, 2019) (funds not available for obligation until September 7); SF-132 Apportionment Schedule FY 2019 (September 6, 2019) (funds not available for obligation until September 11); SF-132 Apportionment Schedule FY 2019 (September 10, 2019) (funds not available for obligation until September 12).

[427] Sandy Dep. Tr. at 131.

[428] Sandy Dep. Tr. at 136-137.

[429] Sandy Dep. Tr. at 136.

[430] Sandy Dep. Tr. at 135-137, 150-155.

[431] Sandy Dep. Tr. at 149-152.

[432] Sandy Dep. Tr. at 152.

[433] Sandy Dep. Tr. at 150-156.

[434] Morrison Dep. Tr. at 266-267.

[435] Morrison Dep. Tr. at 268.

[436] Morrison Dep. Tr. at 267.

[437] Vindman Dep. Tr. at 186.

[438] Vindman Dep. Tr. at 186.

[439] Vindman Dep. Tr. at 187-188.

[440] Morrison Dep. Tr. at 167-168.

[441] Morrison Dep. Tr. at 170-171.

[442] Morrison Dep. Tr. at 265-266.

[443] Morrison Dep. Tr. at 172, 266.

[444] Morrison Dep. Tr. at 266.

[445] Cooper Dep. Tr. at 68.

[446] Croft Dep. Tr. at 86.

[447] Croft Dep. Tr. at 86-87.

[448] Croft Dep. Tr. at 86-87, 101.

[449] Croft Dep. Tr. at 97-98.

[450] Cooper-Hale Hearing Tr. at 14.

[451] Cooper-Hale Hearing Tr. at 13-14.

[452] Cooper-Hale Hearing Tr. at 14.

[453] Cooper-Hale Hearing Tr. at 15.

[454] Vindman Dep. Tr. at 221-22.

[455] *Trump Holds Up Ukraine Military Aid Meant to Confront Russia,* Politico (Aug. 28, 2019) (online at www.politico.com/story/2019/08/28/trump-ukraine-military-aid-russia-1689531).

[456] Holmes Dep. Tr. at 18. ("It is important to understand that a White House visit was critical to President Zelensky. He needed to demonstrate U.S. support at the highest levels, both to advance his ambitious anti-corruption agenda at home and to encourage Russian President Putin to take seriously President Zelensky's peace efforts.")

[457] Kent Dep. Tr. at 202. ("The President of the United States is a longtime acknowledged leader of the free world, and the U.S. is Ukraine's strongest supporter. And so in the Ukraine context, it's very important to show that they can establish a strong relationship with the leader of the United States. That's the Ukrainian argument and desire to have a meeting. The foreign policy argument is it's a very important country in the front lines of Russian malign influence and aggression. And the U.S. spends a considerable amount of our resources supporting Ukraine and therefore it makes sense.")

[458] Hill Dep. Tr. at 158. ("He was just generally concerned about actually not having a meeting because he felt that this would deprive Ukraine, the new Ukrainian Government of the legitimacy that it needed, especially vis-a-vis the Russians. So this gets to, you know, the heart of our national security dilemma. You know, the Ukrainians at this point, you know, are looking at a White House meeting or looking at a meeting with the President of the United States as a recognition of their legitimacy as a sovereign state.")

[459] Vindman Hearing Tr. at 38-39. ("The show of support for President Zelensky, still a brand-new President, frankly, a new politician on the Ukrainian political scene, looking to establish his bona fides as a regional and maybe even a world leader, would want to have a meeting with the United States, the most powerful country in the world and Ukraine's most significant benefactor, in order to be able to implement his agenda.")

[460] Volker Transcribed Interview Tr. at 59.

[461] Volker Transcribed Interview Tr. at 328.

[462] Taylor Dep. Opening Statement at 5. ("In late June, one of the goals of both channels was to facilitate a visit by President Zelensky to the White House for a meeting with President Trump, which President Trump had promised in his congratulatory letter of May 29. The Ukrainians were clearly eager for the meeting to happen. During a conference call with Ambassador Volker, Acting Assistant Secretary of State for European and Eurasian Affairs Phil Reeker, Secretary Perry, Ambassador Sondland, and Counsel of the U.S. Department of State Ulrich Brechbuhl on June 18, it was clear that a meeting between the two presidents was an agreed-upon goal.")

[463] Taylor Dep. Tr. at 25. ("[D]uring my subsequent communications with Ambassadors Volker and Sondland, they relayed to me that the President 'wanted to hear from Zelensky' before scheduling the meeting in the Oval Office. It was not clear to me what this meant.")

[464] Taylor Dep. Tr. at 25.

[465] Holmes Dep. Tr. at 20.

[466] Taylor Dep. Tr. at 25-26.

[467] Taylor Dep. Tr. at 25.

Q: But Ambassador Sondland made it clear not only that he didn't wish to include most of the regular interagency participants but also that no one was transcribing or monitoring the call as they added President Zelensky. What struck you as odd about that?

A: Same concern. That is, in the normal, regular channel, the State Department operations center that was putting the call together would stay on the line, in particular when you were having a conversation with the head of state, they would stay on the line, transcribe, take notes so that there could be a record of the discussion with this head of state. It is an official discussion. When he wanted to be sure that there was not, the State Department operations center agreed.

[468] Taylor Dep. Tr. at 26.

[469] Taylor Dep. Tr. at 127.

[470] Kurt Volker Document Production, Bates KV00000036 (Oct. 2, 2019).

[471] Kurt Volker Document Production, Bates KV00000036 (Oct. 2, 2019).

[472] Taylor Dep. Tr. at 26.

[473] Kurt Volker Document Production, Bates KV00000027 (Oct. 2, 2019).

[474] Volker Transcribed Interview Tr. at 242-243.

[475] Kurt Volker Document Production, Bates KV00000055 (Oct. 2, 2019).

[476] Kurt Volker Document Production, Bates KV00000027 (Oct. 2, 2019).

Taylor: Are you OK with me briefing Ulrich on these conversations? Maybe you

  have already?

Volker: I have not—please feel free

Volker: The key thing is to tee up a phone call w potus and then get visit nailed down

Taylor: I agree. Is Ze on board with a phone call?

Volker: Yes — bogdan was a little skeptical, but Zelensky was ok with it. Now we need to get it on potus schedule...

Taylor: The three amigos are on a roll. Let me know when I can help.

[477] Taylor Dep. Tr. at 65-66. ("Kurt told me that he had discussed how President Zelensky could prepare for the phone call with President Trump. And without going into—without providing me any details about the specific words, did talk about investigations in that conversation ... Kurt suggested that President Trump would like to hear about the investigations.")

[478] Morrison-Volker Hearing Tr. at 94.

Q: In the July 2nd or 3rd meeting in Toronto that you had with President Zelensky, you also mentioned investigations to him, right?

A: Yes

Q: And again, you were referring to the Burisma and the 2016 election.

A: I was thinking of Burisma and 2016.

Q: And you understood that that what the Ukrainians interpreted references to investigations to be, related to Burisma and the 2016 election?

A: I don't know specifically at that time if we had talked that specifically, Burisma/2016. That was my assumption, though, that they would've been thinking that too.

[479] Sondland Hearing Tr. at 27.

[480] Sondland Hearing Tr. at 43.

[481] Sondland Hearing Tr. at 21-22.

[482] Kent Dep. Tr. at 246.

[483] Hill-Holmes Hearing Tr. at 59.

[484] Kent Dep. Tr. at 246-47. ("I do not recall whether the follow-on conversation I had with Kurt about this was in Toronto, or whether it was subsequently at the State Department. But he did tell me that he planned to start reaching out to former Mayor of New York, Rudy Giuliani. And when I asked him why, he said that it was clear that the former mayor had influence on the President in terms of the way the President though of Ukraine. And I think by that moment in time, that was self-evidence to anyone who was working on the issues, and therefore, it made sense to try to engage the mayor. When I raised with Kurt, I said, about what? Because former Mayor Giuliani has a track record of, you know, asking for a visa for a corrupt former prosecutor. He attacked Masha, and he's tweeting that the new President needs to investigate Biden and the 2016 campaign. And Kurt's reaction or response to me at that was, well, if there's nothing there, what does it matter? And if there is something there, it should be investigated. My response to him was asking another country to investigate a prosecution for political reasons undermines our advocacy of the rule of law.")

[485] Kurt Volker Document Production, Bates KV00000036 (Oct. 2, 2019).

[486] Kurt Volker Document Production, Bates KV00000036 (Oct. 2, 2019).

[487] Kurt Volker Document Production, Bates KV00000006 (Oct. 2, 2019).

[488] Volker Transcribed Interview Tr. at 308; Kurt Volker Document Production, Bates KV00000018 (Oct. 2, 2019).

[489] Volker Transcribed Interview Tr. at 138.

[490] Sondland Hearing Tr. at 23.

[491] Hill Dep. Tr. at 63.

[492] Hill Dep. Tr. at 63-67, 155.

[493] Hill Dep. Tr. at 63-67, 155.

Q: Did anything happen in that meeting that was out of the ordinary?

A: Yes. At one point during that meeting, Ambassador Bolton was, you know, basically trying very hard not to commit to a meeting, because, you know – and, again, these meetings have to be well-prepared. They're not just something that you say, yes, we're going to have a meeting without there being a clear understanding of what the content of that meeting is going to be. … And Ambassador Bolton is always – was always very cautious and always very much, you know, by the book and was not going to certainly commit to a meeting right there and then, certainly not one where it wasn't – it was unclear what the content of the meeting would be about, what kind of issues that we would discuss that would be pertaining to Ukrainian-U.S. relations. … Then

Ambassador Sondland blurted out: Well, we have an agreement with the chief of staff for a meeting if these investigations in the energy sector start. And Ambassador Bolton immediately stiffened. He said words to the effect—I can't say word for word what he said because I was behind them sitting on the sofa with our Senior Director of Energy, and we all kind of looked up and thought that was somewhat odd. And Ambassador Bolton immediately stiffened and ended the meeting.

Q: Right then, he just ended the meeting?

A: Yeah. He said: Well, it was very nice to see you. You know, I can't discuss a meeting at this time. We'll clearly work on this. And, you know, kind of it was really nice to see you. So it was very abrupt. I mean, he looked at the clock as if he had, you know, suddenly another meeting and his time was up, but it was obvious he ended the meeting.

[494] Vindman Dep. Tr. at 17. ("The meeting proceeded well until the Ukrainians broached the subject of a meeting between the two Presidents. The Ukrainians saw this meeting as critically important in order to solidify the support for their most important international partner. Ambassador Sondland started -- when Ambassador Sondland started to speak about Ukraine delivering specific investigations in order to secure the meeting with the President, Ambassador Bolton cut the meeting short.")

[495] Volker Transcribed Interview Tr. at 310.

[496] Morrison-Volker Hearing Tr. at 23, 73, 103.

[497] Hill Dep. Tr. at 68. ("And Ambassador Sondland said to Ambassador Volker and also Secretary Perry and the other people who were with him, including the Ukrainians, to come down to—there's a room in the White House, the Ward Room, to basically talk about next steps. And that's also unusual. I mean, he meant to talk to the Ukrainians about next steps about the meeting.")

[498] Hill Dep. Tr. at 68. ("And Ambassador Bolton pulled me back as I was walking out afterwards and said: Go down to the Ward Room right now and find out what they're talking about and come back and talk to me. So I did go down.")

[499] Vindman Dep. Tr. at 64-65.

Q: And what do you recall specifically of what Sondland said to the Ukrainians—

A: Right.

Q: —in the Ward Room?

A: So that is right, the conversation unfolded with Sondland proceeding to kind of, you know, review what the deliverable would be in order to get the meeting, and he talked about the investigation into the Bidens, and, frankly, I can't 100 percent recall because I didn't take notes of it, but Burisma, that it seemed—I mean, there was no ambiguity, I guess, in my mind. He was calling for something, calling for an investigation that didn't exist into the Bidens and Burisma.

Q: Okay. Ambiguity in your mind is different from what you—

A: Sure.

Q: —actually heard?

A: Right. Correct.

Q: What did you hear Sondland say?

A: That the Ukrainians would have to deliver an investigation into the Bidens.

Q: Into the Bidens. So in the Ward Room he mentioned the word "Bidens"?

A: To the best of my recollection, yes.

Q: Okay. Did he mention 2016?

A: I don't recall.

Q: Did he mention Burisma?

A: My visceral reaction to what was being called for suggested that it was explicit. There was no ambiguity.

...

A: Again, based on my visceral reaction, it was explicit what he was calling for. And to the best of my recollection, he did specifically say "investigation of the Bidens."

...

A   So the meeting that occurred in the Ward Room referenced investigations into the Bidens, to the best of my recollection, Burisma and 2016

500 Hill Dep. Tr. at 69.

501 Hill Dep. Tr. at 151-52.

502 Hill Dep. Tr. at 69-70.

503 Vindman Dep. Tr. at 31.

Q: Did Ambassador Sondland—were the Ukrainian officials in the room when he was describing the need for these investigations in order to get the White House meeting?

A: So they were in the room initially. I think, once it became clear that there was some sort of discord amongst the government officials in the room, Ambassador Sondland asked them to step out of the room.

Q: What was the discord?

A: The fact that it was clear that I, as the representative—I, as the representative of the NSC, thought it was inappropriate and that we were not going to get involved in investigations.

Q: Did you say that to Ambassador Sondland?

A: Yes, I did.

504 Vindman Dep. Tr. at 18.

While not specifically disagreeing with any of the content of the discussion in the Ward Room, Ambassador Sondland generally disputed Dr. Hill and Lt. Col. Vindman's accounts, saying that he did not recall "any yelling or screaming ... as others have said." Sondland Hearing Tr. at 23. Neither Dr. Hill nor Lt. Col. Vindman described yelling or screaming in the meetings.

Ambassador Sondland also testified that "those recollections of protest do not square with the documentary record of our interactions with the NSC in the days and weeks that followed." Sondland Hearing Tr. at 23. As an example, Sondland provided text from a July 13 email that he sent—not to Dr. Hill, but to her successor Tim Morrison—which said that the "sole purpose" of the call between President Trump and President Zelensky was to give the former "assurances of 'new sheriff' in town." Sondland Hearing Tr. at 23. The email that Ambassador Sondland provided does not undermine Dr. Hill's or Lt. Col. Vindman's testimony that they objected to Ambassador Sondland's conduct in the Ward Room meeting. The email provided by Ambassador Sondland, however, was sent to Mr. Morrison, not Dr. Hill. Mr. Morrison had not yet started working as NSC Senior Director for Europe and was not at the July 10 meeting.

505 Vindman Dep. Tr. at 29.

A: So I heard him say that this had been coordinated with White House Chief of Staff Mr. Mick Mulvaney.

Q: What did he say about that?

A: He just said that he had had a conversation with Mr. Mulvaney, and this is what was required in order to get a meeting.

506 Hill Dep. Tr. at 69-70.

507 Kurt Volker Document Production, Bates KV00000036 (Oct. 2, 2019).

[7/10/19, 2:26:06 PM] Bill Taylor: Eager to hear if your meeting with Danyliuk and Bolton resulted in a decision on a call.

[7/10/19, 10:26:13 PM] Bill Taylor: How did the meeting go?

[7/10/19, 10:29:44 PM] Kurt Volker: Not good—lets talk—kv

508 Kurt Volker Document Production, Bates KV00000018 (Oct. 2, 2019).

509 Hill Dep. Tr. at 70-72.

510 Hill Dep. Tr. at 126-27.

Q: Okay. But what did you understand him to mean by that?

A: Well, based on what had happened in the July 10th meeting and Ambassador Sondland blurting out that he'd already gotten agreement to have a meeting at the White House for Zelensky if these investigations were started up again, clearly Ambassador Bolton was referring directly to those.

511 Hill Dep. Tr. at 129.

512 Hill Dep. Tr. at 139.   ("I told him exactly, you know, what had transpired and that Ambassador Sondland had basically indicated that there was an agreement with the Chief of Staff that they would have a White House meeting or, you know, a Presidential meeting if the Ukrainians started up these investigations again.")

513 Hill Dep. Tr. at 139.

514 Hill Dep. Tr. at 146-147.

515 Hill Dep. Tr. at 158-59, 161.

Q: What was Mr. Eisenberg's reaction to what you explained to him had and Mr. Griffith had explained to him had occurred the day before?

A: Yeah. He was also concerned. I mean, he wasn't aware that Sondland, Ambassador Sondland was, you know, kind of running around doing a lot of these, you know, meetings and independently. We talked about the fact that, you know, Ambassador Sondland said he'd been meeting with Giuliani and he was very concerned about that. And he said that he would follow up on this.

516 Vindman Dep. Tr. at 37. ("Sir, I think I—I mean, the top line I just offered, I'll restate it, which is that Mr. Sondland asked for investigations, for these investigations into Bidens and Burisma. I actually recall having that particular conversation. Mr. Eisenberg doesn't really work on this issue, so I had to go a little bit into the back story of what these investigations were, and that I expressed concerns and thought it was inappropriate.")

517 Vindman Dep. Tr. at 36.

518 Vindman Dep. Tr. at 38.

Q: Did he say anything to you, that, all right, I'm going to do anything with it?

A: I vaguely recall something about: I'll take a look into it. You know, there might not be anything here. We'll take a look into it, something of that nature. But—and then he offered to, you know, if I have any concerns in the future, you know, that I should be open—I should be—feel free to come back and, you know, share those concerns.

Q: Did either he or anyone from the legal staff circle back to you on this issue?

A: No.

519 Vindman Dep. Tr. at 39-40.

520 Taylor Dep. Tr. at 29. ("In the same July 19th phone call, they gave me an account of the July 10th meeting with the Ukrainian officials at the White House. Specifically, they told me that Ambassador Sondland had connected investigations with an Oval Office meeting for President Zelensky, which so irritated Ambassador Bolton

that he abruptly ended the meeting, telling Dr. Hill and Mr. Vindman that they should have nothing to do with domestic politics.")

[521] Morrison Dep. Tr. at 12.

[522] House Permanent Select Committee on Intelligence, Written Statement of Ambassador Gordon Sondland, *Impeachment*, 116th Cong. (Nov. 20, 2019) ("2. The call between Zelensky and Potus should happen before 7/21. (Parliamentary Elections) Sole purpose is for Zelensky to give Potus assurances of 'new sheriff' in town. Corruption ending, unbundling moving forward and any hampered investigations will be allowed to move forward transparently. Goal is for Potus to invite him to Oval. Volker, Perry, Bolton and I strongly recommend.").

[523] House Permanent Select Committee on Intelligence, Written Statement of Ambassador Gordon Sondland, *Impeachment*, 116th Cong. (Nov. 20, 2019).

[524] Sondland Dep. Tr. at 227.

[525] House Permanent Select Committee on Intelligence, Opening Statement of Ambassador Gordon Sondland, Department of State, *Impeachment*, 116th Cong., at 21 (Nov. 20, 2019).

[526] House Permanent Select Committee on Intelligence, Opening Statement of Ambassador Gordon Sondland, Department of State, *Impeachment*, 116th Cong., at 21 (Nov. 20, 2019).

[527] House Permanent Select Committee on Intelligence, Opening Statement of Ambassador Gordon Sondland, Department of State, *Impeachment*, 116th Cong., at 21 (Nov. 20, 2019).

[528] Sondland Hearing Tr. at 27.

[529] Verizon Document Production. It is unclear whether this call occurred before or after Ambassador Sondland spoke with President Zelensky, and it is also unclear whether the White House caller was an Administration official or the President himself.

[530] Kurt Volker Document Production, Bates KV00000037 (Oct. 2, 2019).

[531] Kurt Volker Document Production, Bates KV00000037 (Oct. 2, 2019).

[532] Volker Transcribed Interview Tr. at 229-230.

[533] Kurt Volker Document Production, Bates KV00000018 (Oct. 2, 2019).

[534] Volker Transcribed Interview Tr. at 202-203.

[535] Volker Transcribed Interview Tr. at 232.

[536] Kurt Volker Document Production, Bates KV00000002 (Oct. 2, 2019).

[537] Kurt Volker Document Production, Bates KV00000018 (Oct. 2, 2019).

[538] Volker Transcribed Interview Tr. at 138-139.

[539] AT&T Document Production, Bates ATTHPSCI_20190930_02705.

[540] Volker Transcribed Interview Tr. at 139.

[541] Kurt Volker Document Production, Bates KV00000018 (Oct. 2, 2019).

[542] Kurt Volker Document Production, Bates KV00000002- KV00000003 (Oct. 2, 2019).

[543] Kurt Volker Document Production, Bates KV00000042 (Oct. 2, 2019).

Volker:	Orchestrated a great call w Rudy and Yermak. They are going to get together when Rudy goes to Madrid in a couple of weeks.
Volker:	In the meantime, Rudy is now advocating for phone call
Volker:	I have call into Fiona's replacement and will call Bolton if needed.
Volker:	But I can tell Bolton and you can tell Mick that Rudy agrees on a call, if that helps
Sondland:	I talked to Tim Morrison. (Fiona's replacement). He is pushing but feel free as well.

[544] Kurt Volker Document Production, Bates KV00000042 (Oct. 2, 2019).

Volker: Orchestrated a great call w Rudy and Yermak. They are going to get together when Rudy goes to Madrid in a couple of weeks.

Volker: In the meantime, Rudy is now advocating for phone call

Volker: I have call into Fiona's replacement and will call Bolton if needed.

Volker: But I can tell Bolton and you can tell Mick that Rudy agrees on a call, if that helps

Sondland: I talked to Tim Morrison. (Fiona's eplacement). He is pushing but feel free as well.

[545] Taylor Dep. Tr. at 30.

[546] Kurt Volker Document Production, Bates KV000000 37 (Oct. 2, 2019).

[547] Taylor Dep. Tr. at 74.

[548] Kent-Taylor Hearing Tr. at 68.

[549] Taylor Dep. Tr. at 177.

[550] Sondland Dep. Tr. at 183.

[551] Sondland Hearing Tr. at 17.

[552] Sondland Hearing Tr. at 18.

[553] Sondland Hearing Tr. at 19; 17.

[554] Sondland Hearing Tr. at 27.

[555] Sondland Hearing Tr. at 26.

[556] Sondland Hearing Tr. at 27.

[557] Taylor Dep. Tr. at 26.

[558] Hill-Holmes Hearing Tr. at 25.

[559] Hill Dep. Tr. at 420-421.

Q: You've mentioned repeatedly concerns that you had about, in particular, Mr. Giuliani and his efforts. When you read the call transcript of July 25th, the call record, which you must have done just a couple weeks ago, did it crystalize in your head in any way a better understanding of what was transpiring while you were there?

A: In terms of providing, you know, more information with hindsight, unfortunately, yes.

Q: And in what way?

A: The specific references, also juxtaposed with the release of the text messages by Ambassador Volker—you know, what I said before—really was kind of my worst fears and nightmares, in terms of, you know, there being some kind of effort not just to subvert the national security process but to try to subvert what really should be, you know, kind of, a diplomatic effort to, you know, kind of, set up a Presidential meeting.

Q: This may—

A: There seems to be an awful lot of people involved in, you know, basically turning a White House meeting into some kind of asset.

Q: What do you mean by "asset"?

A: Well, something that was being, you know, dangled out to the Ukrainian Government. They wanted the White House meeting very much. And this was kind of laying out that it wasn't just a question of scheduling or having, you know, the national security issues worked out, that there were all of these alternative discussions going on behind.

[560] Taylor Dep. Tr. at 174.

[561] Taylor Dep. Tr. at 174.

[562] Kurt Volker Document Production, Bates KV00000042 (Oct. 2, 2019).

[563] Sondland Hearing Tr. at 53-55.

[564] Sondland Hearing Tr. at 52-53.

[565] Morrison Dep. Tr. at 30-31, 101, 247, 256.

[566] Morrison Dep. Tr. at 31.

[567] Morrison Dep. Tr. at 111.

[568] Volker Transcribed Interview Tr. at 102-103; Kurt Volker Document Production, Bates KV00000007 (Oct. 2, 2019).

In his testimony, Ambassador Volker did not explain to the Committees what he had heard about the July 25 call put him in a position to tell Mr. Giuliani that the "right messages" were, in fact, discussed.

Ambassador Volker testified twice about the readouts that he received of the July 25 call. In his deposition, he told the Committees that he received "the same" readout from both the State Department and Mr. Yermak: that there was a message of congratulations to President Zelensky, that President Zelensky promised to fight corruption and that President Trump repeated the invitation to visit the White House. Volker Transcribed Interview Tr. at 102-103. Volker described it as a "superficial" readout. Volker Transcribed Interview Tr. at 19.

In his public testimony, Volker repeated that claim: the readouts from Mr. Yermak and Volker's U.S. sources "were largely the same, that it was a good call, that it was a congratulatory phone call for the President winning the parliamentary election." Volker-Morrison Hearing Tr. at 74. Volker did testify that he "expected" the call to cover the material in his July 25 text message – that the Ukrainians would "investigate/'get to the bottom of what happened' in 2016" – but did not receive anything more than a "barebones" description of what was said. Volker-Morrison Hearing Tr. at 87-88, 75.

If Volker is correctly describing the readouts he received, it is not clear what he heard that gave him the basis to tell Mr. Giuliani that "exactly the right messages" were discussed.

[569] Williams Dep. Tr. at 37-38.

[570] Hill-Holmes Hearing Tr. at 23.

[571] Hill-Holmes Hearing Tr. at 25.

[572] *Trump and Putin Share Joke About Election Meddling, Sparking New Furor*, New York Times (June 28, 2019) (online at www.nytimes.com/2019/06/28/us/politics/trump-putin-election.html) ("As he sat down on Friday with Mr. Putin on the sidelines of an international summit in Japan, Mr. Trump was asked by a reporter if he would tell Russia not to meddle in American elections. 'Yes, of course I will,' Mr. Trump said. Turning to Mr. Putin, he said, with a half-grin on his face and mock seriousness in his voice, 'Don't meddle in the election, President.'").

[573] Morrison Dep. Tr. at 41.

[574] Williams Dep. Tr. at 131.

[575] *See* Vindman Dep. Tr. at 42, 109; Morrison Dep. Tr. at 41.

[576] Vindman Dep. Tr. at 18; Morrison Dep. Tr. at 15.

[577] Vindman Dep. Tr. at 42-43; Morrison-Volker Hearing Tr. at 32.

[578] Morrison Dep. Tr. at 39; Vindman Dep. Tr. at 45.

[579] U.S. Embassy & Consulates in Italy, *Secretary Michael R. Pompeo and Italian Foreign Minister Luigi Di Maio at a Press Availability* (Oct. 2, 2019) (online at https://it.usembassy.gov/secretary-michael-r-pompeo-and-italian-foreign-minister-luigi-di-maio-at-a-press-availability/). Mr. Morrison testified that Dr. Kupperman was not in the Situation Room, but Mr. Morrison was informed after the fact that Dr. Kupperman was listening. Morrison

Dep. Tr. at 39-40. Ms. Williams and Lt. Col. Vindman testified that they both believed Dr. Kupperman was present, but neither had a clear recollection. Williams Dep. Tr. at 64; Vindman Dep. Tr. at 45.

[580] *See* Transcript, *This Week with George Stephanopoulos*, ABC News (Sept. 22, 2019) (online at https://abcnews.go.com/Politics/week-transcript-22-19-secretary-mike-pompeo-gen/story?id=65778332) (Q: And I want to turn to this whistleblower complaint, Mr. Secretary. The complaint involving the president and a phone call with a foreign leader to the director of national intelligence inspector general. That's where the complaint was launched by the whistle-blower. 'The Wall Street Journal' is reporting that President Trump pressed the president of Ukraine eight times to work with Rudy Giuliani to investigate Joe Biden's son. What do you know about those conversations? A: So, you just gave me a report about a I.C. whistle-blower complaint, none of which I've seen....").

[581] *Pompeo Took Part in Ukraine Call, Official Says*, Wall Street Journal (Sept. 30, 2019) (online at www.wsj.com/articles/pompeo-took-part-in-ukraine-call-official-says-11569865002).

[582] The White House, *Memorandum of Telephone Conversation* (July 25, 2019) (online at www.whitehouse.gov/wp-content/uploads/2019/09/Unclassified09.2019.pdf).

[583] The White House, *Memorandum of Telephone Conversation* (July 25, 2019) (online at www.whitehouse.gov/wp-content/uploads/2019/09/Unclassified09.2019.pdf).

[584] The White House, *Memorandum of Telephone Conversation* (July 25, 2019) (online at www.whitehouse.gov/wp-content/uploads/2019/09/Unclassified09.2019.pdf). *See* European Union External Action Service, *EU-Ukraine relations-factsheet* (Sept. 30, 2019) (online at https://eeas.europa.eu/headquarters/headquarters-Homepage/4081/eu-ukraine-relations-factsheet_en).

[585] The White House, *Memorandum of Telephone Conversation* (July 25, 2019) (online at www.whitehouse.gov/wp-content/uploads/2019/09/Unclassified09.2019.pdf).

[586] The White House, *Memorandum of Telephone Conversation* (July 25, 2019) (online at www.whitehouse.gov/wp-content/uploads/2019/09/Unclassified09.2019.pdf); Kent-Taylor Hearing Tr. at 29.

[587] The White House, *Memorandum of Telephone Conversation* (July 25, 2019) (online at www.whitehouse.gov/wp-content/uploads/2019/09/Unclassified09.2019.pdf).

[588] Vindman Dep. Tr. at 114.

[589] The White House, *Memorandum of Telephone Conversation* (July 25, 2019) (online at www.whitehouse.gov/wp-content/uploads/2019/09/Unclassified09.2019.pdf).

[590] *See* Office of the Director of National Intelligence, *Assessing Russian Activities and Intentions in Recent U.S. Elections* (Jan. 6, 2017) (online at www.dni.gov/files/documents/ICA_2017_01.pdf).

[591] The White House, *Memorandum of Telephone Conversation* (July 25, 2019) (online at www.whitehouse.gov/wp-content/uploads/2019/09/Unclassified09.2019.pdf).

[592] *Charges of Ukrainian Meddling? A Russian Operation, U.S. Intelligence Says*, New York Times (Nov. 22, 2019) (online at www.nytimes.com/2019/11/22/us/politics/ukraine-russia-interference.html).

[593] The President of Russia, *Joint News Conference with Hungarian Prime Minister Viktor Orban* (Feb. 2, 2017) (online at http://en.kremlin.ru/events/president/news/53806).

[594] Hill-Holmes Hearing Tr. at 39-40.

[595] *President Trump's Former National Security Advisor 'Deeply Disturbed' by Ukraine Scandal: 'Whole World Is Watching,'* ABC News (Sept. 29, 2019) (online at https://abcnews.go.com/Politics/president-trumps-national-security-advisor-deeply-disturbed-ukraine/story?id=65925477).

[596] Hill Dep. Tr. at 234-235.

[597] The White House, *Memorandum of Telephone Conversation* (July 25, 2019) (online at www.whitehouse.gov/wp-content/uploads/2019/09/Unclassified09.2019.pdf).

[598] The White House, *Memorandum of Telephone Conversation* (July 25, 2019) (online at www.whitehouse.gov/wp-content/uploads/2019/09/Unclassified09.2019.pdf).

[599] The White House, *Memorandum of Telephone Conversation* (July 25, 2019) (online at www.whitehouse.gov/wp-content/uploads/2019/09/Unclassified09.2019.pdf).

[600] The White House, *Memorandum of Telephone Conversation* (July 25, 2019) (online at www.whitehouse.gov/wp-content/uploads/2019/09/Unclassified09.2019.pdf).

[601] The White House, *Memorandum of Telephone Conversation* (July 25, 2019) (online at www.whitehouse.gov/wp-content/uploads/2019/09/Unclassified09.2019.pdf).

[602] The White House, *Memorandum of Telephone Conversation* (July 25, 2019) (online at www.whitehouse.gov/wp-content/uploads/2019/09/Unclassified09.2019.pdf).

[603] The White House, *Remarks by President Trump before Marine One* (Oct. 3, 2019) (online at www.whitehouse.gov/briefings-statements/remarks-president-trump-marine-one-departure-67/).

[604]Hill Dep. Tr. at 400; Kent-Taylor Hearing Tr. at 73.; Hill-Holmes Hearing Tr. at 63-64.; Yovanovitch Hearing Tr. at 49-50; Morrison-Volker Hearing Tr. at 23.

[605] Kent Dep. Tr. at 45.

[606] Kent-Taylor Hearing Tr. at 116.

[607] Yovanovitch Hearing Tr. at 50.

[608] *See* Section I, Chapter 1.

[609] Kent Dep. Tr. at 44-50.

[610] Morrison-Volker Hearing Tr. at 23.

[611] Morrison-Volker Hearing Tr. at 23.

[612] *See* Section I, Chapter 1.

[613] The White House, *Memorandum of Telephone Conversation* (July 25, 2019) (online at www.whitehouse.gov/wp-content/uploads/2019/09/Unclassified09.2019.pdf).

[614] Yovanovitch Dep. Tr. at 192-193.

[615] Yovanovitch Dep. Tr. at 192-193.

[616] Ambassador Volker was the only witness to testify that President Trump's reference to the "prosecutor" during the July 25 call was to Mr. Shokin, not Mr. Lutsenko. See Volker Dep. Tr. at 355. However, Mr. Holmes testified that, on July 26—the day after the call—he spoke with President Zelensky's Chief of Staff Andriy Bohdan who told Holmes that "President Trump had expressed interest during the previous day's phone call in President Zelensky's personnel decisions related to the Prosecutor General's office," which Mr. Holmes understood to refer to Mr. Lutsenko once he saw the July 25 call transcript. Holmes Dep. Tr. at 22, 49. In addition, in a text message to Taylor and Sondland after his July 19 breakfast with Giuliani, Volker emphasized that "Most impt [important] is for Zelensky to say" on the July 25 call "that he will help investigation—and address any specific personnel issues—if there are any." Kurt Volker Document Production, Bates KV00000037 (Oct. 2, 2019).

[617] The White House, *Memorandum of Telephone Conversation* (July 25, 2019) (online at www.whitehouse.gov/wp-content/uploads/2019/09/Unclassified09.2019.pdf).

[618] The White House, *Memorandum of Telephone Conversation* (July 25, 2019) (online at www.whitehouse.gov/wp-content/uploads/2019/09/Unclassified09.2019.pdf).

[619] Hill-Holmes Hearing Tr. at 55.

[620] Holmes Dep. Tr. at 49-50.

[621] Kent-Taylor Hearing Tr. at 25.

[622] Morrison-Volker Hearing Tr. at 19.

[623] Hill-Holmes Hearing Tr. at 18.

[624] *In-Town Pool Report #6—Ukraine Call*, White House Pool Report (July 25, 2019) (online at https://publicpool.kinja.com/subject-in-town-pool-report-6-ukraine-call-1836700221).

[625] Vindman Dep. Tr. at 42-43.

[626] Vindman-Williams Hearing Tr. at 31-33; Morrison-Volker Hearing Tr. at 34.

[627] Vindman Dep. Tr. at 46-47.

[628] Taylor Dep. Tr. at 29.

[629] Vindman Dep. Tr. at 94.

[630] Vindman Dep. Tr. at 46-47.

[631] Vindman-Williams Hearing Tr. at 28.

[632] Vindman Dep. Tr. at 147.

[633] Vindman-Williams Hearing Tr. at 28-29.

[634] Vindman Dep. Tr. at 96-97.

[635] Vindman Dep. Tr. at 97-98.

[636] Morrison-Volker Hearing Tr. at 29.

[637] Morrison Dep. Tr. at 23-24.

[638] Morrison Dep. Tr. at 41-42, 191-192.

[639] Morrison Dep. Tr. at 97.

[640] Morrison Dep. Tr. at 97.

[641] Morrison Dep. Tr. at 101.

[642] Morrison Dep. Tr. at 41.

[643] Morrison Dep. Tr. at 43.

[644] Morrison Dep. Tr. at 44.

[645] Morrison Dep. Tr. at 16.

[646] Morrison Dep. Tr. at 101.

[647] Morrison-Volker Hearing Tr. at 38.

[648] Vindman Dep. Tr. at 121.

[649] Vindman Dep. Tr. at 122.

[650] Vindman Dep. Tr. at 122-123.

[651] Vindman Dep. Tr. at 121.

[652] Vindman Dep. Tr. at 123-124.

[653] Morrison Dep. Tr. at 121.

[654] Morrison Dep. Tr. at 55-56.

[655] Morrison Dep. Tr. at 55-56, 121-123.

[656] Morrison Dep. Tr. at 270.

[657] Williams Dep. Tr. at 16, 63.

[658] Williams Dep. Tr. at 149.

[659] Vindman-Williams Hearing Tr. at 34.

[660] Williams Dep. Tr. at 148.

[661] Vindman-Williams Hearing Tr. at 29.

[662] Williams Dep. Tr. at 54, 149.

[663] Vindman Dep. Tr. at 54-55. ("There's one other substantive item in the next paragraph from Zelensky, where it says 'He or she will look into the situation specifically to the company'—it shouldn't be 'the company.' It should be 'to Burisma that you mentioned.' Because I think, you know, frankly these are not necessarily folks that are familiar with the substance. So President Zelensky specifically mentioned the company Burisma.").

[664] Vindman-Williams Hearing Tr. at 61.

[665] Vindman Dep. Tr. at 89.

[666] Williams Dep. Tr. at 68-69.

Q: Okay. When the transcript was made available to the VP's office, do you remember when that occurred?

A: My colleagues—I can't remember the precise time, but before the end of the day that day my colleagues who help prepare the Vice President's briefing book received a hard copy of the transcript from the White House Situation Room to include in that book. I didn't personally see it, but I understood that they had received it because we wanted to make sure the Vice President got it.

Q: On the 25th or 26th?

A: It was on the 25th.

[667] Vindman Dep. Tr. at 139–141.

[668] Kent Dep. Tr. at 163-165.

[669] Holmes Dep. Tr.at 107.

[670] Holmes Dep. Tr. at 21-22.

[671] Kent-Taylor Hearing Tr. at 38; Hill-Holmes Hearing Tr. at 26.

[672] Morrison-Volker Hearing Tr. at 74. ("Yes. So I was not on the phone call. I had arrived in Ukraine, and I had had that lunch with Mr. Yermak that we saw on the day of the phone call. I had been pushing for the phone call because I thought it was important to renew the personal connection between the two leaders and to congratulate President Zelensky on the parliamentary election. The readout I received from Mr. Yermak and also from the U.S. side—although I'm not exactly sure who it was on the U.S. side, but there was U.S. and a Ukrainian readout—were largely the same, that it was a good call, that it was a congratulatory phone call for the President winning the parliamentary election. President Zelensky did reiterate his commitment to reform and fighting corruption in Ukraine, and President Trump did reiterate his invitation to President Zelensky to come visit him in the White House. That's exactly what I thought the phone call would be, so I was not surprised at getting that as the readout.").

[673] Holmes Dep. Tr. at 22.

[674] Holmes Dep. Tr. at 22, 48-49.

[675] Holmes Dep. Tr. at 49.

[676] Holmes Dep. Tr. at 49.

[677] Holmes Dep. Tr. at 22.

[678] Hill-Holmes Hearing Tr. at 27.

[679] Hill-Holmes Hearing Tr. at 48-49.

[680] Croft Dep. Tr. at 118-119.

[681] Sondland Hearing Tr. at 25; Kent-Taylor Hearing Tr. at 38.

[682] Morrison-Volker Hearing Tr. at 89-90.

[683] Holmes Dep. Tr. at 64.

[684] Kent-Taylor Hearing Tr. at 38.

[685] Hill-Holmes Hearing Tr. at 27.

[686] Hill-Holmes Hearing Tr. at 27.

[687] Hill-Holmes Hearing Tr. at 27-28.

[688] Hill-Holmes Hearing Tr. at 27-28.

[689] Hill-Holmes Hearing Tr. at 27-28.

[690] Holmes Dep. Tr. at 108.

[691] Hill-Holmes Hearing Tr. at 49.

[692] Sondland Hearing Tr. at 25-26.

[693] Hill-Holmes Hearing Tr. at 28.

[694] Hill-Holmes Hearing Tr. at 28.

[695] Hill-Holmes Hearing Tr. at 49. ("The restaurant has sort of glass doors that open onto a terrace, and we were at the first tables on the terrace, so immediately outside of the interior of the restaurant. The doors were all wide open. There were—there was tables, a table for four, while I recall it being two tables for two pushed together. In any case, it was quite a wide table, and the table was set. There was sort of a table runner down the middle. I was directly across from Ambassador Sondland. We were close enough that we could, you know, share an appetizer between us, and then the two staffers were off to our right at this next table.").

[696] Hill-Holmes Hearing Tr. at 28.

[697] Hill-Holmes Hearing Tr. at 28.

[698] Holmes Dep. Tr. at 160.

[699] Hill-Holmes Hearing Tr. at 28.

[700] Hill-Holmes Hearing Tr. at 50.

> Q: Now, you said that you were able to hear President Trump's voice through the receiver. How were you able to hear if it was not on speaker phone?
>
> A: It was several things. It was quite loud when the President came on, quite distinctive. I believe Ambassador Sondland also said that he often speaks very loudly over the phone, and I certainly experienced that. When the President came on, he sort of winced and held the phone away from his ear like this, and he did that for the first couple exchanges. I don't know if he then turned the volume down, if he got used to it, if the President moderated his volume. I don't know. But that's how I was able to hear.

[701] Hill-Holmes Hearing Tr. at 28-29.

[702] *Trump Denies Discussing Ukraine Investigations with Sondland in July Phone Call*, Axios (Nov. 13, 2019) (online at: www.axios.com/trump-denies-ukraine-investigation-sondland-6063f555-2629-4f99-b2f9-fd38739c0548.html).

[703] Sondland Hearing Tr. at 26.

[704] Sondland Hearing Tr. at 46.

[705] Sondland Hearing Tr. at 26.

[706] Sondland Hearing Tr. at 26.

[707] Sondland Hearing Tr. at 48.

[708] Holmes Dep. Tr. at 25.

[709] Holmes Dep. Tr. at 25-26.

[710] Sondland Hearing Tr. at 49-50. Ambassador Sondland opined that, while he may have referred to an investigation that Mr. Giuliani was pushing as an example of an investigation that President Trump cared about, he believed that he would have said "Burisma, not Biden." He testified, however:

> Q: But do you recall saying at least referring to an investigation that Rudy Giuliani was pushing? Is that something that you likely would have said?

> A: I would have, yes. *Id.* at 50.

[711] Sondland Hearing Tr. at 50.

[712] Holmes Dep. Tr. at 67.

[713] Holmes Dep. Tr. at 68-69.

[714] Hill-Holmes Hearing Tr. at 30.

[715] Hill-Holmes Hearing Tr. at 107.

[716] Hill-Holmes Hearing Tr. at 34.

[717] Holmes Dep. Tr. at 80.

[718] Holmes Dep. Tr. at 80-81.

[719] Kurt Volker Document Production, Bates KV00000007 (Oct. 2, 2019).

[720] Kurt Volker Document Production, Bates KV00000007 (Oct. 2, 2019).

[721] Kurt Volker Document Production, Bates KV00000007 (Oct. 2, 2019).

[722] Kurt Volker Document Production, Bates KV00000019 (Oct. 2, 2019).

[723] Volker Transcribed Interview Tr. at 112.

[724] Kurt Volker Document Production, Bates KV00000019 (Oct. 2, 2019).

[725] Morrison-Volker Hearing Tr. at 42.

[726] Morrison-Volker Hearing Tr. at 42.

[727] Morrison-Volker Hearing Tr. at 20-21.

[728] Kurt Volker Document Production, Bates KV00000019 (Oct. 2, 2019).

[729] Kurt Volker Document Production, Bates KV00000007 (Oct. 2, 2019).

[730] AT&T Document Production, Bates ATTHPSCI_20190930_02786.

[731] Kurt Volker Document Production, Bates KV00000007 (Oct. 2, 2019).

[732] Sondland Dep. Tr. at 192-193.

[733] Kurt Volker Document Production, Bates KV00000007 (Oct. 2, 2019).

[734] AT&T Document Production, Bates ATTHPSCI_20190930_02797.

[735] AT&T Document Production, Bates ATTHPSCI_20190930_02797.

[736] *Id.*

[737] AT&T Document Production, Bates ATTHPSCI_20190930_03326.

[738] *Id.*

[739] *Id.*

[740] *Id.*

[741] *Id.*

[742] *Id.*

[743] AT&T Document Production, Bates ATTHPSCI_20190930_02798.

[744] *Id.*

[745] *Id.*

[746] *Id.*

[747] *Id.*

[748] AT&T Document Production, Bates ATTHPSCI_20190930_02799.

[749] AT&T Document Production, Bates ATTHPSCI_20190930_02801.

[750] Kurt Volker Document Production, Bates KV00000019 (Oct. 2, 2019).

[751] Kurt Volker Document Production, Bates KV00000019 (Oct. 2, 2019).

[752] Kurt Volker Document Production, Bates KV00000019 (Oct. 2, 2019).

[753] Kurt Volker Document Production, Bates KV00000019 (Oct. 2, 2019).

[754] AT&T Document Production, Bates ATTHPSCI_20190930_02802-03, 02813, 03326, 03719.

[755] AT&T Document Production, Bates ATTHPSCI_20190930_03326.

[756] AT&T Document Production, Bates ATTHPSCI_20190930_02802.

[757] AT&T Document Production, Bates ATTHPSCI_20190930_02803.

[758] AT&T Document Production, Bates ATTHPSCI_20190930_03719.

[759] *Id.*

[760] AT&T Document Production, Bates ATTHPSCI_20190930_02803.

[761] *Id.*

[762] *Id.*

[763] *Id.*

[764] *Id.*

[765] Kurt Volker Document Production, Bates KV00000004- KV00000005 (Oct. 2, 2019).

[766] Kurt Volker Document Production, Bates KV00000004- KV00000005 (Oct. 2, 2019); AT&T Document Production, Bates ATTHPSCI_20190930_02805-06.

[767] Kurt Volker Document Production, Bates KV00000023 (Oct. 2, 2019).

[768] Kurt Volker Document Production, Bates KV00000023 (Oct. 2, 2019).

[769] Kurt Volker Document Production, Bates KV00000023 (Oct. 2, 2019).

[770] Verizon Document Production.

[771] Kurt Volker Document Production, Bates KV00000042 (Oct. 2, 2019).

[772] Sondland Dep. Tr. at 290; Sondland Hearing Tr. at 100-101.

[773] Kurt Volker Document Production, Bates KV00000042 (Oct. 2, 2019).

[774] Sondland Dep. Tr. at 291.

[775] Sondland Dep. Tr. at 291.

[776] Kurt Volker Document Production, Bates KV00000019 (Oct. 2, 2019).

[777] Kurt Volker Document Production, Bates KV00000019 (Oct. 2, 2019).

[778] Kurt Volker Document Production, Bates KV00000019 (Oct. 2, 2019).

[779] Kurt Volker Document Production, Bates KV00000042 (Oct. 2, 2019).

[780] House Permanent Select Committee on Intelligence, Opening Statement of Ambassador Gordon Sondland, Department of State, *Impeachment*, 116th Cong., at 15 (Nov. 20, 2019).

[781] Kurt Volker Document Production, Bates KV00000042 (Oct. 2, 2019).

[782] Sondland Dep. Tr. at 291-292.

[783] Sondland Dep. Tr. at 291-292.

[784] House Permanent Select Committee on Intelligence, Opening Statement of Ambassador Gordon Sondland, Department of State, *Impeachment*, 116th Cong., at 14 (Nov. 20, 2019).

[785] Kurt Volker Document Production, Bates KV00000005 (Oct. 2, 2019).

[786] AT&T Document Production, Bates ATTHPSCI_20190930_02816.

[787] House Permanent Select Committee on Intelligence, Opening Statement of Ambassador Gordon Sondland, Department of State, *Impeachment*, 116th Cong., at 22 (Nov. 20, 2019).

[788] Sondland Hearing Tr. at 102.

[789] House Permanent Select Committee on Intelligence, Opening Statement of Ambassador Gordon Sondland, Department of State, *Impeachment*, 116th Cong., at 22 (Nov. 20, 2019).

[790] Sondland Hearing Tr. at 28.

[791] Kurt Volker Document Production, Bates KV00000020 (Oct. 2, 2019).

[792] Kurt Volker Document Production, Bates KV00000007 (Oct. 2, 2019).

[793] AT&T Document Production, Bates ATTHPSCI_20190930_02828.

[794] Volker Transcribed Interview Tr. at 113.

[795] Volker Transcribed Interview Tr. at 71-72.

[796] Kurt Volker Document Production, Bates KV00000023 (Oct. 2, 2019).

[797] Kurt Volker Document Production, Bates KV00000023 (Oct. 2, 2019).

[798] Kurt Volker Document Production, Bates KV00000023 (Oct. 2, 2019).

[799] Kurt Volker Document Production, Bates KV00000023 (Oct. 2, 2019).

[800] WhatsApp Security (online at www.whatsapp.com/security/) (accessed Nov. 29, 2019).

[801] Kurt Volker Document Production, Bates KV00000043 (Oct. 2, 2019).

[802] Kurt Volker Document Production, Bates KV00000043 (Oct. 2, 2019).

[803] Kurt Volker Document Production, Bates KV00000023 (Oct. 2, 2019).

[804] Kurt Volker Document Production, Bates KV00000023 (Oct. 2, 2019).

[805] Volker Transcribed Interview Tr. at 43-44, 113-114.

[806] House Permanent Select Committee on Intelligence, Opening Statement of Ambassador Gordon Sondland, Department of State, *Impeachment*, 116th Cong., at 5 (Nov. 20, 2019).

[807] Sondland Hearing Tr. at 18.

[808] Volker Transcribed Interview Tr. at 191, 197-198.

[809] Volker Transcribed Interview Tr. at 191-192.

[810] Volker Transcribed Interview Tr. at 201.

[811] Volker Transcribed Interview Tr. at 198.

[812] Volker Transcribed Interview Tr. at 197.

[813] Department of Justice, *Ukraine Statement* (Sept. 25, 2019).

[814] *Cleaning Up Ukraine in the Shadow of Trump*, The Financial Times (Nov. 28, 2019) (online at www.ft.com/content/eb8e4004-1059-11ea-a7e6-62bf4f9e548a).

[815] *Cleaning Up Ukraine in the Shadow of Trump*, The Financial Times (Nov. 28, 2019) (online at www.ft.com/content/eb8e4004-1059-11ea-a7e6-62bf4f9e548a).

[816] Taylor Dep. Opening Statement at 9.

[817] Taylor Dep. Opening Statement at 9.

[818] Volker Transcribed Interview Tr. at 196-197.

[819] Taylor Dep. Opening Statement at 9.

[820] Kurt Volker Document Production, Bates KV00000043 (Oct. 2, 2019).

[821] Volker Transcribed Interview Tr. at 196-197.

[822] Kent Dep. Tr. at 261

[823] Kent Dep. Tr. at 262-263.

[824] Kent Dep. Tr. at 264.

[825] Kent Dep. Tr. at 264-265.

[826] Kurt Volker Document Production, Bates KV00000020 (Oct. 2, 2019).

[827] Kurt Volker Document Production, Bates KV00000043 (Oct. 2, 2019).

[828] Kurt Volker Document Production, Bates KV00000043 (Oct. 2, 2019).

[829] Kurt Volker Document Production, Bates KV00000043 (Oct. 2, 2019).

[830] Volker Transcribed Interview Opening Statement at 8.

[831] Volker Transcribed Interview Tr. at 44.

[832] Morrison-Volker Hearing Tr. at 21.

[833] Volker Transcribed Interview Tr. at 259-260.

[834] Volker Transcribed Interview Tr. at 260.

[835] Morrison-Volker Hearing Tr. at 128.

[836] Kurt Volker Document Production, Bates KV00000043 (Oct. 2, 2019).

[837] Volker Transcribed Interview Tr. at 199-200.

[838] Hill-Holmes Hearing Tr. at 31-32, 68; Sondland Hearing Tr. at 55-57.

[839] Cooper Dep. Tr. at 71.

[840] Cooper Dep. Tr. at 62, 66.

[841] Cooper Dep. Tr. at 62.

[842] Morrison-Volker Hearing Tr. at 90-91.

[843] House Permanent Select Committee on Intelligence, Written Statement of Ambassador Gordon Sondland, at 23, *Impeachment,* 116th Cong. (Nov. 20, 2019).

[844] House Permanent Select Committee on Intelligence, Written Statement of Ambassador Gordon Sondland, at 23, *Impeachment,* 116th Cong. (Nov. 20, 2019).

[845] Sondland Hearing Tr. at 104.

[846] House Permanent Select Committee on Intelligence, Written Statement of Ambassador Gordon Sondland, at 18, *Impeachment,* 116th Cong. (Nov. 20, 2019).

[847] Sondland Hearing Tr. at 44.

[848] Sondland Hearing Tr. at 75.

[849] Sondland Hearing Tr. at 76.

[850] House Permanent Select Committee on Intelligence, Written Statement of Ambassador Gordon Sondland, at 23, *Impeachment,* 116th Cong. (Nov. 20, 2019).

[851] Hill-Holmes Hearing Tr. at 30.

[852] Hill-Holmes Hearing Tr. at 30.

[853] Sondland Hearing Tr. at 28.

[854] Sondland Hearing Tr. at 106.

[855] Hill-Holmes Hearing Tr. at 31-32.

[856] Hill-Holmes Hearing Tr. at 31.

[857] Kent-Taylor Hearing Tr. at 40.

[858] Taylor Dep. Tr. at 230.

[859] Kent-Taylor Hearing Tr. at 40.

[860] Hill-Holmes Hearing Tr. at 8.

[861] Kurt Volker Document Production, Bates 20 (Aug. 29, 2019).

[862] Volker Transcribed Interview Tr. at 80-81.

A: By the time it hit Politico publicly, I believe it was the end of August. And I got a text message from, it was either the Foreign Minister or—I think it was the future Foreign Minister. And, you know, basically, you're just—you're—I have to verbalize this. You're just trying to explain that we are trying this. We have a complicated system. We have a lot of players in this. We are working this. Give us time to fix it.

Q: So anybody on the Ukrainian side of things ever express like grave concern that this would not get worked out?

A: Not that it wouldn't get worked out, no, they did not. They expressed concern that, since this has now come out publicly in this Politico article, it looks like that they're being, you know, singled out and penalized for some reason. That's the image that that would create in Ukraine.

[863] Taylor Dep. Tr. at 34.

[864] Taylor Dep. Tr. at 137-138.

[865] Taylor Dep. Tr. at 137-138.

[866] Kent-Taylor Hearing Tr. at 174.

[867] Kent-Taylor Hearing Tr. at 40.

[868] Kent-Taylor Hearing Tr. at 40.

[869] Hill-Holmes Hearing Tr. at 31-32.

[870] Hill-Holmes Hearing Tr. at 31-32.

[871] Hill-Holmes Hearing Tr. at 68.

[872] Holmes Dep. Tr. at 58.

[873] Kent-Taylor Hearing Tr. at 40.

[874] *Trump, in August Call with GOP Senator, Denied Official's Claim on Ukraine Aid*, Wall Street Journal (Oct. 4, 2019) (online at www.wsj.com/articles/trump-administration-used-potential-meeting-to-pressure-ukraine-on-biden-texts-indicate-11570205661).

[875] *Trump, in August Call With GOP Senator, Denied Official's Claim on Ukraine Aid*, Wall Street Journal (Oct. 4, 2019) (online at www.wsj.com/articles/trump-administration-used-potential-meeting-to-pressure-ukraine-on-biden-texts-indicate-11570205661).

[876] Letter from Senator Ron Johnson to Ranking Member Jim Jordan, House Committee on Oversight and Reform, and Ranking Member Devin Nunes, House Permanent Select Committee on Intelligence (Nov. 18, 2019) (online at www.ronjohnson.senate.gov/public/_cache/files/e0b73c19-9370-42e6-88b1-b2458eaeeecd/johnson-to-jordan-nunes.pdf).

[877] Letter from Senator Ron Johnson to Ranking Member Jim Jordan, House Committee on Oversight and Reform, and Ranking Member Devin Nunes, House Permanent Select Committee on Intelligence (Nov. 18, 2019) (online at www.ronjohnson.senate.gov/public/_cache/files/e0b73c19-9370-42e6-88b1-b2458eaeeecd/johnson-to-jordan-nunes.pdf).

[878] The White House, *Memorandum of Telephone Conversation* (July 25, 2019) (online at www.whitehouse.gov/wp-content/uploads/2019/09/Unclassified09.2019.pdf).

[879] Office of the Director of National Intelligence, *Background to "Assessing Russian Activities and Intentions in Recent US Elections": The Analytic Process and Cyber Incident Attribution* (Jan. 6, 2017) (online at www.dni.gov/files/documents/ICA_2017_01.pdf).

[880] Letter from Senator Ron Johnson to Ranking Member Jim Jordan, Committee on Oversight and Reform, and Ranking Member Devin Nunes, Permanent Select Committee on Intelligence (Nov. 18, 2019) (online at www.ronjohnson.senate.gov/public/_cache/files/e0b73c19-9370-42e6-88b1-b2458eaeeecd/johnson-to-jordan-nunes.pdf).

[881] Sondland Hearing Tr. at 30.

[882] Volker Transcribed Interview Tr. at 251-252; Kent-Taylor Hearing Tr. at 41.

[883] Williams Dep. Tr. at 74-77.

[884] Williams Dep. Tr.at 76.

[885] Williams Dep. Tr. at 78-79.

[886] Sondland Hearing Tr. at 30.

[887] Sondland Hearing Tr. at 38. *See also* Sondland Hearing Tr. at 57:

A: I don't know exactly what I said to him. This was a briefing attended by many people, and I was invited at the very last minute. I wasn't scheduled to be there. But I think I spoke up at some point late in the meeting and said, it looks like everything is being held up until these statements get made, and that's my, you know, personal belief.

Q: And Vice President Pence just nodded his head?

A: Again, I don't recall any exchange or where he asked me any questions. I think he—it was sort of a duly noted response.

Q: Well, he didn't say, Gordon, what are you talking about?

A: No, he did not.

Q: He didn't say, what investigations?

A: He did not.

[888] *Pence Disputes that Sondland Raised Concerns to Him About Ukraine Aid-Investigations Link*, Wall Street Journal (Nov. 20, 2019) (online at www.wsj.com/livecoverage/gordon-sondland-testifies-impeachment/card/1574268547).

[889] Taylor Dep. Tr. at 190.

[890] Taylor Dep. Tr. at 35.

[891] Taylor Dep. Tr. at 190-191.

[892] Williams Dep. Tr. at 81.

[893] Williams Dep. Tr. at 82.

[894] Williams Dep. Tr. at 82-83.

[895] Williams Dep. Tr. at 83.

[896] Williams Dep. Tr. at 83.

[897] *How a CIA Analyst, Alarmed by Trump's Shadow Foreign Policy, Triggered an Impeachment Inquiry*, Washington Post (Nov. 16, 2019) (online at www.washingtonpost.com/national-security/how-a-cia-analyst-alarmed-by-trumps-shadow-foreign-policy-triggered-an-impeachment-inquiry/2019/11/15/042684a8-03c3-11ea-8292-c46ee8cb3dce_story.html).

[898] Hill-Holmes Hearing Tr. at 31.

[899] Sondland Hearing Tr. at 31.

[900] Morrison Dep. Tr. at 134.

[901] Morrison Dep. Tr. at 155.

[902] Morrison Dep. Tr. at 155.

[903] Morrison Dep. Tr. at 137.

[904] Morrison Dep. Tr. at 182.

[905] Morrison Dep. Tr. at 184.

[906] Morrison Dep. Tr. at 228.

[907] Morrison Dep. Tr. at 154.

[908] Kent-Taylor Hearing Tr. at 42.

[909] Kent-Taylor Hearing Tr. at 42.

[910] Kent-Taylor Hearing Tr. at 57.

[911] Kurt Volker Document Production, Bates 39 (Oct. 4, 2019).

[912] Kent-Taylor Hearing Tr. at 42.

[913] Taylor Dep. Tr. at 190.

[914] Taylor Dep. Tr. at 190.

[915] Taylor Dep. Tr. at 190.

[916] Kent-Taylor Hearing Tr. at 60.

[917] Sondland Hearing Tr. at 59.

[918] Sondland Hearing Tr. at 59-60.

[919] Morrison Dep. Tr. at 190-191.

[920] Morrison-Volker Hearing Tr. at 52.

[921] Morrison-Volker Hearing Tr. at 53-54; Morrison Dep. Tr. at 238.

922 Kent-Taylor Hearing Tr. at 43-44.

923 Kurt Volker Document Production, Bates 53 (Oct. 4, 2019).

924 Kent-Taylor Hearing Tr. at 44.

925 Kent-Taylor Hearing Tr. at 44.

926 Kent-Taylor Hearing Tr. at 44.

927 Sondland Hearing Tr. at 109-110.

928 Sondland Hearing Tr. at 109-110.

929 Sondland Hearing Tr. at 110-111.

930 Kent-Taylor Hearing Tr. at 45.

931 Kent-Taylor Hearing Tr. at 45, 63.

932 Kent-Taylor Hearing Tr. at 45.

933 Sondland Hearing Tr. at 110. Ambassador Volker also testified that Ambassador Sondland used the same analogy to him when discussing the release of the hold on security assistance. Morrison-Volker Hearing Tr. at 96-97.

934 Kurt Volker Document Production, Bates 53 (Oct. 4, 2019).

935 Taylor Dep. Tr. at 209.

936 Kurt Volker Document Production, Bates 53 (Oct. 4, 2019).

937 Kent-Taylor Hearing Tr. at 54.

938 Kent-Taylor Hearing Tr. at 54.

939 Kent-Taylor Hearing Tr. at 54.

940 Kent-Taylor Hearing Tr. at 54.

941 Kurt Volker Document Production, Bates 53 (Oct. 4, 2019).

942 Sondland Dep. Tr. at 217.

943 Sondland Hearing Tr. at 26 ("Was there a quid pro quo? As I testified previously with regard to the requested White House call and the White House meeting, the answer is yes.").

944 Sondland Hearing Tr. at 41.

945 Sondland Hearing Tr. at 112

946 Sondland Hearing Tr. at 61-62.

947 Taylor Dep. Tr. at 39.

948 Taylor Dep. Tr. at 39.

949 Maguire Hearing Tr. at 110; Whistleblower Compl. Appendix 2. Public reporting indicates that "[l]awyers from the White House counsel's office told Mr. Trump in late August about the complaint, explaining that they were trying to determine whether they were legally required to give it to Congress." *Trump Knew of Whistle-Blower Complaint When He Released Aid to Ukraine*, New York Times (Nov. 26, 2019) (online at www.nytimes.com/2019/11/26/us/politics/trump-whistle-blower-complaint-ukraine.html).

950 Letter from Michael Atkinson, Inspector General of the Intelligence Community, to Chairman Adam B. Schiff and Ranking Member Devin Nunes, House Permanent Select Committee on Intelligence (Sept. 9, 2019) (online at https://intelligence.house.gov/uploadedfiles/20190909_-_ic_ig_letter_to_hpsci_on_whistleblower.pdf).

951 Letter from Michael Atkinson, Inspector General of the Intelligence Community, to Chairman Adam B. Schiff and Ranking Member Devin Nunes, House Permanent Select Committee on Intelligence (Sept. 9, 2019) (online at https://intelligence.house.gov/uploadedfiles/20190909_-_ic_ig_letter_to_hpsci_on_whistleblower.pdf).

[952] Sondland Hearing Tr. at 118. *See also Witness Testimony and Records Raise Questions About Account of Trump's 'No Quid Pro Quo' Call*, Washington Post (Nov. 27, 2019) (online at www.washingtonpost.com/politics/witness-testimony-and-records-raise-questions-about-account-of-trumps-no-quid-pro-quo-call/2019/11/27/425545c2-0d49-11ea-8397-a955cd542d00_story.html).

[953] Sondland Hearing Tr. at 118.

[954] Sondland Hearing Tr. at 73.

[955] Statement of Ambassador Gordon Sondland at 1 (Nov. 4, 2019). This addendum did not address the July 26 telephone conversation that Sondland had with President Trump, which he only recalled following the testimony of David Holmes on November 15, 2019.

[956] Statement of Ambassador Gordon Sondland at 3 (Nov. 4, 2019).

[957] Kent-Taylor Hearing Tr. at 43-44; Morrison Dep. Tr. at 190-191.

[958] Morrison Dep. Tr. at 190-191; Kent-Taylor Hearing Tr. at 43-44.

[959] Sondland Hearing Tr. at 109.

[960] Sondland Hearing Tr. at 45, 109.

[961] Kurt Volker Document Production, Bates 20 (Oct. 4, 2019).

[962] Kurt Volker Document Production, Bates 20 (Oct. 4, 2019).

[963] Kurt Volker Document Production, Bates 53 (Oct. 4, 2019).

[964] Kurt Volker Document Production, Bates 53 (Oct. 4, 2019).

[965] The White House, *Press Briefing by Acting Chief of Staff Mick Mulvaney* (Oct. 17, 2019) (online at www.whitehouse.gov/briefings-statements/press-briefing-acting-chief-staff-mick-mulvaney/).

[966] The White House, *Press Briefing by Acting Chief of Staff Mick Mulvaney* (Oct. 17, 2019) (online at www.whitehouse.gov/briefings-statements/press-briefing-acting-chief-staff-mick-mulvaney/).

[967] The White House, *Press Briefing by Acting Chief of Staff Mick Mulvaney* (Oct. 17, 2019) (online at www.whitehouse.gov/briefings-statements/press-briefing-acting-chief-staff-mick-mulvaney/). Ambassador Taylor's testimony contradicted Mr. Mulvaney's statement about the ubiquity of such quid pro quos in American foreign policy. Ambassador Taylor testified that in his decades of military and diplomatic service, he had never seen another example of foreign aid conditioned on the personal or political interests of the President. Kent-Taylor Hearing Tr. at 55. Rather, "We condition assistance on issues that will improve our foreign policy, serve our foreign policy, ensure that taxpayers' money is well-spent." Kent-Taylor Hearing Tr. at 150.

[968] There were early concerns raised in the House and Senate about the frozen aid, even before the news became public. On August 9, the Democratic leadership of the House and Senate Appropriations Committees wrote to OMB and the White House warning that the August 3 letter apportionment might constitute an illegal impoundment of funds. They urged the Trump Administration to adhere to the law and obligate the withheld funding. Letter from Vice Chairman Patrick Leahy, Senate Committee on Appropriations, and Chairwoman Nita M. Lowey, House Committee on Appropriations, to Acting Chief of Staff Mick Mulvaney, The White House, and Acting Director Russell Vought, Office of Management and Budget (Aug. 9, 2019) (online at https://appropriations.house.gov/sites/democrats.appropriations.house.gov/files/documents/SFOPS%20Apportionment%20Letter%20Lowey-Leahy%20Signed%202019.8.9.pdf). On August 19, the Democratic leadership of the House and Senate Budget Committees wrote to OMB and the White House urging the Administration to comply with appropriations law and the Impoundment Control Act. Letter from Chairman John Yarmuth, House Committee on the Budget, and Ranking Member Bernard Sanders, Senate Committee on the Budget, to Acting Chief of Staff Mick Mulvaney, The White House (Aug. 19, 2019) (online at https://budget.house.gov/sites/democrats.budget.house.gov/files/documents/OMB%20Letter_081919.pdf).

[969] Letter from Senators Jeanne Shaheen, Rob Portman, Richard Durbin, Ron Johnson, and Richard Blumenthal to Acting White House Chief of Staff Mick Mulvaney (Sept. 3, 2019) (online at www.shaheen.senate.gov/imo/media/doc/Ukraine%20Security%20Letter%209.3.2019.pdf).

[970] Letter from Senators Jeanne Shaheen, Rob Portman, Richard Durbin, Ron Johnson, and Richard Blumenthal to Acting White House Chief of Staff Mick Mulvaney (Sept. 3, 2019) (online at www.shaheen.senate.gov/imo/media/doc/Ukraine%20Security%20Letter%209.3.2019.pdf).

[971] Letter from Chairman Eliot L. Engel and Ranking Member Michael T. McCaul, House Foreign Affairs Committee to Mick Mulvaney, Director, and Russell Vought, Acting Director, Office of Management and Budget, The White House (Sept. 5, 2019) (online at https://foreignaffairs.house.gov/_cache/files/c/4/c49328c2-941b-4c41-8c00-8c1515f0972f/D1968A9C42455BB3AFC38F97D966857B.ele-mccaul-letter-to-mulvaney-vought-on-ukraine-assistance.pdf).

[972] *Trump Tries to Force Ukraine to Meddle in the 2020 Election*, Washington Post (Sept. 5, 2019) (online at www.washingtonpost.com/opinions/global-opinions/is-trump-strong-arming-ukraines-new-president-for-political-gain/2019/09/05/4eb239b0-cffa-11e9-8c1c-7c8ee785b855_story.html).

[973] Taylor Dep. Tr. at 37-38.

[974] Taylor Dep. Tr. at 38.

[975] *See* Letter from Senator Christopher Murphy, to Chairman Adam B. Schiff, House Permanent Select Committee on Intelligence, and Acting Chairwoman Carolyn Maloney, House Committee on Oversight and Reform (Nov. 19, 2019) (online at www.murphy.senate.gov/download/111919-sen-murphy-letter-to-house-impeachment-investigators-on-ukraine) ("Senator Johnson and I assured Zelensky that Congress wanted to continue this funding, and would press Trump to release it immediately."); Letter from Senator Ron Johnson, to Ranking Member Jim Jordan, Committee on Oversight and Reform, and Ranking Member Devin Nunes, Permanent Select Committee on Intelligence (Nov. 18, 2019) (online at www.ronjohnson.senate.gov/public/_cache/files/e0b73c19-9370-42e6-88b1-b2458eaeeecd/johnson-to-jordan-nunes.pdf) ("I explained that I had tried to persuade the president to authorize me to announce the hold was released but that I was unsuccessful.").

[976] House Permanent Select Committee on Intelligence, *Three House Committees Launch Probe Into Trump and Giuliani Pressure Campaign* (Sept. 9, 2019) (online at https://intelligence.house.gov/news/documentsingle.aspx?DocumentID=685).

[977] Letter from Chairman Eliot L. Engel, House Committee on Foreign Affairs, Chairman Adam B. Schiff, House Permanent Select Committee on Intelligence, and Chairman Elijah E. Cummings, House Committee on Oversight and Reform, to Pat Cipollone, Counsel to the President, The White House (Sept. 9, 2019) (online at https://intelligence.house.gov/uploadedfiles/ele_schiff_cummings_letter_to_cipollone_on_ukraine.pdf).

[978] Letter from Chairman Eliot L. Engel, House Committee on Foreign Affairs, Chairman Adam B. Schiff, House Permanent Select Committee on Intelligence, and Chairman Elijah E. Cummings, House Committee on Oversight and Reform, to Pat Cipollone, Counsel to the President, The White House (Sept. 9, 2019) (online at https://intelligence.house.gov/uploadedfiles/ele_schiff_cummings_letter_to_cipollone_on_ukraine.pdf).

[979] Letter from Chairman Eliot L. Engel, House Committee on Foreign Affairs, Chairman Adam B. Schiff, House Permanent Select Committee on Intelligence, and Chairman Elijah E. Cummings, House Committee on Oversight and Reform, to Pat Cipollone, Counsel to the President, The White House (Sept. 9, 2019) (online at https://intelligence.house.gov/uploadedfiles/ele_schiff_cummings_letter_to_cipollone_on_ukraine.pdf).

[980] Letter from Chairman Eliot L. Engel, House Committee on Foreign Affairs, Chairman Adam B. Schiff, House Permanent Select Committee on Intelligence, and Chairman Elijah E. Cummings, House Committee on Oversight and Reform, to Michael R. Pompeo, Secretary of State (Sept. 9, 2019) (online at https://intelligence.house.gov/uploadedfiles/ele_schiff_cummings_letter_to_sec_pompeo_on_ukraine.pdf).

[981] Morrison Dep. Tr. at 245.

[982] Morrison Dep. Tr. at 245.

[983] Vindman Dep. Tr. at 303.

[984] Vindman Dep. Tr. at 304.

[985] Letter from Michael Atkinson, Inspector General of the Intelligence Community, to Chairman Adam B. Schiff and Ranking Member Devin Nunes, House Permanent Select Committee on Intelligence (Sept. 9, 2019) (online at https://intelligence.house.gov/uploadedfiles/20190909_-_ic_ig_letter_to_hpsci_on_whistleblower.pdf).

[986] Letter from Michael Atkinson, Inspector General of the Intelligence Community, to Chairman Adam B. Schiff and Ranking Member Devin Nunes, House Permanent Select Committee on Intelligence (Sept. 9, 2019) (online at https://intelligence.house.gov/uploadedfiles/20190909_-_ic_ig_letter_to_hpsci_on_whistleblower.pdf); *see also* 50 U.S.C. § 3033(k)(5) (setting forth procedures for reporting of complaints or information with respect to an "urgent concern" to Congressional intelligence committees).

[987] Maguire Hearing Tr. at 14 ("As a result, we consulted with the White House Counsel's Office, and we were advised that much of the information in the complaint was, in fact, subject to executive privilege, a privilege that I do not have the authority to waive. Because of that, we were unable to immediately share the details of the complaint with this committee but continued to consult with the White House counsels in an effort to do so.").

[988] Maguire Hearing Tr. at 15-16 ("Because the allegation on its face did not appear to fall in the statutory framework, my office consulted with the United States Department of Justice Office of Legal Counsel. ... After reviewing the complaint and the Inspector General's transmission letter, the Office of Legal Counsel determined that the complaint's allegations do not meet the statutory definition concerning legal urgent concern, and found that I was not legally required to transmit the material to our oversight committee under the Whistleblower Protection Act.").

[989] Maguire Hearing Tr. at 22-23. *See also CIA's Top Lawyer Made 'Criminal Referral' on Complaint about Trump Ukraine Call*, NBC News (Oct. 4, 2019) (online at www.nbcnews.com/politics/trump-impeachment-inquiry/cia-s-top-lawyer-made-criminal-referral-whistleblower-s-complaint-n1062481) (reporting that the CIA's General Counsel, Courtney Simmons Elwood, informed NSC chief lawyer John Eisenberg about an anonymous whistleblower complaint on August 14, 2019).

[990] Maguire Hearing Tr. at 14, 21-22. On September 26, Acting DNI Maguire testified that he and the ODNI General Counsel first consulted with the White House counsel's office before discussing the whistleblower complaint with the Department of Justice's Office of Legal Counsel:

The Chairman.	I'm just trying to understand the chronology. You first went to the Office of Legal Counsel, and then you went to the White House Counsel?
Acting Director Maguire.	No, no, no, sir. No, sir. No. We went to the White House first to determine—to ask the question—
The Chairman.	That's all I want to know is the chronology. So you went to the White House first. So you went to the subject of the complaint for advice first about whether you should provide the complaint to Congress?
Acting Director Maguire.	There were issues within this, a couple of things: One, it did appear that it has executive privilege. If it does have executive privilege, it is the White House that determines that. I cannot determine that, as the Director of National Intelligence.

Id. at 21-22.

[991] *Trump Knew of Whistle-Blower Complaint When He Released Aid to Ukraine,* New York Times (Nov. 26, 2019) (online at www.nytimes.com/2019/11/26/us/politics/trump-whistle-blower-complaint-ukraine.html).

[992] *Trump Knew of Whistle-Blower Complaint When He Released Aid to Ukraine,* New York Times (Nov. 26, 2019) (online at www.nytimes.com/2019/11/26/us/politics/trump-whistle-blower-complaint-ukraine.html). The Administration repeatedly referenced privilege concerns in connection with the whistleblower complaint. *See, e.g.,* Letter from Jason Klitenic, General Counsel, Office of the Director of National Intelligence, to Chairman Adam B. Schiff, House Permanent Select Committee on Intelligence (Sept. 13, 2019) (noting that "the complaint involves confidential and *potentially privileged* communications by persons outside the Intelligence Community") (emphasis added); Letter from Jason Klitenic, General Counsel, Office of the Director of National Intelligence, to Chairman Adam B. Schiff, House Permanent Select Committee on Intelligence (Sept. 17, 2019) (characterizing subpoena to the Acting DNI for documents as demanding "sensitive and *potentially privileged*" materials and whistleblower complaint as involving "*potentially privileged* matters relating to the interests of other stakeholders within the Executive Branch") (emphasis added).

However, the White House never formally invoked executive privilege as to the whistleblower complaint. *See* Maguire Hearing Tr. at 20 ("Chairman Schiff: So they never asserted executive privilege, is that the answer?

Acting Director Maguire: Mr. Chairman, if they did, we would not have released the letters yesterday and all the information that has been forthcoming.").

[993] Letter from Chairman Adam B. Schiff, House Permanent Select Committee on Intelligence, to Joseph Maguire, Acting Director of National Intelligence (Sept. 10, 2019) (online at https://intelligence.house.gov/uploadedfiles/20190910_-_chm_schiff_letter_to_acting_dni_maguire.pdf).

[994] Letter from Chairman Adam B. Schiff, House Permanent Select Committee on Intelligence, to Joseph Maguire, Acting Director of National Intelligence (Sept. 10, 2019) (online at https://intelligence.house.gov/uploadedfiles/20190910_-_chm_schiff_letter_to_acting_dni_maguire.pdf).

[995] *See* Letter from Jason Klitenic, General Counsel, Office of the Director of National Intelligence, to Chairman Adam B. Schiff, House Permanent Select Committee on Intelligence (Sept. 13, 2019).

[996] Letter from Chairman Adam B. Schiff, House Permanent Select Committee on Intelligence, to Joseph Maguire, Acting Director of National Intelligence (Sept. 13, 2019) (online at https://intelligence.house.gov/uploadedfiles/20190913_-_chm_schiff_letter_to_acting_dni_re_whistleblower_-_subpoena.pdf).

[997] The White House, *Memorandum of Telephone Conversation* (July 25, 2019) (online at www.whitehouse.gov/wp-content/uploads/2019/09/Unclassified09.2019.pdf).

[998] Vindman Dep. Tr. at 305-06; Morrison Dep. Tr. at 242.

[999] Morrison Dep. Tr. at 242.

[1000] *See, e.g.*, Morrison Dep. Tr. at 244; Vindman Dep. Tr. at 306; Williams Dep. Tr. at 147.

[1001] Cooper Dep. Tr. at 68-69.

[1002] Williams Dep. Tr. at 147. Ms. Williams did testify that President Trump's pressure on President Zelensky to open investigations into the Bidens on the July 25 call "shed some light on possible other motivations behind a security assistance hold." Williams Dep. Tr. at 149.

[1003] Sandy Dep. Tr. at 42, 139-140. According to a press report, after Congress began investigating President Trump's scheme, the White House Counsel's Office reportedly opened an internal investigation relating to the July 25 call. As part of that internal investigation, White House lawyers gathered and reviewed "hundreds of documents" that "reveal extensive efforts to generate an after-the-fact justification" for the hold on military assistance for Ukraine ordered by President Trump. These documents reportedly include "early August email exchanges between acting chief of staff Mick Mulvaney and White House budget officials seeking to provide an explanation for withholding the funds after the president had already ordered a hold in mid-July on the nearly $400 million in security assistance." *White House Review Turns Up Emails Showing Extensive Effort to Justify Trump's Decision to Block Ukraine Military Aid*, Washington Post (Nov. 24, 2019) (online at www.washingtonpost.com/politics/white-house-review-turns-up-emails-showing-extensive-effort-to-justify-trumps-decision-to-block-ukraine-military-aid/2019/11/24/2121cf98-0d57-11ea-bd9d-c628fd48b3a0_story.html). The White House has withheld these documents from the Committee, so the Committee cannot verify the accuracy of the reporting as of the publication of this report.

[1004] Sandy Dep. Tr. at 49.

[1005] Sandy Dep. Tr. at 42, 44.

[1006] Sandy Dep. Tr. at 180.

[1007] Vindman Dep. Tr. at 306.

[1008] Cooper Dep. Tr. at 83.

[1009] Cooper Dep. Tr. at 47-48, 58, 112-114; Sandy Dep. Tr. at 34-35, 85-86, 95, 128, 139-131, 133; Morrison Dep. Tr. at 163; Kent Dep. Tr. at 308-309; Reeker Dep. Tr. at 133. News reports indicate that a confidential White House review of President Trump's hold on military assistance to Ukraine has identified hundreds of documents revealing "extensive efforts to generate an after-the-fact justification for the decision and a debate over whether the delay was legal." *White House Review Turns Up Emails Showing Extensive Effort to Justify Trump's Decision to Block Ukraine Military Aid*, Washington Post (Nov. 24, 2019) (online at www.washingtonpost.com/politics/white-house-review-turns-up-emails-showing-extensive-effort-to-justify-trumps-decision-to-block-ukraine-military-aid/2019/11/24/2121cf98-0d57-11ea-bd9d-c628fd48b3a0_story.html). According to "two people briefed on an internal White House review," in August, Acting Chief of Staff Mulvaney "asked … whether there was a legal justification for withholding hundreds of millions of dollars in military aid to Ukraine." *Mulvaney Asked About Legal Justification for Withholding Ukraine Aid*, New York Times (Nov. 24, 2019) (online at www.nytimes.com/2019/11/24/us/politics/mulvaney-ukraine-aid.html). Reports indicate that, "[e]mails show [OMB Director] Vought and OMB staffers arguing that withholding aid was legal, while officials at the National Security Council and State Department protested. OMB lawyers said that it was legal to withhold the aid, as long as they deemed it a 'temporary' hold." *White House Review Turns Up Emails Showing Extensive Effort to Justify Trump's Decision to Block Ukraine Military Aid*, Washington Post (Nov. 24, 2019) (online at www.washingtonpost.com/politics/white-house-review-turns-up-emails-showing-extensive-effort-to-justify-trumps-decision-to-block-ukraine-military-aid/2019/11/24/2121cf98-0d57-11ea-bd9d-c628fd48b3a0_story.html). The White House and State Department's obstruction of Congress has prevented the Committee from obtaining any documents on this matter and, therefore, the Committee cannot verify the accuracy of this reporting as of the publication of this report.

[1010] Cooper Dep. Tr. at 80.

[1011] Sandy Dep. Tr. at 146-147.

[1012] *See* Department of Defense, *DOD Budget Materials (FY2011-FY2018)* (online at https://comptroller.defense.gov/Budget-Materials/). In 1974, President Nixon impounded 15-20 percent of a number of specific programs, which prompted the passage of the Impoundment Control Act of 1974. Congressional Research Service, *The Congressional Budget Act of 1974 (P.L. 93-344) Legislative History and Analysis* (Feb. 26, 1975).

[1013] Department of Defense and Labor, Health and Human Services, and Education Appropriations Act, 2019 and Continuing Appropriations Act, 2019, Pub. L. No. 115-245, § 9013 (2018); Sandy Dep. Tr. at 147.

[1014] Continuing Appropriations Act 2020, and Health Extenders Act of 2019, Pub. L. No. 116-59, § 124 (2019).

[1015] Cooper Dep. Tr. at 98.

[1016] *$35 Million in Pentagon Aid Hasn't Reached Ukraine Despite White House Assurances*, L.A. Times (Nov. 19, 2019) (online at www.latimes.com/politics/story/2019-11-19/documents-show-nearly-40-million-in-ukraine-aid-delayed-despite-white-house-assurances).

[1017] *Zelensky Planned to Announce Trump's 'Quo' on My Show. Here's What Happened*, Washington Post (Nov. 14, 2019) (online at www.washingtonpost.com/opinions/zelensky-was-planning-to-announce-trumps-quid-pro-quo-on-my-show-heres-what-happened/2019/11/14/47938f32-072a-11ea-8292-c46ee8cb3dce_story.html).

[1018] *Zelensky Planned to Announce Trump's 'Quo' on My Show. Here's What Happened*, Washington Post (Nov. 4, 2019) (online at www.washingtonpost.com/opinions/zelensky-was-planning-to-announce-trumps-quid-pro-quo-on-my-show-heres-what-happened/2019/11/14/47938f32-072a-11ea-8292-c46ee8cb3dce_story.html).

[1019] Taylor Dep. Tr. at 40.

[1020] Kent-Taylor Hearing Tr. at 106.

[1021] Kent-Taylor Hearing Tr. at 106.

[1022] Hill-Holmes Hearing Tr. at 33.

[1023] Hill-Holmes Hearing Tr. at 33.

[1024] Taylor Dep. Tr. at 41.

[1025] Taylor Dep. Tr. at 217-18.

[1026] Taylor Dep. Tr. at 217-18.

[1027] Holmes Dep. Tr. at 30.

[1028] *Zelensky Planned to Announce Trump's 'Quo' on My Show. Here's What Happened*, Washington Post (Nov. 4, 2019) (online at www.washingtonpost.com/opinions/zelensky-was-planning-to-announce-trumps-quid-pro-quo-on-my-show-heres-what-happened/2019/11/14/47938f32-072a-11ea-8292-c46ee8cb3dce_story.html).

[1029] Hill-Holmes Hearing Tr. at 33; *see also Zelensky Planned to Announce Trump's 'Quo' on My Show. Here's What Happened*, Washington Post (Nov. 4, 2019) (online at www.washingtonpost.com/opinions/zelensky-was-planning-to-announce-trumps-quid-pro-quo-on-my-show-heres-what-happened/2019/11/14/47938f32-072a-11ea-8292-c46ee8cb3dce_story.html).

[1030] Kent. Dep. Tr. at 333.

[1031] Kent Dep. Tr. at 329-31.

[1032] Kent Dep. Tr. at 330.

[1033] *Zelensky Planned to Announce Trump's 'Quo' on My Show. Here's What Happened*, Washington Post (Nov. 4, 2019) (online at www.washingtonpost.com/opinions/zelensky-was-planning-to-announce-trumps-quid-pro-quo-on-my-show-heres-what-happened/2019/11/14/47938f32-072a-11ea-8292-c46ee8cb3dce_story.html).

[1034] Hill-Holmes Hearing Tr. at 46-47.

[1035] Williams Dep. Tr. at 156.

[1036] Williams Dep. Tr. at 156.

[1037] *Pence Says He's Working to Release Transcripts of His Calls with Ukraine Leader*, Politico (Oct. 9, 2019) (online at www.politico.com/news/2019/10/09/pence-ukraine-zelensky-biden-043684).

[1038] *Pence: I Don't Object To Releasing My Call Transcripts With Zelensky*, Fox Business (Nov. 7, 2019) (online at www.realclearpolitics.com/video/2019/11/07/pence_i_dont_object_to_releasing_my_call_transcripts_with_zelensky.html).

[1039] *Rudy Giuliani's Remarkable Ukraine Interview, Annotated*, Washington Post (Sept. 20, 2019) (online at www.washingtonpost.com/politics/2019/09/20/rudy-giulianis-remarkable-ukraine-interview-annotated/).

[1040] The White House, *Remarks by President Trump and President Duda of Poland Before Bilateral Meeting* (Sept. 23, 2019) (online at www.whitehouse.gov/briefings-statements/remarks-president-trump-president-duda-poland-bilateral-meeting/).

[1041] The White House, *Remarks by President Trump Upon Arriving at the U.N. General Assembly* (Sept. 24, 2019) (online at www.whitehouse.gov/briefings-statements/remarks-president-trump-upon-arriving-u-n-general-assembly-new-york-ny/).

[1042] The White House, *Remarks by President Trump and President Zelensky of Ukraine Before Bilateral Meeting* (Sept 25, 2019) (online at www.whitehouse.gov/briefings-statements/remarks-president-trump-president-zelensky-ukraine-bilateral-meeting-new-york-ny/).

[1043] The White House, *Remarks by President Trump at the Swearing-in Ceremony of Secretary of Labor Eugene Scalia* (Sept 30, 2019) (online at www.whitehouse.gov/briefings-statements/remarks-president-trump-swearing-ceremony-secretary-labor-eugene-scalia/).

[1044] The White House, *Remarks by President Trump and President Niinistö of the Republic of Finland Before Bilateral Meeting* (Oct. 2, 2019) (www.whitehouse.gov/briefings-statements/remarks-president-trump-president-niinisto-republic-finland-bilateral-meeting/).

[1045] The White House, *Remarks by President Trump Before Marine One Departure* (Oct. 3, 2019) (online at www.whitehouse.gov/briefings-statements/remarks-president-trump-marine-one-departure-67/).

[1046] The White House, *Remarks by President Trump Before Marine One Departure* (Oct. 4, 2019) (online at www.whitehouse.gov/briefings-statements/remarks-president-trump-marine-one-departure-68).

[1047] The White House, *Remarks by President Trump Before Marine One Departure* (Oct. 4, 2019) (online at www.whitehouse.gov/briefings-statements/remarks-president-trump-marine-one-departure-68).

[1048] The White House, *Remarks by President Trump Before Marine One Departure* (Oct. 3, 2019) (online at www.whitehouse.gov/briefings-statements/remarks-president-trump-marine-one-departure-67/). These recent statements by President inviting foreign assistance for his personal political interests are consistent with his statements to George Stephanopoulos of ABC News on June 12, when President Trump indicated a desire to receive dirt on a political opponent provided by a foreign country. *ABC News' Oval Office interview with President Trump*, ABC News (Jun. 13, 2019) (online at https://abcnews.go.com/Politics/abc-news-oval-office-interview-president-donald-trump/story?id=63688943).

[1049] Morrison-Volker Hearing Tr. at 46-47, 91-92.

[1050] Vindman Dep. Tr. at 158-19; Holmes Dep. Tr. at 100; Kent-Taylor Hearing Tr. at 43.

[1051] Kent-Taylor Hearing Tr. at 24.

[1052] Hill-Holmes Hearing Tr. at 46.

[1053] Kent-Taylor Hearing Tr. at 165.

[1054] Kent-Taylor Hearing Tr. at 165.

[1055] Kent-Taylor Hearing Tr. at 24.

[1056] Kent-Taylor Hearing Tr. at 55-56.

[1057] Kent-Taylor Hearing Tr. at 164.

[1058] Kent Dep. Tr. at 329; Morrison-Volker Hearing Tr. at 138-139.

[1059] Morrison-Volker Hearing Tr. at 139.

[1060] Morrison-Volker Hearing Tr. at 139.

SECTION II.

THE PRESIDENT'S OBSTRUCTION OF THE HOUSE OF REPRESENTATIVES' IMPEACHMENT INQUIRY

1. Constitutional Authority for Congressional Oversight and Impeachment

> *Article I of the Constitution vests in the House of Representatives the "sole Power of Impeachment." Congress is authorized to conduct oversight and investigations in support of its Article I powers. The Supreme Court—and previous Presidents—have acknowledged these authorities.*

Overview

The House's Constitutional and legal authority to conduct an impeachment inquiry is clear, as is the duty of the President to cooperate with the House's exercise of this authority. The Constitution vests in the House of Representatives the "sole Power of Impeachment" as well as robust oversight powers. As the Founders intended, the courts have agreed, and prior Presidents have acknowledged, the House's sweeping powers to investigate are at their peak during an impeachment inquiry of a President. Congress has also enacted statutes to support its power to investigate and oversee the Executive Branch.

Unlike President Donald J. Trump, past Presidents who were the subject of impeachment inquiries acknowledged Congress' authority to investigate and—to varying degrees—complied with information requests and subpoenas. Even so, the House has previously determined that partial noncooperation can serve as a ground for an article of impeachment against a President as it would upend the separation of powers to allow the President to dictate the scope of an impeachment inquiry. When President Richard Nixon withheld tape recordings and produced heavily edited and inaccurate records, the House Judiciary Committee approved an article of impeachment for obstruction.

Constitutional Power of Congress to Investigate—and to Impeach

Article I of the U.S. Constitution gives the House of Representatives the "sole Power of Impeachment."[1] The Framers intended the impeachment power to be an essential check on a President who might engage in corruption or abuse power. For example, during the Constitutional Convention, George Mason stated:

> No point is of more importance than that the right of impeachment should be continued. Shall any man be above Justice? Above all shall that man be above it, who can commit the most extensive injustice? ... Shall the man who has practised corruption & by that means procured his appointment in the first instance, be suffered to escape punishment, by repeating his guilt?[2]

Congress is empowered to conduct oversight and investigations to carry out its authorities under Article I.[3] In light of the core nature of the impeachment power to the nation's Constitutional system of checks and balances, Congress' investigative authority is at its zenith during an impeachment inquiry.[4]

As the House Judiciary Committee explained during the impeachment of President Nixon:

> Whatever the limits of legislative power in other contexts—and whatever need may otherwise exist for preserving the confidentiality of Presidential conversations—in the context of an impeachment proceeding the balance was struck in favor of the power of inquiry when the impeachment provision was written into the Constitution.[5]

This conclusion echoed an early observation on the floor of the House of Representatives that the "House possessed the power of impeachment solely, and that this authority certainly implied the right to inspect every paper and transaction in any department, otherwise the power of impeachment could never be exercised with any effect."[6]

The House's "sole Power of Impeachment" is the mechanism provided by the Constitution to hold sitting Presidents accountable for serious misconduct. The Department of Justice has highlighted the importance of the impeachment power in justifying the Department's view that a sitting President cannot be indicted or face criminal prosecution while in office.[7] The Department's position that the President is immune from prosecution has not been endorsed by Congress or the courts, but as long as the Department continues to refuse to prosecute a sitting President, Congress has a heightened responsibility to exercise its impeachment power, if necessary, to ensure that no President is "above the law."[8]

The Supreme Court has recognized that Congress has broad oversight authority under the Constitution to inquire about a wide array of topics, even outside the context of impeachment:

> The power of inquiry has been employed by Congress throughout our history, over the whole range of the national interests concerning which Congress might legislate or decide upon due investigation not to legislate; it has similarly been utilized in determining what to appropriate from the national purse, or whether to appropriate. The scope of the power of inquiry, in short, is as penetrating and farreaching as the potential power to enact and appropriate under the Constitution.[9]

The Supreme Court has made clear that Congress' authority to investigate includes the authority to compel the production of information by issuing subpoenas,[10] a power the House has delegated to its committees pursuant to its Constitutional authority to "determine the Rules of its Proceedings."[11]

The Supreme Court has affirmed that compliance with Congressional subpoenas is mandatory:

> It is unquestionably the duty of all citizens to cooperate with the Congress in its efforts to obtain the facts needed for intelligent legislative action. It is their unremitting obligation to respond to subpoenas, to respect the dignity of the Congress and its committees and to testify fully with respect to matters within the province of proper investigation.[12]

Federal courts have held that the "legal duty" to respond to Congressional subpoenas extends to the President's "senior-level aides" and that the failure to comply violates the separation of powers principles in the Constitution.[13] As one court recently explained:

> [W]hen a committee of Congress seeks testimony and records by issuing a valid subpoena in the context of a duly authorized investigation, it has the Constitution's blessing, and ultimately, it is acting not in its own interest, but for the benefit of the People of the United States. If there is fraud or abuse or waste or corruption in the federal government, it is the constitutional duty of Congress to find the facts and, as necessary, take corrective action. Conducting investigations is the means that Congress uses to carry out that constitutional obligation. Thus, blatant defiance of Congress' centuries-old power to compel the performance of witnesses is not an abstract injury, nor is it a mere banal insult to our democracy. It is an affront to the mechanism for curbing abuses of power that the Framers carefully crafted for our protection, and, thereby, recalcitrant witnesses actually undermine the broader interests of the People of the United States.[14]

Laws Passed by Congress

Congress has enacted statutes to support its power to investigate and oversee the Executive Branch. These laws impose criminal and other penalties on those who fail to comply with inquiries from Congress or block others from doing so, and they reflect the broader Constitutional requirement to cooperate with Congressional investigations. For example:

- *Obstructing Congress:* Obstructing a Congressional investigation is a crime punishable by up to five years in prison. An individual is guilty of obstruction if he or she "corruptly, or by threats or force, or by any threatening letter or communication influences, obstructs, or impedes or endeavors to influence, obstruct, or impede" the "due and proper exercise of the power of inquiry under which any inquiry or investigation is being had by either House, or any committee of either House."[15]

- *Concealing Material Facts:* Concealing information from Congress is also punishable by up to five years in prison. This prohibition applies to anyone who "falsifies, conceals, or covers up" a "material fact" in connection with "any investigation or review, conducted pursuant to the authority of any committee, subcommittee, commission or office of the Congress, consistent with applicable rules of the House or Senate."[16]

- *Intimidating and Harassing Witnesses:* Intimidating witnesses in a Congressional investigation is a crime punishable by up to twenty years in prison. This statute applies to anyone who "knowingly uses intimidation, threatens, or corruptly persuades another person, or attempts to do so, or engages in misleading conduct toward another person," with the intent to "influence, delay, or prevent the testimony of any person in an official proceeding."[17] An individual who "intentionally harasses another person and thereby hinders, delays, prevents, or dissuades" a person from "attending or testifying in an official proceeding" is also guilty of a crime punishable by fines and up to three years in prison.[18]

- ***Retaliating Against Employees Who Provide Information to Congress:*** Employees who speak to Congress have the right not to have adverse personnel actions taken against them. Retaliatory actions taken against Executive Branch employees who cooperate with Congress may constitute violations of this law.[19] Any Executive Branch official who "prohibits or prevents" or "attempts or threatens to prohibit or prevent" any officer or employee of the federal government from speaking with Congress could have his or her salary withheld.[20]

Precedent of Previous Impeachments and Other Investigations

Unlike President Trump, past Presidents who were the subject of impeachment inquiries—including Presidents Andrew Johnson, Richard Nixon, and Bill Clinton—acknowledged Congress' authority to investigate and, to varying degrees, complied with information requests and subpoenas.

For example, President Johnson complied with the House's requests for information. According to a report subsequently adopted by the House Judiciary Committee, "There is no evidence that Johnson ever asserted any privilege to prevent disclosure of presidential conversations to the Committee, or failed to comply with any of the Committee's requests."[21]

Similarly, President Clinton provided written responses to 81 interrogatories from the House Judiciary Committee during the House's impeachment inquiry.[22]

Even President Nixon agreed to let his staff testify voluntarily in the Senate Watergate investigation, stating: "All members of the White House Staff will appear voluntarily when requested by the committee. They will testify under oath, and they will answer fully all proper questions."[23] As a result, numerous senior White House officials testified, including White House Counsel John Dean III, White House Chief of Staff H.R. Haldeman, Deputy Assistant to the President Alexander Butterfield, and Chief Advisor to the President for Domestic Affairs John D. Ehrlichman.[24] President Nixon also produced numerous documents and records in response to the House's subpoenas as part of its impeachment inquiry, including more than 30 transcripts of White House recordings and notes from meetings with the President.[25]

However, President Nixon's production of documents was incomplete. For example, he did not produce tape recordings, and transcripts he produced were heavily edited or inaccurate. President Nixon claimed that his noncompliance with House subpoenas was necessary to protect the confidentiality of Presidential conversations, but the House Judiciary Committee rejected these arguments and approved an article of impeachment for obstruction of the House's impeachment inquiry.[26]

In a letter to President Nixon, Judiciary Committee Chairman Peter Rodino explained that it would upend the separation of powers to allow the President to dictate the scope of an impeachment inquiry:

Under the Constitution it is not within the power of the President to conduct an inquiry into his own impeachment, to determine which evidence, and what version or portion of that evidence, is relevant and necessary to such an inquiry. These are matters which, under the Constitution, the House has the sole power to determine.[27]

Consistent with that long-settled understanding, other Presidents have recognized that they must comply with information requests issued in a House impeachment inquiry. In 1846, for example, President James Polk stated in a message to the House:

It may be alleged that the power of impeachment belongs to the House of Representatives, and that with a view to the exercise of this power, that House has the right to investigate the conduct of all public officers under the government. This is cheerfully admitted. In such a case, the safety of the Republic would be the supreme law; and the power of the House in the pursuit of this object would penetrate into the most secret recesses of the executive departments. It could command the attendance of any and every agent of the government, and compel them to produce all papers, public or private, official or unofficial, and to testify on oath to all facts within their knowledge.[28]

Past Presidents have also produced documents and permitted senior officials to testify in connection with other Congressional investigations, including inquiries into Presidential actions.

For example, in the Iran-Contra inquiry, President Ronald Reagan's former National Security Advisor, Oliver North, and the former Assistant to the President for National Security Affairs, John Poindexter, testified before Congress.[29] President Reagan also produced "relevant excerpts of his personal diaries to Congress."[30]

During the Clinton Administration, Congress obtained testimony from top advisors to President Bill Clinton, including Chief of Staff Mack McLarty, Chief of Staff Erskine Bowles, White House Counsel Bernard Nussbaum, and White House Counsel Jack Quinn.[31]

Similarly, in the Benghazi investigation, led by Chairman Trey Gowdy, President Barack Obama made many of his top aides available for transcribed interviews, including National Security Advisor Susan Rice and Deputy National Security Advisor for Strategic Communications Benjamin Rhodes.[32] The Obama Administration also produced more than 75,000 pages of documents in that investigation, including 1,450 pages of White House emails containing communications of senior officials on the National Security Council.[33]

2. The President's Categorical Refusal to Comply

> *President Trump categorically directed the White House, federal departments and agencies, and federal officials not to cooperate with the House's inquiry and not to comply with duly authorized subpoenas for documents or testimony.*

Overview

Donald Trump is the first and only President in American history to openly and indiscriminately defy all aspects of the Constitutional impeachment process, ordering all federal agencies and officials categorically not to comply with voluntary requests or compulsory demands for documents or testimony.

On September 26, President Trump argued that Congress should not be "allowed" to impeach him under the Constitution and that there "should be a way of stopping it—maybe legally, through the courts." A common theme of his defiance has been his claims that Congress is acting in an unprecedented way and using unprecedented rules. However, the House has been following the same investigative rules that Republicans championed when they were in control.

On October 8, White House Counsel Pat Cipollone—acting on behalf of President Trump—sent a letter to House Speaker Nancy Pelosi and the three investigating Committees confirming that President Trump directed his entire Administration not to cooperate with the House's impeachment inquiry. Mr. Cipollone wrote: "President Trump cannot permit his Administration to participate in this partisan inquiry under these circumstances."

Mr. Cipollone's letter elicited immediate criticism from legal experts across the political spectrum. He advanced remarkably politicized arguments and legal theories unsupported by the Constitution, judicial precedent, and more than 200 years of history. If allowed to stand, the President's defiance, as justified by Mr. Cipollone, would represent an existential threat to the nation's Constitutional system of checks and balances, separation of powers, and rule of law.

The House's Impeachment Inquiry of President Trump

In January, the House of Representatives voted to adopt its rules for the 116th Congress. These rules authorized House committees to conduct investigations, hold hearings, issue subpoenas for documents and testimony, and depose witnesses.[34] Significantly, these authorities are similar to those adopted when Republicans controlled the House during previous Congresses.[35]

In April, Special Counsel Robert S. Mueller III, who was appointed by then-Deputy Attorney General Rod J. Rosenstein to investigate Russian interference in the 2016 U.S. Presidential election and potential obstruction of justice by President Trump, issued a two-volume report.[36] In connection with that report, the Committee on the Judiciary began an inquiry into "whether to approve articles of impeachment with respect to the President."[37] The Judiciary

Committee detailed its authority and intent to conduct this investigation in a series of reports, memoranda, and legal filings.[38]

On August 22, Rep. Jerrold Nadler, the Chairman of the Judiciary Committee, sent a letter requesting that the Permanent Select Committee on Intelligence, the Committee on Oversight and Reform, the Committee on Foreign Affairs, and the Committee on Financial Services provide "information, including documents and testimony, depositions, and/or interview transcripts" relevant to the "ongoing impeachment investigation relating to President Trump."[39]

In September, the Intelligence Committee, the Oversight Committee, and the Foreign Affairs Committee sent letters requesting documents and interviews from the White House and the Department of State regarding the actions of President Trump, the President's personal agent, Rudy Giuliani, and others to pressure Ukraine to launch investigations into former Vice President Joe Biden and a debunked conspiracy theory alleging Ukrainian interference in the 2016 election.[40]

On September 22, President Trump admitted to discussing former Vice President Biden and his son with the President of Ukraine during a telephone call on July 25.[41]

On September 24, Speaker Nancy Pelosi stated publicly that the House Committees were "moving forward" to "proceed with their investigations under that umbrella of impeachment inquiry." She explained that, for the past several months, the House had been "investigating in our Committees and litigating in the courts, so the House can gather 'all the relevant facts and consider whether to exercise its full Article I powers, including a constitutional power of the utmost gravity—approval of articles of impeachment.'"[42]

On September 25, the White House made public a Memorandum of Telephone Conversation of President Trump's call with President Zelensky on July 25. As discussed in detail in Section I, this call record documented how President Trump directly and explicitly asked President Zelensky to launch investigations of former Vice President Biden and the 2016 election.[43]

Following the Speaker's announcement and the release of the call record, the Intelligence Committee, the Oversight Committee, and the Foreign Affairs Committee continued their investigation, requesting documents and information, issuing subpoenas, and conducting interviews and depositions. The Committees made clear that this information would be "collected as part of the House's impeachment inquiry and shared among the Committees, as well as with the Committee on the Judiciary as appropriate."[44]

On October 31, the House voted to approve House Resolution 660, directing the Committees "to continue their ongoing investigations as part of the existing House of Representatives inquiry into whether sufficient grounds exist for the House of Representatives to exercise its Constitutional power to impeach Donald John Trump, President of the United States of America." The resolution set forth the process for holding public hearings, releasing deposition transcripts, presenting a report to the Judiciary Committee, holding proceedings within the Judiciary Committee, and submitting to the House of Representatives "such resolutions, articles of impeachment, or other recommendations as it deems proper."[45]

President Trump's Unprecedented Order Not to Comply

President Trump's categorical and indiscriminate order and efforts to block witness testimony and conceal documentary evidence from the Committees investigating his conduct as part of the House's impeachment inquiry stand in contrast to his predecessors and challenge the basic tenets of the Constitutional system of checks and balances.

Even before the House of Representatives launched its investigation regarding Ukraine, President Trump made numerous statements rejecting the fundamental authority of Congress to investigate his actions as well as those of his Administration. For example, on April 24, he stated, in response to Congressional investigations: "We're fighting all the subpoenas."[46] Similarly, during a speech on July 23, he stated: "I have an Article II, where I have to the right to do whatever I want as president."[47]

When the three investigating Committees began reviewing the President's actions as part of the House's impeachment inquiry, President Trump repeatedly challenged the investigation's legitimacy in word and deed. President Trump's rhetorical attacks appeared intended not just to dispute public reports of his misconduct, but to persuade the public that the House lacks authority to investigate the President and the inquiry is therefore invalid and fraudulent. For example, the President described the impeachment inquiry as:

- "a COUP"[48]
- "illegal, invalid, and unconstitutional"[49]
- "an unconstitutional power grab"[50]
- "Ukraine Witch Hunt"[51]
- "a continuation of the Greatest and most Destructive Witch Hunt of all time"[52]
- "a total Witch Hunt Scam by the Democrats"[53]
- "bad for the country"[54]
- "all a hoax"[55]
- "the single greatest witch hunt in American history"[56]
- "Democrat Scam"[57]
- "just another Democrat Hoax"[58]
- "a fraud against the American people"[59]
- "A Witch Hunt Scam"[60]
- "a con being perpetrated on the United States public and even the world"[61]
- "ridiculous"[62]
- "a continuation of the greatest Scam and Witch Hunt in the history of our Country"[63]
- "Ukraine Hoax"[64]
- "No Due Process Scam"[65]
- "the phony Impeachment Scam"[66]
- "the phony Impeachment Hoax"[67]

On September 26, President Trump argued that Congress should not be "allowed" to impeach him under the Constitution: "What these guys are doing—Democrats—are doing to this country is a disgrace and it shouldn't be allowed. There should be a way of stopping it—maybe legally, through the courts."[68]

A common theme of President Trump's defiance has been his claims that Congress is acting in an unprecedented way and using unprecedented rules. However, the House has been following the same investigative rules that Republicans championed when they were in control and conducted aggressive oversight of previous Administrations.[69]

White House Counsel's Letters Implementing the President's Order

On October 8, White House Counsel Pat Cipollone sent a letter to Speaker Pelosi and the three Committees explaining that President Trump had directed his entire Administration not to cooperate with the House's impeachment inquiry. He wrote:

> Consistent with the duties of the President of the United States, and in particular his obligation to preserve the rights of future occupants of his office, President Trump cannot permit his Administration to participate in this partisan inquiry under these circumstances.[70]

On October 10, President Trump confirmed that Mr. Cipollone was indeed conveying his orders, stating:

> As our brilliant White House Counsel wrote to the Democrats yesterday, he said their highly partisan and unconstitutional effort threatens grave and lasting damage to our democratic institutions, to our system of free elections, and to the American people. That's what it is. To the American people. It's so terrible. Democrats are on a crusade to destroy our democracy. That's what's happening. We will never let it happen. We will defeat them.[71]

Mr. Cipollone's letter elicited immediate criticism from legal experts from across the political spectrum.[72]

Mr. Cipollone wrote a second letter to the Committees on October 18, declaring that the White House would refuse to comply with the subpoena issued to it for documents.[73]

On November 1—after the House had already issued several subpoenas to White House and other Executive Branch officials for testimony—the Trump Administration issued a new "Letter Opinion" from Assistant Attorney General Steven A. Engel to Mr. Cipollone. The Office of Legal Counsel opinion sought to extend the reach of the President's earlier direction to defy Congressional subpoenas and to justify noncompliance by officials who could not plausibly be considered among the President's closest advisors.

Mr. Engel's opinion asserted that the House's impeachment inquiry seeks information that is "potentially protected by executive privilege" and claimed the Committees' deposition subpoenas are "invalid" and "not subject to civil or criminal enforcement" because the House's long-standing deposition rules do not allow the participation of attorneys from the White House or other government agencies.[74] These claims are without basis and unsupported by precedent.

The Letter Opinion cited statements from previous Presidents and Attorneys General that directly undercut the Administration's position. For example, President James K. Polk, stated that in an impeachment inquiry the House had power to "penetrate into the most secret recesses of the Executive Departments."[75] In addition, Attorney General Robert H. Jackson, who later served on the Supreme Court, stated that "pertinent information would be supplied in impeachment proceedings, usually instituted at the suggestion of the Department and for the good of the administration of justice."[76]

In his letters conveying the President's direction, Mr. Cipollone advanced remarkably politicized arguments and legal theories unsupported by the Constitution, judicial precedent, and more than 200 years of history. These letters effectuated the President's order and campaign to obstruct and thwart the House's exercise of its sole power of impeachment under the Constitution. They are rebutted as follows:

- *The Impeachment Inquiry is Constitutional:* According to Mr. Cipollone, "the President did nothing wrong," and "there is no basis for an impeachment inquiry."[77] President Trump has repeatedly described his call with President Zelensky as "perfect."[78] Speaking for President Trump, Mr. Cipollone also asserted that the impeachment inquiry is "partisan and unconstitutional," "a naked political strategy that began the day he was inaugurated, and perhaps even before," and that it "plainly seeks to reverse the election of 2016 and to influence the election of 2020."[79]

  However, as this report details in Section I, Congress found abundant evidence of a scheme directed by the President to solicit foreign election interference by pressing the newly-elected President of Ukraine to announce publicly politically-motivated investigations to benefit President Trump's own reelection campaign. Fundamentally, the Constitutional validity of an impeachment inquiry cannot depend on a President's view that he did nothing wrong or on the political composition of the House. Such an extreme reimagining of the Constitution would render the Article I impeachment power meaningless and provide the President with power the Constitution does not grant him to thwart, manipulate, and stonewall an impeachment inquiry conducted by the House, including by concealing information of his own misconduct.[80] Taken to its logical conclusion, the President's position would eliminate the impeachment power in every year during which a political party other than the President's is in power. Under this approach, the impeachments of President Clinton, President Nixon, and President Andrew Johnson would not have been permitted.[81]

  The purpose of an impeachment inquiry is for the House to collect evidence to determine for itself whether the President may have committed an impeachable offense warranting articles of impeachment. Because the Constitution vests the House alone with "the sole Power of Impeachment," it is not for the President to decide whether the House is exercising that power properly or prudently. The President is not free to arrogate the

212

House's power to himself—or to order across-the-board defiance of House subpoenas—based solely on his unilateral characterization of legislative motives or because he opposes the House's decision to investigate his actions.

- ***The Impeachment Inquiry is Properly Authorized:*** According to Mr. Cipollone, the "House has not expressly adopted any resolution authorizing an impeachment investigation" nor has it "delegated such authority to any of your Committees by rule."[82] However, nothing in either the Constitution or the House Rules requires the full House to vote to authorize an impeachment inquiry.[83] The impeachment inquiries into Presidents Andrew Johnson, Nixon, and Clinton all began prior to the House's consideration and approval of a resolution authorizing the investigations.[84] The same is true of many judicial impeachments;[85] indeed, numerous judges have been impeached without any prior vote of the full House authorizing a formal inquiry.[86] Even though Mr. Cipollone's argument is inherently invalid, the House has taken two floor votes that render it obsolete—the first on January 9 to adopt rules authorizing committees to conduct investigations, and the second on October 31 to set forth procedures for open hearings in the Intelligence Committee and for additional proceedings in the Judiciary Committee.[87] Even following passage of House Resolution 660, whereby the House confirmed the preexisting and ongoing impeachment inquiry, the President and the White House Counsel, acting on the President's behalf, have persisted in their obstructive conduct.

- ***President Has No Valid Due Process Claims:*** According to Mr. Cipollone, "the Committees have not established any procedures affording the President even the most basic protections demanded by due process under the Constitution and by fundamental fairness," and the Committees "have denied the President the right to cross-examine witnesses, to call witnesses, to receive transcripts of testimony, to have access to evidence," and "to have counsel present."[88] Yet, there is no requirement that the House provide these procedures during an impeachment inquiry. The Constitution vests the House with "the sole Power of Impeachment," and provides no constraints on how the House chooses to conduct its impeachment process.[89] Nevertheless, Mr. Cipollone's complaints are unfounded as the House has implemented procedural protections for the President in its exercise of its Constitutional power. House Resolution 660 authorizes procedures to "allow for the participation of the President and his counsel."[90] The Committee Report accompanying House Resolution 660 explains that these protections for the President are part of the Judiciary Committee hearing process and are "based on those provided during the Nixon and Clinton inquiries." These procedures include "that the president and his counsel are invited to attend all hearings; the ability for the president's counsel to cross-examine witnesses and object to the admissibility of testimony; and the ability of the president's counsel to make presentations of evidence before the Judiciary Committee, including the ability to call witnesses."[91]

- ***Fact-Finding Was Appropriately Transparent:*** According to Mr. Cipollone, the Committees conducted their proceedings "in secret."[92] This argument fundamentally misconstrues and misapprehends the fact-gathering process required at this initial stage of the House's impeachment inquiry. Unlike in the cases of Presidents Nixon and Clinton, the House conducted a significant portion of the factual investigation itself because no independent prosecutor was appointed to investigate President Trump's conduct regarding Ukraine. Attorney General William P. Barr refused to authorize a criminal investigation into the serious allegations of misconduct, and even this decision was limited to possible violations of federal campaign finance laws.[93] The investigative Committees proceeded consistent with the House's rules of procedure and in keeping with investigative best practices, including the need to reduce the risk that witnesses may try to coordinate or align testimony. As the House explained in its report accompanying House Resolution 660:

> The initial stages of an impeachment inquiry in the House are akin to those preceding a prosecutorial charging decision. Under this process, the House is responsible for collecting the evidence and, rather than weighing the question of returning an indictment, the Members of the House have the obligation to decide whether to approve articles of impeachment.[94]

The Committees have released transcripts of all interviews and depositions conducted during the investigation. As these transcripts make clear, all Members of all three Committees—including 47 Republican Members of Congress—had the opportunity to ask questions, and these transcripts are now available to the President and his counsel. These same procedures were supported by Acting White House Chief of Staff Mick Mulvaney when he served as a Member of the Oversight Committee and by Secretary of State Mike Pompeo when he served as a Member of the Benghazi Select Committee. In fact, some of the same Members and staff currently conducting depositions as part of the present impeachment inquiry participated directly in depositions during the Clinton, Bush, and Obama Administrations.[95] The Intelligence Committee also held public hearings with 12 of these witnesses.

- ***Agency Attorneys Can Be (And Should Be) Excluded from Depositions:*** According to Mr. Cipollone, "it is unconstitutional to exclude agency counsel from participating in congressional depositions."[96] Mr. Cipollone cites no case law to support his position— because there is none. Instead, he relies on a single opinion from the Trump Administration's Office of Legal Counsel and ignores the ample legal authority and historical precedent that clearly support the Committees' actions. For example, the Constitution expressly delegates to Congress the authority to "determine the Rules of its Proceedings,"[97] which includes the power to determine the procedures used for gathering information from witnesses whether via interview, staff deposition, or in a public hearing.[98] The basis for the rule excluding agency counsel is straightforward: it prevents agency officials who are directly implicated in the abuses Congress is investigating from trying to prevent their own employees from coming forward to tell the truth to Congress. The rule protects the rights of witnesses by allowing them to be accompanied in depositions by personal counsel. Agency attorneys have been excluded from Congressional depositions of Executive Branch officials for decades, under both Republicans and Democrats, including Chairmen Dan Burton, Henry Waxman, Darrell Issa, Jason Chaffetz, Trey Gowdy, Kevin Brady, and Jeb Hensarling, among others.[99]

- ***Congress Can Exercise Its Broad Oversight Authority:*** According to Mr. Cipollone, "you simply cannot expect to rely on oversight authority to gather information for an unauthorized impeachment inquiry that conflicts with all historical precedent and rides roughshod over due process and the separation of powers."[100] But, of course, the present impeachment inquiry does neither. Moreover, the Supreme Court has made clear that Congress' "power of inquiry" is "as penetrating and farreaching as the potential power to enact and appropriate under the Constitution."[101] The subject matter of the impeachment inquiry implicates the House's impeachment-specific as well as legislative and oversight authorities and interests. The activity under investigation, for instance, relates to a broad array of issues in which Congress has legislated and may legislate in the future, including government ethics and transparency, election integrity, appropriations, foreign affairs, abuse of power, bribery, extortion, and obstruction of justice. In fact, Members of Congress have already introduced legislation on issues related to the impeachment inquiry.[102] The House does not forfeit its Constitutional authority to investigate and legislate when it initiates an impeachment inquiry.[103] Congress passed sweeping legislative reforms following the scandal over the Watergate break-in and President Nixon's resignation.[104]

- ***"Confidentiality Interests" Do Not Eliminate Congress' Authority:*** According to Mr. Cipollone, the Administration would also not comply with the Committees' demands for documents and testimony because of unspecified Executive Branch "confidentiality interests."[105] There is no basis in the law of executive privilege for declaring a categorical refusal to respond to any House subpoena. In an impeachment inquiry, the House's need for information and its Constitutional authority are at their greatest, and the Executive's interest in confidentiality must yield. Only the President can assert executive privilege, yet he has not done so in the House's impeachment inquiry. Prior to asserting executive privilege, the Executive Branch is obligated to seek to accommodate the legitimate informational needs of Congress, which, as discussed below, it has not done.[106] In any event, much of the information sought by the Committees would not be covered by executive privilege under any theory,[107] and the privilege—where validly asserted on a particularized basis and not outweighed by the legitimate needs of the impeachment inquiry—would protect any legitimate Executive Branch interest in confidentiality.[108]

- ***President's Top Aides Are Not "Absolutely Immune":*** According to Mr. Cipollone, the President's top aides are "absolutely immune" from being compelled to testify before Congress.[109] This extreme position has been explicitly and repeatedly rejected by Congress—which has received testimony from senior aides to many previous Presidents—and by federal courts. In 2008, a federal court rejected an assertion by President George W. Bush that White House Counsel Harriet Miers was immune from being compelled to testify, noting that the President had failed to identify even a single judicial opinion to justify his claim.[110] On November 25, 2019, another federal judge rejected President Trump's claim of absolute immunity for former White House Counsel Don McGahn, concluding: "Stated simply, the primary takeaway from the past 250 years of recorded American history is that Presidents are not kings," and that "Executive branch officials are not absolutely immune from compulsory congressional process—no matter how many times the Executive branch has asserted as much over the years—even if the President expressly directs such officials' non-compliance."[111] Mr. Cipollone's position, adopted by President Trump, has thus been repudiated by Congress and the courts, and is not salvaged by Executive Branch legal opinions insisting upon a wholly fictional ground for non-compliance. In ordering categorical defiance of House subpoenas, President Trump has confirmed the unlimited breadth of his position and his unprecedented view that no branch of government—even the House—is empowered to investigate whether he may have committed constitutional offenses.

In addition to advancing specious legal arguments, President Trump has made no effort to accommodate the House's interests in conducting the impeachment inquiry. For example, the Committees first requested documents from the White House on September 9, but the White House disregarded the request.[112] The Committees made a second request on September 24, but the White House again ignored the request.[113] Finally, on October 4, the Committees transmitted a subpoena for the documents.[114] However, on October 18, the White House Counsel sent a letter stating that "the White House cannot comply with the October 4 subpoena."[115]

Since then, there has been no evidence of a willingness by the President to produce any of the documents covered by the subpoena to the White House. The State Department made passing references to potentially engaging in an "accommodations" process in response to its September 27 subpoena.[116] However, there has been no effort to do so, and departments and agencies have not produced any documents in response to subpoenas issued as part of the House impeachment inquiry. The President also made no apparent effort to accommodate the House's need for witness testimony and instead continued to flatly refuse to allow Executive Branch officials to testify.

3. The President's Refusal to Produce Any and All Subpoenaed Documents

> *Pursuant to the President's orders, the White House, federal departments and agencies, and key witnesses refused to produce any documents in response to duly authorized subpoenas issued pursuant to the House's impeachment inquiry.*

Overview

Following President Trump's categorical order, not a single document has been produced by the White House, the Office of the Vice President, the Office of Management and Budget, the Department of State, the Department of Defense, or the Department of Energy in response to 71 specific, individualized requests or demands for records in their possession, custody, or control. The subpoenas to federal departments and agencies remain in full force and effect. These agencies and offices also blocked many current and former officials from producing records directly to the Committees.

Certain witnesses defied the President's sweeping, categorical, and baseless order and identified the substance of key documents. Other witnesses identified numerous additional documents that the President and various agencies are withholding that are directly relevant to the impeachment inquiry.

The President's personal attorney, Mr. Giuliani, although a private citizen, also sought to rely on the President's order, as communicated in Mr. Cipollone's letter on October 8, to justify his decision to disobey a lawful subpoena for documents.

The White House

On September 9, the Committees sent a letter to White House Counsel Pat Cipollone seeking six categories of documents in response to reports indicating that, "for nearly two years, the President and his personal attorney, Rudy Giuliani, appear to have acted outside legitimate law enforcement and diplomatic channels to coerce the Ukrainian government into pursuing two politically-motivated investigations under the guise of anti-corruption activity."[117] The Committees asked the White House to voluntarily produce responsive documents by September 16.[118] The White House did not provide any response by that date.

On September 24, the Committees sent a follow-up letter requesting that the White House produce the documents by September 26.[119] Again, the White House did not provide any documents or respond by that date.

Having received no response from the White House, then-Chairman Elijah E. Cummings sent a memorandum to Members of the Committee on Oversight and Reform, which has jurisdiction over the Executive Office of the President, explaining that he was preparing to issue a subpoena in light of the White House's non-compliance and non-responsiveness. He wrote:

Over the past several weeks, the Committees tried several times to obtain voluntary compliance with our requests for documents, but the White House has refused to engage with—or even respond to—the Committees.[120]

On October 4, the Committees sent a letter to Acting White House Chief of Staff Mick Mulvaney transmitting a subpoena issued by Chairman Cummings compelling the White House to produce documents by October 18.[121]

As discussed above, on October 8, the White House Counsel sent a letter to Speaker Pelosi and the Committees stating that "President Trump cannot permit his Administration to participate in this partisan inquiry under these circumstances."[122] The White House Counsel also sent a letter on October 18, confirming that "the White House cannot comply with the October 4 subpoena to Acting Chief of Staff Mulvaney."[123]

To date, the White House has not produced a single document in response to the subpoena.[124] Instead, the White House has released to the public only two documents—call records from the President's phone calls with President Zelensky on April 21 and July 25.[125]

Witnesses who testified before the Committees have identified multiple additional documents that the President is withholding that are directly relevant to the impeachment inquiry, including but not limited to:

- briefing materials for President Trump's call with President Zelensky on July 25 prepared by Lt. Col. Alexander S. Vindman, Director for Ukraine at the National Security Council;[126]

- notes relating to the July 25 call taken by Lt. Col. Vindman and Tim Morrison, the former Senior Director for Europe and Russia on the National Security Council;[127]

- an August 15 "Presidential decision memo" prepared by Lt. Col. Vindman and approved by Mr. Morrison conveying "the consensus views from the entire deputies small group" that "the security assistance be released";[128]

- National Security Council staff summaries of conclusions from meetings at the principal, deputy, or sub-deputy level relating to Ukraine, including military assistance;[129]

- call records between President Trump and Ambassador Gordon Sondland, United States Ambassador to the European Union;[130]

- National Security Council Legal Advisor John Eisenberg's notes and correspondence relating to discussions with Lt. Col. Vindman regarding the July 10 meetings in which Ambassador Sondland requested investigations in exchange for a White House meeting;[131]

- the memorandum of conversation from President Trump's meeting in New York with President Zelensky on September 25;[132] and

- as explained below, emails and other messages between Ambassador Sondland and senior White House officials, including Acting Chief of Staff Mick Mulvaney, Senior Advisor to the Chief of Staff Rob Blair, and then-National Security Advisor John Bolton, among other high-level Trump Administration officials.[133]

The Committees also have good-faith reason to believe that the White House is in possession of and continues to withhold significantly more documents and records responsive to the subpoena and of direct relevance to the impeachment inquiry.

The Committees have closely tracked public reports that the White House is in possession of other correspondence and records of direct relevance to the impeachment inquiry. On November 24, for instance, a news report revealed that the White House had conducted a confidential, internal records review of the hold on military assistance in response to the Committees' inquiry. The review reportedly "turned up hundreds of documents that reveal extensive efforts to generate an after-the-fact justification for the decision and a debate over whether the delay was legal."[134]

Office of the Vice President

On October 4, the Committees sent a letter to Vice President Mike Pence seeking 13 categories of documents in response to reports that he and his staff were directly involved in the matters under investigation. The Committees wrote:

> Recently, public reports have raised questions about any role you may have played in conveying or reinforcing the President's stark message to the Ukrainian President. The reports include specific references to a member of your staff who may have participated directly in the July 25, 2019, call, documents you may have obtained or reviewed, including the record of the call, and your September 1, 2019, meeting with the Ukrainian President in Warsaw, during which you reportedly discussed the Administration's hold on U.S. security assistance to Ukraine.[135]

The Committees asked the Vice President to produce responsive documents by October 15.[136] On that date, Matthew E. Morgan, Counsel to the Vice President, responded to the Committees by refusing to cooperate and reciting many of the same baseless arguments as the White House Counsel. He wrote:

> [T]he purported "impeachment inquiry" has been designed and implemented in a manner that calls into question your commitment to fundamental fairness and due process rights. … Never before in history has the Speaker of the House attempted to launch an "impeachment inquiry" against a President without a majority of the House of Representatives voting to authorize a constitutionally acceptable process.[137]

To date, the Vice President has not produced a single document sought by the Committees and has not indicated any intent to do so going forward.

Witnesses who testified before the Committees have identified multiple additional documents that the Vice President is withholding that are directly relevant to the impeachment inquiry, including but not limited to:

- notes taken by Jennifer Williams, Special Advisor to the Vice President for Europe and Russia, during the call between President Trump and President Zelensky on July 25;[138]

- notes taken by Lt. Gen. Keith Kellogg, National Security Advisor to the Vice President, during the call between President Trump and President Zelensky on July 25;[139]

- materials regarding the July 25 call that were placed in the Vice President's briefing book that same day;[140]

- the memorandum of conversation from Vice President Pence's call with President Zelensky on September 18;[141] and

- briefing materials prepared for Vice President Pence's meeting with President Zelensky September 1 in Warsaw, Poland.[142]

The Committees also have good-faith reason to believe that the Office of the Vice President is in possession of and continues to withhold significantly more documents and records responsive to their request and of direct relevance to the impeachment inquiry.

Office of Management and Budget

On October 7, the Committees sent a letter to Russell Vought, Acting Director of the Office of Management and Budget (OMB), conveying a subpoena issued by the Intelligence Committee for nine categories of documents in response to public reports that the President directed OMB to freeze hundreds of millions of dollars in military assistance appropriated by Congress to help Ukraine counter Russian aggression. The Committees wrote:

> According to multiple press reports, at some point in July 2019, President Trump ordered Acting Chief of Staff and Office of Management and Budget (OMB) Director Mick Mulvaney to freeze the military aid to Ukraine, and Mr. Mulvaney reportedly conveyed the President's order "through the budget office to the Pentagon and the State Department, which were told only that the administration was looking at whether the spending was necessary."[143]

The subpoena compelled Acting Director Vought to produce responsive documents by October 15.[144] On that day, OMB Associate Director for Legislative Affairs Jason Yaworske responded by refusing to produce any documents and reciting many of the same baseless arguments as the White House Counsel:

> [T]he President has advised that "[g]iven that your inquiry lacks any legitimate constitutional foundation, any pretense of fairness, or even the most elementary due process protections, the Executive Branch cannot be expected to participate in

it." … President Trump cannot permit his Administration to participate in this partisan inquiry under these circumstances.[145]

To date, Acting Director Vought has not produced a single document sought by the Committees and has not indicated any intent to do so going forward.

Witnesses who testified before the Committees have identified multiple additional documents that Acting Director Vought is withholding that are directly relevant to the impeachment inquiry, including but not limited to:

- a June 19 email from OMB Associate Director of National Security Programs Michael Duffey to DOD Deputy Comptroller Elaine McCusker regarding the fact that "the President had seen a media report and he had questions about the assistance" and expressing "interest in getting more information from the Department of Defense," specifically a "description of the program";[146]

- a July 12 email from White House Assistant to the President and Senior Advisor to the Chief of Staff Robert Blair to Associate Director Duffey explaining that the "President is directing a hold on military support for Ukraine" and not mentioning any other country or security assistance package;[147] and

- an August 7 memorandum drafted in preparation for Acting Director Vought's attendance at a Principals Committee meeting on Ukrainian security assistance, which included a recommendation to lift the military assistance hold.[148]

The Committees also have good-faith reason to believe that the Office of Management and Budget is in possession of and continues to withhold significantly more documents and records responsive to the subpoena and of direct relevance to the impeachment inquiry.

Department of State

On September 9, the Committees sent a letter to Secretary of State Mike Pompeo requesting six categories of documents in response to reports that "President Trump and his personal attorney appear to have increased pressure on the Ukrainian government and its justice system in service of President Trump's reelection campaign" and "the State Department may be abetting this scheme."[149] The Committees requested that Secretary Pompeo produce responsive documents by September 16. The Secretary did not provide any documents or response by that date.

On September 23, the Committees sent a follow-up letter asking Secretary Pompeo to "inform the Committees by close of business on Thursday, September 26, 2019, whether you intend to fully comply with these requests or whether subpoenas will be necessary."[150] The Secretary did not provide any documents or respond by that date.

On September 27, the Committees sent a letter to Secretary Pompeo conveying a subpoena for documents issued by Rep. Eliot Engel, the Chairman of the Committee on Foreign Affairs, compelling the production of documents by October 4.[151]

Since Secretary Pompeo had failed to respond, the Committees also sent separate letters to six individual State Department employees seeking documents in their possession and requesting that they participate in depositions with the Committees.[152]

On October 1, Secretary Pompeo responded to the Committees for the first time. He objected to the Committees seeking documents directly from State Department employees after he failed to produce them, claiming inaccurately that such a request was "an act of intimidation and an invitation to violate federal records laws."[153] He also claimed that the Committees' inquiry was "an attempt to intimidate, bully, and treat improperly the distinguished professionals of the Department of State."[154]

To the contrary, Deputy Assistant Secretary George Kent, one of the State Department professionals from whom the Committees sought documents and testimony, testified that he "had not felt bullied, threatened, and intimidated."[155] Rather, Mr. Kent said that the language in Secretary Pompeo's letter, which had been drafted by a State Department attorney without consulting Mr. Kent, "was inaccurate."[156] Mr. Kent explained that, when he raised this concern, the State Department attorney "spent the next 5 minutes glaring at me" and then "got very angry." According to Mr. Kent, the official "started pointing at me with a clenched jaw and saying, What you did in there, if Congress knew what you were doing, they could say that you were trying to sort of control, or change the process of collecting documents."[157]

With respect to his own compliance with the subpoena for documents, Secretary Pompeo wrote that he "intends to respond to that subpoena by the noticed return date of October 4, 2019."[158]

Later on October 1, the Committees sent a letter to Deputy Secretary of State John J. Sullivan in light of new evidence that Secretary Pompeo participated on President Trump's call with President Zelensky on July 25. The Committees wrote:

> We are writing to you because Secretary Pompeo now appears to have an obvious conflict of interest. He reportedly participated personally in the July 25, 2019 call, in which President Donald Trump pressed President Volodymyr Zelensky of Ukraine to investigate the son of former Vice President Joseph Biden immediately after the Ukrainian President raised his desire for United States military assistance to counter Russian aggression.
>
> If true, Secretary Pompeo is now a fact witness in the impeachment inquiry. He should not be making any decisions regarding witness testimony or document production in order to protect himself or the President. Any effort by the Secretary or the Department to intimidate or prevent witnesses from testifying or withhold documents from the Committees shall constitute evidence of obstruction of the impeachment inquiry.[159]

The following day, at a press conference in Italy, Secretary Pompeo publicly acknowledged that he had been on the July 25 call between Presidents Trump and Zelensky.[160]

On October 7, Committee staff met with State Department officials who acknowledged that they had taken no steps to collect documents in response to the September 9 letter, but instead had waited for the September 27 subpoena before beginning to search for responsive records. During that conversation, the Committees made a good-faith attempt to engage the Department in the constitutionally-mandated accommodations process. The Committees requested, on a priority basis, "any and all documents that it received directly from Ambassador Sondland," as well as "documents—especially those documents identified by the witnesses as responsive—related to Ambassador Yovanovitch and DAS [Deputy Assistant Secretary] Kent." The depositions of these witnesses—Ambassador Sondland, Ambassador Yovanovitch, and Mr. Kent—were scheduled for the days shortly after that October 7 meeting. The Department's representatives stated that they would take the request back to senior State Department officials, but never provided any further response.[161]

To date, Secretary Pompeo has not produced a single document sought by the Committees and has not indicated any intent to do so going forward. In addition, the Department has ordered its employees not to produce documents in their personal possession. For example, on October 14, the Department sent a letter to Mr. Kent's personal attorney warning that "your client is not authorized to disclose to Congress any records relating to official duties."[162]

Moreover, the Department appears to have actively discouraged its employees from identifying documents responsive to the Committees' subpoena. Mr. Kent testified in his deposition that he informed a Department attorney about additional responsive records that the Department had not collected, including an email from Assistant Secretary of State for Consular Affairs David Risch, who "had spoken to Rudy Giuliani several times in January about trying to get a visa for the corrupt former prosecutor general of Ukraine, Viktor Shokin."[163] The Department attorney "objected to [Mr. Kent] raising of the additional information" and "made clear that he did not think it was appropriate for [Mr. Kent] to make the suggestion."[164] Mr. Kent responded that what he was "trying to do was make sure that the Department was being fully responsive."[165]

Certain witnesses defied the President's directive and produced the substance of key documents. For example, Ambassador Sondland attached ten exhibits to his written hearing statement.[166] These exhibits contained replicas of emails and WhatsApp messages between Ambassador Sondland and high-level Trump Administration officials, including Secretary Pompeo, Secretary Perry, Acting Chief of Staff Mick Mulvaney, and former National Security Advisor John Bolton.[167] The exhibits also contained a replica of a WhatsApp message between Ambassador Sondland and Mr. Yermak.[168]

Earlier in the investigation, Ambassador Kurt Volker had produced key text messages with Ambassador Taylor, Ambassador Sondland, President Zelensky's senior aide, Andriy Yermak, Mr. Giuliani, and others very soon after the Committees requested them and prior to Mr. Cipollone's letter on October 8 conveying the President's directive not to comply.[169]

The Department also prevented Ambassador Sondland—a current State Department employee—from accessing records to prepare for his testimony. As described above, federal law imposes fines and up to five years in prison for anyone who corruptly or by threats "impedes or endeavors to influence, obstruct, or impede" the "due and proper exercise of the power of inquiry under which any inquiry or investigation is being had by either House, or any committee of either House."[170] Ambassador Sondland explained that the Department's actions directly impeded his testimony:

> I have not had access to all of my phone records, State Department emails, and other State Department documents. And I was told I could not work with my EU Staff to pull together the relevant files. Having access to the State Department materials would have been very helpful to me in trying to reconstruct with whom I spoke and met, when, and what was said. ...

> My lawyers and I have made multiple requests to the State Department and the White House for these materials. Yet, these materials were not provided to me. They have also refused to share these materials with this Committee. These documents are not classified and, in fairness, should have been made available.[171]

He testified, "I have been hampered to provide completely accurate testimony without the benefit of those documents."[172] Ambassador Sondland also stated:

> Despite repeated requests to the White House and the State Department, I have not been granted access to all of the phone records, and I would like to review those phone records, along with any notes and other documents that may exist, to determine if I can provide more complete testimony to assist Congress.[173]

On November 22, the Department produced 99 pages of emails, letters, notes, timelines, and news articles to a non-partisan, nonprofit ethics watchdog organization pursuant to a court order in a lawsuit filed under the Freedom of Information Act (FOIA).[174] This handful of documents was limited to a narrow window of time and specific people, but it clearly indicates that the Department is withholding documents that are responsive to the Committees' requests.

For example, the Department's FOIA production contains an email from the Office Manager to the Secretary of State to "S_All" sent on March 26 which states that "S is speaking with Rudy Giuliani."[175] It also contains a March 27 email in which Madeleine Westerhout, the Personal Secretary to President Trump, facilitates another phone call between Rudy Giuliani and Secretary Pompeo.[176] These documents are directly responsive to the September 27 subpoena for "all documents and communications, from January 20, 2017 to the present, relating or referring to: Communications between any current or former State Department officials or employees and Rudolph W. Giuliani, including any text messages using personal or work-related devices."[177]

Witnesses who testified before the Committees have identified multiple additional documents that Secretary Pompeo is withholding that are directly relevant to the impeachment inquiry, including but not limited to:

- a cable on August 29 from Bill Taylor, the Chargé d'Affaires for U.S. Embassy in Kyiv, Ukraine, at the recommendation of National Security Advisor John Bolton, sent directly to Secretary Pompeo "describing the folly I saw in withholding military aid to Ukraine at a time when hostilities were still active in the east and when Russia was watching closely to gauge the level of American support for the Ukrainian Government" and telling Secretary Pompeo "that I could not and would not defend such a policy";[178]

- WhatsApp messages and emails that Ambassador Sondland replicated and provided as exhibits to the Intelligence Committee showing key communications between Ambassador Sondland and high-level Trump Administration officials, including Secretary Pompeo, Secretary Perry, Acting Chief of Staff Mick Mulvaney, and National Security Advisor John Bolton, as well as President Zelensky's senior aide, Andriy Yermak;[179]

- notes and memoranda to file from Mr. Kent, Ambassador Taylor, and others, including Ambassador Taylor's "little notebook" in which he would "take notes on conversations, in particular when I'm not in the office," such as meetings with Ukrainians or when out and receiving a phone call," as well as his "small, little spiral notebook" of calls that took place in the office;[180]

- emails among Philip Reeker, Acting Assistant Secretary of State, Bureau of European and Eurasian Affairs; David Hale, Under Secretary of State for Political Affairs; Mr. Kent; and others regarding the unsuccessful effort to issue a public statement in support of Ambassador Yovanovitch, including the "large number of emails related to the press guidance and the allegations about the Ambassador" from the "late March timeframe."[181]

The Committees also have good-faith reason to believe that the Department of State is in possession of and continues to withhold significantly more documents and records responsive to the subpoena and of direct relevance to the impeachment inquiry.

Department of Defense

On October 7, the Committees sent a letter to Secretary of Defense Mark Esper conveying a subpoena issued by the Intelligence Committee for 14 categories of documents in response to reports that the President directed a freeze of hundreds of millions of dollars in military aid appropriated by Congress to help Ukraine counter Russian aggression. The Committees wrote:

Officials at the Departments of State and Defense reportedly were "puzzled and alarmed" after learning about the White House's directive. Defense Department officials reportedly "tried to make a case to the White House that the Ukraine aid was effective and should not be looked at in the same manner as other aid," but "those arguments were ignored."[182]

The subpoena required Secretary Esper to produce responsive documents by October 15. On October 13, Secretary Esper stated in a public interview that the Department would comply with the Intelligence Committee's subpoena:

Q: Very quickly, are you going to comply with the subpoena that the House provided you and provide documents to them regarding to the halt to military aid to Ukraine?

A: Yeah we will do everything we can to cooperate with the Congress. Just in the last week or two, my general counsel sent out a note as we typically do in these situations to ensure documents are retained.

Q: Is that a yes?

A: That's a yes.

Q: You will comply with the subpoena?

A: We will do everything we can to comply.[183]

On October 15, however, Assistant Secretary of Defense for Legislative Affairs Robert R. Hood responded by refusing to produce any documents and reciting many of the same legally unsupportable arguments as the White House Counsel:

In light of these concerns, and in view of the President's position as expressed in the White House Counsel's October 8 letter, and without waiving any other objections to the subpoena that the Department may have, the Department is unable to comply with your request for documents at this time.[184]

To date, Secretary Esper has not produced a single document sought by the Committees and has not indicated any intent to do so going forward, notwithstanding his public promise to "do everything we can to comply."[185]

Witnesses who testified before the Committees have identified multiple additional documents that Secretary Esper is withholding that are directly relevant to the impeachment inquiry, including but not limited to:

- DOD staff readouts from National Security Council meetings at the principal, deputy, or sub-deputy level relating to Ukraine, including military assistance;[186]

- an email from Secretary Esper's Chief of Staff, to Laura K. Cooper, Deputy Assistant Secretary of Defense for Russia, Ukraine, and Eurasia, in late July "asking for follow-up on a meeting with the President," including information on whether "U.S. industry [is] providing any of this equipment," "international contributions" to Ukraine, and "who gave this funding";[187]

- fact sheets and other information provided by Ms. Cooper in response to the email request;[188]

- an email sent to Ms. Cooper's staff on July 25 at 2:31 p.m.—the same day as President's Trump's call with Ukrainian President Zelensky—stating that the Ukrainian Embassy was inquiring about the status of military aid, suggesting that Ukrainian officials were concerned about the status of the military aid much earlier than ever previously acknowledged by the Executive Branch;[189]

- an email sent to Ms. Cooper's staff on July 25 at 4:25 p.m. stating that the Ukrainian Embassy and The Hill newspaper had become aware of the situation with the military assistance funding;[190] and

- an email received by Ms. Cooper's staff on July 3 at 4:23 p.m. from the Department of State explaining that the Department of State "had heard the CN [Congressional Notification] is currently being blocked by OMB."[191]

The Committees also have good-faith reason to believe that the Department of Defense is in possession of and continues to withhold significantly more documents and records responsive to the subpoena and of direct relevance to the impeachment inquiry.

Department of Energy

On October 10, the Committees sent a letter to Secretary of Energy Rick Perry conveying a subpoena issued by the Intelligence Committee for ten categories of documents in response to reports about his involvement with matters under investigation. The Committees wrote:

Recently, public reports have raised questions about any role you may have played in conveying or reinforcing the President's stark message to the Ukrainian President. These reports have also raised significant questions about your efforts to press Ukrainian officials to change the management structure at a Ukrainian state-owned energy company to benefit individuals involved with Rudy Giuliani's push to get Ukrainian officials to interfere in our 2020 election.[192]

The subpoena required Secretary Perry to produce responsive documents by October 18. On that day, Melissa F. Burnison, the Assistant Secretary of Energy for Congressional and Intergovernmental Affairs, responded by refusing to produce any documents and reciting many of the same flawed arguments as the White House Counsel:

Pursuant to these concerns, the Department restates the President's position: "Given that your inquiry lacks any legitimate constitutional foundation, any pretense of fairness, or even the most elementary due process protections, the Executive Branch cannot be expected to participate in it."[193]

To date, Secretary Perry has not produced a single document sought by the Committees and has not indicated any intent to do so going forward.

Witnesses who testified before the Committees have identified multiple documents that Secretary Perry is withholding that are directly relevant to the impeachment inquiry, including but not limited to:

- a document passed directly from Secretary Perry to President Zelensky in a May 2019 meeting with a list of "people he trusts" that President Zelensky could seek advice from on issues of relating to "key Ukrainian energy-sector contacts," according to David Holmes, the Political Counselor at the U.S. Embassy in Kyiv;[194]

- a June 5 email from Philip Reeker, Acting Assistant Secretary of State, Bureau of European and Eurasian Affairs, to Secretary Perry and others, regarding "Zelenskyy's visit to Brussels, and the critical—perhaps historic—role of the dinner and engagement Gordon [Ambassador Sondland] coordinated";[195] and

- a July 19 email from Secretary Perry in which he states "Mick [Acting Chief of Staff Mick Mulvaney] just confirmed the call being set up for tomorrow by NSC" in reference to a call between President Trump and President Zelensky.[196]

The Committees also have good-faith reason to believe that the Department of Energy is in possession of and continues to withhold significantly more documents and records responsive to the subpoena and of direct relevance to the impeachment inquiry.

Rudy Giuliani and His Associates

On September 30, the Committees sent a letter conveying a subpoena issued by the Intelligence Committee to the President's personal attorney, Rudy Giuliani, compelling the production of 23 categories of documents relating to his actions in Ukraine.[197]

On October 15, Mr. Giuliani's counsel responded to the Committees by stating that Mr. Giuliani "will not participate because this appears to be an unconstitutional, baseless, and illegitimate 'impeachment inquiry.'"[198] He also stated: "Mr. Giuliani adopts all the positions set forth in Mr. Cipollone's October 8, 2019 letter on behalf of President Donald J. Trump."[199]

To date, Mr. Giuliani has not produced a single document sought by the Committees and has not indicated any intent to do so going forward.

On September 30, the Committees sent letters to two of Mr. Giuliani's business associates—Igor Fruman and Lev Parnas—requesting testimony and eleven categories of documents from each.[200] The Committees sought documents from Mr. Fruman and Mr. Parnas related to their efforts to influence U.S. elections.

According to press reports, Mr. Parnas and Mr. Fruman reportedly were "assisting with Giuliani's push to get Ukrainian officials to investigate former vice president Joe Biden and his son as well as Giuliani's claim that Democrats conspired with Ukrainians in the 2016 campaign." Press reports also indicate that Mr. Parnas and Mr. Fruman were involved with efforts to press Ukrainian officials to change the management structure at a Ukrainian state-owned energy company, Naftogaz, to benefit individuals involved with Mr. Giuliani's push to get Ukrainian officials to interfere in the 2020 election.[201]

On October 3, counsel to Mr. Fruman and Mr. Parnas responded to Committee staff, explaining his clients' relationship with Mr. Giuliani and President Trump:

> Be advised that Messrs. Parnas and Fruman assisted Mr. Giuliani in connection with his representation of President Trump. Mr. Parnas and Mr. Fruman have also been represented by Mr. Giuliani in connection with their personal and business affairs. They also assisted Joseph DiGenova and Victoria Toensing in their law practice.[202]

With respect to preparing Mr. Fruman and Mr. Parnas' response, their counsel wrote: "The amount of time requires is difficult to determine. [sic] but we are happy to keep you advised of our progress and engage in a rolling production of non-privileged documents."

On October 8, their counsel wrote again to Committee staff, stating:

> This is an update. We continue to meet with Mr. Parnas and Mr. Fruman to gather the facts and documents related to the many subjects and persons detailed in your September 30 letter and to evaluate all of that information in light of the privileges we raised in our last letter.[203]

On October 9, their counsel wrote to Committee staff, stating, "Please be advised that Messrs. Parnas and Fruman agree with and adopt the position of White House Counsel pertaining to Democrat inquiry."[204]

On October 10, the Committees transmitted subpoenas compelling Mr. Fruman and Mr. Parnas to produce eleven categories of documents.[205] That same day, their counsel responded:

> As I did in my recent letter of October 8, 2019, please be advised we were in the formative stages of recovering and reviewing records on October 9 when Messrs. Parnas and Fruman were arrested by the FBI and locked up in Virginia pursuant to Four Count Indictment by a Federal Grand Jury in the Southern District of New York unsealed on October 10, 2019.

> Further their records and other belongings, including materials sought by your subpoenas, were seized pursuant warrants [sic] by the FBI in several locations on the 9th or 10th of October.[206]

To date, Mr. Fruman has not produced a single document in response to his subpoena and has not indicated any intent to do so going forward.

With respect to Mr. Parnas, he obtained new counsel during the course of the impeachment inquiry. His new attorney has asserted that Mr. Parnas will cooperate with the House's inquiry, stating: "We will honor and not avoid the committee's requests to the extent they are legally proper, while scrupulously protecting Mr. Parnas' privileges including that of the Fifth Amendment."[207]

In contrast to Mr. Giuliani and Mr. Fruman, Mr. Parnas has begun rolling production of certain records in his possession, custody, or control in response to the subpoena, which the Committees are evaluating. The Committees expect Mr. Parnas' full compliance with the subpoena.

4. The President's Refusal to Allow Top Aides to Testify

> *At President Trump's direction, twelve current or former Administration officials refused to testify as part of the House's impeachment inquiry, ten of whom did so in defiance of duly authorized subpoenas. The President's orders were coordinated and executed by the White House Counsel and others, and they prevented testimony from officials from the White House, National Security Council, Office of Management and Budget, Department of State, and Department of Energy.*

Overview

No other President in history has issued an order categorically directing the entire Executive Branch not to testify before Congress, including in the context of an impeachment inquiry. President Trump issued just such an order.

As reflected in White House Counsel Pat Cipollone's October 8 letter, President Trump directed all government witnesses to violate their legal obligations by defying House subpoenas—regardless of their office or position.[208] President Trump even extended his order to former officials no longer employed by the federal government. This Administration-wide effort to prevent all witnesses from providing testimony was coordinated and comprehensive.

These witnesses were warned that their refusal to testify "shall constitute evidence that may be used against you in a contempt proceeding" and "may be used as an adverse inference against you and the President."

Despite the President's unprecedented commands, the House gathered a wealth of evidence of his conduct from courageous individuals who were willing to follow the law, comply with duly authorized subpoenas, and tell the truth. Nevertheless, the President's efforts to obstruct witness testimony deprived Congress and the public of additional evidence.

In following President Trump's orders to defy duly authorized Congressional subpoenas, several Administration officials who, to date, remain under subpoena may have placed themselves at risk of being held in criminal contempt of Congress.[209] These witnesses were warned explicitly that their refusal to obey lawful orders to testify "shall constitute evidence that may be used against you in a contempt proceeding" and could also result in adverse inferences being drawn against both them and the President.[210]

Mick Mulvaney, Acting White House Chief of Staff

On November 5, the Committees sent a letter to Mick Mulvaney, the Acting White House Chief of Staff, seeking his appearance at a deposition on November 8.[211] The Committees received no response to this letter.

On November 7, the Intelligence Committee issued a subpoena compelling Mr. Mulvaney's appearance at a deposition on November 8.[212] On November 8, Mr. Mulvaney's personal attorney sent an email to Committee staff stating that "Mr. Mulvaney will not be attending the deposition today, and he is considering the full range of his legal options."[213]

Mr. Mulvaney's personal attorney provided a letter that was sent on November 8 from Mr. Cipollone, stating that "the President directs Mr. Mulvaney not to appear at the Committee's scheduled deposition on November 8, 2019."[214] Mr. Mulvaney's personal attorney also provided a letter sent on November 7 from Steven A. Engel, Assistant Attorney General at the Office of Legal Counsel of the Department of Justice, to Mr. Cipollone, stating, "Mr. Mulvaney is absolutely immune from compelled congressional testimony in his capacity as a senior advisor to the President."[215]

Mr. Mulvaney did not appear at the deposition on November 8, in defiance of the Committees' subpoena. The Committees met, and Chairman Schiff acknowledged Mr. Mulvaney's absence, stating:

> Neither Congress nor the courts recognize a blanket absolute immunity as a basis to defy a congressional subpoena. Mr. Mulvaney and the White House, therefore, have no legitimate legal basis to evade a duly authorized subpoena. The President's direction to Mr. Mulvaney to defy our subpoena can, therefore, only be construed as an effort to delay testimony and obstruct the inquiry, consistent with the White House Counsel's letter dated October 8, 2019.[216]

Chairman Schiff also explained Mr. Mulvaney's knowledge of and role in facilitating the President's conduct:

> Mr. Mulvaney's role in facilitating the White House's obstruction of the impeachment inquiry does not occur in a vacuum. Over the past several weeks, we have gathered extensive evidence of the President's abuse of power related to pressuring Ukraine to pursue investigations that would benefit the President personally and politically and jeopardize national security in doing so. Some of that evidence has revealed that Mr. Mulvaney was a percipient witness to misconduct by the President and may have had a role in certain actions under investigation. The evidence shows that Mr. Mulvaney may have coordinated with U.S. Ambassador to the European Union Gordon Sondland, Rudy Giuliani, and others to carry out President Trump's scheme to condition a White House meeting with President Zelensky on the Ukrainians' pursuit of investigations of the Bidens, Burisma holdings, and purported Ukrainian interference in the 2016 U.S. Presidential election. In addition, evidence suggests that Mr. Mulvaney may have played a central role in President Trump's attempt to coerce Ukraine into launching his desired political investigations by withholding nearly $400 million in vital security assistance from Ukraine that had been appropriated by Congress. At a White House press briefing on October 17, 2019, Mr. Mulvaney admitted publicly that President Trump ordered the hold on Ukraine security assistance to further the President's own personal political interests rather than the national interest. …

Based on the record evidence gathered to date, we can only infer that Mr. Mulvaney's refusal to testify is intended to prevent the Committees from learning additional evidence of President Trump's misconduct and that Mr. Mulvaney's testimony would corroborate and confirm other witnesses' accounts of such misconduct. If the White House had evidence to contest those facts, they would allow Mr. Mulvaney to be deposed. Instead, the President and the White House are hiding and trying to conceal the truth from the American people. Given the extensive evidence the Committees have already uncovered, the only result of this stonewalling is to buttress the case for obstruction of this inquiry.[217]

To date, Mr. Mulvaney has not changed his position about compliance with the subpoena.[218]

Robert B. Blair, Assistant to the President and Senior Advisor to the Chief of Staff

On October 24, the Committees sent a letter to Robert B. Blair, an Assistant to the President and the Senior Advisor to Acting Chief of Staff Mulvaney, seeking Mr. Blair's appearance at a deposition on November 1.[219] On November 2, Mr. Blair's personal attorney sent a letter to the Committees stating:

> Mr. Blair has been directed by the White House not to appear and testify at the Committees' proposed deposition, based on the Department of Justice's advice that the Committees may not validly require an executive branch witness to appear at such a deposition without the assistance of agency counsel. In light of the clear direction he has been given by the Executive Branch, Mr. Blair must respectfully decline to testify, as you propose, on Monday, November 4, 2019.[220]

On November 3, the Committees sent a letter to Mr. Blair's personal attorney transmitting a subpoena compelling Mr. Blair to appear at a deposition on November 4.[221]

On November 4, Mr. Blair did not appear for the scheduled deposition, in defiance of the Committees' subpoena. The Committees met and Chairman Schiff acknowledged Mr. Blair's absence, stating:

> Although the committees requested a copy of the correspondence from the White House and Department of Justice, Mr. Blair's Counsel did not provide it to the Committees. This new and shifting rationale from the White House, like the others it has used to attempt to block witnesses from appearing to provide testimony about the President's misconduct, has no basis in law or the Constitution and is a serious affront to decades of precedent in which Republicans and Democrats have used exactly the same procedures to depose executive branch officials without agency counsel present, including some of the most senior aides to multiple previous Presidents.[222]

Unlike President Trump's directive to Acting Chief of Staff Mulvaney, neither Mr. Blair nor the White House have asserted that Mr. Blair is "absolutely immune" from providing testimony to Congress. To date, Mr. Blair has not changed his position or contacted the Committees about compliance with the subpoena.

Ambassador John Bolton, Former National Security Advisor

On October 30, the Committees sent a letter to the personal attorney of Ambassador John Bolton, the former National Security Advisor to President Trump, seeking his appearance at a deposition on November 7.[223] Later that day, Ambassador Bolton's personal attorney sent an email to Committee staff stating, "As you no doubt have anticipated, Ambassador Bolton is not willing to appear voluntarily."[224]

On November 7, Ambassador Bolton did not appear for the scheduled deposition. On November 8, Ambassador Bolton's personal attorney sent a letter to Douglas Letter, the General Counsel of the House of Representatives, suggesting that, if Ambassador Bolton were subpoenaed, he would file a lawsuit and would comply with the subpoena only if ordered to do so by the court. He referenced a lawsuit filed by another former official, Dr. Charles Kupperman, represented by the same attorney and stated:

> As I emphasized in my previous responses to letters from the House Chairs, Dr. Kupperman stands ready, as does Ambassador Bolton, to testify if the Judiciary resolves the conflict in favor of the Legislative Branch's position respecting such testimony.[225]

To date, Ambassador Bolton has not changed his position or come forward to testify.[226]

John A. Eisenberg, Deputy Counsel to the President for
National Security Affairs and Legal Advisor, National Security Council

On October 30, the Committees sent a letter to John A. Eisenberg, the Deputy Counsel to the President for National Security Affairs and the Legal Advisor at the National Security Council, seeking his appearance at a deposition on November 4.[227] The Committees received no response to this letter.[228]

On November 1, the Committees sent a letter to Mr. Eisenberg transmitting a subpoena compelling his appearance at a deposition on November 4.[229] On November 4, Mr. Eisenberg's personal attorney sent a letter to the Committees, stating:

> Even if Mr. Eisenberg had been afforded a reasonable amount of time to prepare, the President has instructed Mr. Eisenberg not to appear at the deposition. Enclosed with this letter is the President's instruction as relayed by Pat A. Cipollone, Counsel to the President, in a letter dated November 3, 2019. We also enclose a letter, also dated November 3, 2019, from Steven A. Engel, Assistant Attorney General for the Office of Legal Counsel at the Department of Justice, to Mr. Cipollone advising that Mr. Eisenberg is "absolutely immune from compelled congressional testimony in his capacity as a senior advisor to the President." Under these circumstances, Mr. Eisenberg has no other option that is consistent with his legal and ethical obligations except to follow the direction of his client and employer, the President of the United States. Accordingly, Mr. Eisenberg will not be appearing for a deposition at this time.[230]

Enclosed was a letter sent on November 3 from Mr. Cipollone to Mr. Eisenberg's personal attorney stating that "the President directs Mr. Eisenberg not to appear at the Committee's deposition on Monday, November 4, 2019."[231] Also enclosed was a letter sent on November 3 by Assistant Attorney General Steven A. Engel to the Office of Legal Counsel of the Department of Justice to Mr. Cipollone stating:

> You have asked whether the Committee may compel Mr. Eisenberg to testify. We conclude that he is absolutely immune from compelled congressional testimony in his capacity as a senior advisor to the President.[232]

Mr. Eisenberg did not appear for the scheduled deposition, in defiance of the Committees' subpoena. The Committees met and Chairman Schiff acknowledged Mr. Eisenberg's absence, stating:

> Despite his legal obligations to comply, Mr. Eisenberg is not present here today and has therefore defied a duly authorized congressional subpoena. This morning, in an email received at 9:00 a.m., when the deposition was supposed to commence, Mr. Eisenberg's personal attorney sent a letter to the committee stating that President Trump had, quote, "instructed Mr. Eisenberg not to appear at the deposition," unquote. The attorney attached correspondence from White House counsel Pat Cipollone and a letter from the Office of Legal Counsel at Department of Justice. The OLC letter informs the White House that Mr. Eisenberg is purportedly, quote, "absolutely immune from compelled congressional testimony in his capacity as a senior advisor to the President," unquote. …
>
> Moreover, neither Congress nor the courts recognize a blanket, quote, "absolute immunity," unquote, as a basis to defy a congressional subpoena. Mr. Eisenberg and the White House, therefore, have no basis for evading a lawful subpoena. As such, the President's direction to Mr. Eisenberg to defy a lawful compulsory process can only be construed as an effort to delay testimony and obstruct the inquiry, consistent with the White House counsel's letter dated October 8, 2019. As Mr. Eisenberg was informed, the Committees may consider his noncompliance with the subpoena as evidence in a future contempt proceeding. His failure or refusal to appear, moreover, shall constitute evidence of obstruction of the House's impeachment inquiry and may be used as an adverse inference against the President. The subpoena remains in full force. The committees reserve all of their rights, including the right to raise this matter at a future Intelligence Committee proceeding, at the discretion of the chair of the committee.
>
> Mr. Eisenberg's nonappearance today adds to a growing body of evidence of the White House seeking to obstruct the White House's impeachment inquiry. To the extent the White House believes that an issue could be raised at the deposition that may implicate a valid claim of privilege, the White House may seek to assert that privilege with the Committee in advance of the deposition. To date, as has been the case in every other deposition as part of the inquiry, the White House has not done so. Mr. Eisenberg's failure to appear today also flies in the face of historical precedent. Even absent impeachment proceedings, congressional committees have deposed senior White House officials, including White House counsels and senior White House lawyers.[233]

Michael Ellis, Senior Associate Counsel to the President and Deputy Legal Advisor, National Security Council

On October 30, the Committees sent a letter to Michael Ellis, a Senior Associate Counsel to the President and the Deputy Legal Advisor at the National Security Council, seeking his appearance at a deposition on November 4.[234] On November 2, Mr. Ellis' personal attorney sent an email to Committee staff stating:

> [W]e are in receipt of an opinion from the Office of Legal Counsel providing guidance on the validity of a subpoena under the current terms and conditions and based on that guidance we are not in a position to appear for a deposition at this time.[235]

This email followed the November 1 Office of Legal Counsel opinion, discussed above, which sought to extend the reach of the President's earlier direction to defy Congressional subpoenas and provided justification for noncompliance by officials who could not plausibly be considered among the President's closest advisors.

On November 3, Mr. Ellis' personal attorney sent another email to Committee staff stating:

> [O]ur guidance is that the failure to permit agency counsel to attend a deposition of Mr. Ellis would not allow sufficient protection of relevant privileges and therefore render any subpoena constitutionally invalid. As an Executive branch employee Mr. Ellis is required to follow this guidance.[236]

On November 3, the Committees sent a letter to Mr. Ellis' personal attorney transmitting a subpoena compelling his appearance at a deposition on November 4, stating:

> Mr. Ellis' failure or refusal to comply with the subpoena, including at the direction or behest of the President or the White House, shall constitute further evidence of obstruction of the House's impeachment inquiry and may be used as an adverse inference against Mr. Ellis and the President.[237]

On November 4, Mr. Ellis did not appear for the scheduled deposition, in defiance of the Committees' subpoena. The Committees met and Chairman Schiff acknowledged Mr. Ellis' absence, stating:

> Other than the White House's objections to longstanding congressional practice, the committees are aware of no other valid constitutional privilege asserted by the White House to direct Mr. Ellis to defy this subpoena.[238]

To date, Mr. Ellis has not changed his position or contacted the Committees about compliance with the subpoena.

Preston Wells Griffith, Senior Director for International
Energy and Environment, National Security Council

On October 24, the Committees sent a letter to Preston Wells Griffith, the Senior Director for International Energy and Environment at the National Security Council, seeking his appearance at a deposition on November 5.[239] On November 4, Mr. Griffith's personal attorney sent a letter to the Committees stating:

> As discussed with Committee counsel, Mr. Griffith respectfully declines to appear for a deposition before the joint Committees conducting the impeachment inquiry, based upon the direction of White House Counsel that he not appear due to agency counsel not being permitted.[240]

Later that day, the Committees sent a letter to Mr. Griffith's personal attorney transmitting a subpoena compelling his appearance at a deposition on November 5, stating:

> Mr. Griffith's failure or refusal to comply with the subpoena, including at the direction or behest of the President or the White House, shall constitute further evidence of obstruction of the House's impeachment inquiry and may be used as an adverse inference against Mr. Griffith and the President.[241]

On November 5, Mr. Griffith did not appear for the scheduled deposition, in defiance of the Committees' subpoena. The Committees met and Chairman Schiff acknowledged Mr. Griffith's absence, stating:

> Although the committees requested a copy of any written direction from the White House, Mr. Griffith's counsel has not provided any such documentation to the committees. The White House's newly invented rationale for obstructing the impeachment inquiry appears based on a legal opinion that was issued by the Department of Justice Office of Legal Counsel just last Friday, November 1. It is noteworthy and telling that OLC issued this opinion after multiple current and former White House, State Department, and Department of Defense officials testified before the committees, both voluntarily and pursuant to subpoena, all without agency counsel present. The White House's invocation of this self-serving OLC opinion should therefore be seen for what it is: a desperate attempt to staunch the flow of incriminating testimony from the executive branch officials about the President's abuse of power.[242]

To date, Mr. Griffith has not changed his position or contacted the Committees about compliance with the subpoena.

Dr. Charles M. Kupperman, Former Deputy Assistant to the President
for National Security Affairs, National Security Council

On October 16, the Committees sent a letter to Dr. Charles M. Kupperman, a former Deputy Assistant to the President for National Security Affairs, seeking his appearance at a deposition on October 23.[243]

On October 25, the Intelligence Committee issued a subpoena compelling Dr. Kupperman to appear at a deposition on October 28.[244]

Later that day, Dr. Kupperman's personal attorney sent an email to Committee staff attaching a 17-page complaint in federal court seeking a declaratory judgment as to whether he should comply with the subpoena.[245] His counsel wrote:

> Pending the courts' determination as to which Branch should prevail, Dr. Kupperman will not effectively adjudicate the conflict by appearing and testifying before the Committees.[246]

Enclosed as part of the complaint was a letter sent on October 25 from Mr. Cipollone to Dr. Kupperman's personal attorney stating that "the President directs Mr. Kupperman not to appear at the Committee's scheduled hearing on Monday, October 28, 2019."[247] Also enclosed was a letter sent on October 25 from Steven A. Engel, Assistant Attorney General at the Office of Legal Counsel of the Department of Justice, to Mr. Cipollone stating that Dr. Kupperman "is absolutely immune from compelled congressional testimony in his capacity as a former senior advisor to the President."[248]

On October 26, the Committees sent a letter to Dr. Kupperman's personal attorneys, stating:

> In light of the direction from the White House, which lacks any valid legal basis, the Committees shall consider your client's defiance of a congressional subpoena as additional evidence of the President's obstruction of the House's impeachment inquiry.[249]

Later that day, Dr. Kupperman's personal attorney sent a letter to Committee staff, stating: "The proper course for Dr. Kupperman, we respectfully submit, is to lay the conflicting positions before the Court and abide by the Court's judgment as to which is correct."[250] On October 27, Dr. Kupperman's personal attorney sent a letter to Committee staff, writing: "If your clients' position on the merits of this issue is correct, it will prevail in court, and Dr. Kupperman, I assure you again, will comply with the Court's judgment."[251]

On November 5, the Committees sent a letter to Dr. Kupperman's personal attorneys withdrawing the subpoena, stating:

> The question whether the Executive Branch's "absolute immunity" theory has any basis in law is currently before the court in *Committee on the Judiciary v. McGahn*, No. 19-cv-2379 (D.D.C. filed Aug. 7, 2019). In addition to not suffering from the jurisdictional flaws in Dr. Kupperman's suit, *McGahn* is procedurally much further along.[252]

On November 8, Dr. Kupperman's personal attorney sent a letter to Douglas Letter, the General Counsel of the House of Representatives, stating that Dr. Kupperman stands ready to testify "if the Judiciary resolves the conflict in favor of the Legislative Branch's position respecting such testimony."[253]

On November 25, the district court in *McGahn* held that "with respect to senior-level presidential aides, absolute immunity from compelled congressional process simply does not exist." The court explained there is "no basis in the law" for a claim of absolute immunity regardless of the position of the aides in question or whether they "are privy to national security matters, or work solely on domestic issues."[254] To date and notwithstanding the ruling in *McGahn* as it relates to Presidential aides who "are privy to national security matters," Dr. Kupperman continues to refuse to testify, and his case remains pending in federal court.[255]

Russell T. Vought, Acting Director, Office of Management and Budget

On October 11, the Committees sent a letter to Russell T. Vought, the Acting Director of OMB, seeking his appearance at a deposition on October 25.[256] On October 21, an attorney at OMB sent an email to Committee staff stating:

> Per the White House Counsel's October 8, 2019 letter, the President has directed that "[c]onsistent with the duties of the President of the United States, and in particular his obligation to preserve the rights of future occupants of his office, [he] cannot permit his Administration to participate in this partisan inquiry under these circumstances." Therefore, Acting Director Vought will not be participating in Friday's deposition.[257]

That same day, Mr. Vought publicly stated:

> I saw some Fake News over the weekend to correct. As the WH letter made clear two weeks ago, OMB officials—myself and Mike Duffey—will not be complying with deposition requests this week. #shamprocess.[258]

On October 25, the Committees sent a letter transmitting a subpoena compelling Mr. Vought's appearance at a deposition on November 6.[259]

On November 4, Jason A. Yaworske, the Associate Director for Legislative Affairs at OMB, sent a letter to Chairman Schiff stating:

> The Office of Management and Budget (OMB) reasserts its position that, as directed by the White House Counsel's October 8, 2019, letter, OMB will not participate in this partisan and unfair impeachment inquiry. ... Therefore, Mr. Vought, Mr. Duffey, and Mr. McCormack will not appear at their respective depositions without being permitted to bring agency counsel.[260]

On November 5, Mr. Vought did not appear for the scheduled deposition, in defiance of the Committees' subpoena. The Committees met and Chairman Schiff acknowledged Mr. Vought's absence, stating:

> On Monday of this week, OMB reasserted its position that, quote, "as directed by the White House Counsel's October 8, 2019, letter, OMB will not participate in this partisan and unfair impeachment inquiry," unquote. OMB argues that the impeachment inquiry lacks basic due process protections and relies on OLC opinion that the committee cannot

lawfully bar agency counsel from depositions. This new and shifting rationale from the White House, like the others it has used to attempt to block witnesses from appearing to provide testimony about the President's misconduct, has no basis in law or the Constitution and is a serious affront to decades of precedent in which Republicans and Democrats have used exactly the same procedures to depose executive branch officials without agency counsel present, including some of the most senior aides to multiple previous Presidents.[261]

To date, Mr. Vought has not changed his position or contacted the Committees about compliance with the subpoena.

Michael Duffey, Associate Director for National Security Programs, Office of Management and Budget

On October 11, the Committees sent a letter to Michael Duffey, the Associate Director for National Security Programs at OMB, seeking his appearance at a deposition on October 23.[262]

On October 21, an attorney at OMB sent an email to Committee staff stating:

Per the White House Counsel's October 8, 2019 letter, the President has directed that "[c]onsistent with the duties of the President of the United States, and in particular his obligation to preserve the rights of future occupants of his office, [he] cannot permit his Administration to participate in this partisan inquiry under these circumstances." Therefore, Mike Duffey will not be participating in Wednesday's deposition.[263]

On October 25, the Committees sent a letter transmitting a subpoena compelling Mr. Duffey to appear at a deposition on November 5, 2019, stating:

Your failure or refusal to appear at the deposition, including at the direction or behest of the President or the White House, shall constitute evidence of obstruction of the House's impeachment inquiry and may be used as an adverse inference against the President.[264]

On November 4, Jason A. Yaworske, the Associate Director for Legislative Affairs at OMB, sent a letter to Chairman Schiff stating that, "as directed by the White House Counsel's October 8, 2019, letter," Mr. Duffey will not appear at his deposition.[265]

On November 5, Mr. Duffey did not appear for the scheduled deposition, in defiance of the Committees' subpoena. The Committees met and Chairman Schiff acknowledged Mr. Duffey's absence, stating:

This effort by the President to attempt to block Mr. Duffey from appearing can only be interpreted as a further effort by the President and the White House to obstruct the impeachment inquiry and Congress's lawful and constitutional functions.[266]

To date, Mr. Duffey has not changed his position or contacted the Committees about compliance with the subpoena.

Brian McCormack, Associate Director for Natural Resources, Energy, and Science, Office of Management and Budget

On October 24, the Committees sent a letter to Brian McCormack, the Associate Director for Natural Resources, Energy, and Science at OMB, seeking his appearance at a deposition on November 4.[267]

On November 1, the Committees sent a letter transmitting a subpoena compelling Mr. McCormack's appearance at a deposition on November 4.[268]

On November 4, Jason A. Yaworske, the Associate Director for Legislative Affairs at OMB, sent a letter to Chairman Schiff stating that, "as directed by the White House Counsel's October 8, 2019, letter," Mr. McCormack will not appear at his deposition.[269]

On November 4, Mr. McCormack did not appear for the scheduled deposition, in defiance of the Committees' subpoena. The Committees met and Chairman Schiff acknowledged Mr. McCormack's absence, stating:

> At approximately 11:30 a.m. today, committee staff received via email a letter from the Associate Director for Legislative Affairs at OMB. The letter states that, quote, "As directed by the White House counsel's October 8, 2019, letter," unquote, OMB will not participate in the House's impeachment inquiry. The letter further states that, based on the advice of the Office of Legal Counsel that, quote, "the committee cannot lawfully bar agency counsel from these depositions," unquote, Mr. McCormack will not appear at his deposition today without agency counsel present. As Mr. McCormack was informed, the committees may consider his noncompliance with a subpoena as evidence in a future contempt proceeding. His failure or refusal to appear, moreover, shall constitute evidence of obstruction of the House's impeachment inquiry and may be used as an adverse inference against the President.[270]

To date, Mr. McCormack has not changed his position or contacted the Committees about compliance with the subpoena.

T. Ulrich Brechbuhl, Counselor, Department of State

On September 13, the Committees sent a letter to Secretary of State Mike Pompeo seeking transcribed interviews with Counselor T. Ulrich Brechbuhl and other officials.[271] The Committees received no direct, substantive response to this letter.

On September 27, the Committees sent a letter informing Secretary Pompeo that Mr. Brechbuhl's deposition was being scheduled on October 8, stating:

On September 13, the Committees wrote to request that you make State Department employees available for transcribed interviews. We asked you to provide, by September 20, dates by which the employees would be made available for transcribed interviews. You failed to comply with the Committees' request.[272]

That same day, the Committees sent a letter directly to Mr. Brechbuhl seeking his appearance at a deposition on October 8.[273]

On October 1, Secretary Pompeo sent a letter to the Committees stating, "Based on the profound procedural and legal deficiencies noted above, the Committee's requested dates for depositions are not feasible."[274]

Later that day, the Committees sent a letter to Deputy Secretary of State John J. Sullivan stating that the State Department "must immediately halt all efforts to interfere with the testimony of State Department witnesses before Congress."[275]

On October 2, Mr. Brechbuhl's personal attorney sent an email to Committee staff stating:

> My law firm is in the process of being formally retained to assist Mr. Brechbuhl in connection with this matter. It will take us some time to complete those logistics, review the request and associated request for documents, and to meet with our client to insure he is appropriately prepared for any deposition. It will not be possible to accomplish those tasks before October 8, 2019. Thus, as I am sure that you can understand, Mr. Brechbuhl will not be able to appear on that date as he requires a sufficient opportunity to consult with counsel. Moreover, given the concerns expressed in Secretary Pompeo's letter of October 1, 2019, to Chairman Engel, any participation in a deposition would need to be coordinated with our stakeholders.[276]

On October 8, Committee staff sent an email to Mr. Brechbuhl's personal attorney stating: "The Committees have agreed to reschedule Mr. Brechbuhl's deposition to Thursday, October 17. Please confirm that Mr. Brechbuhl intends to appear voluntarily."[277] On October 9, Committee staff sent an email to Mr. Brechbuhl's personal attorney asking him to "confirm by COB today whether Mr. Brechbuhl intends to appear voluntarily."[278] Later that day, Mr. Brechbuhl's personal attorney sent an email to Committee staff stating, "I am still seeking clarification from the State Department regarding this deposition."[279]

On October 25, the Committees sent a letter to Mr. Brechbuhl's personal attorney transmitting a subpoena compelling Mr. Brechbuhl's appearance at a deposition on November 6.[280]

On November 5, Mr. Brechbuhl's personal attorney sent a letter to the Committees stating:

> Mr. Brechbuhl respects the important Constitutional powers vested in the United States Congress. And, indeed, he would welcome the opportunity to address through testimony

an existing inaccuracy in the public record—the false claim that Mr. Brechbuhl in any way personally participated in the telephone call between President Trump and President Zelensky that occurred on July 25, 2019. However, Mr. Brechbuhl has received a letter of instruction from the State Department, directing that he not appear. The State Department letter of instruction asserts significant Executive Branch interests as the basis for direction not to appear and also asserts that the subpoena Mr. Brechbuhl received is invalid. The letter is supported by analysis from the United States Department of Justice. We are also aware that litigation has recently been initiated in the United States District Court for the District of Columbia that may bear on resolving the significant issues now arising between the Committees and the President. Given these circumstances, Mr. Brechbuhl is not able to appear on November 6, 2019.[281]

On November 6, Mr. Brechbuhl did not appear for the scheduled deposition, in defiance of the Committees' subpoena. The Committees met and Chairman Schiff acknowledged Mr. Brechbuhl's absence, stating:

> The committees requested a copy of the State Department's letter and the Department of Justice analysis, but Mr. Brechbuhl's attorney has not responded. While the letter from Mr. Brechbuhl's attorney provides only vague references to unidentified executive branch interests and a DOJ analysis as the basis for the State Department's blocking of Mr. Brechbuhl's testimony, the Department's latest obstruction of this inquiry appears to be predicated on the opinion issued by the Department of Justice Office of Legal Counsel just last Friday, November 1, well after the subpoena was issued to Mr. Brechbuhl. It is noteworthy and telling that the OLC issued this opinion only after multiple State Department officials testified in this inquiry, both voluntarily and pursuant to subpoena, all without agency counsel present. Indeed, this morning, the third-highest-ranking official at the State Department, Under Secretary David Hale, appeared and has begun testifying in accordance with his legal obligations pursuant to a subpoena.[282]

The Committees sent Mr. Brechbuhl's personal attorney two separate inquiries asking him to provide a copy of the "letter of instruction" that Mr. Brechbuhl claimed to have received from the State Department directing him to defy a congressional subpoena.[283] Mr. Brechbuhl's personal attorney furnished the Committees with a copy of the letter on December 2. The State Department's letter to Mr. Brechbuhl is dated November 4, 2019.[284]

To date, Mr. Brechbuhl has not changed his position or contacted the Committees about compliance with the subpoena.

Secretary Rick Perry, Department of Energy

On November 1, the Committees sent a letter to Secretary of Energy Rick Perry seeking his appearance at a deposition on November 6, stating:

> Your failure or refusal to appear at the deposition, including at the direction or behest of the President or the White House, shall constitute evidence of obstruction of the House's impeachment inquiry and may be used as an adverse inference against the President.[285]

243

On November 5, an attorney at the Department of Energy sent a letter to the Committees stating:

> Please be advised that the Secretary will not appear on Wednesday, November 6, 2019, at 2:00 pm for a deposition to be conducted jointly by the Permanent Select Committee on Intelligence, the Committee on Foreign Affairs, and the Committee on Oversight and Reform.[286]

To date, Secretary Perry has not changed his position or come forward to testify.

5.   **The President's Unsuccessful Attempts to Block Key Witnesses**

> *Despite President Trump's explicit orders that no Executive Branch employees should cooperate with the House's impeachment inquiry and efforts by federal agencies to limit the testimony of those who did, multiple key officials complied with duly authorized subpoenas and provided critical testimony at depositions and public hearings. These officials adhered to the rule of law and obeyed lawful subpoenas.*

Overview

Despite President Trump's orders that no Executive Branch employees should cooperate with the House's impeachment inquiry, multiple key officials complied with duly authorized subpoenas and provided critical testimony at depositions and public hearings. These officials not only served their nation honorably, but they fulfilled their oath to support and defend the Constitution of the United States.

In addition to the President's broad orders seeking to prohibit all Executive Branch employees from testifying, many of these witnesses were personally directed by senior political appointees not to cooperate with the House's impeachment inquiry. These directives frequently cited or enclosed copies of Mr. Cipollone's October 8 letter conveying the President's order not to comply.

For example, the State Department, relying on President Trump's order, attempted to block Ambassador Marie Yovanovitch from testifying, but she fulfilled her legal obligations by appearing at a deposition on October 11 and a hearing on November 15. More than a dozen current and former officials followed her courageous example by testifying at depositions and public hearings over the course of the last two months. The testimony from these witnesses produced overwhelming and clear evidence of President Trump's misconduct, which is described in detail in Section I of this report.

Ambassador Marie Yovanovitch, Former
U.S. Ambassador to Ukraine, Department of State

On September 13, the Committees sent a letter to Secretary of State Mike Pompeo seeking a transcribed interview with Ambassador Marie Yovanovitch and other State Department officials.[287] The Committees received no direct, substantive response to this letter.

On September 27, the Committees sent a letter informing Secretary Pompeo that Ambassador Yovanovitch's deposition was being scheduled on October 2, stating:

> On September 13, the Committees wrote to request that you make State Department employees available for transcribed interviews. We asked you to provide, by September 20, dates by which the employees would be made available for transcribed interviews. You failed to comply with the Committees' request.[288]

Also on September 27, the Committees sent a letter directly to Ambassador Yovanovitch seeking her appearance at a deposition on October 2.[289]

On October 1, Secretary Pompeo sent a letter to the Committees stating:

Therefore, the five officials subject to your letter may not attend any interview or deposition without counsel from the Executive Branch present to ensure that the Executive Branch's constitutional authority to control the disclosure of confidential information, including deliberative matters and diplomatic communications, is not impaired.[290]

After further discussions with Ambassador Yovanovitch's counsel, her deposition was rescheduled for October 11. On October 10, Brian Bulatao, the Under Secretary of State for Management, sent a letter to Ambassador Yovanovitch's personal attorney directing Ambassador Yovanovitch not to appear for her deposition and enclosing Mr. Cipollone's October 8 letter stating that President Trump and his Administration would not participate in the House's impeachment inquiry. Mr. Bulatao's letter stated:

Accordingly, in accordance with applicable law, I write on behalf of the Department of State, pursuant to the President's instruction reflected in Mr. Cipollone's letter, to instruct your client (as a current employee of the Department of State), consistent with Mr. Cipollone's letter, not to appear before the Committees under the present circumstances.[291]

That same day, October 10, when asked whether he intended to block Ambassador Yovanovitch from testifying the next day, President Trump stated: "You know, I don't think people should be allowed. You have to run a country, I don't think you should be allowed to do that."[292]

On the morning of Ambassador Yovanovitch's deposition on October 11, the Committees sent a letter to her personal attorney transmitting a subpoena compelling her appearance, stating:

In light of recent attempts by the Administration to direct your client not to appear voluntarily for the deposition, the enclosed subpoena now compels your client's mandatory appearance at today's deposition on October 11, 2019.[293]

Later on October 11, Ambassador Yovanovitch's personal attorney sent a letter to Mr. Bulatao, stating:

In my capacity as counsel for Ambassador Marie Yovanovitch, I have received your letter of October 10, 2019, directing the Ambassador not to appear voluntarily for her scheduled deposition testimony on October 11, 2019 before the Committee on Foreign Affairs, the Permanent Select Committee on Intelligence, and the Committee on Oversight and Reform in connection with the House of Representatives's impeachment inquiry. Just this morning, the Ambassador received a subpoena issued by the House Permanent Select Committee on Intelligence, requiring her to appear for the deposition as scheduled. Although the Ambassador has faithfully and consistently honored her professional duties as a State Department employee—including at all times following her abrupt termination as U.S. Ambassador to Ukraine—she is unable to obey your most recent directive. As the recipient of a duly issued congressional subpoena, Ambassador Yovanovitch is, in my judgment, legally obligated to attend the depositions as scheduled.[294]

Ambassador Yovanovitch participated in the deposition on October 11, in compliance with the Committees' subpoena.[295] During her deposition, Ambassador Yovanovitch's personal attorney confirmed that "she received a direction by the Under Secretary to decline to appear voluntarily."[296]

On November 15, the Committees transmitted a subpoena to Ambassador Yovanovitch compelling her to testify at a public hearing of the Intelligence Committee that same day.[297] Ambassador Yovanovitch complied with the Committees' subpoena and testified at the public hearing. During the hearing, Chairman Schiff acknowledged Ambassador Yovanovitch's compliance, stating:

Ambassador, I want to thank you for your decades of service. I want to thank you, as Mr. Maloney said, for being the first one through the gap. What you did in coming forward and answering a lawful subpoena was to give courage to others that also witnessed wrongdoing, that they, too, could show the same courage that you have, that they could stand up, speak out, answer questions, they could endure whatever threats, insults may come their way. And so in your long and distinguished career you have done another great public service in answering the call of our subpoena and testifying before us today.[298]

Ambassador Gordon Sondland, U.S. Ambassador to the European Union, Department of State

On September 27, 2019, the Committees sent a letter informing Secretary Pompeo that Ambassador Gordon Sondland's deposition was being scheduled on October 10.[299] That same day, the Committees sent a letter directly to Ambassador Sondland seeking his appearance at the deposition.[300] On October 1, Secretary Pompeo sent a letter to the Committees stating that Ambassador Sondland "may not attend" the deposition.[301]

After further discussions with Ambassador Sondland's personal attorney, his deposition was rescheduled for October 8. On October 7, Mr. Bulatao sent a letter to Ambassador Sondland's personal attorney, stating:

Based on consultations with the White House, the State Department hereby instructs your client, Ambassador Gordon Sondland, not to appear tomorrow for his voluntary deposition based on the Executive Branch confidentiality interests remaining to be addressed, including, in particular, the Committee's refusal to permit agency counsel to appear.[302]

On October 8, Ambassador Sondland's personal attorney sent an email to the Committees stating:

> I am incredibly disappointed to report that, overnight, the State Department advised that it will direct Ambassador Sondland not to appear before the Committee this morning. While we have not yet gotten written confirmation of that direction, we wanted to advise you of this development at the earliest opportunity. As the sitting US Ambassador to the EU and employee of the State Department, Ambassador Sondland is required to follow this direction. I hope that whatever concerns the Department has can be resolved promptly and that Ambassador Sondland's testimony can be scheduled at the earliest opportunity. I am very sorry for the inexcusably late notice, but we are sharing this with you as soon as it was confirmed to us. Ambassador Sondland is personally disappointed that he will not be able to answer the Committee's questions this morning.[303]

On October 8, the Committees sent a letter to Ambassador Sondland transmitting a subpoena compelling his appearance at a deposition on October 16, stating:

> The Committees have not received any communication directly from the White House or the State Department about this matter. In light of Secretary Pompeo's direct intervention to block your appearance before our Committees, we are left with no choice but to compel your appearance at a deposition pursuant to the enclosed subpoena.[304]

On October 14, the Committees sent a letter to Ambassador Sondland stating:

> We hereby write to memorialize our agreement with your counsel, Mr. Robert Luskin, Esq., to adjourn the date and time of your document production and deposition to October 17, 2019, at 9:30 a.m. at the Capitol, HVC-304.[305]

Ambassador Sondland participated in the deposition on October 17, in compliance with the Committees' subpoena.[306] During the deposition, Ambassador Sondland's personal attorney stated:

> But we also wish to emphasize that it's his belief, and ours, that the Committee should have access to all relevant documents, and he regrets that they have not been provided in advance of his testimony. Having those documents would lead to a more fulsome and accurate inquiry into the matters at hand. Indeed, Ambassador Sondland has not had access to all of the State Department records that would help him refresh his recollection in anticipation of this testimony.[307]

During the deposition, Ambassador Sondland stated:

> I was truly disappointed that the State Department prevented me at the last minute from testifying earlier on October 8, 2019. But your issuance of a subpoena has supported my appearance here today, and I'm pleased to provide the following testimony.[308]

On November 4, Ambassador Sondland's personal attorney transmitted to the Committees a sworn declaration from Ambassador Sondland, which supplemented his deposition testimony and noted that despite "repeated requests to the White House and the State Department," he still had not been granted access to records he sought to review to determine if he could "provide more complete testimony to assist Congress."[309]

On November 20, the Committees transmitted a subpoena to Ambassador Sondland compelling him to testify at a public hearing of the Intelligence Committee that same day.[310] Ambassador Sondland complied with the Committees' subpoena and testified at the public hearing. During the hearing, Ambassador Sondland described the direction he received from the White House:

> Q: Ambassador Sondland, in your deposition, you lamented, quote: I was truly disappointed that the State Department prevented me at the last minute from testifying earlier on October 8, 2019, but your issuance of a subpoena has supported my appearance here today, and I am pleased to provide the following testimony. So it is clear that the White House, the State Department did not want you to testify at that deposition. Is that correct?
>
> A: That is correct.
>
> Q: And since then, you have on numerous occasions during your opening statement today indicated that you have not been able to access documents in the State Department. Is that correct?
>
> A: Correct.
>
> Q: So you have been hampered in your ability to provide testimony to this committee. Is that correct?
>
> A: I have been hampered to provide completely accurate testimony without the benefit of those documents.[311]

George P. Kent, Deputy Assistant Secretary of State, Bureau of European and Eurasian Affairs, Department of State

On September 13, 2019, the Committees sent a letter to Secretary of State Pompeo seeking a transcribed interview with Deputy Assistant Secretary of State George Kent and other State Department officials.[312] The Committees received no direct, substantive response to this letter.

On September 27, the Committees sent a letter informing Secretary Pompeo that Mr. Kent's deposition was being scheduled on October 7.[313] That same day, the Committees sent a letter directly to Mr. Kent seeking his appearance at the deposition on that date.[314] Later that day, Mr. Kent sent an email to Committee staff acknowledging receipt of the Committees' request and copying an official from the Office of Legislative Affairs at the Department of State.[315] On October 1, Secretary Pompeo sent a letter to the Committees stating that Mr. Kent "may not attend" the deposition.[316]

After consulting with Mr. Kent's personal attorney, the Committees rescheduled his deposition for October 15.[317] On October 10, Under Secretary Bulatao sent a letter to Mr. Kent's personal attorney enclosing the White House Counsel's letter of October 8, and stating:

> I write on behalf of the Department of State, pursuant to the President's instruction reflected in Mr. Cipollone's letter, to instruct your client (as a current employee of the Department of State), consistent with Mr. Cipollone's letter, not to appear before the Committees under the present circumstances.[318]

On October 15, the Committees sent a letter to Mr. Kent's personal attorney transmitting a subpoena compelling him to appear at a deposition on that date.[319]

Mr. Kent participated in the deposition on October 15, in compliance with the Committees' subpoena.[320] During the deposition, he stated:

> As you all know, I am appearing here in response to your congressional subpoena. If I did not appear I would have been exposed to being held in contempt. At the same time, I have been instructed by my employer, the U.S. Department of State, not to appear. I do not know the Department of State's views on disregarding that order.[321]

On November 13, the Committees transmitted a subpoena to Mr. Kent compelling him to testify at a public hearing before the Intelligence Committee on that day.[322] Mr. Kent complied with the Committees' subpoena and testified at the public hearing. During the hearing, Mr. Kent described the direction he received from the White House, stating that he "received, initially, a letter directing me not to appear. And once the committees issued a subpoena, I was under legal obligation to appear, and I am here today under subpoena."[323]

Ambassador William B. Taylor, Jr., Chargé d'Affaires for U.S. Embassy in Kyiv, Department of State

On October 4, 2019, the Committees sent a letter to Deputy Secretary of State John Sullivan seeking a deposition with Ambassador William B. Taylor, Jr. on October 15.[324] That same day, the Committees sent a letter directly to Ambassador Taylor seeking his appearance at the deposition.[325]

On October 14, after consulting with Ambassador Taylor's counsel, the Committees sent a letter to Ambassador Taylor stating: "We hereby write to adjourn the date and time of your deposition to Tuesday, October 22, 2019, at 9:30 a.m. at the Capitol, HVC-304."[326]

On October 22, the Committees transmitted a subpoena to Ambassador Taylor's personal attorneys compelling Ambassador Taylor to appear at a deposition on that date, stating:

> In light of recent attempts by the Administration to direct witnesses not to appear voluntarily for depositions, the enclosed subpoena compels your client's mandatory appearance at today's deposition.[327]

Ambassador Taylor participated in the deposition on October 22, in compliance with the Committees' subpoena. During the deposition, Ambassador Taylor's personal attorney stated, in regard to communications with the Department of State:

> They sent us the directive that said he should not appear under I think the quote is under the present circumstances. We told the majority that we could not appear; he'd been instructed not to. We saw the pattern.[328]

On November 13, the Committees transmitted a subpoena to Ambassador Taylor compelling him to testify at a public hearing of the Intelligence Committee that same day.[329] Ambassador Taylor complied with the Committees' subpoena and testified at the public hearing. During the hearing, Ambassador Taylor described the direction he received from the State Department:

> Q: Ambassador, were you also asked not to be part of the deposition?
> A: Mr. Quigley, I was told by the State Department: Don't appear under these circumstances. That was in the letter to me. And when I got the subpoena, exactly as Mr. Kent said, that was different circumstances and obeyed a legal subpoena. So, yes, sir, I'm here for that reason.[330]

Catherine Croft and Christopher Anderson, Department of State

On October 24, 2019, the Committees sent letters to the personal attorney representing two State Department officials, Catherine Croft and Christopher Anderson, seeking their attendance at depositions on October 30 and November 1, respectively.[331]

On October 25, their attorney sent a letter to the Committees acknowledging receipt of the Committees' requests and stating that "we are in the process of contacting the Office of the Legal Advisor of the Department of State in an effort to learn the disposition of that Office with regard to the Committee's request."[332]

On October 28, Under Secretary Bulatao sent letters to the personal attorney for Ms. Croft and Mr. Anderson. Both letters enclosed the White House Counsel's October 8 letter and stated:

> Pursuant to Mr. Cipollone's letter and in light of these defects, we are writing to inform you and Ms. Croft of the Administration-wide direction that Executive Branch personnel "cannot participate in [the impeachment] inquiry under these circumstances."[333]

On October 30, the Committees transmitted subpoenas to the personal attorney for Ms. Croft and Mr. Anderson compelling their appearance at depositions on October 30, stating:

> In light of recent attempts by the Administration to direct witnesses not to appear voluntarily for depositions, the enclosed subpoenas compel your clients' mandatory appearance.[334]

Ms. Croft and Mr. Anderson participated in their depositions on October 30, in compliance with the Committees' subpoenas.[335] During Ms. Croft's deposition, her personal attorney stated:

> On October 28th, 2019, Ms. Croft received a letter through her lawyers from Under Secretary of State Brian Bulatao, in which we were instructed that Ms. Croft cannot participate in the impeachment inquiry being conducted by the House of Representatives and these committees. Under Secretary Bulatao's letter stated that these instructions were issued pursuant to a directive from the Office of White House Counsel. Nonetheless, Ms. Croft has been served with a valid subpoena, and so she is obliged to be here today.[336]

During Mr. Anderson's deposition, his personal attorney stated:

> On October 28th, 2019, Mr. Anderson received a letter, through his lawyers, from Under Secretary of State Brian Bulatao in which we were instructed that Mr. Anderson cannot participate in the impeachment inquiry being conducted by the House of Representatives and these committees. Under Secretary Bulatao's letter stated that these instructions were issued pursuant to a directive from the Office of White House Counsel. Nonetheless, Mr. Anderson has been served with a valid subpoena, and so he is obliged to be here today.[337]

Laura K. Cooper, Deputy Assistant Secretary of Defense for Russia, Ukraine, and Eurasia, Department of Defense

On October 11, the Committees sent a letter to Deputy Assistant Secretary of Defense Laura K. Cooper seeking her attendance at a deposition on October 18.[338]

After consulting with Ms. Cooper's personal attorney, the Committees rescheduled her deposition for October 23.

On October 22, Deputy Secretary of Defense David L. Norquist sent a letter to Ms. Cooper's personal attorney, stating:

> This letter informs you and Ms. Cooper of the Administration-wide direction that Executive Branch personnel "cannot participate in [the impeachment] inquiry under these circumstances" [Tab C]. In the event that the Committees issue a subpoena to compel Ms. Cooper's appearance, you should be aware that the Supreme Court has held, in *United States v. Rumely*, 345 U.S. 41 (1953), that a person cannot be sanctioned for refusing to comply with a congressional subpoena unauthorized by House Rule or Resolution.[339]

On October 23, the Committees sent an email transmitting a subpoena compelling Ms. Cooper to appear at a deposition on that date, stating:

In light of recent attempts by the Administration to direct witnesses not to appear voluntarily for depositions, the enclosed subpoena compels your client's mandatory appearance at today's deposition.[340]

Ms. Cooper participated in the deposition on October 23, in compliance with the Committees' subpoena.[341]

During her deposition, Ms. Cooper stated with regard to the Department of Defense, "They instructed me yesterday not to participate."[342]

On November 20, the Committees transmitted a subpoena to Ms. Cooper compelling her to testify at a public hearing before the Intelligence Committee on that day.[343] Ms. Cooper complied with the Committees' subpoena and testified at the public hearing.[344]

Mark Sandy, Deputy Associate Director of National Security Programs, Office of Management and Budget

On November 5, the Committees sent a letter to Mark Sandy, the Deputy Associate Director of National Security Programs at OMB, seeking his appearance at a deposition on November 8.[345] On November 6, Mr. Sandy responded to confirm receipt of the Committees' letter.[346]

On November 7, an attorney at OMB sent an email to Committee staff stating:

In light of the Committee's rules that prohibit agency counsel from being present in a deposition of an executive branch witness and consistent with the November 1, 2019 OLC letter opinion addressing this issue, OMB has directed Mr. Sandy not to appear at tomorrow's deposition.[347]

After consulting with Mr. Sandy's personal attorney, the Committees rescheduled his deposition for November 16.

On November 16, the Committees sent an email transmitting a subpoena compelling Mr. Sandy to appear at a deposition on that date, stating:

In light of recent attempts by the Administration to direct witnesses not to appear voluntarily for depositions, the enclosed subpoena compels your client's mandatory appearance.[348]

Mr. Sandy participated in the deposition on November 16, in compliance with the Committees' subpoena.[349] During his deposition, Mr. Sandy also testified that the Administration sent his personal attorney an official communication with further direction, stating: "It did direct me to have my personal counsel ask for a postponement until agency counsel could accompany me."[350]

Dr. Fiona Hill, Former Deputy Assistant to the President and
Senior Director for Europe and Russian Affairs, National Security Council

On October 9, 2019, the Committees sent a letter seeking Dr. Hill's testimony at a deposition on October 14.[351] On October 13, Dr. Hill's personal attorney informed the White House that she intended to appear at the scheduled deposition.[352] On October 14, the White House sent a letter to Dr. Hill's personal attorney stating that "Dr. Hill is not authorized to reveal or release any classified information or any information subject to executive privilege."[353] Also on October 14, the Committees sent Dr. Hill a subpoena seeking her testimony the same day.[354] Dr. Hill complied and participated in the deposition.[355]

On November 18, Dr. Hill's personal attorney sent a letter to the White House stating that Dr. Hill had been invited to provide testimony at a public hearing on November 21, and stating: "We continue to disagree with regard to the parameters of executive privilege as you articulated it on October 14 and our prior telephone calls."[356] On November 20, the White House sent a letter to Dr. Hill's personal attorney stating that Dr. Hill "continues to be bound by important obligations to refrain from disclosing classified information or information subject to executive privilege in her upcoming testimony before the House Permanent Select Committee on Intelligence."[357] On November 21, the Committees sent Dr. Hill a subpoena seeking her testimony the same day.[358] Dr. Hill also complied with this subpoena and testified at the public hearing.[359]

Lieutenant Colonel Alexander S. Vindman,
Director for Ukraine, National Security Council

On October 16, 2019, the Committees sent a letter seeking Lt. Col. Alexander Vindman's testimony at a deposition on October 24.[360] After discussions with Lt. Col. Vindman's personal attorneys, the deposition was rescheduled to October 29. On October 29, the Committees sent Lt. Col. Vindman a subpoena seeking his testimony the same day.[361] Lt. Col. Vindman complied.[362] In addition, on November 19, the Committees conveyed a subpoena seeking Lt. Col. Vindman's testimony at a public hearing that same day.[363] Lt. Col. Vindman also complied with this subpoena and testified at the public hearing.[364]

Timothy Morrison, Former Deputy Assistant to the President
and Senior Director for Europe and Russia, National Security Council

On October 16, 2019, the Committees sent a letter to Timothy Morrison seeking his testimony at a deposition on October 25.[365] After discussions with Mr. Morrison's personal attorney, the deposition was rescheduled to October 31. On October 31, the Committees sent Mr. Morrison a subpoena seeking his testimony the same day.[366] Mr. Morrison complied.[367] In addition, on November 19, the Committees conveyed a subpoena seeking Mr. Morrison's testimony at a public hearing that same day.[368] Mr. Morrison also complied with this subpoena and testified at the public hearing.[369]

David Hale, Under Secretary for Political Affairs, Department of State

On November 1, 2019, the Committees sent a letter seeking Under Secretary David Hale's testimony at a deposition on November 6.[370] On November 5, Mr. Hale's counsel wrote to the Committees, stating that Mr. Hale would be willing to testify pursuant to a subpoena.[371]

On November 6, the Committees sent Mr. Hale a subpoena seeking his testimony the same day.[372] Mr. Hale complied.[373] In addition, on November 20, the Committees conveyed a subpoena seeking Mr. Hale's testimony at a public hearing that same day.[374] Mr. Hale also complied with this subpoena and testified at the public hearing.[375]

David Holmes, Counselor for Political Affairs at the
U.S. Embassy in Kyiv, Ukraine, Department of State

On November 12, 2019, the Committees sent a letter to Political Counselor David Holmes' personal attorney seeking his testimony at a deposition on November 15.[376] On November 15, the Committees conveyed a subpoena to Mr. Holmes' personal attorney seeking his testimony the same day.[377] Mr. Holmes complied.[378] In addition, on November 21, the Committees conveyed a subpoena seeking Mr. Holmes' testimony at a public hearing that same day.[379] Mr. Holmes also complied with this subpoena and testified at the public hearing.[380]

Ambassador P. Michael McKinley, Former Senior Advisor
to the Secretary of State, Department of State

On October 12, 2019, Committee staff emailed Ambassador P. Michael McKinley requesting his voluntary participation in a transcribed interview on October 16.[381] On October 14, the Committees sent a letter formalizing this request.[382] On October 16, Ambassador McKinley participated in the scheduled transcribed interview.[383]

Ambassador Philip T. Reeker, Acting Assistant Secretary,
Bureau of European and Eurasian Affairs, Department of State

On October 16, 2019, the Committees sent a letter seeking Ambassador Philip T. Reeker's testimony at a deposition on October 23.[384] On October 25, the Committees sent Ambassador Reeker a subpoena seeking his testimony on October 26.[385] Ambassador Reeker complied and testified at the scheduled deposition.[386]

Ambassador Kurt Volker, Former U.S. Special Representative
for Ukraine Negotiations, Department of State

On September 13, 2019, the Committees wrote a letter to Secretary Pompeo requesting the testimony of four witnesses, including Ambassador Kurt Volker.[387] On September 27, the Committees sent a follow up letter to Secretary Pompeo, noting that Ambassador Volker's deposition had been scheduled for October 3.[388] On that same day, the Committees sent a letter directly to Ambassador Volker, seeking his testimony at the deposition scheduled for October 3.[389]

On October 1, Secretary Pompeo responded to the Committees, refusing to make Ambassador Volker available on the requested date.[390] On October 2, the Department of State wrote a letter to Ambassador Volker's counsel instructing Ambassador Volker not to reveal classified or privileged information and prohibiting Ambassador Volker from producing any government documents.[391]

On October 2, Ambassador Volker produced copies of text messages in response to the Committees' request.[392] On October 3, Ambassador Volker voluntarily participated in a transcribed interview.[393] In addition, on November 19, Ambassador Volker testified voluntarily at a public hearing.[394]

Jennifer Williams, Special Advisor for Europe and Russia, Office of the Vice President

On November 4, 2019, the Committees sent a letter to Jennifer Williams seeking her testimony at a deposition on November 7.[395] On November 7, the Committees sent Ms. Williams a subpoena seeking her testimony the same day.[396] Ms. Williams complied.[397] On November 11, Ms. Williams sent a letter to Chairman Schiff to make one amendment to her deposition testimony.[398] In addition, on November 19, the Committees conveyed a subpoena seeking Ms. William's testimony at a public hearing on November 19.[399] Ms. Williams also complied with this subpoena and testified at the public hearing.[400]

6. The President's Intimidation of Witnesses

> *President Trump publicly attacked and intimidated witnesses who came forward to comply with duly authorized subpoenas and testify about his conduct. The President also threatened and attacked an Intelligence Community whistleblower.*

Overview

President Trump engaged in a brazen effort to publicly attack and intimidate witnesses who came forward to comply with duly authorized subpoenas and testify about his conduct, raising grave concerns about potential violations of the federal obstruction statute and other criminal laws intended to protect witnesses appearing before Congressional proceedings. President Trump issued threats, openly discussed possible retaliation, made insinuations about witnesses' character and patriotism, and subjected them to mockery and derision. The President's attacks were broadcast to millions of Americans—including witnesses' families, friends, and coworkers—and his actions drew criticism from across the political spectrum, including from his own Republican supporters.

It is a federal crime to intimidate or seek to intimidate any witness appearing before Congress. This statute applies to all citizens, including federal officials. Violations of this law can carry a criminal sentence of up to 20 years in prison.

This campaign of intimidation risks discouraging witnesses from coming forward voluntarily, complying with mandatory subpoenas for documents and testimony, and disclosing evidence that may support consideration of articles of impeachment.

Ambassador Marie Yovanovitch, Former U.S. Ambassador to Ukraine, Department of State

As discussed above, President Trump removed Marie Yovanovitch as the U.S. Ambassador to Ukraine in May 2019 following a concerted effort by Rudy Giuliani, his associates Lev Parnas and Igor Fruman, and others to spread false conspiracy theories about her. The smearing of the Ambassador was part of the larger campaign undertaken by Mr. Giuliani at President Trump's direction and in his capacity as President Trump's representative. During her deposition on October 11, Ambassador Yovanovitch explained that she felt threatened and "very concerned" after she read President Trump's statements about her during his July 25 call with President Zelensky, including President Trump's claim that "she's going to go through some things."[401]

On November 15, Ambassador Yovanovitch testified at a public hearing that she was "shocked" and "devastated" by the President's statements about her:

> I was shocked and devastated that I would feature in a phone call between two heads of state in such a manner, where President Trump said that I was bad news to another world

leader and that I would be "going through some things." So I was—it was—it was a terrible moment. A person who saw me actually reading the transcript said that the color drained from my face. I think I even had a physical reaction. I think, you know, even now, words kind of fail me.[402]

Ambassador Yovanovitch was also asked about her reaction to the President's comment that she would "go through some things." She acknowledged feeling threatened, stating: "It didn't sound good. It sounded like a threat."[403]

As Ambassador Yovanovitch was in the process of testifying before the Committee, President Trump tweeted an attack against her. He wrote:

Everywhere Marie Yovanovitch went turned bad. She started off in Somalia, how did that go? Then fast forward to Ukraine, where the new Ukrainian President spoke unfavorably about her in my second phone call with him. It is a U.S. President's absolute right to appoint ambassadors.[404]

During the hearing, Chairman Schiff asked Ambassador Yovanovitch for her reaction to the President's attacks:

Q: Ambassador, you've shown the courage to come forward today and testify, notwithstanding the fact you were urged by the White House or State Department not to; notwithstanding the fact that, as you testified earlier, the President implicitly threatened you in that call record. And now, the President in real-time is attacking you. What effect do you think that has on other witnesses' willingness to come forward and expose wrongdoing?
A: Well, it's very intimidating.
Q: It's designed to intimidate, is it not?
A: I—I—I mean, I can't speak to what the President is trying to do, but I think the effect is to be intimidating.
Q: Well, I want to let you know, Ambassador, that some of us here take witness intimidation very, very seriously.[405]

In response to the President's attacks, Rep. Liz Cheney, Chair of the House Republican Caucus, stated that the President "was wrong" and that Ambassador Yovanovitch "clearly is somebody who's been a public servant to the United States for decades and I don't think the President should have done that."[406] Rep. Francis Rooney, also a Republican, stated: "I don't necessarily think it's right to be harassing or beating up on our professional diplomatic service."[407]

Even after these rebukes, the President continued to attack and threaten Ambassador Yovanovitch. For example, in an interview on November 22, President Trump stated: "This was not an angel, this woman, okay? And there are a lot of things that she did that I didn't like. And we will talk about that at some time."[408]

Lieutenant Colonel Alexander S. Vindman,
Director for Ukraine, National Security Council

On October 29, President Trump tweeted that Lt. Col. Alexander Vindman is a "Never Trumper."[409] When asked by a reporter what evidence he had for his claim, the President responded: "We'll be showing that to you real soon. Okay?"[410] President Trump continued attacking Lt. Col. Vindman during his testimony on November 19, seeking to question his loyalty to the United States. The President retweeted: "Lt. Col. Vindman was offered the position of Defense Minister for the Ukrainian Government THREE times!"[411] Allies of the President also questioned Lt. Col. Vindman's loyalty to the country and amplified the smear.[412]

For his part, Lt. Col. Vindman stated during his testimony:

I want to take a moment to recognize the courage of my colleagues who have appeared and are scheduled to appear before this Committee. I want to state that the vile character attacks on these distinguished and honorable public servants is reprehensible.[413]

Ambassador William B. Taylor, Jr., Chargé d'Affaires for
U.S. Embassy in Kyiv, Department of State

On October 23, one day after Ambassador William Taylor's deposition, the President sent a tweet comparing "Never Trumper Republicans" to "human scum."[414] An hour later, he described Ambassador Taylor in a tweet as a "Never Trumper."[415]

On October 25, the President discussed Ambassador Taylor's testimony with reporters, and again dismissed the Ambassador as a "Never Trumper." After a reporter noted that Secretary of State Mike Pompeo had hired Ambassador Taylor, the President responded: "Hey, everybody makes mistakes." He then had the following exchange about Ambassador Taylor:

Q: Do you want him out now as the top diplomat?
A: He's a Never Trumper. His lawyer is the head of the Never Trumpers. They're a dying breed, but they're still there.[416]

On the morning of November 13, just before Ambassador Taylor and George Kent testified at a public hearing, the President tweeted: "NEVER TRUMPERS!"[417]

Jennifer Williams, Special Advisor for
Europe and Russia, Office of the Vice President

On November 17, two days before Jennifer Williams testified at a public hearing, President Trump sent a tweet attacking her and stating that "she should meet with the other Never Trumpers, who I don't know & mostly never even heard of, & work out a better presidential attack!"[418] During the hearing, Rep. Jim Himes asked Ms. Williams what impression the President's tweet had made on her. She responded: "It certainly surprised me. I was not expecting to be called out by name." Rep. Himes noted that the tweet "surprised me, too, and it looks an awful lot like witness intimidation and tampering, and an effort to try to get you to perhaps shape your testimony today."[419]

Threats of Retaliation

The President suggested that witnesses who testified as part of the impeachment inquiry could face retaliation. For example, on November 16, the President sent a pair of tweets indicating that three witnesses appearing before the impeachment inquiry could face dismissals as a result of their testimony. The President tweeted language he attributed to radio host Rush Limbaugh:

> "My support for Donald Trump has never been greater than it is right now. It is paramountly obvious watching this, these people have to go. You elected Donald Trump to drain the Swamp, well, dismissing people like Yovanovitch is what that looks like. Dismissing people like Kent ... and Taylor, dismissing everybody involved from the Obama holdover days trying to undermine Trump, getting rid of those people, dismissing them, this is what it looks like. It was never going to be clean, they were never going to sit by idly and just let Trump do this!" Rush L[420]

Intelligence Community Whistleblower

In addition to his relentless attacks on witnesses who testified in connection with the House's impeachment inquiry, the President also repeatedly threatened and attacked a member of the Intelligence Community who filed an anonymous whistleblower complaint raising an "urgent concern" regarding the President's conduct. The whistleblower filed the complaint confidentially with the Inspector General of the Intelligence Community, as authorized by the relevant whistleblower law. Federal law prohibits the Inspector General from revealing the whistleblower's identity.[421] Federal law also protects the whistleblower from retaliation.[422]

On September 9, the Inspector General notified Congress that this individual had filed a credible complaint regarding an "urgent concern," but that the Acting Director of National Intelligence was withholding the complaint from Congress—contrary to his statutory obligation to have submitted the complaint to the congressional intelligence committees by no later than September 2.[423] On September 13, 2019, the Intelligence Committee issued a subpoena to the Acting Director of National Intelligence for the whistleblower's complaint and other records.[424]

On September 26, the Intelligence Committee received the declassified whistleblower complaint and made it available to the public.[425]

That day, the President issued a chilling threat against the whistleblower and those who provided information to the whistleblower regarding the President's misconduct, suggesting that they could face the death penalty for treason. President Trump stated:

> I want to know who's the person who gave the whistle-blower the information because that's close to a spy. You know what we used to do in the old days when we were smart with spies and treason, right? We used to handle it a little differently than we do now.[426]

In response, the Committees warned President Trump to stop attacking the whistleblower, stating:

> The President's comments today constitute reprehensible witness intimidation and an attempt to obstruct Congress' impeachment inquiry. We condemn the President's attacks, and we invite our Republican counterparts to do the same because Congress must do all it can to protect this whistleblower, and all whistleblowers. Threats of violence from the leader of our country have a chilling effect on the entire whistleblower process, with grave consequences for our democracy and national security.[427]

Yet the President's attacks did not stop. Instead, he continued to threaten the whistleblower, publicly questioned the whistleblower's motives, disputed the accuracy of the whistleblower's account, and encouraged others to reveal the whistleblower's identity. The President's focus on the whistleblower has been obsessive, with the President making more than 100 public statements about the whistleblower over a period of just two months. For example, the President stated:

- "I want to meet not only my accuser, who presented SECOND & THIRD HAND INFORMATION, but also the person who illegally gave this information, which was largely incorrect, to the 'Whistleblower.' Was this person SPYING on the U.S. President? Big Consequences!"[428]
- "I think it's outrageous that a Whistleblower is a CIA agent."[429]
- "But what they said is he's an Obama person. It was involved with Brennan; Susan Rice, which means Obama. But he was like a big—a big anti-Trump person. Hated Trump."[430]
- "The Whistleblower got it sooo wrong that HE must come forward. The Fake News Media knows who he is but, being an arm of the Democrat Party, don't want to reveal him because there would be hell to pay. Reveal the Whistleblower and end the Impeachment Hoax!"[431]
- "But the whistleblower should be revealed because the whistleblower gave false stories. Some people would call it a fraud; I won't go that far. But when I read it closely, I probably would. But the whistleblower should be revealed."[432]
- "I think that the whistleblower gave a lot of false information."[433]
- "The whistleblower is not a whistleblower. He's a fake. … Everybody knows who the whistleblower is. And the whistleblower is a political operative."[434]

In response to a request from Intelligence Committee Ranking Member Devin Nunes to call the whistleblower to testify at an open hearing, Chairman Schiff underscored the danger posed by the President's threats against the whistleblower and why the whistleblower's testimony was now unnecessary:

> The Committee also will not facilitate efforts by President Trump and his allies in Congress to threaten, intimidate, and retaliate against the whistleblower who courageously raised the initial alarm. It remains the duty of the Intelligence Committee to protect whistleblowers, and until recently, this was a bipartisan priority. The

whistleblower has a right under laws championed by this Committee to remain anonymous and to be protected from harm.

The impeachment inquiry, moreover, has gathered an ever-growing body of evidence—from witnesses and documents, including the President's own words in his July 25 call record—that not only confirms, but far exceeds, the initial information in the whistleblower's complaint. The whistleblower's testimony is therefore redundant and unnecessary. In light of the President's threats, the individual's appearance before us would only place their personal safety at grave risk.[435]

Until President Trump's attacks on the whistleblower, Republicans and Democrats were united in protecting whistleblowers' right to report abuses of power and be free from retaliation.[436] For example, Rep. Nunes, serving in 2017 as Chairman of the Intelligence Committee, spoke in defense of whistleblowers, stating: "We want people to come forward and we will protect the identity of those people at all cost."[437] He also stated:

As you know, and I've said this several times, we don't talk about sources at this committee. … The good thing is, is that we have continued to have people come forward, voluntarily, to this committee and we want to continue that and I will tell you that that will not happen if we tell you who our sources are and people that come—come to the committee.[438]

Other Republican Members of Congress have opposed efforts to expose the whistleblower. For example, Senator Charles Grassley stated:

This person appears to have followed the whistleblower protection laws and ought to be heard out and protected. We should always work to respect whistleblowers' requests for confidentiality. Any further media reports on the whistleblower's identity don't serve the public interest—even if the conflict sells more papers or attracts clicks.[439]

Senator Richard Burr, the Chair of the Senate Select Committee on Intelligence, affirmed that he would "never" want the identity of the whistleblower revealed and stated, "We protect whistleblowers. We protect witnesses in our committee."[440]

Senator Mitt Romney also called for support of the whistleblower's rights, stating: "[W]histleblowers should be entitled to confidentiality and privacy, because they play a vital function in our democracy."[441]

SECTION II ENDNOTES

[1] U.S. Const. Art. I, § 2, cl. 5.

[2] Statement of George Mason, Madison Debates (July 20, 1787).

[3] *McGrain v. Daugherty*, 273 U.S. 135 (1927) ("We are of [the] opinion that the power of inquiry—with process to enforce it—is an essential and appropriate auxiliary to the legislative function."); *Eastland v. United States Servicemen's Fund*, 421 U.S. 491 (1975) ("the power to investigate is inherent in the power to make laws"); *Committee on the Judiciary v. McGahn*, Case No. 1:19-cv-02379, Memorandum Opinion, Doc. No. 46 (D.D.C. Nov. 25, 2019) ("[T]he House of Representatives has the constitutionally vested responsibility to conduct investigations of suspected abuses of power within the government, and to act to curb those improprieties, if required."). As of this report, an appeal is pending in the D.C. Circuit. No. 19-5331 (D.C. Cir.).

[4] *Cf. Nixon v. Fitzgerald*, 457 U.S. 731 (1982) ("Vigilant oversight by Congress also may serve to deter Presidential abuses of office, as well as to make credible the threat of impeachment."); *Senate Select Committee on Presidential Campaign Activities v. Nixon*, 498 F.2d 725 (D.C. Cir. 1974) (discussing in dicta the "inquiry into presidential impeachment" opened by the House Judiciary Committee regarding President Nixon and explaining, "The investigative authority of the Judiciary Committee with respect to presidential conduct has an express constitutional source."); *In re Report & Recommendation of June 5, 1972 Grand Jury Concerning Transmission of Evidence to House of Representatives*, 370 F. Supp. 1219 (D.D.C. 1974) ("[I]t should not be forgotten that we deal in a matter of the most critical moment to the Nation, an impeachment investigation involving the President of the United States. It would be difficult to conceive of a more compelling need than that of this country for an unswervingly fair inquiry based on all the pertinent information."). In 1833, Justice Joseph Story reasoned—while explaining why pardons cannot confer immunity from impeachment—that, "The power of impeachment will generally be applied to persons holding high office under the government; and it is of great consequence that the President should not have the power of preventing a thorough investigation of their conduct, or of securing them against the disgrace of a public conviction by impeachment, should they deserve it. The constitution has, therefore, wisely interposed this check upon his power." Joseph L. Story, 3 *Commentaries on the Constitution of the United States* § 1501 (1873 ed., T.M. Cooley (ed.)).

[5] House Committee on the Judiciary, *Impeachment of Richard M. Nixon, President of the United States*, 93rd Cong. (1974) (H. Rep. 93-1305).

[6] Statement of Rep. William Lyman, Annals of Congress, 4th Cong. 601 (1796).

[7] Department of Justice, Office of Legal Counsel, *A Sitting President's Amenability to Indictment and Criminal Prosecution* (Oct. 16, 2000) (explaining that a President "who engages in criminal behavior falling into the category of 'high Crimes and Misdemeanors'" is "always subject to removal from office upon impeachment by the House and conviction by the Senate") (online at www.justice.gov/sites/default/files/olc/opinions/2000/10/31/op-olc-v024-p0222_0.pdf).

[88] *Id.* ("Moreover, the constitutionally specified impeachment process ensures that the immunity [of a sitting President from prosecution] would not place the President 'above the law.'"). President Trump's personal lawyers have staked out the more extreme position that the President may not be investigated by law enforcement agencies while in office. For example, President Trump's personal attorney asserted in court that the President could not be investigated by local authorities if he committed murder while in office. *If Trump Shoots Someone on 5th Ave., Does He Have Immunity? His Lawyer Says Yes,* New York Times (Oct. 23, 2019) (online at www.nytimes.com/2019/10/23/nyregion/trump-taxes-vance.html). A federal district court and appeals court rejected this argument. *Trump v. Vance*, 941 F.3d 631 (2nd Cir. 2019) ("presidential immunity does not bar the enforcement of a state grand jury subpoena directing a third party to produce non-privileged material, even when the subject matter under investigation pertains to the President"); *Trump v. Vance*, 395 F. Supp. 3d 283 (S.D.N.Y. 2019) (calling the President's claims of "unqualified and boundless" immunity from judicial process "repugnant to the nation's governmental structure and constitutional values"). The case is currently being appealed.

[9] *Barenblatt v. U.S*, 360 U.S. 109 (1959).

[10] *McGrain v. Daugherty*, 273 U.S. 135 (1927) ("A legislative body cannot legislate wisely or effectively in the absence of information respecting the conditions which the legislation is intended to affect or change; and where the legislative body does not itself possess the requisite information—which not infrequently is true—recourse must

be had to others who do possess it. Experience has taught that mere requests for such information often are unavailing, and also that information which is volunteered is not always accurate or complete; so some means of compulsion are essential to obtain what is needed."); *Eastland v. United States Servicemen's Fund*, 421 U.S. 491 (1975) ("the subpoena power may be exercised by a committee acting, as here, on behalf of one of the Houses"); *Committee on the Judiciary v. Miers,* 558 F. Supp. 2d 84 (D.D.C. 2008) ("In short, there can be no question that Congress has a right—derived from its Article I legislative function—to issue and enforce subpoenas, and a corresponding right to the information that is the subject of such subpoenas. ... Congress's power of inquiry is as broad as its power to legislate and lies at the very heart of Congress's constitutional role. Indeed, the former is necessary to the proper exercise of the latter: according to the Supreme Court, the ability to compel testimony is 'necessary to the effective functioning of courts and legislatures.'") (citation omitted).

[11] U.S. Const. Art. I, § 5, cl. 2.

[12] *Watkins v. United States*, 354 U.S. 178 (1957).

[13] *See Committee on the Judiciary v. Miers,* 558 F. Supp. 2d 84 (D.D.C. 2008) ("Thus, federal precedent dating back as far as 1807 contemplates that even the Executive is bound to comply with duly issued subpoenas.").

[14] *Committee on the Judiciary v. McGahn*, Case No. 1:19-cv-02379, Memorandum Opinion, Doc. No. 46 (D.D.C. Nov. 25, 2019). As of this report, an appeal is pending in the D.C. Circuit. No. 19-5331 (D.C. Cir.).

[15] 18 U.S.C. § 1505.

[16] 18 U.S.C. § 1001 (also prohibiting making "any materially false, fictitious, or fraudulent statement or representation" or making or using "any false writing or document knowing the same to contain any materially false, fictitious, or fraudulent statement or entry" in connection with a Congressional investigation).

[17] 18 U.S.C. § 1512(b); *See also* 18 U.S.C. § 1515(a) (defining "official proceeding" to include "a proceeding before the Congress").

[18] 18 U.S.C. § 1512(d).

[19] *See, e.g.*, 5 U.S.C. § 2302; 10 U.S.C. § 1034; P.L. 113-126.

[20] P.L. 116-6, § 713 ("No part of any appropriation contained in this or any other Act shall be available for the payment of the salary of any officer or employee of the Federal Government, who ... prohibits or prevents, or attempts or threatens to prohibit or prevent, any other officer or employee of the Federal Government from having any direct oral or written communication or contact with any Member, committee, or subcommittee of the Congress in connection with any matter pertaining to the employment of such other officer or employee or pertaining to the department or agency of such other officer or employee in any way, irrespective of whether such communication or contact is at the initiative of such other officer or employee or in response to the request or inquiry of such Member, committee, or subcommittee.").

[21] House Committee on the Judiciary, *Impeachment of Richard M. Nixon, President of the United States,* 93rd Cong. (1974) (H. Rep. 93-1305).

[22] House Committee on the Judiciary, *Impeachment of William Jefferson Clinton, President of the United States*, 105th Cong. (1998) (H. Rep. 105-830).

[23] The White House, *The President's Remarks Announcing Developments and Procedures to be Followed in Connection with the Investigation* (Apr. 17, 1973). President Nixon initially stated that members of his "personal staff" would "decline a request for a formal appearance before a committee of the Congress," but reversed course approximately one month later. The White House, *Statement by the President, Executive Privilege* (Mar. 12, 1973).

[24] *See, e.g.*, Senate Select Committee on Presidential Campaign Activities, Testimony of John Dean, *Watergate and Related Activities, Phase I: Watergate Investigation*, 93rd Cong. (June 25, 1973); Senate Select Committee on Presidential Campaign Activities, Testimony of H.R. Haldeman, *Watergate and Related Activities, Phase I: Watergate Investigation*, 93rd Cong. (July 30, 1973); Senate Select Committee on Presidential Campaign Activities, Testimony of Alexander Butterfield, *Watergate and Related Activities, Phase I: Watergate Investigation*, 93rd Cong. (July 16, 1973); Senate Select Committee on Presidential Campaign Activities, Testimony of John Ehrlichman, *Watergate and Related Activities, Phase I: Watergate Investigation*, 93rd Cong. (July 24, 1973).

[25] *See* House Committee on the Judiciary, *Impeachment of Richard M. Nixon, President of the United States,* 93rd Cong. (1974) (H. Rep. 93-1305).

[26] *Id.*

[27] *Id.* (quoting letter from Chairman Peter W. Rodino, Jr., House Committee on the Judiciary, to President Richard M. Nixon (May 30, 1974)).

[28] H.R. Jour., 29th Cong., 1st Sess., 693 (Apr. 20, 1846).

[29] Senate Select Committee on Secret Military Assistance to Iran and the Nicaraguan Opposition and House Select Committee to Investigate Covert Arms Transactions with Iran, Testimony of Oliver North, *Iran-Contra Investigation: Joint Hearings Before the House Select Committee to Investigate Covert Arms Transactions with Iran and the Senate Select Committee on Secret Military Assistance to Iran and the Nicaraguan Oppositions,* 100th Cong. (July 7, 1987); Senate Select Committee on Secret Military Assistance to Iran and the Nicaraguan Opposition and House Select Committee to Investigate Covert Arms Transactions with Iran, Testimony of John Poindexter, *Iran-Contra Investigation: Joint Hearings Before the House Select Committee to Investigate Covert Arms Transactions with Iran and the Senate Select Committee on Secret Military Assistance to Iran and the Nicaraguan Oppositions,* 100th Cong. (July 15, 1987).

[30] *Committee on the Judiciary v. McGahn,* Civ. No. 1:19-cv-02379, Memorandum Opinion, Doc. No. 46 (D.D.C. Nov. 25, 2019). As of this report, an appeal is pending in the D.C. Circuit. No. 19-5331 (D.C. Cir.).

[31] Committee on Government Reform, Democratic Staff, *Congressional Oversight of the Clinton Administration* (Jan. 17, 2006) (online at https://wayback.archive-it.org/4949/20141031200116/http://oversight-archive.waxman.house.gov/documents/20060117103516-91336.pdf) (noting that Republican Dan Burton, Chairman of the Committee on Government Reform, deposed 141 Clinton Administration officials during his tenure).

[32] Select Committee on the Events Surrounding the 2012 Terrorist Attack in Benghazi, *Final Report of the Select Committee on the Events Surrounding the 2012 Terrorist Attack in Benghazi,* 114th Cong. (2016) (H. Rep. 114-848) (noting that the Select Committee interviewed or received testimony from 107 people—none of whom was instructed not to appear—including 57 current and former State Department officials such as Secretary of State Hillary Clinton, Chief of Staff and Counselor to the Secretary of State Cheryl Mills, Deputy Chief of Staff and Director of Policy Planning, Jacob Sullivan, and Deputy Chief of Staff for Operations Huma Abedin; 24 Defense Department officials such as Secretary Leon Panetta and General Carter Ham; and 19 Central Intelligence Agency officials such as Director David Petraeus and former Deputy Director Michael Morell).

[33] *Id.* (including productions of 71,640 pages of State Department documents, 300 pages of CIA intelligence analyses, 200 pages of FBI documents, 900 pages of Defense Department documents, and 750 pages of National Security Agency documents).

[34] *See, e.g.,* House rule X, clause 2(a) (assigning "general oversight responsibilities" to committees); House Rule XI, clause 2(m) (authorizing Committees to "hold such hearings as it considers necessary" and to "require, by subpoena or otherwise, the attendance and testimony of such witnesses and the production of such books, records, correspondence, memoranda, papers, and documents as it considers necessary"); H.Res. 6 (2019) (granting deposition authority to committees); 116th Congress Regulations for Use of Deposition Authority, Congressional Record (Jan. 25, 2019) (establishing procedures for committee depositions).

[35] *See, e.g.,* House Rules (2017); H.Res. 5 (2017); 115th Congress Staff Deposition Authority Procedures, Congressional Record (Jan. 13, 2017).

[36] Special Counsel Robert S. Mueller III, Department of Justice, *Report on The Investigation Into Russian Interference In The 2016 Presidential Election,* Vol. I (March 2019) (online at www.justice.gov/storage/report.pdf); Special Counsel Robert S. Mueller, III, Department of Justice, *Report on The Investigation Into Russian Interference In The 2016 Presidential Election,* Vol. II (March 2019) (online at www.justice.gov/storage/report_volume2.pdf).

[37] *See* H. Res. 430; *see also* H. Rep. 116-105 (2019) (the purposes of the Judiciary Committee's investigation include "considering whether any of the conduct described in the Special Counsel's Report warrants the Committee in taking any further steps under Congress' Article I powers," including "whether to approve articles of impeachment with respect to the President or any other Administration official").

[38] *See* Letter from Chairman Jerrold Nadler, House Committee on the Judiciary, to Chairman Adam B. Schiff, House Permanent Select Committee on Intelligence, Chairman Maxine Waters, House Committee on Financial Services, Chairman Elijah E. Cummings, House Committee on Oversight and Reform, and Chairman Eliot L. Engel, House Committee on Foreign Affairs (Aug. 22, 2019) (online at https://judiciary.house.gov/sites/democrats.judiciary.house.gov/files/documents/FiveChairsLetter8.22.pdf).

[39] *Id.*

[40] Letter from Chairman Eliot L. Engel, House Committee on Foreign Affairs, Chairman Adam B. Schiff, House Permanent Select Committee on Intelligence, and Chairman Elijah E. Cummings, House Committee on Oversight and Reform, to Pat A. Cipollone, Counsel to the President, The White House (Sept. 9, 2019) (online at https://intelligence.house.gov/uploadedfiles/ele_schiff_cummings_letter_to_cipollone_on_ukraine.pdf); Letter from Chairman Eliot L. Engel, House Committee on Foreign Affairs, Chairman Adam B. Schiff, House Permanent Select Committee on Intelligence, and Chairman Elijah E. Cummings, House Committee on Oversight and Reform, to Secretary Michael R. Pompeo, Department of State (Sept. 9, 2019) (online at https://intelligence.house.gov/uploadedfiles/ele_schiff_cummings_letter_to_sec_pompeo_on_ukraine.pdf); Letter from Chairman Eliot L. Engel, Committee on Foreign Affairs, Chairman Adam B. Schiff, Permanent Select Committee on Intelligence, and Chairman Elijah E. Cummings, Committee on Oversight and Reform, to Secretary Michael R. Pompeo, Department of State (Sept. 13, 2019) (online at https://oversight.house.gov/sites/democrats.oversight.house.gov/files/2019-09-13.EEC%20ELE%20Schiff%20re%20Ukraine.pdf).

[41] The White House, *Remarks by President Trump Before Marine One Departure* (Sept. 22, 2019) (online at www.whitehouse.gov/briefings-statements/remarks-president-trump-marine-one-departure-66/) ("We had a great conversation. The conversation I had was largely congratulatory. It was largely corruption—all of the corruption taking place. It was largely the fact that we don't want our people, like Vice President Biden and his son, creating to the corruption already in the Ukraine.").

[42] Speaker of the House Nancy Pelosi, *Pelosi Remarks Announcing Impeachment Inquiry* (Sept. 24, 2019) (online at www.speaker.gov/newsroom/92419-0).

[43] The White House, *Memorandum of Telephone Conversation* (July 25, 2019) (online at www.whitehouse.gov/wp-content/uploads/2019/09/Unclassified09.2019.pdf).

[44] *See, e.g.*, Letter from Chairman Elijah E. Cummings, House Committee on Oversight and Reform, Chairman Adam B. Schiff, House Permanent Select Committee on Intelligence, and Chairman Eliot L. Engel, House Committee on Foreign Affairs, to Mick Mulvaney, Acting Chief of Staff, The White House (Oct. 4, 2019) (online at https://oversight.house.gov/sites/democrats.oversight.house.gov/files/documents/2019-10-04.EEC%20Engel%20Schiff%20to%20Mulvaney-WH%20re%20Subpoena.pdf).

[45] H. Res. 660 (2019).

[46] *Trump Vows Stonewall of 'All' House Subpoenas, Setting Up Fight Over Powers*, New York Times (Apr. 24, 2019) (online at www.nytimes.com/2019/04/24/us/politics/donald-trump-subpoenas.html).

[47] *While Bemoaning Mueller Probe, Trump Falsely Says the Constitution Gives Him 'The Right to do Whatever I Want'*, Washington Post (July 23, 2019) (online at www.washingtonpost.com/politics/2019/07/23/trump-falsely-tells-auditorium-full-teens-constitution-gives-him-right-do-whatever-i-want/).

[48] Donald J. Trump, Twitter (Oct. 1, 2019) (online at https://twitter.com/realDonaldTrump/status/1179179573541511176).

[49] *At Louisiana Rally, Trump Lashes Out at Impeachment Inquiry and Pelosi,* New York Times (Oct. 11, 2019) (online at www.nytimes.com/2019/10/11/us/trump-rally-louisiana-lake-charles.html).

[50] Donald J. Trump, Twitter (Oct. 18, 2019) (online at https://twitter.com/realDonaldTrump/status/1185374394350215169) (purporting to quote former Rep. Jason Chaffetz).

[51] Donald J. Trump, Twitter (Sept. 21, 2019) (online at https://twitter.com/realDonaldTrump/status/1175409914384125952).

[52] Donald J. Trump, Twitter (Sept. 24, 2019) (online at https://twitter.com/realDonaldTrump/status/1176559970390806530).

[53] Donald J. Trump, Twitter (Sept. 24, 2019) (online at https://twitter.com/realDonaldTrump/status/1176623010230525953).

[54] The White House, *Remarks by President Trump and President Salih of Iraq Before Bilateral Meeting* (Sept. 24, 2019) (online at www.whitehouse.gov/briefings-statements/remarks-president-trump-president-salih-iraq-bilateral-meeting-new-york-ny-2/).

[55] The White House, *Remarks by President Trump and President Bukele of El Salvador Before Bilateral Meeting* (Sept. 25, 2019) (online at www.whitehouse.gov/briefings-statements/remarks-president-trump-president-bukele-el-salvador-bilateral-meeting-new-york-ny/).

[56] The White House, *Remarks by President Trump in a Multilateral Meeting on the Bolivarian Republic of Venezuela* (Sept. 25, 2019) (online at www.whitehouse.gov/briefings-statements/remarks-president-trump-multilateral-meeting-bolivarian-republic-venezuela-new-york-ny/).

[57] Donald J. Trump, Twitter (Sept. 26, 2019) (online at https://twitter.com/realDonaldTrump/status/1177285017636093953).

[58] Donald J. Trump, Twitter (Oct. 1, 2019) (online at https://twitter.com/realDonaldTrump/status/1179023004241727489).

[59] Donald J. Trump, Twitter (Oct. 5, 2019) (online at https://twitter.com/realDonaldTrump/status/1180482408522629120).

[60] Donald J. Trump, Twitter (Oct. 8, 2019) (online at https://twitter.com/realDonaldTrump/status/1181761045486080002).

[61] The White House, *Remarks by President Trump at Signing of Executive Orders on Transparency in Federal Guidance and Enforcement* (Oct. 9, 2019) (online at www.whitehouse.gov/briefings-statements/remarks-president-trump-signing-executive-orders-transparency-federal-guidance-enforcement/).

[62] Donald J. Trump, Twitter (Oct. 9, 2019) (online at https://twitter.com/realDonaldTrump/status/1181913137483829250).

[63] Donald J. Trump, Twitter (Oct. 9, 2019) (online at https://twitter.com/realdonaldtrump/status/1181969511697788928).

[64] Donald J. Trump, Twitter (Oct. 20, 2019) (online at https://twitter.com/realDonaldTrump/status/1186035686396321793).

[65] Donald J. Trump, Twitter (Nov. 12, 2019) (online at https://twitter.com/realDonaldTrump/status/1194214569591394304).

[66] Donald J. Trump, Twitter (Nov. 24, 2019) (online at https://twitter.com/realDonaldTrump/status/1198733640722718725).

[67] Donald J. Trump, Twitter (Nov. 26, 2019) (online at https://twitter.com/realDonaldTrump/status/1199352977934487553).

[68] The White House, *Remarks by President Trump Upon Air Force One Arrival* (Sept. 26, 2019) (online at www.whitehouse.gov/briefings-statements/remarks-president-trump-upon-air-force-one-arrival-prince-georges-county-md/).

[69] *See, e.g.,* Co-Equal, *Investigative Rules and Practices Followed by House Republicans* (online at www.co-equal.org/guide-to-congressional-oversight/investigative-rules-and-practices-followed-by-house-republicans). *See also* Committee on Government Reform, Democratic Staff, *Congressional Oversight of the Clinton Administration* (Jan. 17, 2006) (online at https://wayback.archive-it.org/4949/20141031200116/http://oversight-archive.waxman.house.gov/documents/20060117103516-91336.pdf) (noting that House Republicans conducted hundreds of confidential depositions of both political appointees and career officials without agency counsel present, with one Committee alone conducting over 140 depositions of Clinton Administration officials).

[70] Letter from Pat A. Cipollone, Counsel to the President, The White House, to House Speaker Nancy Pelosi, Chairman Adam B. Schiff, House Permanent Select Committee on Intelligence, Chairman Eliot L. Engel, House Committee on Foreign Affairs Committee, and Chairman Elijah E. Cummings, House Committee on Oversight and Reform (Oct. 8, 2019) (online at www.whitehouse.gov/wp-content/uploads/2019/10/PAC-Letter-10.08.2019.pdf).

[71] *Speech: Donald Trump Holds a Political Rally in Minneapolis, Minnesota*, Factbase Videos (Oct. 10, 2019) (online at www.youtube.com/watch?time_continue=742&v=_y8Al_mGwmc&feature=emb_logo).

[72] Gregg Nunziata, a former legal counsel and senior policy advisor to Senator Marco Rubio, stated: "This letter is bananas. A barely-lawyered temper tantrum." Gregg Nunziata, Twitter (Oct. 8, 2019) (online at https://twitter.com/greggnunziata/status/1181685021926662144). Jonathan Turley, a law professor who has represented House Republicans, stated: "A President cannot simply pick up his marbles and leave the game because he does not like the other players. A refusal to cooperate with a constitutionally mandated process can itself be an abuse of power." *White House Issues Defiant Letter Refusing to Cooperate in Impeachment Proceedings,* Res Ipsa Loquitur (Oct. 9, 2019) (online at https://jonathanturley.org/2019/10/09/white-house-issues-defiant-letter-refusing-to-cooperate-in-impeachment-proceedings/). Preet Bharara, the former U.S. Attorney for the Southern District of New York, stated, "It's one of the worst letters I've seen from the White House counsel's office." George Conway, a prominent conservative attorney, called Mr. Cipollone's letter "a disgrace to the country, a disgrace to the presidency, and a disgrace to the legal profession." He accused the White House of "clearly engaging in obstructionist tactics." *Diagnosing Trump (with George Conway),* Stay Tuned with Preet Bharara (Oct. 9, 2019) (online at https://cafe.com/stay-tuned-transcript-diagnosing-trump-with-george-conway/). Mr. Conway also stated: "I cannot fathom how any self-respecting member of the bar could affix his name to this letter. It's pure hackery, and it disgraces the profession." George T. Conway, III, Twitter (Oct. 8, 2019) (online at https://twitter.com/gtconway3d/status/1181685229687394307).

[73] Letter from Pat A. Cipollone, Counsel to the President, The White House, to Acting Chairwoman Carolyn Maloney, House Committee on Oversight and Reform, Chairman Adam B. Schiff, House Permanent Select Committee on Intelligence Chairman Eliot L. Engel, Chairman, House Committee on Foreign Affairs (Oct. 18, 2019).

[74] Department of Justice, Office of Legal Counsel, *Exclusion of Agency Counsel from Congressional Depositions in the Impeachment Context* (Nov. 1, 2019) (online at www.justice.gov/olc/file/1214996/download).

[75] Department of Justice, Office of Legal Counsel, *Legal Aspects of Impeachment: An Overview* (1974) (quoting President James K. Polk) (online at www.justice.gov/olc/page/file/980036/download).

[76] *Position of the Executive Department Regarding Investigative Reports*, 40 Op. Atty Gen. 45 (1941).

[77] Letter from Pat A. Cipollone, Counsel to the President, The White House, to House Speaker Nancy Pelosi, Chairman Adam B. Schiff, House Permanent Select Committee on Intelligence, Chairman Eliot L. Engel, House Committee on Foreign Affairs Committee, and Chairman Elijah E. Cummings, House Committee on Oversight and Reform (Oct. 8, 2019) (online at www.whitehouse.gov/wp-content/uploads/2019/10/PAC-Letter-10.08.2019.pdf).

[78] *See, e.g.,* The White House, *Remarks by President Trump and President Salih of Iraq Before Bilateral Meeting* (Sept. 24, 2019) (online at www.whitehouse.gov/briefings-statements/remarks-president-trump-president-salih-iraq-bilateral-meeting-new-york-ny/) ("The phone call was perfect."); The White House, *Remarks by President Trump Upon Arriving at the U.N. General Assembly* (Sept. 24, 2019) (online at www.whitehouse.gov/briefings-statements/remarks-president-trump-upon-arriving-u-n-general-assembly-new-york-ny/) ("That call was perfect."); Donald J. Trump, Twitter (Nov. 11, 2019) (online at https://twitter.com/realDonaldTrump/status/1193615188311912449) ("The call to the Ukrainian President was PERFECT.").

[79] Letter from Pat A. Cipollone, Counsel to the President, The White House, to House Speaker Nancy Pelosi, Chairman Adam B. Schiff, House Permanent Select Committee on Intelligence, Chairman Eliot L. Engel, House Committee on Foreign Affairs Committee, and Chairman Elijah E. Cummings, House Committee on Oversight and Reform (Oct. 8, 2019) (online at www.whitehouse.gov/wp-content/uploads/2019/10/PAC-Letter-10.08.2019.pdf).

[80] *See* House Committee on the Judiciary, *Impeachment of Richard M. Nixon, President of the United States*, 93rd Cong. (1974) (H. Rep. 93-1305) (Impeachment Article III: "In refusing to produce these papers and things, Richard M. Nixon, substituting his judgment as to what materials were necessary for the inquiry, interposed the powers of the presidency against the lawful subpoenas of the House of Representatives, thereby assuming to himself functions and judgments necessary to the exercise of the sole power of impeachment vested by the Constitution in the House of Representatives.").

[81] In this case, one Republican Member of the House of Representatives supported impeaching President Trump—Rep. Justin Amash from Michigan. In explaining his support, Rep. Amash noted the importance of upholding Congress' "duties under our Constitution" rather than "loyalty to a political party." After Rep. Amash announced his support for impeachment, President Trump denounced him as a "total lightweight" and a "loser." Rep. Amash subsequently declared that he was leaving the Republican party. *See* Justin Amash, Twitter (May 18, 2019) (online at https://twitter.com/justinamash/status/1129831626844921862); *Trump Calls Representative Justin Amash a 'Loser' Over Impeachment Talk,* New York Times (May 19, 2019) (online at www.nytimes.com/2019/05/19/us/politics/trump-justin-amash-impeachment.html*); Justin Amash: Our politics is in a partisan death spiral. That's why I'm leaving the GOP*, Washington Post (July 4, 2019) (online at www.washingtonpost.com/opinions/justin-amash-our-politics-is-in-a-partisan-death-spiral-thats-why-im-leaving-the-gop/2019/07/04/afbe0480-9e3d-11e9-b27f-ed2942f73d70_story.html).

[82] Letter from Pat A. Cipollone, Counsel to the President, The White House, to Acting Chairwoman Carolyn Maloney, House Committee on Oversight and Reform, Chairman Adam B. Schiff, House Permanent Select Committee on Intelligence, Chairman Eliot L. Engel, Chairman, House Committee on Foreign Affairs (Oct. 18, 2019).

[83] Jefferson's Manual of Parliamentary Practice § 603 (stating that "various events have been credited with setting an impeachment in motion," including "facts developed and reported by an investigating committee of the House"). On October 25, 2019, a federal district court affirmed that "no governing law requires" the House to hold a such a vote. *In re Application of the Committee on the Judiciary, United States House of Representatives*, 2019 U.S. Dist. LEXIS 184857 (D.D.C. 2019). More than 300 legal scholars agreed, concluding that "the Constitution does not mandate the process for impeachment and there is no constitutional requirement that the House of Representatives authorize an impeachment inquiry before one begins." *An Open Letter from Legal Scholars on Trump Impeachment Inquiry* (Oct. 17, 2019) (online at www.law.berkeley.edu/wp-content/uploads/2019/10/Open-Letter-from-Legal-Scholars-re-Impeachment.pdf).

[84] *In re Application of the Committee on the Judiciary, United States House of Representatives,* 2019 U.S. Dist. LEXIS 184857 (D.D.C. 2019).

[85] *See, e.g.,* 3 Deschler Ch. 14 § 5 (discussing impeachment of Justice William O. Douglas).

[86] *See, e.g.*, H. Res. 87, 101st Cong. (1989) (impeachment of Judge Walter L. Nixon, Jr.); H. Res. 461, 99th Cong. (1986) (impeachment of Judge Harry E. Claiborne).

[87] H. Res. 6 (2019); H. Res. 660 (2019). In addition, on June 11, 2019, the House approved House Resolution 430, which, in part, authorized the House Committee on the Judiciary to seek judicial enforcement of subpoenas in the ongoing investigation related to Special Counsel Mueller's report. The resolution granted the Committee "any and all necessary authority under Article I of the Constitution" to seek judicial enforcement. The accompanying report by the House Committee on Rules explained that this authority is intended to further the Judiciary Committee's ongoing investigation, the purpose of which includes assessing whether to recommend "articles of impeachment with respect to the President." H. Rep. 116-108, quoting H. Rep. 116-105.

[88] Letter from Pat A. Cipollone, Counsel to the President, The White House, to House Speaker Nancy Pelosi, Chairman Adam B. Schiff, House Permanent Select Committee on Intelligence, Chairman Eliot L. Engel, House Committee on Foreign Affairs Committee, and Chairman Elijah E. Cummings, House Committee on Oversight and Reform (Oct. 8, 2019) (online at www.whitehouse.gov/wp-content/uploads/2019/10/PAC-Letter-10.08.2019.pdf). President Trump has also made these claims directly, stating: "we had a great two weeks watching these crooked politicians, not giving us due process, not giving us lawyers, not giving us the right to speak, and destroying their witnesses," and "we weren't allowed any rights." *Speech: Donald Trump Holds a Political Rally in Sunrise, Florida*, Factbase Videos (Nov. 26, 2019) (online atwww.youtube.com/watch?v=zoRcCRULQl8&feature=youtu.be).

[89] Indeed, Mr. Cipollone articulated no basis under the Constitution for his various "due process" demands—and there is no such basis, especially when the House is engaged in a fact-finding investigation as part of its efforts to ascertain whether to consider articles of impeachment. *See* H. Rept. 116-266 (2019).

[90] H. Res. 660 (2019).

[91] H. Rept. 116-266 (2019) ("The purpose of providing these protections is to ensure that the president has a fair opportunity to present evidence to the Judiciary Committee if it must weigh whether to recommend articles of impeachment against him to the full House.").

[92] Letter from Pat A. Cipollone, Counsel to the President, to House Speaker Nancy Pelosi, Chairman Adam B. Schiff, House Permanent Select Committee on Intelligence, Chairman Eliot L. Engel, House Committee on Foreign Affairs, and Chairman Elijah E. Cummings, Committee on Oversight and Reform (Oct. 8, 2019) (online at www.whitehouse.gov/wp-content/uploads/2019/10/PAC-Letter-10.08.2019.pdf).

[93] In a September 25, 2019, statement, a Department of Justice spokesperson stated: "The Attorney General was first notified of the President's conversation with Ukrainian President Zelensky several weeks after the call took place, when the Department of Justice learned of a potential referral. The President has not spoken with the Attorney General about having Ukraine investigate anything relating to former Vice President Biden or his son. The President has not asked the Attorney General to contact Ukraine—on this or any other matter. The Attorney General has not communicated with Ukraine—on this or any other subject. Nor has the Attorney General discussed this matter, or anything relating to Ukraine, with Rudy Giuliani." As to the President's conduct with regard to Ukraine, the Department stated: "In August, the Department of Justice was referred a matter relating to a letter the Director of National Intelligence had received from the Inspector General for the Intelligence Community regarding a purported whistleblower complaint. The Inspector General's letter cited a conversation between the President and Ukrainian President Zelensky as a potential violation of federal campaign finance law, while acknowledging that neither the Inspector General nor the complainant had firsthand knowledge of the conversation. Relying on established procedures set forth in the Justice Manual, the Department's Criminal Division reviewed the official record of the call and determined, based on the facts and applicable law, that there was no campaign finance violation and that no further action was warranted. All relevant components of the Department agreed with this legal conclusion, and the Department has concluded the matter." Statement of Kerri Kupec, Spokesperson, Department of Justice (Sept. 25, 2019) (as emailed by the Department of Justice to the House Permanent Select Committee on Intelligence).

[94] H. Rept. 116-266 (2019) (The report continued: "As previously described, an impeachment inquiry is not a criminal trial and should not be confused with one. The president's liberty is not at stake and the constitutional protections afforded a criminal defendant do not as a matter of course apply. The constitutionally permitted consequences of impeachment are limited to immediate removal from office and potentially being barred from holding future federal office. Moreover, it is the Senate that conducts the trial to determine whether the conduct outlined in the articles warrant the president's removal from office, which requires a 2/3 majority vote. Indeed, given the nature of the ongoing investigation into the Ukraine matter, President Trump has received additional procedural protections. During closed door depositions held by HPSCI and others related to the Ukraine matter, minority members have been present and granted equal time to question witnesses brought before the committees. This is unlike the process in the preceding two presidential impeachment inquiries, which relied significantly upon information gathered by third-party investigators.").

[95] *See* Committee on Government Reform, Democratic Staff, *Congressional Oversight of the Clinton Administration* (Jan. 17, 2006) (online at https://wayback.archive-it.org/4949/20141031200116/http://oversight-archive.waxman.house.gov/documents/20060117103516-91336.pdf) (explaining that when Rep. Dan Burton served as Chairman of the Committee on Government Reform, the Committee deposed 141 Clinton Administration officials without agency counsel present—including White House Chief of Staff Mack McLarty; White House Chief of Staff Erskine Bowles; White House Counsel Bernard Nussbaum; White House Counsel Jack Quinn; Deputy White House Counsel Bruce Lindsey; Deputy White House Counsel Cheryl Mills; Deputy White House Chief of Staff Harold Ickes; Chief of Staff to the Vice President Roy Neel; and Chief of Staff to the First Lady Margaret Williams).

[96] Letter from Pat A. Cipollone, Counsel to the President, The White House, to House Speaker Nancy Pelosi, Chairman Adam B. Schiff, House Permanent Select Committee on Intelligence, Chairman Eliot L. Engel, House Committee on Foreign Affairs, and Chairman Elijah E. Cummings, Committee on Oversight and Reform

(Oct. 8, 2019) (online at www.whitehouse.gov/wp-content/uploads/2019/10/PAC-Letter-10.08.2019.pdf). On November 1, 2019, after the House approved H. Res. 660, the Administration continued to press this spurious claim, with the Office of Legal Counsel issuing an opinion asserting that "Congressional committees participating in an impeachment inquiry may not validly compel executive branch witnesses to testify about matters that potentially involve information protected by executive privilege without the assistance of agency counsel." Department of Justice, Office of Legal Counsel, *Exclusion of Agency Counsel from Congressional Depositions in the Impeachment Context* (Nov. 1, 2019) (online at www.justice.gov/olc/file/1214996/download). As discussed in this section, this position is entirely unsupported by judicial precedent and erroneous.

[97] U.S. Const., Art. I, sec. 5, cl. 2.

[98] The regulations that govern House depositions state: "Only members, Committee staff designated by the chair or ranking minority member, an official reporter, the witness, and the witness's counsel are permitted to attend. Observers or counsel for other persons, including counsel for government agencies, may not attend." 116th Congress Regulations for Use of Deposition Authority, Congressional Record, H1216 (Jan. 25, 2019) (online at www.congress.gov/116/crec/2019/01/25/CREC-2019-01-25-pt1-PgH1216-2.pdf).

[99] Committee on Oversight and Reform, *Committee Depositions in the House of Representatives: Longstanding Republican and Democratic Practice of Excluding Agency Counsel* (Nov. 5, 2019) (online at https://oversight.house.gov/sites/democrats.oversight.house.gov/files/Committee%20Depositions%20in%20the%20 House%20of%20Representatives_Longstanding%20Republican%20and%20Democratic%20Practice%20of%20Exc luding%20Agency%20Counsel.pdf).

[100] Letter from Pat A. Cipollone, Counsel to the President, The White House, to House Speaker Nancy Pelosi, Chairman Adam B. Schiff, House Permanent Select Committee on Intelligence, Chairman Eliot L. Engel, House Committee on Foreign Affairs Committee, and Chairman Elijah E. Cummings, House Committee on Oversight and Reform (Oct. 8, 2019).

[101] *Barenblatt v. United States*, 360 U.S. 109 (1959).

[102] *See, e.g.*, S. 2537 (requiring an investigation by the State Department Inspector General into the withholding of aid to Ukraine, directing the President to immediately obligate previously appropriated funds, and authorizing funds to counter Russian influence); H.R. 3047 (providing support to Ukraine to defend its independence, sovereignty, and territorial integrity).

[103] *In re Application of the Committee on the Judiciary, United States House of Representatives*, 2019 U.S. Dist. LEXIS 184857 (D.D.C. 2019), quoting *Trump v. Mazars United States*, 2019 U.S. App. LEXIS 30475 (D.D.C. 2019) ("Nothing 'in the Constitution or case law ... compels Congress to abandon its legislative role at the first scent of potential illegality and confine itself exclusively to the impeachment process.'").

[104] *See, e.g.*, the 1974 Amendments to the Freedom of Information Act, P.L. 93-502; Ethics in Government Act of 1978, P.L. 95-52; Presidential Records Act of 1978, P.L. 95-591; Federal Election Campaign Act Amendments of 1974, P.L. 93-443.

[105] Letter from Pat A. Cipollone, Counsel to the President, The White House, to House Speaker Nancy Pelosi, Chairman Adam B. Schiff, House Permanent Select Committee on Intelligence, Chairman Eliot L. Engel, House Committee on Foreign Affairs Committee, and Chairman Elijah E. Cummings, House Committee on Oversight and Reform (Oct. 8, 2019) (online at www.whitehouse.gov/wp-content/uploads/2019/10/PAC-Letter-10.08.2019.pdf); Letter from Pat A. Cipollone, Counsel to the President, The White House, to Acting Chairwoman Carolyn Maloney, House Committee on Oversight and Reform, Chairman Adam B. Schiff, House Permanent Select Committee on Intelligence Chairman Eliot L. Engel, Chairman, House Committee on Foreign Affairs (Oct. 18, 2019).

[106] *United States v. American Tel. & Tel. Co.*, 567 F.2d 121 (D.C. Cir. 1977) ("Rather, each branch should take cognizance of an implicit constitutional mandate to seek optimal accommodation through a realistic evaluation of the needs of the conflicting branches in the particular fact situation.").

[107] For example, on November 22, 2019, the Department of State produced to a private party 99 pages of emails, letters, notes, timelines, and news articles under a court order pursuant to the Freedom of Information Act. *State Department Releases Ukraine Documents to American Oversight*, American Oversight (Nov. 22, 2019) (online at www.americanoversight.org/state-department-releases-ukraine-documents-to-american-oversight).

271

[108] Even if the President were to make a colorable assertion of executive privilege, which he has not, the Supreme Court has held that the privilege is not absolute. In the context of a grand jury subpoena, the Supreme Court found that the President's "generalized assertion of privilege must yield to the demonstrated, specific need for evidence in a pending criminal trial." *United States v. Nixon*, 418 U.S. 683 (1974). Similarly, the D.C. Circuit has held that executive privilege is a "qualified" privilege and that "courts must balance the public interests at stake in determining whether the privilege should yield in a particular case, and must specifically consider the need of the party seeking privileged evidence." *In re Sealed Case*, 121 F.3d 729 (D.C. Cir. 1997). As described above, Congress' need for information during an impeachment inquiry is particularly "compelling." *In re Report & Recommendation of June 5, 1972 Grand Jury Concerning Transmission of Evidence to House of Representatives*, 370 F. Supp. 1219 (D.D.C. 1974) ("[I]t should not be forgotten that we deal in a matter of the most critical moment to the Nation, an impeachment investigation involving the President of the United States. It would be difficult to conceive of a more compelling need than that of this country for an unswervingly fair inquiry based on all the pertinent information.").

[109] *See, e.g.,* Letter from Pat A. Cipollone, Counsel to the President, The White House, to William Pittard, Counsel to Mick Mulvaney, Acting Chief of Staff, The White House (Nov. 8, 2019) (asserting that Acting Chief of Staff Mick Mulvaney "is absolutely immune from compelled congressional testimony with respect to matters related to his service as a senior advisor to the President" and that "[s]ubjecting a senior presidential advisor to the congressional subpoena power would be akin to requiring the President himself to appear before Congress on matters relating to the performance of his constitutionally assigned executive functions").

[110] *Committee on the Judiciary v. Miers*, 558 F. Supp. 2d 53 (D.D.C. 2008) ("The Executive cannot identify a single judicial opinion that recognizes absolute immunity for senior presidential advisors in this or any other context. That simple yet critical fact bears repeating: the asserted absolute immunity claim here is entirely unsupported by existing case law. In fact, there is Supreme Court authority that is all but conclusive on this question and that powerfully suggests that such advisors do not enjoy absolute immunity. The Court therefore rejects the Executive's claim of absolute immunity for senior presidential aides.").

[111] *Committee on the Judiciary v. McGahn,* Case No. 1:19-cv-02379, Memorandum Opinion, Doc. No. 46 (D.D.C. Nov. 25, 2019). As of this report, an appeal is pending in the U.S. Court of Appeals for the D.C. Circuit. No. 19-5331 (D.C. Cir.).

[112] Letter from Chairman Eliot L. Engel, House Committee on Foreign Affairs, Chairman Adam B. Schiff, House Permanent Select Committee on Intelligence, and Chairman Elijah E. Cummings, House Committee on Oversight and Reform, to Pat A. Cipollone, Counsel to the President, The White House (Sept. 9, 2019) (online at https://intelligence.house.gov/uploadedfiles/ele_schiff_cummings_letter_to_cipollone_on_ukraine.pdf).

[113] Letter from Chairman Eliot L. Engel, House Committee on Foreign Affairs, Chairman Adam B. Schiff, House Permanent Select Committee on Intelligence, and Chairman Elijah E. Cummings, House Committee on Oversight and Reform, to Pat A. Cipollone, Counsel to the President, The White House (Sept. 24, 2019) (online at https://intelligence.house.gov/uploadedfiles/2019-09-24.eec_engel_schiff_to_cipollone-wh_re_potus_ukraine.pdf).

[114] Letter from Chairman Elijah E. Cummings, House Committee on Oversight and Reform, Chairman Adam B. Schiff, House Permanent Select Committee on Intelligence, and Chairman Eliot L. Engel, House Committee on Foreign Affairs, to Pat A. Cipollone, Counsel to the President, The White House (Oct. 4, 2019) (online at https://oversight.house.gov/sites/democrats.oversight.house.gov/files/documents/2019-10-04.EEC%20Engel%20Schiff%20to%20Mulvaney-WH%20re%20Subpoena.pdf).

[115] Letter from Pat A. Cipollone, Counsel to the President, The White House, to Acting Chairwoman Carolyn Maloney, House Committee on Oversight and Reform, Chairman Adam B. Schiff, House Permanent Select Committee on Intelligence, and Chairman Eliot L. Engel, House Committee on Foreign Affairs, (Oct. 18, 2019).

[116] Email from Bureau of Legislative Affairs, Department of State, to Committee Staff (Oct. 2, 2019).

[117] Letter from Chairman Eliot L. Engel, House Committee on Foreign Affairs, Chairman Adam B. Schiff, House Permanent Select Committee on Intelligence, and Chairman Elijah E. Cummings, House Committee on Oversight and Reform, to Pat A. Cipollone, Counsel to the President, The White House (Sept. 9, 2019) (online at https://intelligence.house.gov/uploadedfiles/ele_schiff_cummings_letter_to_cipollone_on_ukraine.pdf).

[118] *Id.*

[119] Letter from Chairman Eliot L. Engel, House Committee on Foreign Affairs, Chairman Adam B. Schiff, House Permanent Select Committee on Intelligence, and Chairman Elijah E. Cummings, House Committee on Oversight and Reform, to Pat A. Cipollone, Counsel to the President, The White House (Sept. 24, 2019).

[120] Memorandum from Chairman Elijah E. Cummings to Members of the House Committee on Oversight and Reform, Notice of Intent to Issue Subpoenas (Oct. 2, 2019) (online at https://oversight.house.gov/sites/democrats.oversight.house.gov/files/documents/2019-10-02.COR%20WH%20Subpoena%20Memo%20and%20Schedule.pdf).

[121] Letter from Chairman Elijah E. Cummings, House Committee on Oversight and Reform, Chairman Adam B. Schiff, House Permanent Select Committee on Intelligence, and Chairman Eliot L. Engel, House Committee on Foreign Affairs, to Pat A. Cipollone, Counsel to the President, The White House (Oct. 4, 2019) (online at https://oversight.house.gov/sites/democrats.oversight.house.gov/files/documents/2019-10-04.EEC%20Engel%20Schiff%20to%20Mulvaney-WH%20re%20Subpoena.pdf).

[122] Letter from Pat A. Cipollone, Counsel to the President, The White House, to Speaker Nancy Pelosi, Chairman Adam B. Schiff, House Permanent Select Committee on Intelligence, Chairman Eliot L. Engel, House Committee on Foreign Affairs, and Chairman Elijah E. Cummings, House Committee on Oversight and Reform (Oct. 8, 2019) (online at www.whitehouse.gov/wp-content/uploads/2019/10/PAC-Letter-10.08.2019.pdf).

[123] Letter from Pat A. Cipollone, Counsel to the President, The White House, to Acting Chairwoman Carolyn Maloney, House Committee on Oversight and Reform, Chairman Adam B. Schiff, House Permanent Select Committee on Intelligence, and Chairman Eliot L. Engel, House Committee on Foreign Affairs, (Oct. 18, 2019).

[124] On September 13, the Intelligence Committee issued a subpoena pursuant to its oversight authority to the Acting Director of National Intelligence to compel the production of a complaint submitted by an Intelligence Community whistleblower, as well as other records. The Intelligence Committee issued this subpoena before Speaker Pelosi announced on September 24 that the Intelligence Committee and other committees would be continuing their work under the umbrella of the impeachment inquiry being conducted by the Judiciary Committee. As a result, this subpoena should not be conflated with subpoenas issued as part of the impeachment inquiry. *See* Letter from Chairman Adam B. Schiff, House Permanent Select Committee on Intelligence, to Joseph Maguire, Acting Director of National Intelligence, Office of the Director of National Intelligence (Sept. 13, 2019).

[125] The White House, *Memorandum of Telephone Conversation* (Apr. 21, 2019) (online at http://cdn.cnn.com/cnn/2019/images/11/15/4-21-19.trump-zelensky.call.pdf); The White House, *Memorandum of Telephone Conversation* (July 25, 2019) (online at www.whitehouse.gov/wp-content/uploads/2019/09/Unclassified09.2019.pdf).

[126] Vindman-Williams Hearing Tr. at 31-32.

[127] Vindman Dep. Tr. at 53; Morrison Dep. Tr. at 19-20.

[128] Vindman Dep. Tr. at 186-187; Morrison Dep. Tr. at 166-167.

[129] *See, e.g.*, Cooper Dep. Tr. at 42-43.

[130] Sondland Hearing Tr. at 78-79.

[131] Vindman Dep. Tr. at 36-37.

[132] Holmes Dep. Tr. at 31.

[133] House Permanent Select Committee on Intelligence, Opening Statement of Ambassador Gordon Sondland, Department of State, *Impeachment*, 116th Cong. (Nov. 20, 2019).

[134] The review reportedly uncovered "early August email exchanges between acting chief of staff Mick Mulvaney and White House budget officials seeking to provide an explanation for withholding the funds after the president had already ordered a hold in mid-July on the nearly $400 million in security assistance." The review also reportedly included interviews with "some key White House officials involved in handling Ukraine aid and dealing with complaints and concerns in the aftermath of the call between Trump and Zelensky." *White House Review Turns Up Emails Showing Extensive Effort to Justify Trump's Decision to Block Ukraine Military Aid,* Washington Post (Nov. 24, 2019) (online at www.washingtonpost.com/politics/white-house-review-turns-up-emails-showing-

extensive-effort-to-justify-trumps-decision-to-block-ukraine-military-aid/2019/11/24/2121cf98-0d57-11ea-bd9d-c628fd48b3a0_story.html).

[135] Letter from Chairman Eliot L. Engel, House Committee on Foreign Affairs, Chairman Adam B. Schiff, House Permanent Select Committee on Intelligence, and Chairman Elijah E. Cummings, House Committee on Oversight and Reform, to Vice President Michael Pence, Office of the Vice President (Oct. 4, 2019) (online at https://oversight.house.gov/sites/democrats.oversight.house.gov/files/documents/2019-10-.04.EEC%20Engel%20Schiff%20%20re%20Request%20to%20VP%2010-04-19%20Letter%20and%20Schedule.pdf).

[136] Id.

[137] Letter from Matthew E. Morgan, Counsel to the Vice President, Office of the Vice President, to Chairman Elijah E. Cummings, House Committee on Oversight and Reform, Chairman Eliot L. Engel, House Committee on Foreign Affairs, and Chairman Adam B. Schiff, House Permanent Select Committee on Intelligence (Oct. 15, 2019).

[138] Vindman-Williams Hearing Tr. at 61.

[139] Williams Dep. Tr. at 129.

[140] Vindman-Williams Hearing Tr. at 15.

[141] Vindman-Williams Hearing Tr. at 23-24.

[142] Williams Dep. Tr. at 74-75.

[143] Letter from Chairman Adam B. Schiff, House Permanent Select Committee on Intelligence, Chairman Eliot L. Engel, House Committee on Foreign Affairs, and Chairman Elijah E. Cummings, House Committee on Oversight and Reform, to Acting Director Russell T. Vought, Office of Management and Budget (Oct. 7, 2019) (online at https://intelligence.house.gov/uploadedfiles/2019-10-07.eec_engel_schiff_to_vought-_omb_re_subpoena.pdf).

[144] Id.

[145] Letter from Jason Yaworske, Associate Director for Legislative Affairs, Office of Management and Budget, to Chairman Adam B. Schiff, House Permanent Select Committee on Intelligence (Oct. 15, 2019).

[146] Sandy Dep. Tr. at 23-26.

[147] Sandy Dep. Tr. at 36-41.

[148] Sandy Dep. Tr. at 57-60, 62-63.

[149] Letter from Chairman Eliot L. Engel, House Committee on Foreign Affairs, Chairman Adam B. Schiff, House Permanent Select Committee on Intelligence, and Chairman Elijah E. Cummings, House Committee on Oversight and Reform, to Secretary Michael R. Pompeo, Department of State (Sept. 9, 2019) (online at https://intelligence.house.gov/uploadedfiles/ele_schiff_cummings_letter_to_sec_pompeo_on_ukraine.pdf).

[150] Letter from Chairman Eliot L. Engel, House Committee on Foreign Affairs, Chairman Adam B. Schiff, House Permanent Select Committee on Intelligence, and Chairman Elijah E. Cummings, House Committee on Oversight and Reform, to Secretary Michael R. Pompeo, Department of State (Sept. 23, 2019).

[151] Letter from Chairman Eliot L. Engel, House Committee on Foreign Affairs, Chairman Adam B. Schiff, House Permanent Select Committee on Intelligence, and Chairman Elijah E. Cummings, House Committee on Oversight and Reform, to Secretary Michael R. Pompeo, Department of State (Sept. 27, 2019) (online at https://oversight.house.gov/sites/democrats.oversight.house.gov/files/documents/2019-09-27.EEC%20Engel%20Schiff%20%20to%20Pompeo-%20State%20re%20Document%20Subpoena.pdf).

[152] Letter from Chairman Adam B. Schiff, House Permanent Select Committee on Intelligence, Chairman Elijah E. Cummings, House Committee on Oversight and Reform, and Chairman Eliot L. Engel, House Committee on Foreign Affairs, to Ambassador Gordon Sondland, Department of State (Oct. 8, 2019) (online at https://oversight.house.gov/sites/democrats.oversight.house.gov/files/documents/2019-10-08.EEC%20Engel%20Schiff%20to%20Sondland%20re%20Subpoena.pdf); Letter from Chairman Eliot L. Engel,

House Committee on Foreign Affairs, Chairman Adam B. Schiff, House Permanent Select Committee on Intelligence, and Chairman Elijah E. Cummings, House Committee on Oversight and Reform, to Ambassador William Taylor, Department of State (Oct. 4, 2019); Letter from Chairman Eliot L. Engel, House Committee on Foreign Affairs, Chairman Adam B. Schiff, House Permanent Select Committee on Intelligence, and Chairman Elijah E. Cummings, House Committee on Oversight and Reform, to Counselor T. Ulrich Brechbuhl, Department of State (Sept. 27, 2019) (online at https://intelligence.house.gov/uploadedfiles/20190927_-_eec_engel_schiff_to_brechbuhl_re_individual_deposition_request.pdf); Letter from Chairman Eliot L. Engel, House Committee on Foreign Affairs, Chairman Adam B. Schiff, House Permanent Select Committee on Intelligence, and Chairman Elijah E. Cummings, House Committee on Oversight and Reform, to Deputy Assistant Secretary George P. Kent, Department of State (Sept. 27, 2019); Letter from Chairman Eliot L. Engel, House Committee on Foreign Affairs, Chairman Adam B. Schiff, House Permanent Select Committee on Intelligence, and Chairman Elijah E. Cummings, House Committee on Oversight and Reform, to Ambassador Kurt Volker, Department of State (Sept. 27, 2019); Letter from Chairman Eliot L. Engel, House Committee on Foreign Affairs, Chairman Adam B. Schiff, House Permanent Select Committee on Intelligence, and Chairman Elijah E. Cummings, House Committee on Oversight and Reform, to Ambassador Marie Yovanovitch, Department of State (Sept. 27, 2019).

[153] Letter from Secretary Michael R. Pompeo, Department of State, to Chairman Eliot L. Engel, House Committee on Foreign Affairs (Oct. 1, 2019) (Secretary Pompeo sent identical letters to Chairman Elijah. E. Cummings, House Committee on Oversight and Reform, and Chairman Adam B. Schiff, House Permanent Select Committee on Intelligence, the same day).

[154] *Id.*

[155] Kent Dep. Tr. at 27.

[156] Kent Dep. Tr. at 33-34.

[157] Kent Dep. Tr. at 34-35.

[158] Letter from Secretary Michael R. Pompeo, Department of State, to Chairman Eliot L. Engel, House Committee on Foreign Affairs (Oct. 1, 2019) (Secretary Pompeo sent identical letters to Chairman Elijah. E. Cummings, House Committee on Oversight and Reform, and Chairman Adam B. Schiff, House Permanent Select Committee on Intelligence, the same day).

[159] Letter from Chairman Eliot L. Engel, House Committee on Foreign Affairs, Chairman Adam B. Schiff, House Permanent Select Committee on Intelligence, and Chairman Elijah E. Cummings, House Committee on Oversight and Reform, to Deputy Secretary John J. Sullivan, Department of State (Oct. 1, 2019) (online at https://foreignaffairs.house.gov/_cache/files/4/6/4683bc86-be2a-49fc-9e76-7cdbf669592f/98BEBD8006DE62BA36BEBD175775F744.2019-10-1-ele-abs-eec-to-depsec-sullivan.pdf).

[160] *Pompeo: 'I Was on the Phone Call' with Trump and Ukrainian President*, CNN (Oct. 2, 2019) (online at www.cnn.com/2019/10/02/politics/mike-pompeo-ukraine-call/index.html).

[161] Email from Committee Staff to Bureau of Legislative Affairs, Department of State (Oct. 7, 2019).

[162] Letter from Brian Bulatao, Under Secretary of State for Management, Department of State, to Andrew Wright, Counsel to Deputy Assistant Secretary George P. Kent, Department of State (Oct. 14, 2019).

[163] Kent Dep. Tr. at 30-31, 46.

[164] Kent Dep. Tr. at 32.

[165] Kent Dep. Tr. at 35.

[166] House Permanent Select Committee on Intelligence, Opening Statement of Ambassador Gordon Sondland, Department of State, *Impeachment*, 116th Cong. (Nov. 20, 2019).

[167] *Id.*

[168] *Id.* In addition, Dr. Fiona Hill, the former Senior Director for European and Russian Affairs at the National Security Council, produced calendar entries relating to relevant meetings. Fiona Hill Document Production, Bates Hill0001 through Hill0049 (Oct. 13, 2019).

[169] Kurt Volker Document Production, Bates KV00000001-KV00000065 (Oct. 3, 2019).

[170] 18 U.S.C. § 1505.

[171] House Permanent Select Committee on Intelligence, Opening Statement of Ambassador Gordon Sondland, Department of State, *Impeachment*, 116th Cong., at 3-4 (Nov. 20, 2019).

[172] Sondland Hearing Tr. at 160.

[173] Declaration of Ambassador Gordon Sondland, Department of State, at 3 (Nov. 4, 2019).

[174] *State Department Releases Ukraine Documents to American Oversight*, American Oversight (Nov. 22, 2019) (online at www.americanoversight.org/state-department-releases-ukraine-documents-to-american-oversight); *American Oversight v. Dep't of State*, Case No. 19-cv-2934, Doc. No. 15 (D.D.C. November 25, 2019).

[175] Email from Office Manager to the Secretary of State to S_All (Mar. 26, 2019) (online at www.americanoversight.org/wp-content/uploads/2019/11/AO_State_Ukraine_Docs_11-22.pdf).

[176] Email from Madeleine Westerhout to State Department Official, (Mar. 27, 2019) (online at www.americanoversight.org/wp-content/uploads/2019/11/AO_State_Ukraine_Docs_11-22.pdf).

[177] Letter from Chairman Eliot L. Engel, House Committee on Foreign Affairs, Chairman Adam B. Schiff, House Permanent Select Committee on Intelligence, and Chairman Elijah E. Cummings, House Committee on Oversight and Reform, to Secretary Michael R. Pompeo, Department of State (Sept. 27, 2019) (online at https://oversight.house.gov/sites/democrats.oversight.house.gov/files/documents/2019-09-27.EEC%20Engel%20Schiff%20%20to%20Pompeo-%20State%20re%20Document%20Subpoena.pdf).

[178] Taylor Dep. Tr. at 33-34.

[179] House Permanent Select Committee on Intelligence, Opening Statement of Ambassador Gordon Sondland, Department of State, *Impeachment*, 116th Cong., at 20-23 (Nov. 20, 2019).

[180] Taylor Dep. Tr. at 45-46.

[181] Hale Dep. Tr. at 147-148.

[182] Letter from Chairman Adam B. Schiff, House Permanent Select Committee on Intelligence, Chairman Eliot L. Engel, House Committee on Foreign Affairs, and Chairman Elijah E. Cummings, House Committee on Oversight and Reform, to Secretary Mark Esper, Department of Defense (Oct. 7, 2019) (online at https://intelligence.house.gov/uploadedfiles/2019-10-07.eec_engel_schiff_to_esper-dod_re_subpoena.pdf).

[183] *Transcript: Secretary of Defense Mark Esper on "Face the Nation," October 13, 2019*, CBS News (Oct. 13, 2019) (online at www.cbsnews.com/news/transcript-secretary-of-defense-mark-esper-on-face-the-nation-october-13-2019/).

[184] Letter from Robert R. Hood, Assistant Secretary of Defense for Legislative Affairs, Department of Defense, to Chairman Adam B. Schiff, House Permanent Select Committee on Intelligence, Chairman Eliot L. Engel, House Committee on Foreign Affairs, and Chairman Elijah E. Cummings, House Committee on Oversight and Reform (Oct. 15, 2019).

[185] *Transcript: Secretary of Defense Mark Esper on "Face the Nation," October 13, 2019*, CBS News (Oct. 13, 2019) (online at www.cbsnews.com/news/transcript-secretary-of-defense-mark-esper-on-face-the-nation-october-13-2019/).

[186] *See, e.g.*, Cooper Dep. Tr. at 42-43.

[187] Cooper Dep. Tr. at 33.

[188] Cooper Dep. Tr. at 33-38.

[189] Cooper Hearing Tr. at 13-14.

[190] Cooper Hearing Tr. at 14.

[191] Cooper Hearing Tr. at 14.

192 Letter from Chairman Eliot L. Engel, House Committee on Foreign Affairs, Chairman Adam B. Schiff, House Permanent Select Committee on Intelligence, and Chairman Elijah E. Cummings, House Committee on Oversight and Reform, to Secretary Rick Perry, Department of Energy (Oct. 10, 2019) (online at https://oversight.house.gov/sites/democrats.oversight.house.gov/files/documents/2019-10-10.EEC%20Engel%20Schiff%20to%20Perry-DOE%20Joint%20Cover%20Letter%20re%20Subpoena.pdf).

193 Letter from Melissa F. Burnison, Assistant Secretary for Congressional and Intergovernmental Affairs, Department of Energy, to Chairman Eliot L. Engel, House Committee on Foreign Affairs, Chairman Adam B. Schiff, House Permanent Select Committee on Intelligence, and Chairman Elijah E. Cummings, House Committee on Oversight and Reform (Oct. 18, 2019).

194 Hill-Holmes Hearing Tr. at 160.

195 House Permanent Select Committee on Intelligence, Opening Statement of Ambassador Gordon Sondland, Department of State, *Impeachment*, 116th Cong. (Nov. 20, 2019).

196 House Permanent Select Committee on Intelligence, Opening Statement of Ambassador Gordon Sondland, Department of State, *Impeachment*, 116th Cong. (Nov. 20, 2019).

197 Letter from Chairman Chairman Adam B. Schiff, House Permanent Select Committee on Intelligence, Eliot L. Engel, House Committee on Foreign Affairs, and Chairman Elijah E. Cummings, House Committee on Oversight and Reform, to Rudy Giuliani (Sept. 30, 2019) (online at https://oversight.house.gov/sites/democrats.oversight.house.gov/files/documents/20190930%20-%20Giuliani%20HPSCI%20Subpoena%20Letter.pdf).

198 Letter from Jon A. Sale, Counsel to Rudy Giuliani, to Committee Staff (Oct. 15, 2019).

199 *Id.*

200 Letter from Chairman Adam B. Schiff, House Permanent Select Committee on Intelligence, Chairman Eliot L. Engel, House Committee on Foreign Affairs, and Chairman Elijah E. Cummings, House Committee on Oversight and Reform, to Igor Fruman (Sept. 30, 2019) (online at https://oversight.house.gov/sites/democrats.oversight.house.gov/files/documents/20190930%20-%20Fruman%20Letter%20and%20Doc%20Request%20Schedule.pdf); Letter from Chairman Adam B. Schiff, House Permanent Select Committee on Intelligence, Chairman Eliot L. Engel, House Committee on Foreign Affairs, and Chairman Elijah E. Cummings, House Committee on Oversight and Reform, to Lev Parnas (Sept. 30, 2019) (online at https://oversight.house.gov/sites/democrats.oversight.house.gov/files/documents/20190930%20-%20Parnas%20Letter%20and%20Doc%20Request%20Schedule.pdf).

201 Letter from Chairman Adam B. Schiff, House Permanent Select Committee on Intelligence, Chairman Eliot L. Engel, House Committee on Foreign Affairs, and Chairman Elijah E. Cummings, House Committee on Oversight and Reform, to John M. Dowd, Counsel to Igor Fruman and Lev Parnas (Oct. 10, 2019) (online at https://intelligence.house.gov/uploadedfiles/2019-10-09.eec_engel_schiff_to_parnas_fruman_re_subpoena.pdf).

202 Letter from John M. Dowd, Counsel to Igor Fruman and Lev Parnas, to Committee Staff (Oct. 3, 2019).

203 Letter from John M. Dowd, Counsel to Igor Fruman and Lev Parnas, to Committee Staff (Oct. 8, 2019).

204 Email from John M. Dowd, Counsel to Igor Fruman and Lev Parnas, to Committee Staff (Oct. 9, 2019).

205 Email from Committee Staff to John M. Dowd, Counsel to Igor Fruman and Lev Parnas (Oct. 10, 2019).

206 Email from John M. Dowd, Counsel to Igor Fruman and Lev Parnas, to Committee Staff (Oct. 10, 2019).

207 *Exclusive: Giuliani Associate Parnas Will Comply with Trump Impeachment Inquiry—Lawyer*, Reuters (Nov. 4, 2019) (online at www.reuters.com/article/us-usa-trump-impeachment-parnas-exclusiv/exclusive-giuliani-associate-now-willing-to-comply-with-trump-impeachment-inquiry-lawyer-idUSKBN1XE297). On November 23, 2019, Mr. Parnas' attorney informed the press that "Mr. Parnas learned from former Ukrainian Prosecutor General Victor Shokin that [Ranking Member Devin] Nunes had met with Shokin in Vienna last December." According to the report, "Parnas says he worked to put Nunes in touch with Ukrainians who could help Nunes dig up dirt on Biden and Democrats in Ukraine, according to Bondy." *Exclusive: Giuliani Associate Willing to Tell Congress Nunes Met with Ex-Ukrainian Official to Get Dirt on Biden,* CNN (Nov. 23, 2019) (online at

www.cnn.com/2019/11/22/politics/nunes-vienna-trip-ukrainian-prosecutor-biden/index.html). On November 24, 2019, Mr. Parnas' attorney told press that his client had arranged skype and phone calls earlier this year between Ranking Member Nunes' staff and Ukraine's chief anti-corruption prosecutor, Nazar Kholodnytsky, as well as a deputy in Ukraine's Prosecutor General's office, Konstantin Kulik. According to Mr. Parnas' attorney, Ranking Member Nunes had actually planned a trip to Ukraine instead of the calls, but cancelled the trip when his staff realized it would require alerting Chairman Schiff about the travel. *Giuliani Associate Parnas Wants to Testify that Nunes Aides Hid Ukraine Meetings on Biden Dirt from Schiff*, CNBC (Nov. 24, 2019) (online at www.cnbc.com/2019/11/24/giuliani-ally-would-testify-that-nunes-staffers-hid-ukraine-meetings-from-schiff.html).

[208] Letter from Pat A. Cipollone, Counsel to the President, The White House, to House Speaker Nancy Pelosi, Chairman Adam B. Schiff, House Permanent Select Committee on Intelligence, Chairman Eliot L. Engel, House Committee on Foreign Affairs Committee, and Chairman Elijah E. Cummings, House Committee on Oversight and Reform (Oct. 8, 2019) (online at www.whitehouse.gov/wp-content/uploads/2019/10/PAC-Letter-10.08.2019.pdf).

[209] *See* 2 U.S.C. §§ 192, 194. Witnesses who received subpoenas that were subsequently withdrawn would not face a similar risk of being held in contempt of Congress.

[210] *See, e.g.*, Email from Committee Staff to Mick Mulvaney, Acting Chief of Staff, The White House (Nov. 7, 2019) ("Your failure or refusal to comply with the subpoena, including at the direction or behest of the President, shall constitute further evidence of obstruction of the House's impeachment inquiry and may be used as an adverse inference against you and the President. Moreover, your failure to appear shall constitute evidence that may be used against you in a contempt proceeding.").

[211] Letter from Chairman Eliot L. Engel, House Committee on Foreign Affairs, Chairman Adam B. Schiff, House Permanent Select Committee on Intelligence, and Acting Chairwoman Carolyn B. Maloney, House Committee on Oversight and Reform, Mick Mulvaney, Acting Chief of Staff, The White House (Nov. 5, 2019) (online at https://oversight.house.gov/sites/democrats.oversight.house.gov/files/2019-11-05.CBM%20Engel%20Schiff%20to%20Mulvaney-WH%20re%20Depo%20Notice.pdf).

[212] House Permanent Select Committee on Intelligence, Subpoena to Mick Mulvaney, Acting Chief of Staff, The White House (Nov. 7, 2019).

[213] Email from William Pittard, Counsel to Mick Mulvaney, Acting Chief of Staff, The White House, to Committee Staff (Nov. 8, 2019).

[214] Letter from Pat A. Cipollone, Counsel to the President, The White House, to William Pittard, Counsel to Mick Mulvaney, Acting Chief of Staff, The White House (Nov. 8, 2019) (online at www.whitehouse.gov/wp-content/uploads/2019/10/PAC-Letter-10.08.2019.pdf).

[215] Letter from Steven A. Engel, Assistant Attorney General, Office of Legal Counsel, Department of Justice, to Pat A. Cipollone, Counsel to the President, The White House (Nov. 7, 2019).

[216] Mulvaney Dep. Tr. at 5.

[217] Mulvaney Dep. Tr. at 7-9.

[218] On November 8, 2019, Mr. Mulvaney filed a motion in federal court seeking to join a lawsuit, discussed below, filed by Dr. Charles Kupperman seeking a declaratory judgment as to whether he should comply with the Committees' subpoena. On November 11, 2019, Mr. Mulvaney withdrew his request to join the case. *White House Chief of Staff Mulvaney Drops Bid to Join Kupperman Impeachment Lawsuit,* Washington Post (Nov. 11, 2019) (online at www.washingtonpost.com/local/legal-issues/bolton-and-kupperman-reject-white-house-chief-of-staff-mulvaneys-bid-to-join-impeachment-lawsuit/2019/11/11/cdf40226-04ac-11ea-8292-c46ee8cb3dce_story.html).

[219] Letter from Chairman Eliot L. Engel, House Committee on Foreign Affairs, Chairman Adam B. Schiff, House Permanent Select Committee on Intelligence, and Acting Chairwoman Carolyn B. Maloney, House Committee on Oversight and Reform, to Robert B. Blair, Assistant to the President and Senior Advisor to the Chief of Staff, The White House (Oct. 24, 2019).

[220] Letter from Whitney C. Ellerman, Counsel to Robert B. Blair, Assistant to the President and Senior Advisor to the Chief of Staff, The White House, to Chairman Eliot L. Engel, House Committee on Foreign Affairs,

Chairman Adam B. Schiff, House Permanent Select Committee on Intelligence, and Acting Chairwoman Carolyn B. Maloney, House Committee on Oversight and Reform (Nov. 2, 2019).

[221] Letter from Chairman Adam B. Schiff, House Permanent Select Committee on Intelligence, Acting Chairwoman Carolyn B. Maloney, House Committee on Oversight and Reform, and Chairman Eliot L. Engel, House Committee on Foreign Affairs, to Whitney C. Ellerman, Counsel to Robert B. Blair, Assistant to the President and Senior Advisor to the Chief of Staff, The White House (Nov. 3, 2019); House Permanent Select Committee on Intelligence, Subpoena to Robert B. Blair, Assistant to the President and Senior Advisor to the Chief of Staff, The White House (Nov. 3, 2019).

[222] Blair Dep. Tr. at 6-7.

[223] Letter from Chairman Eliot L. Engel, House Committee on Foreign Affairs, Chairman Adam B. Schiff, House Permanent Select Committee on Intelligence, and Acting Chairwoman Carolyn B. Maloney, House Committee on Oversight and Reform, to Charles J. Cooper and Michael W. Kirk, Counsel to Ambassador John Bolton, Former National Security Advisor, The White House (Oct. 30, 2019).

[224] Email from Charles J. Cooper, Counsel to Ambassador John Bolton, Former National Security Advisor, The White House, to Committee Staff (Oct. 30, 2019).

[225] Letter from Charles J. Cooper, Counsel to Ambassador John Bolton, Former National Security Advisor, The White House, to Douglas N. Letter, General Counsel, House of Representatives (Nov. 8, 2019).

[226] In early November 2019, Ambassador Bolton's personal attorney also informed Committee staff that if the Committees were to issue a subpoena to compel his testimony, he would seek to join the lawsuit filed by Dr. Kupperman. On November 24, 2019, Chairman Schiff stated, "We've certainly been in touch with his lawyer and what we've been informed by his lawyer—because we invited him and he did not choose to come in and testify, notwithstanding the fact that his deputy Fiona Hill and his other deputy Colonel Vindman and Tim Morrison and others on the National Security Council have shown the courage to come in—is if we subpoena him, they will sue us in court." *Schiff Pushes Bolton to Testify But Will Not Go to Court to Force Him*, CNN (Nov. 24, 2019) (online at www.cnn.com/2019/11/24/politics/adam-schiff-house-democrats-impeachment-state-of-the-union-cnntv/index.html).

[227] Letter from Chairman Eliot L. Engel, House Committee on Foreign Affairs, Chairman Adam B. Schiff, House Permanent Select Committee on Intelligence, and Acting Chairwoman Carolyn B. Maloney, House Committee on Oversight and Reform, to John A. Eisenberg, Deputy Counsel to the President for National Security Affairs and Legal Advisor to the National Security Council, National Security Council, The White House (Oct. 30, 2019).

[228] Eisenberg Dep. Tr. at 6 ("Mr. Eisenberg never acknowledged receipt or otherwise responded to the committees' deposition request, nor did any official at the White House.").

[229] Letter from Chairman Eliot L. Engel, House Committee on Foreign Affairs, Chairman Adam B. Schiff, House Permanent Select Committee on Intelligence, and Acting Chairwoman Carolyn B. Maloney, House Committee on Oversight and Reform, to John A. Eisenberg, Deputy Counsel to the President for National Security Affairs and Legal Advisor to the National Security Council, National Security Council, The White House (Nov. 1, 2019); House Permanent Select Committee on Intelligence, Subpoena to John A. Eisenberg, Deputy Counsel to the President for National Security Affairs and Legal Advisor to the National Security Council, The White House (Nov. 1, 2019).

[230] Letter from William A. Burck, Counsel to John A. Eisenberg, Deputy Counsel to the President for National Security Affairs and Legal Advisor to the National Security Council, National Security Council, The White House, to Chairman Eliot L. Engel, House Committee on Foreign Affairs, Chairman Adam B. Schiff, House Permanent Select Committee on Intelligence, and Acting Chairwoman Carolyn B. Maloney, House Committee on Oversight and Reform (Nov. 4, 2019).

[231] Letter from Pat A. Cipollone, Counsel to the President, The White House, to William A. Burck, Counsel to John A. Eisenberg, Deputy Counsel to the President for National Security Affairs and Legal Advisor to the National Security Council, National Security Council, The White House (Nov. 3, 2019).

[232] Letter from Steven A. Engel, Assistant Attorney General, Office of Legal Counsel, Department of Justice, to Pat A. Cipollone, Counsel to the President, the White House (Nov. 3, 2019).

[233] Eisenberg Dep. Tr. at 6-8.

[234] Letter from Chairman Eliot L. Engel, House Committee on Foreign Affairs, Chairman Adam B. Schiff, House Permanent Select Committee on Intelligence, and Acting Chairwoman Carolyn B. Maloney, House Committee on Oversight and Reform, to Michael Ellis, Senior Associate Counsel to the President and Deputy Legal Advisor to the National Security Council, National Security Council, The White House (Oct. 30, 2019).

[235] Email from Paul Butler, Counsel to Michael Ellis, Senior Associate Counsel to the President and Deputy Legal Advisor to the National Security Council, National Security Council, The White House, to Committee Staff (Nov. 2, 2019).

[236] Email from Paul Butler, Counsel to Michael Ellis, Senior Associate Counsel to the President and Deputy Legal Advisor to the National Security Council, National Security Council, The White House, to Committee Staff (Nov. 3, 2019).

[237] Letter from Chairman Adam B. Schiff, House Permanent Select Committee on Intelligence, Acting Chairwoman Carolyn B. Maloney, House Committee on Oversight and Reform, Chairman Eliot L. Engel, House Committee on Foreign Affairs, to Paul W. Butler, Counsel to Michael Ellis, Senior Associate Counsel to the President and Deputy Legal Advisor to the National Security Council, National Security Council, The White House (Nov. 3, 2019); House Permanent Select Committee on Intelligence, Subpoena to Michael Ellis, Senior Associate Counsel to the President and Deputy Legal Advisor to the National Security Council, National Security Council, The White House (Nov. 3, 2019).

[238] Ellis Dep. Tr. at 7.

[239] Letter from Chairman Eliot L. Engel, House Committee on Foreign Affairs, Chairman Adam B. Schiff, House Permanent Select Committee on Intelligence, and Acting Chairwoman Carolyn B. Maloney, House Committee on Oversight and Reform, to Preston Wells Griffith, Senior Director for International Energy and Environment, National Security Council (Oct. 24, 2019).

[240] Letter from Karen D. Williams, Counsel to Preston Wells Griffith, Senior Director for International Energy and Environment, National Security Council, to Chairman Eliot L. Engel, House Committee on Foreign Affairs, Chairman Adam B. Schiff, House Permanent Select Committee on Intelligence, and Acting Chairwoman Carolyn B. Maloney, House Committee on Oversight and Reform (Nov. 4, 2019).

[241] Letter from Chairman Adam B. Schiff, House Permanent Select Committee on Intelligence, Acting Chairwoman Carolyn B. Maloney, House Committee on Oversight and Reform, and Chairman Eliot L. Engel, House Committee on Foreign Affairs, to Karen D. Williams, Counsel to Preston Wells Griffith, Senior Director for International Energy and Environment, National Security Council (Nov. 4, 2019); House Permanent Select Committee on Intelligence, Subpoena to Preston Wells Griffith, Senior Director for International Energy and Environment, National Security Council (Nov. 4, 2019).

[242] Griffith Dep. Tr. at 5-6.

[243] Letter from Chairman Eliot L. Engel, House Committee on Foreign Affairs, Chairman Adam B. Schiff, House Permanent Select Committee on Intelligence, and Chairman Elijah E. Cummings, House Committee on Oversight and Reform, to Dr. Charles M. Kupperman, Former Deputy Assistant to the President for National Security Affairs, National Security Council (Oct. 16, 2019).

[244] Email from Committee Staff to Charles J. Cooper and Michael W. Kirk, Counsel to Dr. Charles M. Kupperman, Former Deputy Assistant to the President for National Security Affairs, National Security Council (Oct. 25, 2019); House Permanent Select Committee on Intelligence, Subpoena to Dr. Charles M. Kupperman, Former Deputy Assistant to the President for National Security Affairs, National Security Council (Oct. 25, 2019).

[245] Compl., *Kupperman v. U.S. House of Representatives et al.*, No. 19 Civ. 3224 (D.D.C. filed Oct. 25, 2019).

[246] Email from Michael W. Kirk, Counsel to Dr. Charles M. Kupperman, Former Deputy Assistant to the President for National Security Affairs, National Security Council, to Committee Staff (Oct. 25, 2019).

[247] Letter from Pat A. Cipollone, Counsel to the President, The White House, to Charles J. Cooper, Counsel to Dr. Charles M. Kupperman, Former Deputy Assistant to the President for National Security Affairs, National Security Council (Oct. 25, 2019).

[248] Letter from Steven A. Engel, Assistant Attorney General, Office of Legal Counsel, Department of Justice, to Pat A. Cipollone, Counsel to the President, The White House (Oct. 25, 2019).

[249] Letter from Chairman Adam B. Schiff, House Permanent Select Committee on Intelligence, Chairman Eliot L. Engel, House Committee on Foreign Affairs, and Acting Chairwoman Carolyn B. Maloney, House Committee on Oversight and Reform, to Charles J. Cooper and Michael W. Kirk, Counsel to Dr. Charles M. Kupperman, Former Deputy Assistant to the President for National Security Affairs, National Security Council (Oct. 26, 2019).

[250] Letter from Charles J. Cooper, Counsel to Dr. Charles M. Kupperman, Former Deputy Assistant to the President for National Security Affairs, National Security Council, to Committee Staff (Oct. 26, 2019).

[251] Letter from Charles J. Cooper, Counsel to Dr. Charles M. Kupperman, Former Deputy Assistant to the President for National Security Affairs, National Security Council, to Committee Staff (Oct. 27, 2019).

[252] Letter from Chairman Eliot L. Engel, House Committee on Foreign Affairs, Chairman Adam B. Schiff, House Permanent Select Committee on Intelligence, and Acting Chairwoman Carolyn B. Maloney, House Committee on Oversight and Reform to Charles J. Cooper and Michael W. Kirk, Counsel to Dr. Charles M. Kupperman, Former Deputy Assistant to the President for National Security Affairs, National Security Council, (Nov. 5, 2019).

[253] Letter from Charles J. Cooper, Counsel to Dr. Charles M. Kupperman, Former Deputy Assistant to the President for National Security Affairs, National Security Council, to Douglas N. Letter, General Counsel, House of Representatives (Nov. 8, 2019).

[254] *Committee on the Judiciary v. McGahn*, Memorandum Opinion (D.D.C. Nov. 25, 2019) ("To make the point as plain as possible, it is clear to this Court for the reasons explained above that, with respect to senior-level presidential aides, absolute immunity from compelled congressional process simply does not exist. Indeed, absolute testimonial immunity for senior-level White House aides appears to be a fiction that has been fastidiously maintained over time through the force of sheer repetition in OLC opinions, and through accommodations that have permitted its proponents to avoid having the proposition tested in the crucible of litigation. And because the contention that a President's top advisors cannot be subjected to compulsory congressional process simply has no basis in the law, it does not matter whether such immunity would theoretically be available to only a handful of presidential aides due to the sensitivity of their positions, or to the entire Executive branch. Nor does it make any difference whether the aides in question are privy to national security matters, or work solely on domestic issues."). As of this report, an appeal is pending in the D.C. Circuit. No. 19-5331 (D.C. Cir.).

[255] *See, Kupperman v. U.S. House of Representatives, et al.*, No. 19 Civ. 3224 (D.D.C.). As of this report, the House Defendants' Motion to Dismiss (Nov. 14, 2019), ECF No. 41, remains pending. Although the Committee will not reissue the subpoena to Dr. Kupperman and the court case is moot, he could choose to appear on a voluntary basis to assist Congress in the discharge of its Constitutional responsibilities.

[256] Letter from Chairman Eliot L. Engel, House Committee on Foreign Affairs, Chairman Adam B. Schiff, House Permanent Select Committee on Intelligence, and Chairman Elijah E. Cummings, House Committee on Oversight and Reform, to Acting Director Russell T. Vought, Office of Management and Budget (Oct. 11, 2019).

[257] Email from Jessica L. Donlon, Deputy General Counsel for Oversight, Office of Management and Budget, to Committee Staff (Oct. 21, 2019).

[258] Russell T. Vought, Twitter (Oct. 21, 2019) (online at https://twitter.com/RussVought45/status/1186276793172578306?s=20).

[259] Letter from Chairman Eliot L. Engel, House Committee on Foreign Affairs, Chairman Adam B. Schiff, House Permanent Select Committee on Intelligence, and Acting Chairwoman Carolyn B. Maloney, House Committee on Oversight and Reform, to Acting Director Russell T. Vought, Office of Management and Budget (Oct. 25, 2019).

[260] Letter from Jason A. Yaworske, Associate Director for Legislative Affairs, Office of Management and Budget, to Chairman Adam B. Schiff, House Permanent Select Committee on Intelligence (Nov. 4, 2019).

[261] Vought Dep. Tr. at 10-11.

[262] Letter from Chairman Eliot L. Engel, House Committee on Foreign Affairs, Chairman Adam B. Schiff, House Permanent Select Committee on Intelligence, and Chairman Elijah E. Cummings, House Committee on Oversight and Reform, to Associate Director Michael Duffey, Office of Management and Budget (Oct. 11, 2019).

[263] Email from Jessica L. Donlon, Deputy General Counsel for Oversight, Office of Management and Budget, to Committee Staff (Oct. 21, 2019).

[264] Letter from Chairman Eliot L. Engel, House Committee on Foreign Affairs, Chairman Adam B. Schiff, House Permanent Select Committee on Intelligence, and Acting Chairwoman Carolyn B. Maloney, House Committee on Oversight and Reform, to Michael Duffey, Associate Director of National Security Programs, Office of Management and Budget (Oct. 25, 2019) (online at https://intelligence.house.gov/uploadedfiles/20191025_-_letter_duffey_re_subpoena.pdf); House Permanent Select Committee on Intelligence, Subpoena to Michael Duffey, Associate Director of National Security Programs, Office of Management and Budget (Oct. 25, 2019).

[265] Letter from Jason A. Yaworske, Associate Director for Legislative Affairs, Office of Management and Budget, to Chairman Adam B. Schiff, House Permanent Select Committee on Intelligence (Nov. 4, 2019).

[266] Duffey Dep. Tr. at 7.

[267] Letter from Chairman Eliot L. Engel, House Committee on Foreign Affairs, Chairman Adam B. Schiff, House Permanent Select Committee on Intelligence, and Acting Chairwoman Carolyn B. Maloney, House Committee on Oversight and Reform, to Brian McCormack, Associate Director for Natural Resources, Energy, and Science, Office of Management and Budget (Oct. 24, 2019).

[268] Letter from Chairman Eliot L. Engel, House Committee on Foreign Affairs, Chairman Adam B. Schiff, House Permanent Select Committee on Intelligence, and Acting Chairwoman Carolyn B. Maloney, House Committee on Oversight and Reform, to Brian McCormack, Associate Director for Natural Resources, Energy, and Science, Office of Management and Budget (Nov. 1, 2019); House Permanent Select Committee on Intelligence, Subpoena to Brian McCormack, Associate Director for Natural Resources, Energy, and Science, Office of Management and Budget (Nov. 1, 2019).

[269] Letter from Jason A. Yaworske, Associate Director for Legislative Affairs, Office of Management and Budget, to Chairman Adam B. Schiff, House Permanent Select Committee on Intelligence (Nov. 4, 2019).

[270] McCormack Dep. Tr. at 6.

[271] Letter from Chairman Eliot L. Engel, House Committee on Foreign Affairs, Chairman Adam B. Schiff, House Permanent Select Committee on Intelligence, and Chairman Elijah E. Cummings, House Committee on Oversight and Reform, to Secretary Michael R. Pompeo, Department of State (Sept. 13, 2019).

[272] Letter from Chairman Eliot L. Engel, House Committee on Foreign Affairs, Chairman Adam B. Schiff, House Permanent Select Committee on Intelligence, and Chairman Elijah E. Cummings, House Committee on Oversight and Reform, to Secretary Michael R. Pompeo, Department of State (Sept. 27, 2019) (internal citations omitted) (online at https://oversight.house.gov/sites/democrats.oversight.house.gov/files/documents/2019-09-27.EEC%20Engel%20Schiff%20%20to%20Pompeo-%20State%20re%20Depositions.pdf).

[273] Letter from Chairman Eliot L. Engel, House Committee on Foreign Affairs, Chairman Adam B. Schiff, House Permanent Select Committee on Intelligence, and Chairman Elijah E. Cummings, House Committee on Oversight and Reform, to T. Ulrich Brechbuhl, Counselor, Department of State (Sept. 27, 2019).

[274] Letter from Secretary Michael R. Pompeo, Department of State, to Chairman Eliot L. Engel, House Committee on Foreign Affairs (Oct. 1, 2019) (Secretary Pompeo sent identical letters to Chairman Elijah. E. Cummings, House Committee on Oversight and Reform, and Chairman Adam B. Schiff, House Permanent Select Committee on Intelligence, the same day).

[275] Letter from Chairman Eliot L. Engel, House Committee on Foreign Affairs, Chairman Adam B. Schiff, House Permanent Select Committee on Intelligence, and Chairman Elijah E. Cummings, House Committee on Oversight and Reform, to Deputy Secretary of State John J. Sullivan, Department of State (Oct. 1, 2019) (online at https://oversight.house.gov/sites/democrats.oversight.house.gov/files/documents/2019-10-01%20ELE%20ABS%20EEC%20TO%20DEPSEC%20SULLIVAN.pdf).

[276] Email from Ronald J. Tenpas, Counsel to T. Ulrich Brechbuhl, Counselor, Department of State, to Committee Staff (Oct. 2, 2019).

[277] Email from Committee Staff, to Ronald J. Tenpas, Counsel to T. Ulrich Brechbuhl, Counselor, Department of State (Oct. 8, 2019).

[278] Email from Committee Staff, to Ronald J. Tenpas, Counsel to T. Ulrich Brechbuhl, Counselor, Department of State (Oct. 9, 2019).

[279] Email from Ronald J. Tenpas, Counsel to T. Ulrich Brechbuhl, Counselor, Department of State, to Committee Staff (Oct. 9, 2019).

[280] Letter from Chairman Eliot L. Engel, House Committee on Foreign Affairs, Chairman Adam B. Schiff, House Permanent Select Committee on Intelligence, and Acting Chairwoman Carolyn B. Maloney, House Committee on Oversight and Reform, to T. Ulrich Brechbuhl, Counselor, Department of State (Oct. 25, 2019); House Permanent Select Committee on Intelligence, Subpoena to T. Ulrich Brechbuhl, Counselor, Department of State (Oct. 25, 2019).

[281] Letter from Ronald J. Tenpas, Counsel to T. Ulrich Brechbuhl, Counselor, Department of State to Chairman Adam B. Schiff, House Permanent Select Committee on Intelligence, Chairman Eliot L. Engel, House Committee on Foreign Affairs, and Acting Chairwoman Carolyn B. Maloney, House Committee on Oversight and Reform (Nov. 5, 2019).

[282] Brechbuhl Dep. Tr. at 4-5.

[283] Email from Committee staff to Ronald J. Tenpas, Counsel to T. Ulrich Brechbuhl, Counselor, Department of State (Nov. 5, 2019); Email from Committee Staff to Ronald J. Tenpas, Counsel to T. Ulrich Brechbuhl, Counselor (Nov. 22, 2019).

[284] Letter from Brian Bulatao, Under Secretary of State for Management, to Ronald J. Tenpas, Counsel to T. Ulrich Brechbuhl, Counselor, Department of State (Nov. 4, 2019.)

[285] Letter from Chairman Eliot L. Engel, House Committee on Foreign Affairs, Chairman Adam B. Schiff, House Permanent Select Committee on Intelligence, and Acting Chairwoman Carolyn B. Maloney, House Committee on Oversight and Reform, to Secretary Rick Perry, Department of Energy (Nov. 1, 2019).

[286] Letter from General Counsel Bill Cooper, Department of Energy, to Chairman Adam B. Schiff, House Permanent Select Committee on Intelligence, Chairman Eliot L. Engel, House Committee on Foreign Affairs, and Acting Chairwoman Carolyn B. Maloney, House Committee on Oversight and Reform (Nov. 5, 2019).

[287] Letter from Chairman Eliot L. Engel, House Committee on Foreign Affairs, Chairman Adam B. Schiff, House Permanent Select Committee on Intelligence, and Chairman Elijah E. Cummings, House Committee on Oversight and Reform, to Secretary Michael R. Pompeo, Department of State (Sept. 13, 2019).

[288] Letter from Chairman Eliot L. Engel, House Committee on Foreign Affairs, Chairman Adam B. Schiff, House Permanent Select Committee on Intelligence, and Chairman Elijah E. Cummings, House Committee on Oversight and Reform, to Secretary Michael R. Pompeo, Department of State (Sept. 27, 2019) (internal citations omitted).

[289] Letter from Chairman Eliot L. Engel, House Committee on Foreign Affairs, Chairman Adam B. Schiff, House Permanent Select Committee on Intelligence, and Chairman Elijah E. Cummings, House Committee on Oversight and Reform, to Ambassador Marie Yovanovitch, Former U.S. Ambassador to Ukraine, Department of State (Sept. 27, 2019).

[290] Letter from Secretary Michael R. Pompeo, Department of State, to Chairman Eliot L. Engel, House Committee on Foreign Affairs (Oct. 1, 2019) (Secretary Pompeo sent identical letters to Chairman Elijah. E. Cummings, House Committee on Oversight and Reform, and Chairman Adam B. Schiff, House Permanent Select Committee on Intelligence, the same day).

[291] Letter from Brian Bulatao, Under Secretary of State for Management, Department of State, to Lawrence S. Robbins, Counsel to Ambassador Marie Yovanovitch, Former U.S. Ambassador to Ukraine, Department of State (Oct. 10, 2019).

[292] The White House, *Remarks by President Trump Before Marine One Departure* (Oct. 10, 2019) (online at www.whitehouse.gov/briefings-statements/remarks-president-trump-marine-one-departure-69/).

[293] Letter from Chairman Adam B. Schiff, House Permanent Select Committee on Intelligence, Chairman Eliot L. Engel, House Committee on Foreign Affairs, and Chairman Elijah E. Cummings, House Committee on Oversight and Reform, to Lawrence S. Robbins, Counsel to Ambassador Marie Yovanovitch, Former U.S. Ambassador to Ukraine, Department of State (Oct. 11, 2019); House Permanent Select Committee on Intelligence, Subpoena to Ambassador Marie Yovanovitch, Former U.S. Ambassador to Ukraine, Department of State (Oct. 11, 2019).

[294] Letter from Lawrence S. Robbins, Counsel to Ambassador Marie Yovanovitch, Former U.S. Ambassador to Ukraine, Department of State, to Brian Bulatao, Under Secretary of State for Management, Department of State (Oct. 11, 2019) (citations omitted).

[295] Yovanovitch Dep. Tr.

[296] *Id.* at 70.

[297] Email from Committee Staff to Lawrence S. Robbins, Counsel to Ambassador Marie Yovanovitch, Former U.S. Ambassador to Ukraine, Department of State (Nov. 15, 2019); House Permanent Select Committee on Intelligence, Subpoena to Ambassador Marie Yovanovitch, Former U.S. Ambassador to Ukraine, Department of State (Nov. 15, 2019).

[298] Yovanovitch Hearing Tr. at 157-158.

[299] Letter from Chairman Elijah E. Cummings, House Committee on Oversight and Reform, Chairman Eliot L. Engel, House Committee on Foreign Affairs, and Chairman Adam B. Schiff, House Permanent Select Committee on Intelligence, to Secretary Michael R. Pompeo, Department of State (Sept. 27, 2019) (internal citations omitted) (online at https://oversight.house.gov/sites/democrats.oversight.house.gov/files/documents/2019-09-27.EEC%20Engel%20Schiff%20%20to%20Pompeo-%20State%20re%20Depositions.pdf).

[300] Letter from Chairman Elijah E. Cummings, House Committee on Oversight and Reform, Chairman Eliot L. Engel, House Committee on Foreign Affairs, and Chairman Adam B. Schiff, House Permanent Select Committee on Intelligence, to Ambassador Gordon Sondland, U.S. Ambassador to the European Union, Department of State (Sept. 27, 2019).

[301] Letter from Secretary Michael R. Pompeo, Department of State, to Chairman Eliot L. Engel, House Committee on Foreign Affairs (Oct. 1, 2019) (Secretary Pompeo sent identical letters to Chairman Elijah. E. Cummings, House Committee on Oversight and Reform, and Chairman Adam B. Schiff, House Permanent Select Committee on Intelligence, the same day).

[302] Letter from Brian Bulatao, Under Secretary of State for Management, Department of State, to Robert Luskin, Counsel to Ambassador Gordon Sondland, U.S. Ambassador to the European Union, Department of State (Oct.7, 2019).

[303] Email from Robert Luskin, Counsel to Ambassador Gordon Sondland, U.S. Ambassador to the European Union, Department of State, to Committee Staff (Oct. 8, 2019).

[304] Letter from Chairman Adam B. Schiff, House Permanent Select Committee on Intelligence, Chairman Elijah E. Cummings, House Committee on Oversight and Reform, and Chairman Eliot L. Engel, House Committee on Foreign Affairs, to Ambassador Gordon Sondland, U.S. Ambassador to the European Union, Department of State (Oct. 8, 2019); House Permanent Select Committee on Intelligence, Subpoena to Ambassador Gordon Sondland, U.S. Ambassador to the European Union, Department of State (Oct. 11, 2019).

[305] Letter from Chairman Adam B. Schiff, House Permanent Select Committee on Intelligence, Chairman Elijah E. Cummings, House Committee on Oversight and Reform, and Chairman Eliot L. Engel, House Committee on Foreign Affairs, to Ambassador Gordon Sondland, U.S. Ambassador to the European Union, Department of State (Oct. 14, 2019).

[306] Sondland Dep. Tr.

[307] *Id.* at 16.

[308] *Id.* at 17.

[309] Letter from Robert Luskin, Counsel to Ambassador Gordon Sondland, U.S. Ambassador to the European Union, Department of State, to Chairman Adam B. Schiff, House Permanent Select Committee on

Intelligence (Nov. 4, 2019); Declaration of Ambassador Gordon Sondland, U.S. Ambassador to the European Union, Department of State (Nov. 4, 2019).

[310] House Permanent Select Committee on Intelligence, Subpoena to Ambassador Gordon Sondland, U.S. Ambassador to the European Union, Department of State (Nov. 20, 2019).

[311] Sondland Hearing Tr. at 160.

[312] Letter from Chairman Eliot L. Engel, House Committee on Foreign Affairs, Chairman Adam B. Schiff, House Permanent Select Committee on Intelligence, and Chairman Elijah E. Cummings, House Committee on Oversight and Reform, to Secretary Michael R. Pompeo, Department of State (Sept. 13, 2019).

[313] Letter from Chairman Eliot L. Engel, House Committee on Foreign Affairs, Chairman Adam B. Schiff, House Permanent Select Committee on Intelligence, and Chairman Elijah E. Cummings, House Committee on Oversight and Reform, to Secretary Michael R. Pompeo, Department of State (Sept. 27, 2019) (online at https://oversight.house.gov/sites/democrats.oversight.house.gov/files/documents/2019-09-27.EEC%20Engel%20Schiff%20%20to%20Pompeo-%20State%20re%20Depositions.pdf) (internal citations omitted).

[314] Letter from Chairman Eliot L. Engel, House Committee on Foreign Affairs, Chairman Adam B. Schiff, House Permanent Select Committee on Intelligence, and Chairman Elijah E. Cummings, House Committee on Oversight and Reform, to George P. Kent, Deputy Assistant Secretary of State, Bureau of European and Eurasian Affairs, Department of State (Sept. 27, 2019).

[315] Email from George P. Kent, Deputy Assistant Secretary of State, Bureau of European and Eurasian Affairs, Department of State, to Committee Staff (Sept. 27, 2019).

[316] Letter from Secretary Michael R. Pompeo, Department of State, to Chairman Eliot L. Engel, House Committee on Foreign Affairs (Oct. 1, 2019) (Secretary Pompeo sent identical letters to Chairman Elijah. E. Cummings, House Committee on Oversight and Reform, and Chairman Adam B. Schiff, House Permanent Select Committee on Intelligence, the same day).

[317] Email from Committee Staff to Andrew M. Wright, Counsel to George P. Kent, Deputy Assistant Secretary of State, Bureau of European and Eurasian Affairs, Department of State (Oct. 8, 2019).

[318] Letter from Brian Bulatao, Under Secretary of State for Management, Department of State, to Andrew M. Wright, Counsel to George P. Kent, Deputy Assistant Secretary of State, Bureau of European and Eurasian Affairs, Department of State (Oct. 10, 2019).

[319] Letter from Chairman Adam B. Schiff, House Permanent Select Committee on Intelligence, Chairman Eliot L. Engel, House Committee on Foreign Affairs, and Chairman Elijah E. Cummings, House Committee on Oversight and Reform, to Andrew M. Wright, Counsel to George P. Kent, Deputy Assistant Secretary of State, Bureau of European and Eurasian Affairs, Department of State (Oct. 15, 2019); House Permanent Select Committee on Intelligence, Subpoena to George P. Kent, Deputy Assistant Secretary of State, Bureau of European and Eurasian Affairs, Department of State (Oct. 15, 2019).

[320] Kent Dep. Tr.

[321] *Id.* at 17.

[322] House Permanent Select Committee on Intelligence, Subpoena to George P. Kent, Deputy Assistant Secretary of State, Bureau of European and Eurasian Affairs, Department of State (Nov. 20, 2019).

[323] Kent-Taylor Hearing Tr. at 142-143.

[324] Letter from Chairman Eliot L. Engel, House Committee on Foreign Affairs, Chairman Adam B. Schiff, House Permanent Select Committee on Intelligence, and Chairman Elijah E. Cummings, House Committee on Oversight and Reform, to John J. Sullivan, Deputy Secretary of State, Department of State (Oct. 4, 2019).

[325] Letter from Chairman Eliot L. Engel, House Committee on Foreign Affairs, Chairman Adam B. Schiff, House Permanent Select Committee on Intelligence, and Chairman Elijah E. Cummings, House Committee on Oversight and Reform, to Ambassador William B. Taylor, Jr., Chargé d'Affaires, U.S. Embassy, Kyiv, Department of State (Oct. 4, 2019).

[326] Letter from Chairman Adam B. Schiff, House Permanent Select Committee on Intelligence, Chairman Elijah E. Cummings, House Committee on Oversight and Reform, and Chairman Eliot L. Engel, House Committee on Foreign Affairs, to Ambassador William B. Taylor, Jr., Ambassador William B. Taylor, Jr., Chargé d'Affaires, U.S. Embassy, Kyiv, Department of State (Oct. 14, 2019).

[327] Email from Committee Staff to John B. Bellinger, III, and Jeffrey H. Smith, Counsel to Ambassador William B. Taylor, Jr., Chargé d'Affaires, U.S. Embassy, Kyiv, Department of State (Oct. 22, 2019); House Permanent Select Committee on Intelligence, Subpoena to Ambassador William B. Taylor, Jr., Chargé d'Affaires, U.S. Embassy, Kyiv, Department of State (Oct. 22, 2019).

[328] Taylor Dep. Tr. at 83.

[329] House Permanent Select Committee on Intelligence, Subpoena to Ambassador William B. Taylor, Jr., Chargé d'Affaires, U.S. Embassy, Kyiv, Department of State (Nov. 13, 2019).

[330] Kent-Taylor Hearing Tr. at 143.

[331] Letter from Chairman Eliot L. Engel, House Committee on Foreign Affairs, Chairman Adam B. Schiff, House Permanent Select Committee on Intelligence, and Acting Chairwoman Carolyn B. Maloney, House Committee on Oversight and Reform, to Mark J. MacDougall, Counsel to Catherine Croft, Foreign Service Officer, Department of State (Oct. 24, 2019); Letter from Chairman Eliot L. Engel, House Committee on Foreign Affairs, Chairman Adam B. Schiff, House Permanent Select Committee on Intelligence, and Acting Chairwoman Carolyn B. Maloney, House Committee on Oversight and Reform, to Mark J. MacDougall, Counsel to Christopher Anderson, Foreign Service Officer, Department of State (Oct. 24, 2019).

[332] Letter from Mark J. MacDougall, Counsel to Catherine Croft, Foreign Service Officer, Department of State, and Christopher Anderson, Foreign Service Officer, Department of State, to Committee Staff (Oct. 25, 2019).

[333] Letter from Brian Bulatao, Under Secretary of State for Management, Department of State, to Mark J. MacDougall, Counsel to Catherine Croft, Foreign Service Officer, Department of State (Oct. 28, 2019) (bracketed text in original); Letter from Brian Bulatao, Under Secretary of State for Management, Department of State, to Mark J. MacDougall, Counsel to Christopher Anderson, Foreign Service Officer, Department of State (Oct. 28, 2019) (bracketed text in original); *see* Letter from Pat A. Cipollone, Counsel to the President, The White House, to Speaker Nancy Pelosi, Chairman Elijah E. Cummings, House Committee on Oversight and Reform, Chairman Eliot L. Engel, House Committee on Foreign Affairs, and Chairman Adam B. Schiff, House Permanent Select Committee on Intelligence (Oct. 8, 2019).

[334] Email from Committee Staff to Mark J. MacDougall and Abbey McNaughton, Counsel to Catherine Croft, Foreign Service Officer, Department of State and Christopher Anderson, Foreign Service Officer, Department of State (Oct. 30, 2019); House Permanent Select Committee on Intelligence, Subpoena to Catherine Croft, Foreign Service Officer, Department of State (Oct. 30, 2019); House Permanent Select Committee on Intelligence, Subpoena to Christopher Anderson, Foreign Service Officer, Department of State (Oct. 30, 2019).

[335] Croft Dep. Tr.; Anderson Dep. Tr.

[336] Croft Dep. Tr. at 12.

[337] Anderson Dep. Tr. at 11-12.

[338] Letter from Chairman Eliot L. Engel, House Committee on Foreign Affairs, Chairman Adam B. Schiff, House Permanent Select Committee on Intelligence, and Chairman Elijah E. Cummings, House Committee on Oversight and Reform, to Laura K. Cooper, Deputy Assistant Secretary of Defense for Russia, Ukraine, Eurasia, Department of Defense (Oct. 11, 2019).

[339] Letter from Deputy Secretary of Defense David L. Norquist to Daniel Levin, Counsel to Laura K. Cooper, Deputy Assistant Secretary of Defense for Russia, Ukraine, Eurasia, Department of Defense (Oct. 22, 2019).

[340] Email from Committee Staff to Dan Levin, Counsel to Laura K. Cooper, Deputy Assistant Secretary of Defense for Russia, Ukraine, Eurasia, Department of Defense (Oct. 23, 2019); House Permanent Select Committee on Intelligence, Subpoena to Laura K. Cooper, Deputy Assistant Secretary of Defense for Russia, Ukraine, Eurasia, Department of Defense (Oct. 23, 2019).

[341] Cooper Dep. Tr.

[342] *Id.* at 108.

[343] Email from Committee Staff to Dan Levin, Counsel to Laura K. Cooper, Deputy Assistant Secretary of Defense for Russia, Ukraine, Eurasia, Department of Defense (Nov. 20, 2019); House Permanent Select Committee on Intelligence, Subpoena to Laura K. Cooper, Deputy Assistant Secretary of Defense for Russia, Ukraine, Eurasia, Department of Defense (Nov. 20, 2019).

[344] Cooper-Hale Hearing Tr.

[345] Letter from Chairman Adam B. Schiff, House Permanent Select Committee on Intelligence, Acting Chairwoman Carolyn B. Maloney, House Committee on Oversight and Reform, and Chairman Eliot L. Engel, House Committee on Foreign Affairs, to Mark Sandy, Deputy Associate Director of National Security Programs, Office of Management and Budget (Nov. 5, 2019).

[346] Email from Mark Sandy, Deputy Associate Director of National Security Programs, Office of Management and Budget, to Committee Staff (Nov. 6, 2019).

[347] Email from Jessica L. Donlon, Deputy General Counsel for Oversight, Office of Management and Budget, to Committee Staff (Nov. 7, 2019).

[348] Email from Committee Staff to Barbara Van Gelder, Counsel to Mark Sandy, Deputy Associate Director of National Security Programs, Office of Management and Budget (Nov. 16, 2019); House Permanent Select Committee on Intelligence, Subpoena to Mark Sandy, Deputy Associate Director of National Security Programs, Office of Management and Budget (Nov. 16, 2019).

[349] Sandy Dep. Tr.

[350] Sandy Dep. Tr. at 161.

[351] Letter from Chairman Eliot L. Engel, House Committee on Foreign Affairs, Chairman Adam B. Schiff, House Permanent Select Committee on Intelligence, and Chairman Elijah E. Cummings, House Committee on Oversight and Reform, to Dr. Fiona Hill, Former Deputy Assistant to the President and Senior Director for Europe and Russian Affairs, National Security Council (Oct. 9, 2019).

[352] Letter from Lee S. Wolosky, Counsel to Dr. Fiona Hill, Former Deputy Assistant to the President and Senior Director for Europe and Russian Affairs, National Security Council, to Michael M. Purpura, Deputy Counsel and Deputy Assistant to the President, The White House, and Patrick F. Philbin, Deputy Counsel and Deputy Assistant to the President, The White House (Oct. 13, 2019).

[353] Letter from Michael M. Purpura, Deputy Counsel and Deputy Assistant to the President, The White House, to Lee S. Wolosky, Counsel to Dr. Fiona Hill, Former Deputy Assistant to the President and Senior Director for Europe and Russian Affairs, National Security Council (Oct. 14, 2019).

[354] Email from Committee Staff to Lee S. Wolosky and Samuel S. Ungar, Counsel to Dr. Fiona Hill, Former Deputy Assistant to the President and Senior Director for Europe and Russian Affairs, National Security Council (Oct. 14, 2019); House Permanent Select Committee on Intelligence, Subpoena to Dr. Fiona Hill, Former Deputy Assistant to the President and Senior Director for Europe and Russian Affairs, National Security Council (Oct. 14, 2019).

[355] Hill Dep. Tr.

[356] Letter from Lee S. Wolosky, Counsel to Dr. Fiona Hill, Former Deputy Assistant to the President and Senior Director for Europe and Russian Affairs, National Security Council, to Michael M. Purpura, Deputy Counsel and Deputy Assistant to the President, The White House (Nov. 18, 2019).

[357] Letter from Michael M. Purpura, Deputy Counsel and Deputy Assistant to the President, The White House, to Lee S. Wolosky, Counsel to Dr. Fiona Hill, Former Deputy Assistant to the President and Senior Director for Europe and Russian Affairs, National Security Council (Nov. 20, 2019).

[358] Email from Committee Staff to Lee S. Wolosky and Samuel S. Ungar, Counsel to Dr. Fiona Hill, Former Deputy Assistant to the President and Senior Director for Europe and Russian Affairs, National Security Council (Nov. 21, 2019); House Permanent Select Committee on Intelligence, Subpoena to Dr. Fiona Hill, Former

Deputy Assistant to the President and Senior Director for Europe and Russian Affairs, National Security Council (Nov. 21, 2019).

[359] Hill-Holmes Hearing Tr.

[360] Letter from Chairman Eliot L. Engel, House Committee on Foreign Affairs, Chairman Adam B. Schiff, House Permanent Select Committee on Intelligence, and Chairman Elijah E. Cummings, House Committee on Oversight and Reform, to Lieutenant Colonel Alexander S. Vindman, Director for Ukraine, National Security Council (Oct. 16, 2019).

[361] Email from Committee Staff, to Michael Volkov and Matt Stankiewicz, Counsel to Lieutenant Colonel Alexander S. Vindman, Director for Ukraine, National Security Council (Oct. 29, 2019); House Permanent Select Committee on Intelligence, Subpoena to Lieutenant Colonel Alexander S. Vindman, Director for Ukraine, National Security Council (Oct. 29, 2019).

[362] Vindman Dep. Tr. (During the deposition, Lieutenant Colonel Vindman stated: "I was subpoenaed to appear here. You know, absent a subpoena, I would believe I was operating under the President's guidance to not appear, but I was subpoenaed and I presented myself." Vindman Dep. Tr. at 232).

[363] Email from Committee Staff, to Michael Volkov and Matt Stankiewicz, Counsel to Lieutenant Colonel Alexander S. Vindman, Director for Ukraine, National Security Council (Nov. 19, 2019); House Permanent Select Committee on Intelligence, Subpoena to Lieutenant Colonel Alexander S. Vindman, Director for Ukraine, National Security Council (Nov. 19, 2019).

[364] Vindman-Williams Hearing Tr.

[365] Letter from Chairman Eliot L. Engel, House Committee on Foreign Affairs, Chairman Adam B. Schiff, House Permanent Select Committee on Intelligence, and Chairman Elijah E. Cummings, House Committee on Oversight and Reform, to Timothy Morrison, Former Deputy Assistant to the President and Senior Director for Europe and Russia, National Security Council (Oct. 16, 2019).

[366] Email from Committee Staff to Barbara Van Gelder, Counsel to Timothy Morrison, Former Deputy Assistant to the President and Senior Director for Europe and Russia, National Security Council (Oct. 31, 2019); House Permanent Select Committee on Intelligence, Subpoena to Timothy Morrison, Former Deputy Assistant to the President and Senior Director for Europe and Russia, National Security Council (Oct. 31, 2019).

[367] Morrison Dep. Tr.

[368] Email from Committee Staff to Barbara Van Gelder, Counsel to Timothy Morrison, Former Deputy Assistant to the President and Senior Director for Europe and Russia, National Security Council (Nov. 19, 2019); House Permanent Select Committee on Intelligence, Subpoena to Timothy Morrison, Former Deputy Assistant to the President and Senior Director for Europe and Russia, National Security Council (Nov. 19, 2019).

[369] Morrison-Volker Hearing Tr.

[370] Letter from Chairman Eliot L. Engel, House Committee on Foreign Affairs, Chairman Adam B. Schiff, House Permanent Select Committee on Intelligence, and Acting Chairwoman Carolyn B. Maloney, House Committee on Oversight and Reform, to David Hale, Under Secretary of State for Political Affairs, Department of State (Nov. 1, 2019).

[371] Letter from Brian A. Glasser, Counsel to David Hale, Under Secretary of State for Political Affairs, Department of State, to Chairman Adam B. Schiff, House Permanent Select Committee on Intelligence, Chairman Eliot L. Engel, House Committee on Foreign Affairs, and Acting Chairwoman Carolyn B. Maloney, House Committee on Oversight and Reform (Nov. 5, 2019).

[372] Email from Committee Staff to Brian Glasser and Cary Joshi, Counsel for David Hale, Under Secretary of State for Political Affairs, Department of State (Nov. 6, 2019); House Permanent Select Committee on Intelligence, Subpoena to David Hale, Under Secretary of State for Political Affairs, Department of State (Nov. 6, 2019).

[373] Hale Dep. Tr.

[374] Email from Committee Staff to Brian A. Glasser, Counsel to David Hale, Under Secretary of State for Political Affairs, Department of State (Nov. 20, 2019); House Permanent Select Committee on Intelligence, Subpoena to David Hale, Under Secretary of State for Political Affairs, Department of State (Nov. 20, 2019).

[375] Cooper-Hale Hearing Tr.

[376] Letter from Chairman Adam B. Schiff, House Permanent Select Committee on Intelligence, Acting Chairwoman Carolyn B. Maloney, House Committee on Oversight and Reform, and from Chairman Eliot L. Engel, House Committee on Foreign Affairs, to Kenneth L. Wainstein, Counsel to David Holmes, Political Counselor at the U.S. Embassy in Kyiv, Ukraine, Department of State (Nov. 12, 2019).

[377] Email from Committee Staff to Kenneth L. Wainstein, Paul J. Nathanson, and Katherine Swan, Counsel to David Holmes, Political Counselor at the U.S. Embassy in Kyiv, Ukraine, Department of State (Nov. 15, 2019); House Permanent Select Committee on Intelligence, Subpoena to David Holmes, Political Counselor at the U.S. Embassy in Kyiv, Ukraine, Department of State (Nov. 15, 2019).

[378] Holmes Dep. Tr.

[379] Email from Committee Staff to Kenneth L. Wainstein, Paul J. Nathanson, and Katherine Swan, Counsel to David Holmes, Political Counselor at the U.S. Embassy in Kyiv, Ukraine, Department of State (Nov. 21, 2019); House Permanent Select Committee on Intelligence, Subpoena to David Holmes, Political Counselor at the U.S. Embassy in Kyiv, Ukraine, Department of State (Nov. 21, 2019).

[380] Hill-Holmes Hearing Tr.

[381] Email from Committee Staff to Ambassador P. Michael McKinley, Former Senior Advisor to the Secretary of State, Department of State (Oct. 12, 2019).

[382] Letter from Chairman Eliot L. Engel, House Committee on Foreign Affairs, Chairman Adam B. Schiff, House Permanent Select Committee on Intelligence, and Chairman Elijah E. Cummings, House Committee on Oversight and Reform, to John B. Bellinger, III, Counsel to Ambassador P. Michael McKinley, Former Senior Advisor to the Secretary of State, Department of State (Oct. 14, 2019).

[383] McKinley Transcribed Interview Tr.

[384] Letter from Chairman Eliot L. Engel, House Committee on Foreign Affairs, Chairman Adam B. Schiff, House Permanent Select Committee on Intelligence, and Chairman Elijah E. Cummings, House Committee on Oversight and Reform, to Ambassador Philip T. Reeker, Acting Assistant Secretary, Bureau of European and Eurasian Affairs, Department of State (Oct. 16, 2019).

[385] Letter from Chairman Adam B. Schiff, House Permanent Select Committee on Intelligence, Chairman Eliot L. Engel, House Committee on Foreign Affairs, and Acting Chairwoman Carolyn B. Maloney, House Committee on Oversight and Reform, to Margaret E. Daum, Counsel to Ambassador Philip T. Reeker, Acting Assistant Secretary, Bureau of European and Eurasian Affairs, Department of State (Oct. 25, 2019); House Permanent Select Committee on Intelligence, Subpoena to Ambassador Philip T. Reeker, Acting Assistant Secretary, Bureau of European and Eurasian Affairs, Department of State (Oct. 25, 2019).

[386] Reeker Dep. Tr.

[387] Letter from Chairman Eliot L. Engel, House Committee on Foreign Affairs, Chairman Adam B. Schiff, House Permanent Select Committee on Intelligence, and Chairman Elijah E. Cummings, House Committee on Oversight and Reform, to Secretary Michael R. Pompeo, Department of State (Sept. 13, 2019).

[388] Letter from Chairman Eliot L. Engel, House Committee on Foreign Affairs, Chairman Adam B. Schiff, House Permanent Select Committee on Intelligence, and Chairman Elijah E. Cummings, House Committee on Oversight and Reform, to Secretary Michael R. Pompeo, Department of State (Sept. 27, 2019).

[389] Letter from Chairman Eliot L. Engel, House Committee on Foreign Affairs, Chairman Adam B. Schiff, House Permanent Select Committee on Intelligence, and Chairman Elijah E. Cummings, House Committee on Oversight and Reform, to Ambassador Kurt Volker, U.S. Special Representative for Ukraine Negotiations, Department of State (Sept. 27, 2019).

[390] Letter from Secretary Michael F. Pompeo, Department of State, to Chairman Eliot L. Engel, House Committee on Foreign Affairs (Oct. 1, 2019) (Identical letters transmitted to Chairman Schiff and Chairman Cummings).

[391] Letter from Marik A. String, Acting Legal Advisor, Department of State, to Margaret E. Daum, Counsel to Ambassador Kurt Volker, U.S. Special Representative for Ukraine Negotiations, Department of State (Oct. 2, 2019).

[392] Letter from Margaret E. Daum, Counsel to Ambassador Kurt Volker, U.S. Special Representative for Ukraine Negotiations, Department of State, to Chairman Eliot L. Engel, House Committee on Foreign Affairs, Chairman Adam B. Schiff, House Permanent Select Committee on Intelligence, and Chairman Elijah E. Cummings, House Committee on Oversight and Reform (Oct. 2, 2019); Kurt Volker Document Production, Bates KV00000001 – KV00000065 (Oct. 2, 2019).

[393] Volker Transcribed Interview Tr.

[394] Morrison-Volker Hearing Tr.

[395] Letter from Chairman Adam B. Schiff, House Permanent Select Committee on Intelligence, and Acting Chairwoman Carolyn B. Maloney, House Committee on Oversight and Reform, and Chairman Eliot L. Engel, House Committee on Foreign Affairs, to Justin Shur, Counsel to Jennifer Williams, Special Advisor for Europe and Russia, Office of the Vice President (Nov. 4, 2019).

[396] Email from Committee Staff to Justin Shur, Counsel to Jennifer Williams, Special Advisor for Europe and Russia, Office of the Vice President (Nov. 7, 2019); House Permanent Select Committee on Intelligence, Subpoena to Jennifer Williams, Special Advisor for Europe and Russia, Office of the Vice President (Nov. 7, 2019).

[397] Williams Dep. Tr.

[398] Letter from Jennifer Williams, Special Advisor for Europe and Russia, Office of the Vice President, Justin Shur, Emily K. Damrau, and Caleb Hayes-Deats, Counsel to Jennifer Williams, Special Advisor for Europe and Russia, Office of the Vice President, to Chairman Adam B. Schiff, House Permanent Select Committee on Intelligence (Nov. 11, 2019).

[399] Email from Committee Staff to Justin Shur and Caleb Hayes-Deats, Counsel to Jennifer Williams, Special Advisor for Europe and Russia, Office of the Vice President (Nov. 19, 2019); House Permanent Select Committee on Intelligence, Subpoena to Jennifer Williams, Special Advisor for Europe and Russia, Office of the Vice President (Nov. 19, 2019).

[400] Vindman-Williams Hearing Tr.

[401] Yovanovitch Dep. Tr. at 193.

[402] Yovanovitch Hearing Tr. at 37-38.

[403] Yovanovitch Hearing Tr. at 38.

[404] Donald J. Trump, Twitter (Nov. 15, 2019) (online at https://twitter.com/realDonaldTrump/status/1195356198347956224).

[405] Yovanovitch Hearing Tr. at 46.

[406] *The Latest: Ousted Ukraine Ambassador Has Her Say in Hearing,* Associated Press (Nov. 16, 2019) (online at https://apnews.com/2f420045618b4106b6fa7419a3d75b8e).

[407] *Impeachment Inquiry Hearing with Former US Ambassador to Ukraine*, CNN (Nov. 15, 2019) (online at www.cnn.com/politics/live-news/impeachment-hearing-11-15-19/h_fb32b149181437e02e5d937c6fc64f35). During a recess in the hearing at which Ambassador Yovanovitch was testifying, a federal jury returned a verdict of guilty against President Trump's longest-serving political advisor, Roger Stone, on seven criminal counts, including witness tampering and obstruction of Congress' investigation into Russian interference in the 2016 election and possible links to President Trump's campaign. Mr. Stone used threats and intimidation to attempt to persuade a witness to withhold information and lie to Congress. He has yet to be sentenced. *See Roger Stone Guilty on All Counts of Lying to Congress, Witness Tampering*, Washington Post (Nov. 15, 2019) (online at www.washingtonpost.com/local/public-safety/roger-stone-jury-weighs-evidence-and-a-defense-move-to-make-case-

about-mueller/2019/11/15/554fff5a-06ff-11ea-8292-c46ee8cb3dce_story.html). Mr. Stone was convicted of giving false and misleading statements to the Intelligence Committee, failing to produce and lying about the existence of records responsive to Committee requests, and attempting to persuade a witness to give false testimony to the Committee. Among other acts of witness tampering, Mr. Stone told the witness to "Stonewall it. Plead the Fifth" and to "be honest w fbi" that "there was no back channel." He also called the witness a "rat" and "stoolie" and threatened retaliation. United States v. Roger Stone, Indictment, No. 1:19-cr-00018-ABJ (Jan. 24, 2019). Mr. Stone was convicted of violating 18 U.S.C. § 1505 (obstruction), 18 U.S.C. § 1001 (false statements), and 18 U.S.C. § 1512(b) (witness tampering).

[408] Fox and Friends, Fox News (Nov. 22, 2019) (online at www.youtube.com/watch?v=WNqKhRcpktU).

[409] Donald J. Trump, Twitter (Oct. 23, 2019) (online at https://twitter.com/realDonaldTrump/status/1189167309455331328).

[410] The White House, Remarks by President Trump Before Marine One Departure (Nov. 3, 2019) (online at www.whitehouse.gov/briefings-statements/remarks-president-trump-marine-one-departure-74/).

[411] Donald J. Trump, Twitter (Nov. 19, 2019) (retweeting Dan Scavino Jr., Twitter (Nov. 19, 2019) (online at https://twitter.com/Scavino45/status/1196860213233684480)).

[412] See, e.g, Berman Shocked by Republican's Attacks on US War Vet, CNN (Oct. 29, 2019) (online at www.cnn.com/videos/politics/2019/10/29/duffy-berman-spar-over-vindman-loyalty newday-vpx.cnn) (former Rep. Sean Duffy claiming that Lt. Col Vindman "has an affinity, I think for the Ukraine," that "it seems very clear that he is incredibly concerned about Ukrainian defense," and that "I don't know that he's concerned about American policy"); see also Rudy Giuliani, Twitter (Oct. 30, 2019) (online at https://twitter.com/RudyGiuliani/status/1189732605383630850) (claiming that Lt. Col. Vindman was "giving advice to two countries" and stating that "I thought he worked for US").

[413] House Permanent Select Committee on Intelligence, Written Statement of Lieutenant Colonel Alexander S. Vindman, Impeachment, 116th Cong. (Nov. 19, 2019).

[414] Donald J. Trump, Twitter (Oct. 23, 2019) (online at https://twitter.com/realDonaldTrump/status/1187063301731209220).

[415] Donald J. Trump, Twitter (Oct. 23, 2019) (online at https://twitter.com/realDonaldTrump/status/1187080923961012228).

[416] The White House, Remarks by President Trump Before Marine One Departure (Oct. 25, 2019) (online at www.whitehouse.gov/briefings-statements/remarks-president-trump-marine-one-departure-72/).

[417] Donald J. Trump, Twitter (Nov. 13, 2019) (online at https://twitter.com/realdonaldtrump/status/1194608482793795584).

[418] Donald J. Trump, Twitter (Nov. 17, 2019) (online at https://twitter.com/realDonaldTrump/status/1196155347117002752).

[419] Vindman-Williams Hearing Tr. at 97.

[420] Donald J. Trump, Twitter (Nov. 16, 2019) (online at https://twitter.com/realDonaldTrump/status/1195727871765073921); Donald J. Trump, Twitter (Nov. 16, 2019) (online at https://twitter.com/realDonaldTrump/status/1195727879780360193).

[421] 50 U.S.C. § 3033(g)(3) (when a complaint is received from a member of the Intelligence Community, "the Inspector General shall not disclose the identity of the employee without the consent of the employee, unless the Inspector General determines that such disclosure is unavoidable during the course of the investigation or the disclosure is made to an official of the Department of Justice responsible for determining whether a prosecution should be undertaken").

[422] 50 U.S.C. § 3234(b).

[423] Letter from Michael K. Atkinson, Inspector General of the Intelligence Community, to Chairman Adam B. Schiff, House Permanent Select Committee on Intelligence, and Ranking Member Devin Nunes, House Permanent Select Committee on Intelligence (Sept. 9, 2019); see also 50 U.S.C. § 3033(k)(5)(C) ("Upon receipt of

the transmittal from the ICIG, the Director *shall* within 7 calendar days of such receipt, forward such transmittal to the congressional intelligence committees, together with any comments the Director considers appropriate.")

[424] Letter from Chairman, Adam B. Schiff, House Permanent Select Committee on Intelligence, to Joseph Maguire, Acting Director of National Intelligence, Office of the Director of National Intelligence (Sept. 13, 2019).

[425] House Permanent Select Committee on Intelligence, *House Intelligence Committee Releases Whistleblower Complaint* (Sept. 26, 2019) (online at https://intelligence.house.gov/news/documentsingle.aspx?DocumentID=708).

[426] *Listen: Audio of Trump Discussing Whistleblower at Private Event: 'That's Close to a Spy,'* Los Angeles Times (Sept. 26, 2019) (online at www.latimes.com/politics/story/2019-09-26/trump-at-private-breakfast-who-gave-the-whistle-blower-the-information-because-thats-almost-a-spy).

[427] House Permanent Select Committee on Intelligence, *Chairmen Warn President to Stop Attacking Whistleblower and Witnesses to His Misconduct and to Halt Efforts to Obstruct Impeachment Inquiry* (Sept. 26, 2019) (online at https://intelligence.house.gov/news/documentsingle.aspx?DocumentID=709).

[428] Donald J. Trump, Twitter (Sept. 29, 2019) (online at https://twitter.com/realDonaldTrump/status/1178442765736333313?s=20).

[429] Donald J. Trump, Twitter (Oct. 4, 2019) (online at https://twitter.com/realDonaldTrump/status/1180123504924151809).

[430] The White House, *Remarks by President Trump Before Marine One Departure* (Nov. 3, 2019) (online at www.whitehouse.gov/briefings-statements/remarks-president-trump-marine-one-departure-74/).

[431] Donald J. Trump, Twitter (Nov. 3, 2019) (online at https://twitter.com/realdonaldtrump/status/1191000516580519937).

[432] The White House, *Remarks by President Trump Before Marine One Departure* (Nov. 3, 2019) (online at www.whitehouse.gov/briefings-statements/remarks-president-trump-marine-one-departure-74/).

[433] The White House, *Remarks by President Trump Before Marine One Departure* (Nov. 4, 2019) (online at www.whitehouse.gov/briefings-statements/remarks-president-trump-marine-one-departure-75/).

[434] The White House, *Remarks by President Trump After Tour of Apple Manufacturing Plant* (Nov. 20, 2019) (online www.whitehouse.gov/briefings-statements/remarks-president-trump-tour-apple-manufacturing-plant-austin-tx/).

[435] Letter from Chairman Adam B. Schiff to Ranking Member Devin Nunes, House Permanent Select Committee on Intelligence (Nov. 9, 2019).

[436] In 2017, every Republican Member of Congress joined a unanimous vote in the House of Representatives to increase penalties for retaliation against whistleblowers. U.S. House of Representatives, Roll Call Vote Approving S. 585, The Dr. Chris Kirkpatrick Whistleblower Protection Act of 2017 (Oct. 12, 2017) (420 yeas, 0 nays) (online at www.govtrack.us/congress/votes/115-2017/h568).

[437] *House Intelligence Chair News Conference*, C-SPAN (Mar. 24, 2017) (online at www.c-span.org/video/?425953-1/paul-manafort-volunteered-intelligence-committee-chairman-nunes).

[438] *Id.*

[439] Office of Senator Chuck Grassley, *Grassley Statement Regarding Intel Community Whistleblower* (Oct. 1, 2019) (online at www.grassley.senate.gov/news/news-releases/grassley-statement-regarding-intel-community-whistleblower).

[440] *Senate Intel Chair Doesn't Want Whistleblower's Identity Disclosed*, The Hill (Nov. 7, 2019) (online at https://thehill.com/homenews/senate/469455-senate-intel-chair-doesnt-want-whistleblowers-identity-disclosed).

[441] *Republicans Break with Trump and Rand Paul on Whistleblower Unmasking*, Politico (Nov. 5, 2019) (online at www.politico.com/news/2019/11/05/rand-paul-trump-whistleblower-065917).

APPENDIX A: KEY PEOPLE AND ENTITIES

Anderson, Christopher J.	Special Advisor for Ukraine Negotiations, Department of State, August 2017-July 2019

Atkinson, Michael K.	Inspector General of the Intelligence Community, May 2018-present

Avakov, Arsen	Ukrainian Minister of Internal Affairs, February 2014-present

Bakanov, Ivan	Head of Security Service of Ukraine, August 2019-present; First Deputy Chief of the Security Service of Ukraine, May 2019-August 2019

Barr, William P.	Attorney General, Department of Justice, February 2019-present

Biden, Hunter	Son of former Vice President Joe Biden

Biden, Joseph R., Jr.	U.S. Vice President, January 2009-January 2017

Blair, Robert B.	Assistant to the President and Senior Advisor to the Chief of Staff, February 2019-present

Bohdan (Bogdan), Andriy	Head of Ukrainian Presidential Administration, May 2019-present

Bolton, John	National Security Advisor, March 2018-September 2019

Brechbuhl, T. Ulrich	Counselor, Department of State, May 2018-present

Bulatao, Brian	Under Secretary of State for Management, Department of State, May 2019-present

Burisma Holdings	Ukrainian energy company

Cipollone, Pat	White House Counsel, December 2018-present

Clinton, Hillary Rodham	Democratic Presidential candidate, November 2016

Cooper, Laura K.	Deputy Assistant Secretary of Defense for Russia, Ukraine, Eurasia, Department of Defense, 2016-present

Croft, Catherine M.	Special Advisor for Ukraine Negotiations, Department of State, July 2019-present; Ukraine director, National Security Council, July 2017-July 2018

293

CrowdStrike	Cybersecurity company; object of conspiracy theories claiming that CrowdStrike framed Russia in hack of the DNC server in the 2016 U.S. election
Danyliuk (Danylyuk), Oleksandr "Sasha"	Secretary, Ukrainian National Security and Defense Council, May 2019-September 2019
diGenova, Joseph	Attorney allegedly working for President Trump to obtain information from Ukrainian officials on the Bidens
Duffey, Michael	Associate Director, National Security Programs, Office of Management and Budget, May 2019-present
Eisenberg, John	Legal Advisor to the National Security Council and Deputy Counsel to the President for National Security Affairs, February 2017-present
Ellis, Michael	Senior Associate Counsel to the President and Deputy Legal Advisor to the National Security Council, March 2017-present
Elwood, Courtney Simmons	General Counsel, Central Intelligence Agency, June 2017-present
Engel, Steven A.	Assistant Attorney General, Office of Legal Counsel, Department of Justice, November 2017-present
Esper, Mark	Secretary of Defense, Department of Defense, July 2019-present; Acting Secretary of Defense, June 2019-July 2019
Fruman, Igor	Giuliani associate named in indictment unsealed on October 10, 2019
Giuliani, Rudolph "Rudy"	President Trump's agent and personal attorney
Griffith, P. Wells	Senior Director for International Energy and Environment, National Security Council, April 2018-present
Hale, David M.	Under Secretary of State for Political Affairs, Department of State, August 2018-present
Hannity, Sean	Host of *Hannity*, Fox News, January 2009-present
Hill, Fiona	Deputy Assistant to the President and Senior Director for European and Russian Affairs, National Security Council, April 2017-July 2019
Hochstein, Amos J.	Supervisory Board Member, Naftogaz, November 2017-present

Holmes, David A.	Political Counselor, U.S. Embassy in Kyiv, Ukraine, August 2017-present
Johnson, Ron	Senator from Wisconsin, Chairman, Senate Homeland Security and Governmental Affairs Committee, January 2015-present
Kellogg, Keith	National Security Advisor to the Vice President, April 2018-present
Kenna, Lisa D.	Executive Secretary in the Office of the Secretary, Department of State, June 2017-present
Kent, George P.	Deputy Assistant Secretary of State, Bureau of European and Eurasian Affairs, September 2018-present; Deputy Chief of Mission in Kyiv, Ukraine, 2015-2018
Kholodnitsky, Nazar	Head, Ukrainian Specialized Anti-Corruption Prosecutor's Office, November 2015-present
Klitenic, Jason	General Counsel, Office of the Director of National Intelligence
Kulyk, Konstiantyn	Deputy Head of the Ukrainian Department of International Legal Cooperation of the Prosecutor General's Office, November 2018-November 2019
Kupperman, Charles M.	Deputy National Security Advisor, January 2019-September 2019
Kushner, Jared	Assistant to the President and Senior Advisor, 2017-present
Kvien, Kristina	Deputy Chief of Mission, U.S. Embassy in Kyiv, May 2019-present
Lutsenko, Yuriy	Ukrainian Prosecutor General, May 2016-August 2019
McCormack, Brian	Associate Director for Natural Resources, Office of Management and Budget, September 2019-present; Chief of Staff, Department of Energy, March 2017-September 2019
McKinley, P. Michael	Senior Advisor to the Secretary, Department of State, May 2018-October 2019
McKusker, Elaine A.	Deputy Under Secretary of Defense (Comptroller), Department of Defense, August 2017-present
Maguire, Joseph	Acting Director of National Intelligence, August 2019-present

Manafort, Paul	Chairman, Donald J. Trump presidential campaign, May 2016-August 2016; convicted in August 2018 on two counts of bank fraud, five counts of tax fraud, and one count of failure to disclose a foreign bank account
Morrison, Tim	Deputy Assistant to the President for National Security, National Security Council, July 2019-October 2019
Mueller, Robert S., III	Special Counsel, Department of Justice, May 2017-May 2019
Mulvaney, John Michael "Mick"	Acting Chief of Staff, White House, January 2019-present
Murphy, Chris	Senator from Connecticut, Ranking Member, Subcommittee on Near East, South Asia, Central Asia, and Counterterrorism, Senate Committee on Foreign Relations, formerly Ranking Member, Subcommittee on Europe and Regional Security Cooperation, Senate Committee on Foreign Relations, January 2017-January 2019
Naftogaz	Ukrainian state-owned national gas company
Parnas, Lev	Giuliani associate named in indictment unsealed on October 10, 2019
Patel, Kashyap "Kash"	Senior Director for Counterterrorism, National Security Council, July 2019-present; former Staff, Directorate of International Organizations and Alliances, National Security Council, February 2019-July 2019; former National Security Advisor, House Permanent Select Committee on Intelligence, March 2018-January 2019; former Senior Counsel for Counterterrorism, House Permanent Select Committee on Intelligence, April 2017-March 2018
Pence, Michael R.	Vice President, January 2017-present
Pennington, Joseph	Chargé d'Affaires, of the U.S. Embassy in Ukraine, May 2019
Perez, Carol Z.	Director General of the Foreign Service and Director of Human Services, January 2019-present
Perry, James Richard "Rick"	Secretary of Energy, March 2017-December 2019
Pompeo, Michael	Secretary of State, April 2018-present
Poroshenko, Petro	President of Ukraine, June 2014-May 2019

Portman, Robert	U.S. Senator from Ohio, January 2011-present; Chairman, Permanent Subcommittee on Investigations, Senate Homeland Security and Governmental Affairs Committee, January 2015-present
Purpura, Michael	Deputy Counsel to the President, December 2018-present
Putin, Vladimir	Russian President, May 2012-present
Reeker, Philip T.	Acting Assistant Secretary, Bureau of European and Eurasian Affairs, Department of State, March 2019-present
Rood, John C.	Under Secretary of Defense for Policy, Department of Defense, January 2018-present
Sandy, Mark	Deputy Associate Director for National Security at the Office of Management and Budget, December 2013-present; Acting Director of the Office of Management and Budget, January 2017-February 2017
Sekulow, Jay	Personal attorney for President Trump
Shokin, Viktor	Ukrainian Prosecutor General of Ukraine, February 2015-March 2016
Short, Marc	Chief of Staff to Vice President Mike Pence, February 2019-present
Solomon, John	Author of articles promoting debunked conspiracy theories about the Bidens, Crowdstrike, and the 2016 U.S. election
Sondland, Gordon	U.S. Ambassador to the European Union, July 2018-present
String, Marik	Acting Legal Advisor, Office of the Legal Advisor, Department of State, June 2019-present
Sullivan, John J.	Deputy Secretary of State, Department of State, June 2017-present
Taylor, William B., Jr.	Chargé d'Affaires for the U.S. Embassy in Kyiv, Ukraine, June 2019-present
"Three Amigos"	Secretary of Energy Rick Perry, Ambassador Gordon Sondland, and Ambassador Kurt Volker
Toensing, Victoria	Attorney allegedly working "off the books" for President Trump to obtain information from Ukrainian officials on the Bidens

Trump, Donald J.	U.S. President, January 2017-present
Trump, Donald J., Jr.	Son of President Trump
Vindman, Alexander S.	Director for Ukraine, National Security Council, July 2018-present; Lieutenant Colonel, U.S. Army
Volker, Kurt	U.S. Special Representative for Ukraine Negotiations, Department of State, July 2017-September 2019
Vought, Russell T.	Acting Director, Office of Management and Budget, January 2019-present
Whistleblower	Author of complaint declassified by the Office of the Director of National Intelligence on September 25, 2019
Williams, Jennifer	Special Advisor for Europe and Russia, Office of the Vice President, April 2019-present
Yermak, Andriy	Assistant to the President of Ukraine, May 2019-present
Yovanovitch, Marie L.	U.S. Ambassador to Ukraine, August 2016-May 2019
Zakaria, Fareed	Host, *Fareed Zakaria GPS*, June 2008-present
Zelensky, Volodymyr	President of Ukraine, May 2019-present

APPENDIX B: ABBREVIATIONS AND COMMON TERMS

AntAC	Anti-Corruption Action Center
CDA	Chargé d'Affaires / Acting Ambassador
CIA	Central Intelligence Agency
Chargé d'Affaires	Acting Ambassador
CN	Congressional Notification
COM	Chief of Mission
DAS	Deputy Assistant Secretary
DC	Deputies Committee
DCM	Deputy Chief of Mission
DNI	Director of National Intelligence
DNC	Democratic National Committee
DOD	Department of Defense
DOE	Department of Energy
DOJ	Department of Justice
DOS	Department of State
DSCA	Defense Security Cooperation Agency
EDI	European Deterrence Initiative
ERI	European Reassurance Initiative
FBI	Federal Bureau of Investigation
FMF	Foreign Military Financing
FMS	Foreign Military Sales
FSB	Russian Federal Security Service
IC	Intelligence Community
ICIG	Inspector General for the Intelligence Community
IO	Bureau of International Organizations
IG	Inspector General
Legatt	Legal Attaché
LNG	Liquefied Natural Gas
MEMCON	Memorandum of Conversation
MLAT	Mutual Legal Assistance Treaty
NABU	National Anti-Corruption Bureau of Ukraine
NBU	National Bank of Ukraine
NDAA	National Defense Authorization Act
NSC	National Security Council
ODNI	Office of the Director of National Intelligence
OFAC	Office of Foreign Assets Control
OMB	Office of Management and Budget
OSCE	Organization for Security and Co-operation in Europe
OVP	Office of the Vice President
PAC	Political Action Committee
PC	Principals Committee
PCC	Policy Coordination Committee
PDB	President's Daily Briefing
PDM	Presidential Decision Memorandum

PGO	Prosecutor General's Office
SAPO	Specialized Anti-Corruption Prosecutor's Office
SBU	Security Service of Ukraine
SDN	Specially Designated Nationals and Blocked Persons
SMM	Special Monitoring Mission
SOC	Summary of Conclusions
SVTC	Secure Video Teleconference
TCG	Trilateral Contact Group
UNSCR	United Nations Security Council Resolution
USAI	Ukraine Security Assistance Initiative
USAID	United States Agency for International Development
WHSR	White House Situation Room
YES	Yalta European Strategy